NATIONAL HUGUENOT SOCIETY BIBLE RECORDS

Abstracted from the Files of the Society

Edited by

Arthur Louis Finnell
Registrar General

CLEARFIELD

Printed for
Clearfield Company, Inc. by
Genealogical Publishing Co., Inc.
Baltimore, Maryland
1996

Reprinted for
Clearfield Company, Inc. by
Genealogical Publishing Co., Inc.
Baltimore, Maryland
1997, 2001, 2004

International Standard Book Number: 0-8063-4636-1

Made in the United States of America

Foreword
Huguenot Bible Records
The 1993–1994 President General's Challenge Project

No single record of Huguenot history and genealogy is dearer to our Society than those found in Bibles of our Huguenot ancestors. To be sure, important documents abound from government and land offices, from ships' lists, and from personal family histories.

Yet the records kept lovingly by mothers and fathers, by newlyweds, by older matriarchs and patriarchs, in our family Bibles hold a special place in hereditary research.

Our National Huguenot Society is unique among lineage societies in that we are a religious hereditary society—descendants of French Huguenots who are themselves of the Protestant faith. These qualifications delineate us even from other Huguenot societies. Our religious history, brought into the present generation, enlivens all that we stand for, as individuals and as an organization. Our ancestors' faith in God, abiding hope in Christ and protection of the Holy Spirit allowed them to prevail against numerous odds in Europe and the New World. This same faith, hope and protective guidance undergirds our lives today.

It is with great happiness that I launched the publishing of our Huguenot family Bible records as the President General's Challenge Project in 1993. My heartfelt thanks to all those State Societies who contributed to the project and my high praise to Arthur Louis Finnell, Registrar General of our venerable Society, for assembling the materials.

(The Rev.) Travis Talmadge DuPriest, Jr.
President General, 1993–1995

Introduction

Over the years since the organization of the National Huguenot Society, the files have continued to collect proofs on claimed ancestors. The Society maintains two collections of files as part of the archives. First is the "Proof Files" for the qualified Huguenots accepted by the National Society. The Society does try to maintain proof files on the qualified ancestors that in many cases contain evidence used for the first two to four generations. In addition, many miscellaneous copies of family Bible records are included, for later generations, as submitted by members. The National Society has not, prior to Oct. 1992, saved the documentation submitted with all applications. The Society is now maintaining these files, but they have done so only since Oct. 1992. The second collection is a collection of files with materials on families that have at one time been considered Huguenots, or are alleged Huguenots, and await additional documentation to clear up their claims. These files in many cases are found to contain family Bible records for individuals who have attempted to join the Society on this line. This file also continues to grow and becomes more complete as time goes by.

The following pages contain transcripts of the Bible records as found in the archives of the National Huguenot Society. The records in this publication have been transcribed from photocopies of the original records or typescripts of the original records as submitted by a member. Many of the records are only partial copies of the Bible records; no information is available as to the owner at the time of the copies or at the present time, unless noted. In some cases limited additional materials are attached; i.e., copies of epitaphs from tombstones or copies of local records. These have been transcribed also.

Each entry is followed by a reference indicating where the records can be found and located. Many of the copies are in very poor condition and will not photocopy again, so any request for copies must be discouraged. You are welcome to visit the Society library and archives and look at the files yourself.

The records that have been transcribed for this volume are in many cases photocopies and sometimes very hard to read; this is the best transcript possible. If you have additions or corrections, they would be welcomed and would be included in any future volume of Society bible records. Please direct all correspondence to the editor at the Society address.

Arthur Louis Finnell
National Huguenot Society
9033 Lyndale Avenue South #108
Bloomington, MN 55420-3535

Abbreviations

b. = born
d. = died
m. = married
yrs = years
mo = months
dys = days
dau = daughter

The standard two-letter abbreviations are used for the states, and standard three-letter abbreviations are used for the months.

NOTE: In some cases numbers are used for the months; these seem to be Quaker records, and this format has been retained.

AYERS BIBLE

No Title Page or Dates

BIRTHS

Fred Ward AYERS was born 24 March 1867
Albert Edward AYERS was born 17 Oct 1868
Abigail Josephine AYERS was born 10 April 1870
Frank AYERS was born 1 Jan 1873
Archie Allan AYERS was born 17 July 1877
Rollin Willard AYERS was born 21 July 1874
Cora Etta AYERS was born 20 Dec 1884
Edward AYERS, son of Thomas M. & Abigail FORESTER AYERS was born 23 Oct 1833
in the Parish of Minster Isle of Shippy, Kent Co, England
Maria Louisa (MASSEY) AYERS was born 23 Oct 1841 near Jacksonville, Morgan Co, IL, US

MARRIAGES

Mr Edward Ayers to Miss Maria Louisa MASSEY 31 Dec 1865 by Rev D.H. Hamilton; Jacksonville, IL
Abigail Josephine AYERS to Frank E. YOUNG 19 March 1893 at Lyon Co, KS by Rev Kline of Admire
Albert E. AYERS was married to Lilly FISHER at Harpers, KS 9 June 1898
Fred W. AYERS to Helen GOUDER of Sterling, KS at Lawrence, KS 10 Oct 1898
Frank AYERS to Miss Cora M. DOUGHTY at Madison, KS 19 Aug 1903
Rollin Willard AYERS to Mary Robinette TALIAFERRO at Topeka, KS 13 Feb 1912 by Rev V.C. Taliaferro and Rev Dr Fiske

Also attached is a photo of two Tombstones: Levina A.

MASSEY / born10 May 1817 / died 4 Feb 1901 and Stephen S. MASSEY / died 14 Oct 1878/ Aged 64yrs 7mos 26days **(Misc Bible File)**

RUTAN BIBLE

No Title Page, Publisher, or date of publication

BIRTHS

Samuel RUTAN was born 8 Jan 1710
Maria STOUGHTENBURGH, his wife was born 2 Sep 1712
Samuel RUTAN, their son born 3 Jul 1752
Maria RUTAN was born 25 Nov 1754
Abram RUTAN was born 28 Feb 1776
Silvanus J. RUTAN was born 7 Mar 1816
Sarah J. RUTAN was born 12 Mar 1824
William Henry RUTAN was born 10 Jan 1853
Lizzie Ogdon Johnson RUTAN was born 27 May 1866
Norman Edward RUTAN born 16 Oct 1892
Althea E, RUTAN was born 30 Oct 1890
Clinton Norman RUTAN was born 9 Jun 1918

DEATHS

Abraham RUTAN died 11 Feb 1713
His beloved wife Mary died 4 May 1713
Samuel RUTAN, their son died 1 Dec 1777
Maria S. RUTAN, his wife died 18 Mar 1779
Samuel RUTAN the younger died 13 Oct 1814
Maria, his wife died 2 Jan 1834
Abram RUTAN died 3 Jan 1845
Margaret E. RUTAN died 11 Jun 1843
Silvanus J. RUTAN, their son died 6 Oct 1886
Sarah I. RUTAN died 6 Jul 1865

William Henry RATAN died 30 Apr 1936
Elizabeth O. RUTAN died 20 JaN 1919

MARRIAGES

Maria STOUGHTENBURGH and Samuel RUTAN married 2 Sep 1733
Samuel RUTAN and Mary BRUYN married 3 May 1775
Abram RUTAN married Margaret ENNIS 14 May 1799
Sylvanus James RUTAN married Sarah Isabel MANSFIELD 4 Oct 1842
William H. RUTAN married Lizzie O. JOHNSON 20 Oct 1891
Norman Edward RUTAN married Althea Edwards SMITH 14 Apr 1915

(Misc Bible File / 2-400)

BROWN / MIMS FAMILY BIBLE

No Title Page or Date

John J. BROWN, son of Milelus & Elizabeth BROWN, b.8 Nov 1810, Buckingham Co, VA
Martha Nichloas MOSELEY; dau of Robert & Judith MOSELEY; b.23 Mar 1814, Buckingham Co, VA.
Williamina Henningham BROWN; dau of Jon J. & M.N. BROWN; b.23 Oct 1836, Buckingham Co, VA
Judith Scott BROWN; dau of J.J. & M.N. BROWN, b.31 Mar 1838, Buchingham Co, VA
Martha Nicholas BROWN, dau of J.J. & M.N. BROWN; b.17 Oct 1839, Buckingham Co, VA
Robert Burley BROWN, son of J.J. & M.N. BROWN, b.18 Aug 1841, Buckingham, Co, VA
Elizabeth Lewis BROWN; dau of J.J. & M.N.BROWN, b.26 Mar 1844, Richmond, VA
Ann Bentley BROWN; dau of J.J. & M.N.BROWN, b.11 Jun

1846, Richmond, VA
William Titus BROWN; son of John J. & M.N. BROWN; b.21 Feb 1848, Richmond, VA
Mary Gillispson BROWN; dau of J.J. & M.N. BROWN, b.29 Mar 1850, Richmond, VA
Lusene Fontaine COOPER; dau of J.R. & W.H. COOPER, b.1 Mar 1860 [Sciven] Co GA
Walter Irving COOPER, son of J.R. & W.H. COOPER, b.8 Jul 1861, [Sciven] Co, GA
Roberta Ossilla COOPER; dau of J.R. & W.H. COOPER b. [blank]
Willie Randolph COOPER; dau of J.R.& W.H. COOPER, b.31 Aug 1865, [Siswen] Co, GA
Frank, son of Thos S. & Judith S. MIMS, b.13 Aug 1876, Scriven Co, GA
Frank MINS, Jr, son of Frank & Hattie MIMS, b.5 Jul 1901
Thos S. MIMS, son of Britton & Edison Goodlyn MIMS, b.31 Jul 1820, Bainwell Dist, SC
John O. MANER, Jr; son of John O. & Sallie M. MANER, b.6 Mar 1902
Emma Jean MANER; dau of John O. & Sallie M. MANER, b.26 Jul 1904
Gilifford Amelia MIMS; dau of Thos S. & Mary E. MIMS, b.23 Dec 1842
James Augustus MIMS; son of Thos S. & Mary E. MIMS, b.28 Dec 1843
William Horace MIMS; son of Thos S. & Mary E. MIMS, b.27 Jun 1845
Thos Shachack MIMS, son of Thos S. & Mary E. MIMS, b.20 Apr 1847
Milton MIMS, son of Thos S. & Mary E. MIMS, b.20 Oct 1848
Ollive Ophuia MIMS; dau of Thos S. & Mary E. MIMS, b.23

Jan 1850
Eugenia Carloine MIMS; dau of Thos J. & Mary E. MIMS, b.17 Jul 1852
Samuel Walter MIMS; son of Thos S.& Mary E. MIMS; b.26 Mar 1855
Mary Gillispie MIMS; dau of Thos S. & Judith S. MIMS, b.28 Sep 1866, Sciven Co, GA
Willie Miles MIMS; dau of Thos S. & Judith S. MIMS, b.25 Dec 1867, Sciven Co, GA
Lou Eve MIMS; dau of Thos S. & Judith S. MIMS, b.1 Sep 1869, Sciven Co, GA
Lucy Southwell MIMS; dau of Thos S. & Judith S. MIMS b.29 Aug 1871, Sciven Co, GA
Sallie Elizabeth MIMS; dau of Thos S. & Judith S. MIMS, b.28 Aug 1873, Scrivers Co, GA
Leslie Brown MIMS; son of Thos S. & Judith S. MIMS b.23 Feb 1875
Lillie Ora MIMS; dau of Thos S & Mary E. MIMS, b.28 Dec 1862
Ella Mattie MIMS; dau of Thos S. & Mary E. MIMS, b.18 Jul 1860

MARRIAGES

John J. BROWN to Martha Nicholas MOSLEY, 25 Nov 1835
John J. BROWN to Lucy Catherine JOHNSON, 14 Jun 1855
J.R. COOPER of Scriven Co, GA to Willie A. BROWN of Ruchingham Co, VA, 25 Nov 1858
Samuel S. LINE of Scriven Co, GA to Nannie B. BROWN of Buckingham Co, VA, 24 Jan 1866
Wm Stells BROWN to Kate ROBERTS, 2 Jan 1875, Savannah, GA
Thos S. MIMS
Allen L. MIMS to Carrie F. COLDING, 24 Dec 1886
John Ogilvie MANE to Sadie E. MIMS, 25 Dec 1900

Thos S. MIMS of Scriven Co, GA to Judith S. BROWN of Buckingham Co, VA; 21 Sep 1865
E.C. MIMS to H.P MALAIR [?] of Stecker, FL, 23 Mar 1887
Willie S. MIMS to H.H. CHANCE, 3 Jan 1889
Ella M. MIMS to A.J. MIXSON, 2 Feb 1783
Lucy S, MIMS to J. Lee WILLI, 6 May 1894
DEATHS
Elizabeth Seevis BROWN, d.19 Jan 1847; age 2y 9m 24d
Martha Nicholas BROWN, wife of John J. BROWN, d.13 Oct 1851; age 40y 6m 21d
Mary Cillessia BROWN, d.2 Jul 1855; age 5y 3m 4d
Martha Nicholas BROWN; Dau of J.J. & M.M. BROWN; d.27 Dec 1855; age 16yrs 2m 8d
John J. BROWN; son of Melatus & Elizabeth BROWN, d.14 Feb 1875, age 65yrs
Wm Stiles BROWN; son of Jno J. & Martha N. BROWN, d. Savannah, GA of Yellow Fever, 20 Sep 1876; age 28yrs 7m
Willie H. COOPER, wife of J.R. COOPER, d.18 Sep 1865
Leslie Brown MIMS; son of Thos S. & Judith S. MIMS; d.20 Sep 1875, age 6mo 28d
Britton MIMS, SR; d.2Mar 1837, Barnwell Dist, SC
Edison Goodwyn MIMS, wife of Britton MINS, d.6 May 1835 Barnwell Dist, SC (b.15 Dec 1798)
Britton MIMS, son of Thos S. & Mary S. MIMS, d.2 Nov 1852
Mary Elizabeth Lines MIMS, wife of Thos S. MIMS, d.13 Dec 1863 (b.11 Jan 1825)
Lilly Ora MIMS; dau of Thos S. & Mary E. MIMS, d.1 Sep 1867, Scriven Co, GA
Clifford Amelia, dau of Thos S. & Mary E. MIMS, d.2 Feb 1846
William W. MIMS, son of Britton & Edison MIMS, d.29 Aug 1846

Dr. B.R. MIMS; son of B.R. & E.G. MIMS, d.30 Jan 1873
Sue Eve MIMS; dau of Thos S. & Judith S. MIMS, d.1 Mar 1873, age 2y 6m
Mary Lessie MIMS; dau of Thos S. & Judith S. MIMS, d.31 Oct 1877, age 8y 1m 3d
T.S. MIMS, Jr, d.6 Nov 1895, Screven Co, GA
Hiram Robert BROWN, son of W. & R.R. BROWN, d.in Savannah, GA 28 Oct 1876, age 11m
Judith Scott MIMS, wife of Thos S. MIMS, d.12 Mar 1879, age 40y 11m 12d
Wm H. MIMS, d.11 Nov 1896 Waco, TX
J.M. BROWN b.1752; d.1820
Edison Goodwyn SOUTHWELL, wife of Britton MIMS, Sr, b.15 Oct 1798; d.6 May 1835, bur Old Mims Family Cemetery, Allendale Co, NC.
Dr Thos S. MIMS, d.17 Dec 1906, age 86yrs, 4m 17d
Mary Elizabeth LINES, wife of Dr Thos MIMS, dau of Samuel & Caroline LINES, b.11 Jan 1825; d.13 Dec 186[-]
(Misc Bible File)

SLATEN BIBLE

HOLY BIBLE by National Publishing Co. Chicago, IL Jones Junkins & Co 1869

MARRIAGES

Christopher J. SLATEN to Elizabeth P. EATON on 29 July 1868 at Grafton, IL
Elizabeth EATON SLATON, b.2 Jun 1842, Phelps, NY; d.7 Jun 1917, Grafton, IL
Christopher J. SLATEN, b.26 Mar 1840, Grafton, IL, d.4 Apr 1924, Grafton,IL
Misc Bible File)

NETTLETON BIBLE

No Title Page or Date

BIRTHS

Alpha NETTLETON born OH, d. Kingsouth, OH
Benjamin SMITH b.1 Jan 1791, CT
Sally M. SMITH , b.28 Sep 1791, CT
Orin DuBOIS, b.28 Feb 1820
Mary E. DuBOIS, b.March 1828
Booth NETTLETON, b.21 Nov 1819
Louisa Maria NETTLETON, b.24 Jan 182[-]
Eugene Booth NETTLETON, b.1 Aug 1858, Galesburg, Knox Co, IL
Blanche DuBois NETTLETON, b.4 Sep 1876
Blanche & Adele NETTLETON, b. 4 Apr 1878
Irene NETTLETON, b.11 Mar 1890

DEATHS

Alpha NETTLETON, d.at Kingsville, OH
Sarah Booth NETTLETON, d. at Kingsville, OH
Benj SMITH, d.25 Mar 1850, Mentor, OH, age 59y 3m
Sally M. W. SMITH, d.16 Jan 18[--], Lexon, OH; age 50yrs
Louise Marie NETTLETON, d.at DuBois, PA, 17 Apr 1877
Booth NETTLETON, d.Nov 1881, Harrisburg, PA
Orin DuBOIS, d. Aug 1882, San Jose, CA

MARRIAGES

Benj & S. M. W. SMITH married 15 Jun 1808, New Haven, CT
Booth NETTLETON & Louisa M. SMITH married 13 Jul 1857, Mentor, OH
Eugene B. NETTLETON and Blanche DuBOIS married 27 Oct 1875 at DuBois, PA
(Misc Bible File / 18-141)

GRAVES BIBLE

No Title Page or Date

BIRTHS

Willard Prudy GRAVES, b.31 Jul 1838, [Mebraville], NH
Lucy Melvina LIBBY, b.20 Nov 1838, Joy, ME
Willard GRAVES, JR, b.26 Sep 1865, Alexandria, VA
Myetilla Melonia GRAVES, b.4 Mar 1868
Herbert Cornelius GRAVES, b.17 Aug 1869
Lucy Mariah GRAVES, b.3 Aug 1871
Mary Ellen GRAVES, b.14 Aug 1873
Willard Prady GRAVES, Jr, b.3 Feb 1878

MARRIAGES

Willard Pardy GRAVES to Lucy Melvina LIBBY, 19 Dec 1864 at Manchester, NH by Rev Mr Wallace
Herbert C. GRAVES to Clara Edith WALTER, 4 Sep 1894 at Washington DC
Mary Ellen GRAVES to Fred M. McGROW, 25 Jun 1902 at Alexanderia, VA
Asenath Moore GRAVES to George Albert CHADWICK, 29 May 1905 at Alexanderia, VA

DEATHS

Willard GRAVES,JR d.14 Feb 1866
Lucy Melvina GRAVES, d.26 Feb 1912
Willard P. GRAVES,JR, d.20 Jun 1913
Herbert C. GRAVES, d.26 Jul 1919 in England
Willard Purdy GRAVES, Sr, d.12 Jan 1922
Myrtilla Melvina GRAVES, d.7 Dec 1939
Lucy Mariah GRAVES, d.27 Jun 1946
Mary Ellan GRAVES, d.24 Jul 1946

BIRTHS

Herbert C. GRAVES, b.17 Aug 1869
Clara E. GRAVES, b.14 Dec 1873
Lucy Engel GRAVES, b.25 Jul 1895, Cleveland, OH

Henry Walter GRAVES, b.22 Nov 1896, Cleveland, OH
Herbert Cornelius GRAVES, Jr, b.9 Jul 1898, Cleveland, OH
Clara Edith GRAVES, b.14 Jun 1902, Washington, DC
Asenath Libby GRAVES, b.13 Aug 1908, Washington, DC
Alvin Cushman GRAVES, b.4 Nov 1909, Washington, DC
MARRIAGES
Lucy Engle GRAVES to William Hay TOLIAFURO, 6 Jun 1919
Henry Walter GRAVES to Marguerite Spatz ERB, 7 Sep 1918
Herbert Cornelius GRAVES, Jr to Josephine Lee YOST, 31 Dec 1929
Clara Edith GRAVES to Arthur Alan BAKER, 29 Sep 1925
Asenath Libby GRAVES to Edwin Thor McKNIGHT, 16 May 1931
Alvin Cushman GRAVES to Elizabeth RIDDLE, 27 Sep 1937

Children born to Henry Walter GRAVES and Marguerite ERB GRAVES:
Eleanor Marguerite GRAVES, b.9 Jun 1919, Philadelphia, PA
John Robert GRAVES, b.3 Dec 1925, Philadelphia, PA
MARRIAGES
Eleanor Marguerite GRAVES to Gordon Rudolph SANCTUARY, 19 Oct 1940
John Robert GRAVES to Anita Claire BELLETTI, 16 Sep 1947
(Misc Bible FILE / 3-559)

ROGERS / LOTT BIBLE

No Title Page or Date

BIRTHS
Guy Lott ROGERS, b.23 Nov 1885
Clarence Elms ROGERS, b.31 Oct 1887

Hazel Elizabeth ROGERS, b.27 Jun 1891
Freddie Lee ROGERS, b.13 Nov 1892
Bessie Francis ROGERS, b.29 Nov 1896
BIRTHS
Charles G. LOTT, b.27 Jul 1832
Elizabeth WILSON, b.30 Mar 1831
Cecelia Elvira LOTT, dau of C.G. & Elizabeth LOTT, b.3 May 1856
Francis Elizabeth LOTT, Dau of C.G. & Eliz LOTT, b.9 Apr 1858
(Mics Bible File / 19=33)

COFFIN BIBLE

No Title Page or Dates

BIRTHS
Clarence M. COFFIN, b.1 Oct 1851, Racine, WI
Francis Durissa COFFIN, b.10 Feb 1850; d. 30 Sep 193___
Perry H. COFFIN, b.7 Aug 1877, Centerville, MI
Alice [ ] COFFIN, b.30 Jun 1879
Latham C. COFFIN, b.5 Feb 1882
Bessie I. COFFIN, b.31 Mar 1889, Hudson, MI
Lurissa Catherine COFFIN, b.15 May 1908
Catherine Butram COFFIN, b.11 Sep 1912, Petersburg, MI
Bernice Mice COFFIN, b.24 Mar 1917, Sheldon, MI
William Robert McCLURE, b.30 Dec 1941, Detriot, MI
Carolyn Alice McCLURE, b.20 Oct 1943, Detroit, MI
Donald James McCLURE, b.16 Aug 1945
Pamela Avaline McCLURE, b.2 Jan 1950
Paul Frederick BEEMAN, b.16 Apr 1948, Modesto, CA
Roger Latham BEEMAN, b.28 Jul 1948. Modesto, CA
DEATHS
Clarence M. COFFIN, d.4 Nov 1924, Dania, FL

Francis Durissa COFFIN, d.30 Sep 1936, Detroit, MI
(Misc Bible File)

BERRIAN BIBLE

No Title Page or Date

BIRTHS

Ada Louisa BERRIAN, b.21 Oct 1866, Boltenville. Washington Co, WI

James Wendell BERRIAN, b.21 Jan 1871, Medota, LaSalle Co, IL

Arleigh BERRIAN, b.20 May 1873, Chitheral, Otter Tail Co, MN

Lulu Jennie BERRIAN, b.26 Oct 1875, Golden Dale Klickital Co, WA Territory

George Waller BERRIAN, b.14 Jan 1880, Columbus, WA Terr.

Clarence Howard BERRIAN, b.25 Jan 1888, Columbus, WA Terr

James V. BERRIAN, b.7 Jun 1823, Burghumtown, NY

Imlda Leona WENDELL, b.29 Sep 1840, Warren, Herkemer Co, NY

PHOTO attached:

Tombstone for James A. BERRIAN / b.7 Jun 1828 / d.18 May 1883.

b. Binghamton, Broome Co, NY

d. Goldendale, Klickitat Co, WA Ter

bur. Columbus Cemetery, Maryhill, WA

James W. BERRIAN, d.15 Apr 1848, Peoria, Peoria Co, IL
(Misc Bible File)

WASHER BIBLE

No Title Page or Date

MARRIAGES

George P. WASHER to Emma J. THIBES, 27 Oct 1869
Harold W. ADAMS to Beatrice MITTON, 16 Nov 1922

BIRTHS

Martha E. WASHER, b.20 Jan 1871
George P. WASHER, Jr, b.9 Jul 1873
Mary J. WASHER, b.5 Nov 1876
Etta May WASHER, b.18 Sep 1879
Harry Victor WASHER, b.2 Apr 1884
George P. WASHER, b.18 Jan 1847
Emma J. WASHER, b.5 Oct 1850
Peter WASHER, b.4 Aug [----]
[-----------] b. Apr 1791
George Henry McARTHUR, b.3 Jul 1899
Harold ADAMS, b.21 Dec 1902, Orange, NJ
Virginia H. ADAMS, b.15 Mar 1924, Newark, NJ
Harold Roger ADAMS, b.20 Nov 1920, Neward, NJ
Dorothy Etta ADAMS, b.10 Feb 1928, Newark, NJ

DEATHS

Henry Victor WASHER, d.1 Nov 1886, Age 2y 7ms
George H. McARTHUR, d.1 Aug 1906, Age 7y 1m
George P. WASHER, Sr, d.15 Jun 1923, Age 76yrs
Mrs Emma J. WASHER, d.28 Nov 1928, age 78yrs
Mary J. WASHER McARTHUR, d.23 Sep 1932; age 55yrs
George Peter WASHER, Jr, d.10 Mar 1945
(Misc Bible File / 2-713)

STEWART BIBLE

Hitchcock's New and Complete Analysis of the Holy Bible

New York, 1873

BIRTHS

Samuel STEWART, b.7 Apr 1827
Delila S. BOONE, wife of Samuel STEWART, b.7 Feb 1835
CHILDREN OF THE ABOVE
Mary J. STEWART, b.10 Dec 1853
Joel F. STEWART, b.27 Sep 1855
Nopealeon STEWART, b.2 Jun 1857
Amelia R. STEWART, b.28 Oct 1858
Theodore W. STEWART, b.1 Jan 1861
Joshua D. STEWART, b.12 Feb 1863
William S. STEWART, b.5 Feb 1865
Edith C. STEWART, b.11 Dec 1867

BIRTHS

May STEWART, b.12 May 1871
Elizabeth J. STEWART, b.29 Sep 1877
CHILDREN OF JOHN & BELLE TODD
Marcus Troy TODD, b.22 Sep 1885
Mollie Constance TODD, b.23 Oct 1888
Nellie May TODD, b.13 Aug 1890
CHILDREN OF T. & MARIA STEWART
Roger Boone STEWART, b.18 Oct 1890
CHILDREN OF MAY & WM WILLES
Stewart WELLIS, b.
CHILDREN OF J.D. & MAY STEWART
(none listed)

MARRIAGES

Samuel STEWART to Delila S. BOONE, 3 Oct 1852
children of the above
Mary J. STEWART to D. SHARPLES, m.20 Apr 1880
Amelia B. STEWART to John S. TODD, m.4 Dec 1884

MARRIAGES

Theodore W. STEWART to Maria G. GAGE, m.1 Jan 1890
David J. STEWART to May _____
May STEWART to William M. WILLIS, m.9 Jun 1896
Elizabeth J. STEWART to Ernest P. McCARTHY, m.2 Sep 1896
Vivian Myers SUMMONS to Stewart Boone McCARTY, m.4 Apr 1920
Edith Lucretia McCARTY to Charles Randull HOZAN, m.29 Sep 1934
MISCELLANOUS
Stewart B. McCARTY, son of E.P. & E.G. McCARTY, b.28 Aug 1898
Edith Lueretia McCARTY, b.6 Sep 1902
Lillian B. SHARPLES, b.20 Apr 1881
Miria Waide SHARPLES, b.14 Oct 1882
[Jefferson] SHARPLES, b.11 Aug 1884
Stewart Boone McCARTY, Jr, son of Stewart Boone McCARTY & Vivian SIMMONS McCARTY, b.13 Jul 1926
(Misc Bible File / 3-545)

TAYLOR BIBLE

No Title Page or Date

FAMILY RECORDS
David TAYLOR, b.6 Nov 1750; d.2 Oct 1839
Rosannah GILBERT, b.10 Jan 1753, d.28 Aug 1838
David TAYLOR, b.8 Apr 1774
Gilbert TAYLOR, b.27 Dec 1776, d.13 Oct 1840
Sarah TAYLOR, b.30 Jan 1780
Rachael TAYLOR, b.12 Sep 1783, d.22 Mar 1873
Lucy TAYLOR, b.16 Dec 1784
Stephen TAYLOR,b.21 Aug 1786
George TAYLOR, b.25 Apr 1788

Ralph TAYLOR, b.18 Nov 1790
Hannah TAYLOR, b.15 Mar 1796
Annie TAYLOR, b.17 Mar 1798
Gilbert TAYLOR, b.27 Dec 1776, d.13 Oct 1840
Clorissa GIBBS, b.29 Dec 1781, d.17 Mar 1857
Fanny TAYLOR, b.19 Nov 1800
Marla TAYLOR, b.21 Mar 1803
Olive TAYLOR, b.8 Jun 1805
Eunice Lucy TAYLOR, b.29 Apr 1808
Clinton Gilbert TAYLOR, b.23 Jul 1811
David Gibbs TAYLOR, b.3 Sep 1816, d. at birth
Cyrus Wells TAYLOR, b.1 Feb 1819
Alfred Zena TAYLOR, b.7 Jun 1823
Clinton Gilbert TAYLOR, b.23 Jul 1810, d.15 Jul 1882
Eliza Maria BARNES, b.28 Mar 1811, d.5 Sep 1905

Edgington Township, Rock Island Co, IL 10 Mar 1853 moved out to my Farm

Leona Arabell TAYLOR, b.27 Aug 1836
Annetta Eliza TAYLOR, b.2 Feb 1839
Marquis Barnes TAYLOR, b.11 Aug 1841
Grandison Marger TAYLOR, b.24 Jul 1845
Arthur LeRoy TAYLOR, b.5 Apr 1848
Asa Gilbert TAYLOR, b.30 Mar 1851
Ella Coburn TAYLOR, b.24 Nov 1855; d.14 Jul 1934
(Misc Bible File / 18 - 29)

BROWN BIBLE

NEW TESTAMENT, Philadelphia, M. Carey, 1814

<u>FAMILY RECORDS</u>

Birth of the Children of Mitehus BROWN and Elizabeth

LEWIS, his wife
of Buckingham Co, VA
William Lewis BROWN, b.7 Feb 1806
Mary Ann BROWN, b.7 Jul 1807
Sally Lewis BROWN, b.18 Feb 1809
John Garman BROWN, b.8 Nov 1810
Marsha [---] BROWN, b.4 May 1813
Metelus Bently BROWN, b.6 Apr 1815
Elizabeth Moseley BROWN, b.11 Aug 1817
Henry Benejah BROWN, b.5 Mar 1820

MARRIAGES

Mitelus BROWN to Elizabeth L. MOSELEY, 7 Mar 1805
Garland B. PRICE to Mary Ann BROWN, 23 Dec 1823
Thompeson BROWN to Sarah L. BROWN, 21 Dec 1831
William L. BROWN to Emeline G. GILLS, 19 Dec 1832
John J. BROWN to Martha N. MOSELEY, 25 Nov 1835
Smith W. BROWN to Martha M. BROWN, 19 Dec 1839
William A. CHAMBERS to Elizabeth M. BROWN, 28 May 1840

DEATHS

John J. BROWN, son of Benajah BROWN, d.28 Jul 1807, age 30yrs
Sarah GARMAN, dau of Benajah BROWN, d.5 Jan 1808
Polly FORD, dau of Benajah BROWN, d.11 Jun 1814
Binajah BROWN, The Father, d.6 Jul 1814
Thos J. PRICE, d.1 Mar 1817
Patsy PRICE, d.17 Jun 1817
Polly FORD, d.6 Jun 1814
Mitclus BROWN, son of Benajah BROWN, d.31 Mar 1822
Mary BROWN, The Mother, d.1 Oct 1825
William B. PRICE, son of Thos PRICE, d.16 Aug 1827
William MASELY, d. Jul 1828
Mariah BAGBY, d.7 Sep 1828

Edward A. MOSELEY, son of William, d.24 Mar 1833
Garland B. PRICE, son of Thomas PRICE, d.25 Mar 1835, Age 34yrs
John M. MOSELEY, son of Edward A. MOSELEY, d.13 Feb 1843
Elizabeth M. CHAMBERS, d.10 Apr 1844, age 27yrs
Wm L BROWN, d.16 Oct 1845, age 40yrs
Elizabeth L. BROWN, wife of Mitclus BROWN, d. Jun 1848
Martha M. BROWN, d.15 Apr 1850
Henry B. BROWN, 13 [?] 1867
(Misc Bible File)

THE BESSELLIEU BIBLE

No Title Page or Date. A Huguenot Bible owned in the 1970's by Mr Bessellieu of St Petersburg, FL

BIRTHS

[----] BESSELLIEU was born 12 May 1773, Charleston
Mark Anthony BESSELLIEU was born 22 Oct 1774, St Thomas
CHARLES BESSELLIEU was born 14 May 1776, Berrisfolds Bounty, St Thomas
Philip Anthony BESSELLIEU born 27 Feb 1778, St Thomas
Lewis BESSELLIEU born 26 Mar 1779, St Thomas
[---] E. BESSELLIEU born 29 Jan 1782, St Thomas
Anne Martha BESSELLIEU b.25 Feb 1784, Wentworth Street, Charleston
Marta Catharine BESSELLIEU born 30 Jan 1786, Beaufour St, Charleston
El[---] Mai Nardine who married to Eliza KOWNIAN, 1 Jan 1820

23 Feb 1748/9 4 o'clock a son born to Samuel & Jane

HENDERSON
Joanna HENDERSON born 4 Aug 1732
Joanna CHECHE born 24 Dec 1723
Charles REILY and Joanna REILY married 10 Jul 1763, Charlestown
Charles REILY born 9 Aug 1765 in Charleston
Charles REILY departed this life 24 Sep 1783, age 76yrs
Philip John BESSELLIEU was born 14 Feb 1788, Charleston, SC
Philip Anthony BESSELLIEU departed this life 15 Feb 1795
[---], his wife, my beloved mother Susannah GISSENDENNER died [--] Jan 1829, age 77y, 8m
(Besselieu file)

OGILVIE BIBLE

HOLY BIBLE published by Hubbard Bros, 1873 at one time owned by Bessie R. Gray, Shreveport, LA

Robert C. JORDAN, b.27 Jun 1869, Hoener, LA, married 16 Nov 1893 to
Eloise OGILVIE JORDAN, b.16 Nov 1874, Gilveer, TX
Robert C. JORDAN, Jr, b.29 Aug 1894, Shreveport, LA
Eloise JORDAN, b.15 Mar 1902, Shreveport, LA
E.R. RATCLIFF, b.10 Mar 1874, Glaster, MS, d.6 Oct 1943, married 15 Dec 1898 to
Bessie O. RATCLIFF, b.22 Aug 1877, Shreveport, LA, d.2 Jul 1902
Bessie O. RATCLIFF, dau of E.R. & Bessie RATCLIFF, b.8 Jul 1902
W.B. OGILVIE, b.25 Nov 1847, Coweto Co, GA, d.1 Feb 1899; married 3 Jul 1890 to
E.V. CULBERSON, b.2 Jul 1849, Troup Co, GA, d.20 Feb

1906
Acheah Lou (Mai) OGILVIE, b.18 Aug 1872, Upshur Co, TX; d.9 Aug 1935, married 29 Apr 1891
Eloise OGILVIE, b.16 Nov 1874, Upshur Co, TX, d.16 Jun 1916, married 16 Nov 1893
Bessie CULBERSON OGILVIE, b.25 Aug 1877, Shreveport, LA; d.9 Jul 1902, married 15 Dec 1898
Russell J. OGILVIE, b.3 Dec 1883, Shreveport, LA, d.5 Feb 1941, married 9 Oct 1906
Parents of Ella C. OGILVIE
W.P. CULBERSON, b.29 Mar 1819, d.21 Sep 1898, married 14 Oct 1845 to
Susan E. DARDEN, b.22 Oct 1825, d.22 Feb 1889
Parents of Susan E. DARDEN
James H. DARDEN, b.15 Aug 1801; d. Jun 1864, married 25 Mar 1824 to
Anna GASTON b.16 Sep 1802, d.18 Jul 1884
Children of W.P. & Susan CULBERSON
Bernice Achsah, b.21 Jun 1846
James Isaac, b.4 Feb 1848, d.12 May 1901
Ella Veronica, b.2 Jul 1849, d.20 Feb 1906
Mary Anne, b.14 Feb 1851
Columbus Young, b.18 Aug 1855
Elizabeth Susan, b.25 Feb 1857
William Pinkney, b.4 Mar 1859
Walter Lee, b.10 Dec 1861
Albert Leonidas, b.24 Jan 1865, d.1 Sep 1899
Thomas Augustus, b.2 Aug 1855

Marriage Certificate
W.B. OGILVIE and Ella V. CULBERSON
married at Gilmer, Upshur Co, TX 3 Jul 1870
In Presence of

E.H. Hopson, C. Smithy, A.D. Gaskill, Elder MECS
(Misc Bible File)

PARK FAMILY BIBLE I

Records from the Bible belonging to Joel Parks of Scipio, Cayuga Co, NY and Point Dover, Ontario Co, NY. One double page was cut out at one time the remaining was copies as found. The bible then owned by Dorothy I. Vandercook of Glen Ellyn, IL. The Bible printed by Holbrook, Brattleborough, VT, 1816.

Joel PARK married in the twenty third year of his age to Cloe FOSTER in the twenth year of her age in the year one thousand Seven Hundred and Eighty four the Last Day of October 1784

And she Died and was buried the First day of January 1832

Daniel PARKS b.1 Oct 1785
Juliana PARKS, b.14 Feb 1787, d.19 Apr 1823
Leonora PARKS, b.14 Oct 1788
Moses PARKS, b.16 Dec 1790, d.20 Nov 1819
Nancy PARKS, b.1 Nov 1792
Loregalma PARKS, b.25 Jan 1795 [or 1796], d.24 Aug 1797 [?]
William PARKS, 24 Jan 1798
Elisha F. PARKS, b.8 Jan 1800 , he died in his 88th year
<u>MARRIAGES</u>
Juliana PARKS to David HENDERSON, 22 Dec 1803
Leonora PARKS to Benjamin P. MARTIN, Apr 1815
Daniel PARKS to Nancy PHELPS, 31 Mar 1808

Jennie Adalade HOUGHTON, b.26 Jul 1868
Horace Herbert HOUGHTON, b.3 Apr 1870, d.21 1955, Adams, MA
Horace HOUGHTON married to Lena May IVERSON 30 Sep 1894

Elisah F. PARKS married in [++++++++] to Sally McDOWELL
Mrs Elizabeth AVICHOUSER d.20 Nov 1894
married 13 Oct 1867 to Charles HOUGHTON
(Misc Bible File / 13-207)

CLARKSON BIBLE

THE COTTAGE BIBLE, Printed and published by Case, Tiffany and Co, Hartford, CT, 1853
Family Bible of Smith and Lydia CLARKSON
Smith CLARKSON, b.3 Dec 1819
Lydia LARKIN, b.24 Jan 1824
Smith CLARKSON, b.10 Sep 1843
Cornelia CLARKSON, b.28 Feb 1848
Sarah CLARKSON, b. Feb 1850
Mary Augusta CLARKSON, b.1 Aug 1854
Fred CLARKSON, b. Mar 1857
Harry CLARKSON, b.9 Nov 1862
MARRIAGES
Smith CLARKSON to Lydia LARKIN 1842
Smith CLARKSON to Mary Jane LOUNSBERRY 1881 in New York City
Cornelia CLARKSON to Harry Herman SMITH 1869, Perth Amboy, [NJ]
Sarah CLARKSON to Henry Clay BATTELLE, 1878 in Jersey City, [NJ]

Mary Augusta CLARKSON to John William CAMPBELL,12 Jun 1879, Jersey City
Harry CLARKSON to Anna Marie KLAPROTH, 13 Dec 1882, Jersey City
DEATHS
Smith CLARKSON d.7 Apr 1888, Newark, [NJ]
Lydia Larkin CLARKSON, d.5 Mar 1898, Newark
Sarah d.5 May 1887 [?]
Frederick, d.28 Aug 1906, Scranton, PA
Cornelia, d.1 Dec 1908
Mary Augusta, d.8 Jul 1913, Newark
Smith, d. Jan 1925, Jersey City
Harry, d. Jun 1929, Upper Darby, PA

Nelle Lange CAMPBELL, b.19 Mar 1880, married 14 Sep 1921 to Rev Lyman Whitney ALLEN, married Second 18 Jun 1940 to Col Philander BETTS
Anna CLARKSON, b.5 Nov 1883; dau of Harry; married 6-8-1904 Richard Jones BOND
(Misc Bible File / 2-335)

CLARKSON BIBLE II

copied from a Bible owned in 1947 by Mrs R.P. Vroom, Maplewood, NJ. The Bible Published by Charles Ewer, Boston, no date given.
only record prior to 1833 were copied in the Transcript we have.
Randolph CLARKSON, b.4 Aug 1759
Catherine, wife of Randolph CLARKSON, b.15 Sep 1762
Randolph CLARKSON and Catherine LOW married 1 Apr 1783

Children of Randolph and Catherine CLARKSON:
Margaret, b.31 Mar 1784
John, b.30 Jul 1786
Phebe, b.28 Oct 1788
Isaac Freeman, b.11 Nov 1790
William, b.1 Mar 1793
Catharine, b.3 Sep 1795
Rachel, b.31 Jul 1798
Randolph, b.4 Oct 1800
James, b.1 Aug 1804

Randolph CLARKSON, d.13 Mar 1833, age 74y 7m 9d
Widow Catharine Low CLARKSON, d.26 May 1846, age 84y 8m 11ds
(Misc Bible File / 2-335)

VAN NESS BIBLE

No Title Page or Date copied in Nov 1955 by Edward N. AcAllister

BIRTHS

Evert H. VAN NESS, b.24 Sep 1772
Caty SMITH, b.9 Oct 1778
Henry VAN NESS, b.11 May 1778
Sophia VAN NESS, b.24 Dec 1799
Rachel VAN NESS, b.11 Feb 1802
Jacob Smith VAN NESS, b.12 Mar 1804
William VAN NESS, b.31 Aug 1807
James VAN NESS, b.4 Jul 1810
Francis VAN NESS, b.7 Dec 1812
Isaac VAN NESS, b.23 Feb 1818
Elias VAN NESS, b.29 Jun 1820

DEATHS

Elias VAN NESS, d.4 Oct 1820
Henry E. VAN NESS, d.19 Dec 1836, aged 38yrs 7m 8dys
Caty SMITH, wife of Evert H. VAN NESS, d.8 Dec 1855, aged 77yrs,2mos
Evert H. VAN NESS, d.27 Aug 1862; aged 89yrs 11m 3dys
(Misc Bible File / 2-456)

NIEUKIRK AND FOSTER BIBLE

Bible published by Mathew Carey, Philadelphia, 1803 The original in 1924 was in the possession of the Salem County, New Jersey Historical Society. Copied by Mary R. C. Clayton in May 1924.

"This Bible is the property of Matthew NIEUKIRK, November 1803, now the property of Judah FOSTER, May 5th, 1808"

Matthew NIEUKIRK and Catherine his wife were married 18 Dec 1785
Samuel NIEUKIRK and Rachel his wife were married 30 May 1809
Judah FOSTER and Christiana his wife were married 17 Mar 1812
Benjamin NIEUKIRK and Rebecca his wife were married 1 Jan 1814
Judah FOSTER and Hannah his wife were married 4 Apr 1814
Judah Foster and Saloma his wife were married 4 March 1830
Judah FOSTER and Barbary his wife were married 1 Oct 1833

BIRTHS

Matthew NIEUKIRK b.28 Feb 1763
Catherine his wife b.21 Nov 1767
Rachel, their Daughter,b.4 Mar 1787
Hannah, their Daughter b.22 Sep 1789
Christiana, their Daughter, b.17 Sep 1791

Benjamin, their Son, b.18 Dec 1794
Matthew and Mary were b.29 Jul 1799
Matthew, the younger, b.26 Aug 1801
Judah FOSTER, b.29 Mar 1788
Cyrus Benjamin NIEUKIRK Rebecca his wife b.6 Dec 1823
Cyrus their son, b.4 Apr 1814
Harrison, their son, b.18 Apr 1811
John, their son, b.24 May 1815
Margaret, their daughter, b.29 Aug 1820
Samuel NIEUKIRK and Rachel his wife was married 31 May 1809
Ethan, their son, b.5 Mar 1810
George W.I., their son, b.11 Nov 1811
Elizabeth, their daughter, b.4 Mar 1813
Christiana, their daughter, b.29 Dec 1814
Charles, their son, b.2 Mar 1816
Constant W., their son, b.27 Dec 1818
Samuel, their son, b.17 Apr 1820
Christiana FOSTER, daughter of Judah FOSTER and Christiana his wife, b.4 Apr 1813
Catherine, daughter of Judah FOSTER and Hannah his wife, b.15 May 1815
Matthew N., their son, b.1 Jun 1817
Rolins L., their son, b.27 Aug 1819
Hannah, their daughter, b.4 Apr 1821
Ira FOSTER, their son, b.6 Jun 1823

DEATHS

Matthew the elder and son of Matthew and Catherine NIEUKIRK, d.29 Jul 1799
Mary, their daughter, d.4 Jul 1800
Matthew, the younger, their son, d. Oct 1802
Christiana FOSTER, departed this life 8 Apr 1813
Margaret, the daughter of Benjamin and Rebecca NIEUKIRK,

d.2 Jun 1821
Rachel daughter of Matthew and Catherine NIEUKIRK, d.4 Sep 1823
Ethan, son of Samuel and Rachel NIEUKIRK, d.19 Aug 1811
Benjamin son of Matthew and Catherine NIEUKIRK, d.18 Jan 1824
Catherine NIEUKIRK, d.28 Apr. 1828
Hannah FOSTER, d.24 Nov,1828, wife of Judah FOSTER
Saloma, wife of Judah FOSTER, d.16 Feb 1833
Barbara FOSTER, wife of Judah FOSTER, d.31 May 1857
Hannah Avis, dau of Judah FOSTER, d. Jun 1853
Ira FOSTER, son of Judah FOSTER, d.4 Feb 1857
Christiana FOSTER, Daughter of Judah FOSTER and Christiana his wife, d.28 Apr 1813
Matthew N. FOSTER, son of Judah FOSTER, d.2 Mar 1882

BIRTHS

Jane daughter of Judah FOSTER and Saloma, his wife, b.3 Dec 1830
Harriet C. daughter of Judah FOSTER and Saloma his wife, b.11 Apr 1832
(Misc Bible File / 2-453)

MANNING BIBLE

Copied from a Bible at that time in the possession of Mrs Harry J. Manning, Oreland, PA. The Bible Published and sold by H. & E. Phinney, Cooperstown, NY, 1834

MARRIAGES

David MANNING, son of Jeremiah MANNING to
Rhoda RUNYON, dau of Reune B. RUNYON, married 8 Feb 1834

BIRTHS

David MANNING, b.28 Feb 1806

Rhoda MANNING, b.31 Aug 1809
Samuel MANNING, b.3 Aug 1834
David MANNING, b.18 Apr 1837
Elizabeth MANNING, b.11 Sep 1839
Reune B. MANNING, b.8 Jan 1844
William Henry MANNING, b.10 Nov 1845
<u>DEATHS</u>
David MANNING, d.21 Apr 1837
(Misc Bible File / 2-465)

CAMPBELL FAMILY BIBLE

Copied from a Bible in the possession of Mary Louise Tappen about 1956
Bible published by M. Carey, Philadelphia, 1813
Neil CAMPBELL, b.16 May 1768 (Monday)
Prudence CAMPBELL, b.9 Dec 1763
Their Daughter, Mary CAMPBELL, b.22 Sep 1799
Elizabeth CAMPBELL, b.13 May 1804 (Thursday)
Samuel Ayers TAPPEN, b.2 Mar 1798
Elizabeth C. TAPPEN, b.30 May 1804
Their son Neil Campbell TAPPEN, b.21 Jan 1823 (Tuesday)
William Manning TAPPEN, b.14 Feb 1824 (Saturday)
Alexander Barton TAPPEN, b.30 Nov 1826 (Thursday)
Theodore TAPPEN, b.24 Mar 1829 (Tuesday)
Randolph TAPPEN, b.4 Feb 1832 (Saturday)
Monro TAPPEN, b.10 May 1836 (Tuesday)
Adelbert Burnet TAPPEN, b.13 Jun 1838 (Wednesday)
Anna Elizabeth TAPPEN, b.23 Apr 1840 (Thursday)
(Misc Bible File)

WINSTON FAMILY BIBLE

Copied from the "BIG BIBLE" of Alice Taylor Winston Pettus. Bible owned by Agnes W. Robert of Birmingham, AL. Copied by Nell Winston McMahan Fallaw.

MARRIAGES

Anthony WINSTON, Sr to Alice TAYLOR, 27 Feb 1747

Anthony WINSTON, Jr, son of Anthony and Alice WINSTON to Kezziah JONES, 11 Mar 1776

Anthony WINSTON, son of Anthony and Kezziah WINSTON to Sally A. WATSON, 27 Aug 1806

Alice Taylor WINSTON to John J. PETTUS, 21 Dec 1812

BIRTHS

Anthony WINSTON, Sr, son of Isaac and Sarah WINSTON, b.29 Sep 1723

Alice Taylor WINSTON, dau of James and Alice TAYLOR, b.21 May 1730

CHILDREN of Anthony and Alice WINSTON

Sarah WINSTON, b.9 Feb 1748

Anthony WINSTON, b.25 Nov 1750

Alice WINSTON, b.20 Mar 1752

Martha WINSTON, b.8 Jan 1755

Mary WINSTON, b.3 Jun 1759

DEATHS

Anthony WINSTON, Sr, d.29 Jul 1783, aged 60yrs

Alice TAYLOR, his wife, d.24 Oct 1764, aged 34yrs

Alice WINSTON, daughter of Edmund WINSTON, d. Feb 1784

Anthony WINSTON, 2nd, d.20 Dec 1828

Kezziah WINSTON, d.21 Oct 1826, age 66yrs

CHILDREN of Anthony WINSTON, 2nd and Kessiah JONES:

Anthony, b.Dec 1782

John J., b.31 May 1785

Edmund, d. at four months

William, b.21 Mar 1789
Alice Taylor, b.21 Dec 1780
Joel Walker, b. 5 Dec 1792
Isaac, b.22 Jan 1795
Mary Walker, b.6 Nov 1796
Edmund, b.1 Jan 1801
Thomas Jones, b.2 Sep 1804
(Misc Bible File)

JAMES McDONNELL WINSTON BIBLE

No Title Page or Date,Original Bible owned by Mrs J. B. Morton of Birmingham, AL
entries copied by Nell Winston McMahan Fallaw.

MARRIAGES

James McDONNELL WINSTON to Rebecca Virginia BRODNAX, 16 Oct 1845 at home of Anthony Augustus Winston

BIRTHS

Anthony Augustus, b.26 Aug 1848
William Overton, b.20 Jan 1852
Annie Gage, b.20 Feb 1854
Fleta, b.7 May 1858
Fannie, b.12 Nov 1860
Ella Watson, b.24 Feb 1864
Olive James, b.6 Sep 1869

DEATHS

Anthony Augustus, d.18 Feb 1849
Fleta, d.4 Oct 1865, age 7yrs
(Misc Bible Files)

FLOURNOY BIBLE

No Title Page or Date

Obituary

Ellen Flournoy THORNTON, d.18 Sep 1885, Infant dau of D. McCarty THORNTON & Ellen F. THORNTON, age 17mos 21dys

Daniel McCARTY F. THORNTON married to Ellen FLOURNOY, 4 Jul 1883, Richmond, VA

BIRTHS

Ellen Flournoy THORNTON, b.28 Mar 1884
Daniel MaCarty Fitzhugh THORNTON, b.22 Apr 1885
Mary Dade THORNTON, b.24 Nov 1886
Parke Poindexter THORNTON, b.2 Feb 1888
Eliza Archer THORNTON, b.22 Sep 1889
Sarah Flournoy THORNTON, b.8 Jun 1892
Richard Flournoy THORNTON, b.11 Feb 1894
Lawrence Dade THORNTON, b.26 Oct 1895
James Mayo THORNTON, b.13 Nov 1897
Virginia Elizabeth THORNTON, b.21 Nov 1899

DEATHS

Ellen Flournoy THORNTON, d.18 Sep 1885, age 17mos
Richard Flournoy THORNTON, d.12 Jan 1895, age 11mos 21dys
Lawrence Dade THORNTON, d.29 Jun 1896, age 8mos 3dys
(Laurent Flournoy file)

KIDD FAMILY BIBLE

Holman's Edition THE HOLY BIBLE. Published by A.J. Holman & Co, Philadelphia, 1884

MARRIAGE

Robert W. KIDD [Crewe?], VA to Martyne BRADSHAW of

[Crewe?], VA on 3 Jun 1896 at Bristol, TN by Rev W.R. Laird
Charley Hunter A.S.J. Wheeler
BIRTHS
Robt Wm, son of Wm & Martha KIDD, b.29 Apr 1863
Martyne, dau of Edward & Rosa L. BRADSHAW, b.22 May [---]
Howard Leigh, son of R.W. & Jennie M. KIDD, b.18 Mar 1886
William Richard, son of R.W. & Jennie M. KIDD, b.10 Sep 1888
Annie May, dau of R.W. & Jennie M. KIDD, b.7 Nov 1890
Robert Millard, son of R.W. & Jennie M. KIDD, b.22 Apr 1893
Martha Lois, dau of Robt Wm & Martyne B. KIDD, b.19 Jun 1897
Martyne, dau of Robt Wm & Martyne KIDD, b.25 Dec 1899
Alton Bradshaw, son of Robt Wm KIDD & Martyne BRADSHAW, b. [----]
(Laurent Flournoy File)

STONE BIBLE

THE NEW TESTAMENT, published by Mathew Carey, Philadelphia 1810
At one time owned by Mrs Grace Streety Tuggle.

Philip Taylor STONE, b. 20 Mar 1811
Penelope Candice STONE, b.4 Mar 1813
William Thomas STONE, b.29 Jul 1815
Anderson STONE, b.28 Jun 1817
J. Osborne STONE, b.22 Nov 1822
David Lawrence STONE, b.29 Jul 1824

Charles Lewis STONE, b.3 May 1826
Willis Anderson STONE, b.13 Apr 1828
John Michael STONE, b.6 Sep 1830
Laurent Flournoy FIle)

HUDSPETH FAMILY BIBLE

No Title Page or Date

BIRTHS

George R. HUDSPETH, b.7 Sep 1851
John Green HUDSPETH, b.25 Jul 1854
Sophia Elizabeth HUDSPETH, b.3 Apr 1857, d.24 Nov 1863
Ella Bell HUDSPETH, b.8 Oct 1864
Simon Buckner HUDSPETH, b.23 Feb 1862, d.3 Jun 1863
Cindarella HUDSPETH, b.16 Apr 1825
Samuel M. HUDSPETH, b.18 Sep 1815
Fred Allen FORD, b.22 Jun 1891, Blue Spring, MO
Anna Georgie FORD, b.20 Jun 1894 in Cottage by the Bridge on Little Blue near Lake City, MO
Caey Jonathan Maurice FORD, b.26 Aug 1896
Elizabeth Leona FORD, b.6 Feb 1904, married to Marvin E. DUEKLE, 21 May 1930

MARRIAGES

S.M. HUDSPETH to Sarah E, HUDSPETH, 12 Jul 1841

Infant Dau, b.22 May 1842, d. same day
George T.J. HUDSPETH, b.8 Sep 1847
Infant son, b.9 Feb 1850, d. Feb 1850
Cindarilla HUDSPETH, late PAYNE, d.27 Jun 1859
Anna L. HUDSPETH to Clarence M. FROST in Columbia, TN at Christian Church, 15 Jul 1885 by George Reynolds
Linn TANRELHILL to J. Frank EVANS
John C. FORD to Ella B. HUDSPETH, 27 Feb 1890, at

residence of Geo B. Hudspeth, by Rev Leonard
Geo. HUDSPETH to Rufus P. MORROW, Nov 1887
Sterling CLARK to Mary WOOD, 17 Aug 1780, Warren Co, NC
(Laurent Flournoy File / 20-69)

ROSSER ADAMS MALONE FAMILY BIBLE

No Title Page or Date, Copy from a bible at that time owned by Thomas Pace Malone of Albany GA. Copies by Elizabeth Smith Weaver. No Title Page with records

Marriage Certificate
Rosser Adams MALONE to Mary Eliza COLLIER, 23 Dec 1879 at Centerville, Talbot Co, GA

Rosser A. MALONE, Sr, d.20 Apr 1920

CHILDREN of Rosser A. MALONE & Mary COLLIER MALONE
Rosser Adamd MALONE, Jr., b.7 Dec 1880, Allendale, SC; d.19 Feb 1929, m.7 Jul 1905
Linnie Florence MALONE, 13 Jan 1883, Centerville, Talbot Co, GA, m.8 Jul 1903
Charles Person MALONE, b.3 Mar 1884, d.30 Jun 1887
Harry Callier MALONE, b.5 Aug 1887, Talbotton, GA, m.9 Jun 1915
James Eugene MALONE, 21 Jul 1890, Macon, GA, m. May 1916
Mamie Leonora MALONE, 21 Jun 1892, Macon, GA, d.29 Dec 1892
Jane Hudson MALONE, 9 Dec 1894, Albany, GA, d.14 Aug

1896
Hudson Jenkins MALONE, b.30 Nov 1898, Albany, GA, m.25 Sep 1920
Thomas Pace MALONE, b.13 Dec 1900, Albanym GA,m.19 Mar 1924
MARRIAGES
Rosser Adams MALONE, Jr to Elizabeth MIRIAM; then to Elizabeth SPEER
Linnie Florence MALONE to Leon Perdue SMITH
Harry Callier MALONE to Allie Leonard DAUGHERTY [Daughtry]
Thomas Eugene MALONE to Minnie H. CROWDER
Hudson Jenkins MALONE to Katie Sue REESE
Thomas Pace MALONE to Marie PAYETTE
BIRTHS
To Rosser A. MALONE, Jr & E.M. MALONE
Rosser A. MALONE III ; Herry Kenwood MALONE
To Leon P. SMITH & Linnie M. SMITH
Rufus Eugene SMITH, Mary Elizabeth SMITH,Rosser Malome SMITH, Maidee SMITH
To Harry C. MALONE & Allie D. MALONE
Allie Daughtry MALONE b.28 Mar 1920
Harry Callier MALONE, b.18 Aug 1825 Both b. Albany GA
To Hudson J. MALONE & Katie Sue MALONE
Mary Brown MALONE, b.28 Aug 1924, Albany GA
Thomas P. MALONE & Marie B. MALONE
Anne Marie MALONE, b.3 Apr 1927, Albany, GA
Jean MALONE, b.18 Dec 1932, Waycross, GA
(Laurent Flournoy File)

CHARLES J. MALONE BIBLE

No Title Page or Date, Copied by Mrs Harry C.

Malone of Albany, GA.

Rosser Adams MALONE, b.8 Jul 1854
Charles J. MALONE, b.14 Oct 1811, d.3 Oct 1873, Americus, GA
Jane Ann HUDSON MALONE, b.5 June 1819, d.11 Aug 1877, Macon, GA

Charles J. MALONE married Jane Ann HUDSON, 15 Mar 1838 at Eatonton, Putnam Co, GA by Rev Miles Grees
(Laurent Flournoy File)

THOMPSON - JUSTICE - VEREEN BIBLES

No Title page or Date, what seems to be entries from three Bibles interfiled; No Title Pages attached

MARRIAGES

Moore THOMPSON to Louise C. SLOAN, 16 Apr 1911
Eloise THOMPSON to Frank K. JENKINS, 30 Dec 1938
R.G. THOMPSON to Katherine FIZER, 12 Sep 1938
Moore THOMPSON, Jr to Georgia Mae CHAPPELL, Oct 1944
James B. THOMPSON to Frances CEGER, 27 Jun 1951

BIRTHS

R.G. SLOAN, b.[--] Oct 1851
E.E. SLOAN, b.21 Jun 1864
B.G. SLOAN, b.21 Jun 1883
Louise C. SLOAN, b.20 Sep 1888
R.G. SLOAN married to Ella JUSTICE, 2 Feb 1882
Moore THOMPSON, b.18 Aug 1883
Louise SLOAN THOMPSON, b.20 Sep 1888
Eloise THOMPSON, b.3 Jan 1912

R.G.THOMPSON, b.1 Oct 1913
Moore THOMPSON, Jr, b.13 Oct 1915
Jane Beverly THOMPSON, b.27 Feb 1930

This Certifies that Francis JUSTICE and Amanda F. VEREEN were united in Marriage according to he laws of North Carolina at Joseph J. VEREEN on 4 Feb 1858

Thomas G. Roy

T.M. JUSTICE, b.11 Dec 1858
E.E. JUSTICE. b.2 Jun 1861
[line unreadable]
Elizie JUSTICE. b.[-] Nov 1865
Bonnie JUSTICE. b.21 Jan 1868

BIBLE of William and Elizabeth VARIN written on first page:
William VEREEN, b.3 Nov 1729, son of Jeremiah & Mary VEREEN
Elizabeth LEWIS, b. Nov 1734, dau of Charles & Martha LEWIS
CHILDREN:
William VEREEN, b.27 Jan 1756
Charles VEREEN, b.29 Oct 1757
Jeremiah VEREEN, b.3 Jun 1760
Martha Elizabeth VEREEN, b.31 Mar 1762
John VEREEN, b.12 May 1765
Elizabeth VEREEN, b.21 Dec 1767
Mary VEREEN, b.10 Dec 1774
Daniel VEREEN, b.20 Aug 1777
<u>MARRIAGES</u>
William VEREEN was married to Elizabeth LEWIS, 20 Nov 1754
<u>DEATHS</u>
William VEREEN, Sr, d.20 Sep 1789, on Sunday about noon

Elizabeth, wife of Wm VEREEN, Sr, d. 7 Jun [----]; aged 45yrs 5mos, 7dys
Martha Elizabeth, wife of Daniel MARRALL, d.Saturday Morning about Sunrise 1786, aged 22yrs, 8mos, 17dys
Jeremiah VEREEN, d.14 Aug 1813, at 10 o'clock in the evening, aged 54yrs, 2mos, 11dys
Joseph Jeremiah VEREEN, son of Jeremiah and Elizabeth VEREEN, b.16 Jul 1812
Elizabeth L. VEREEN, dau of Elizabeth B. VEREEN, d.25 Jun 1854
Amelia L. Thomas, d. 9 Aug ___
This bible is owned by Jackson H. VEREEN of Mandarin, FL
(Jacques Vareen file)

YOST FAMILY BIBLE

No Title Page or Date

BIRTHS

Ephraim YOST, b.4 Jun 1819 in Wayne, Lycoming Co, PA
Hulah J. CALKIN, b.20 Dec 1824 in Columbia, Bradford Co, PA
Thomas F. YOST, b.21 Jul 1845, Manchester, Tioga Co, PA
George A. YOST, b.8 Mar 1847, Shippen, Tioga Co, PA
Isaac R. YOST, b.19 Jul 1849, Wells, Bradford Co, PA
James E. YOST,b.16 Sep 1850, Wells, Bradford Co, PA
Mary J. YOST, b.26 Dec 1851, Wells, Bradford Co, PA
Stephen H. YOST, b.11 Nov 1854, Wells, Bradford Co, PA
Emma M. YOST, b.12 Oct 1857, Michigan Precint, State of ILL, Livingston Co

MARRIAGES

Ephraim YOST to Huldah J. CALKINS, married by Rev Wm Crum at Troy, Bradford Co, PA on 16 Oct 1844
George Albert YOST son of Ephraim and Huldah YOST,

married to Maria L. PARKER by Rev Gray at OTTAWA, IL [----] 1870
Mary J. YOST, dau of Ephraim and Huldah J. YOST married Isaac Shiles BALL on 21 Sep 1870 by Rev Force at Ottawa, IL
Thomas F. YOST, oldest son of Ephraim and H.J. YOST married Fida SEARS, Mar 1873 at Ottawa, IL
Emma M. YOST, dau of Ephraim and Hulda YOST married to Clare A. COOPER, 13 Oct 1878 at Marsells, IL
(John Vassell file)

PLUE FAMILY BIBLE

No Title Page or Date, copied by Miss Hazel M. Plue, 16 Aug 1963. The original bible in the possession of Mrs Vella Plue, Hubbardton, VT
FAMILY RECORD
MARRIAGES
Freeman PLUE to Kate C. ALLEN, 30 Aug 1868
Ashley C. PLUE to Winifred M. McDONALD, 14 Mar 1892
George F. PLUE to Cora MAYHEW, 22 Nov 1897
Allen C. PLUE to Bessie M. BASCOM, 2 Oct 1900
Allen C. PLUE to Vella Mallory BUTTERFIELD, 28 Mar 1945

CHILDREN of Ashley C. PLUE
Harry HOWARD to Vera M. PLUE, 27 Aug 1913
Freeman E. PLUE to Florence WHITCOMB, 24 Feb 1917
Herbert HUGHES to Helen McDONALD PLUE, 26 Nov 1919
Howard MARCIELLA to Christine Katherine PLUE, 2Jan 1922
BIRTHS
CHILDREN of Freeman and Kate PLUE

Ashley C. PLUE, b.27 Jul 1869
Jennie A. PLUE, b.6 Dec 1871
George F. PLUE, b.22 Mar 1875
Charles A. PLUE, b.11 Sep 1877
CHILDREN of Ashley C. and Winifred PLUE
Vivian Aileen PLUE, b.1 Nov 1892
Vera Howard PLUE, b.25 Mar 1894
Freeman Eugene PLUE, b.12 Nov 1895
Hazel Marie PLUE, 22 Apr 1897
Helen McDonald PLUE, b.10 May 1899
Winifred May PLUE, b.1 Feb 1909
<u>DEATHS</u>
Freeman PLUE, d.3 Jun 1877
Kenneth M. PLUE, d.19 Feb 1926
Kate C. PLUE, d.8 Apr 1927
Jennie A. PLUE, d.24 Apr 1947
Winnifred M. PLUE, d.14 Feb 1909

Winifred May McDONALD, b.13 Aug 1871 at Benson, VT
Ashley C. PLUE, d.13 Mar 1932 at Benson, VT
(John Vassell file)

BANVARD BIBLE

The original in the Banvard Papers (B219) at The Minnesota Historical Society manuscript Collection. No Title Page

Daniel & Elizabeth BANVARD was married 25 Dec 1791

David, b.22 Dec 1792, 2 o'clock in the morning

Daniel, b.23 Oct 1794
Elizabeth, b.11 Feb 1797
Jane, b.13 Feb 1800
Margaret, b.21 May 1802
Mary Ann, b.14 Jun 1804, d.31 Mar 1805
Catherine, b.20 Jan 1806
Peter, b.6 Mar 1808
Joseph, b.9 May 1810
Jesse, b.11 Apr 1813
John, b.15 Nov 1815
(David Banvard file)

NATHAN DEPRIEST BIBLE

NEW TESTAMENT Published by Mark and Charles Kerr, Edinburgh, MDCCXCII
Original in possession of Rev Travis T. DuPriest of Racine, WI

Levana DePRIEST, b.25 Sep 1800
John Buryan DePRIEST, b.25 May 1802
Lorianna DePRIEST, b.18 May 1804
James Henry DePRIEST, b.6 Jan 1806
Jestus [---] DePRIEST, b.13 Aug 1809
Dusella [---] DePRIEST, b.5 Jan 18[--]
Charles Austin DePRIEST, b. [-] Dec 1815
Talachi DePRIEST, b.1 Sep 1817

HOLY BIBLE Published by American Bible Society, New York, 1852
Original in possessions of Rev Travis T. DuPriest of Racine, WI

[------] DuPRIEST, b.5 Feb 1841
Chas A. DuPRIEST, b. [--] Oct 1843
John F. DuPRIEST, b.5 May 1846
Alexander B. DuPRIEST, b.23 Aug 1848
Lucy Ann DuPRIEST, b.9 Jun 1850
Mary J. L. DuPRIEST, b.18 Jul 1852
William DuPRIEST, b.8 Sep 185[-]
(DuPriest File)

PAYSANT BIBLE

HOLY BIBLE Published by B.B. Mussey & Co., Boston, 1847
Copies given by Lewis F. Parsly of Oak Ridge, TN

FAMILY RECORD MARRIAGES
Peter PAYZANT to C. J. SMITH, 20 Oct 1819
Grace E. PAYZANT, b.28 Oct 1840
Rachel M. PAYZANT, b.13 Jun 1850
Lewis L. PAYZANT, b.11 Jan 1855
John Y. PAYZANT, b.27 Aug 1868
CHILDREN of L. S. PAYZANT
Florence A. PAYZANT. b.28 Oct 18[--]
Clara A. PAYZANT, b.21 Feb 1892
CHILDREN of Lewis SMITH and Mary Jane PAYZANT
Florence AUSTIN to William L. BARSS by E.M. Sanyder, 28 Oct 1879
Clara ALASTES to Edward A. ANDERSON,by C.H. William, 21 Oct 1890
Lewis King PAYZANT to Florence D. BELCHER by Rev Maitell,14 Sep 1897
Henry Allison PAYZANT to Eugaine Lee McCULLOCH by Rev Simpson, 23 Feb 1899

Minnie Marila PAYZANT to Ford J. WARD, 30 Nov 1902
BIRTHS
Peter PAYZANT, b.12 Dec 1793
Cath. J. SMITH, b.5 Oct 1797
Grace E. PAYZANT, b.31 Oct 1820
Margaret H. PAYZANT, b.5 May 1822
John L. PAYZANT, b.17 Oct 1823
Rachel M. PAYZANT, b.2 Jan 1825
Lewis L. PAYZANT, b.21 Nov 1830
Sarah J. PAYZANT, b.23 Nov 1832
John Y. PAYZANT, b.9 Feb 1837
CHILDREN of Lewis L and Mary J. PAYZANT
Florence Austin PAYZANT, b.31 Jan 1856
Clara Alcestia PAYZANT, b.8 Sep 1858
Sarah Kate PAYZANT, b.4 Feb 1860
Blowers Smith PAYZANT, b.14 Aug 1861
Lewis King PAYZANT, b.20 Oct 1862

Henry Allison PAYZANT, b.23 Sep 1872
Minnie Marita PAYZANT, b.28 Oct 1877

CHILDREN of Lewis K. and Florence Betcher PAYZANT
Lewis Belcher PAYZANT, b.14 Jun 1898
Claire Eleanor M. PAYZANT, b.6 Apr 1900
John William PAYZANT, b.11 Nov 1901
Donald Anderson PAYZANT, b.20 Oct 1903
Edward Anderson PAYZANT, b.23 May 1911
Grace Edith PAYZANT, b.9 Jun 1912
Florence Carolyn PAYZANT, b.8 Dec 1919
CHILDREN of John W. and Sidney (SHAW) PAYZANT
Lewis John PAYZANT, b.8 Jun 1924
Geoffrey Barss PAYZANT, b.7 Mar 1926
Sidney Jane PAYZANT, b.30 Jul 1941

John Shaw PAYZANT, b.3 Sep 1944
CHILDREN of Lewis John and Joan MURRAY PAYZANT, married 21 Jul 1948
Lewis Peter Murray PAYZANT, b.11 Oct 1949
Philip William PAYZANT, b.22 May 1951
Aida Kercut PAYZANY, b.16 Jul 1953
Janet Sidney PAYZANT, b.15 Apr 1956
Antoinette PAYZANT. b.6 Mar 1959
CHILDREN of Geoffrey Barss and Mary Louise CHRISTIE PAYZANT, married 19 Aug 1948
Stephen Geoffrey PAYZANT, b.22 Dec 1952
John Chrsitie PAYZANT, b.29 Mar 1955
Bleinda Jane PAYZANT, b.28 Feb 1961
(Louis Payzant File)

AGEE BIBLE

No Title Page or Date

CHILDREN'S NAMES
Minnie Jenerene AGEE, b.25 Nov 1909
Benjamin Franklin AGEE, b.20 Mar 1911
Eula Delema AGEE, b.10 Aug 1912
Olive Clarinda AGEE, b.11 Sep 1915
Carmon Silvanus AGEE, b.1 Feb 1914
Ruby Joyce AGEE, b.13 Dec 1916
Nina Isabell AGEE, b.3 Dec 1917
Vivian Marie AGEE, 9 Jul 1919
child b. & d. 9 Jul 1921
Elenor Frances AGEE, b.23 May 1922
James Adrian AGEE, b.9 Oct 1924
Amy Avis [June] AGEE, b.30 Jun 1926
Esther Naomi AGEE, 13 Nov 1928
Mary Elizabeth AGEE, b.6 Jun 1932

John AGEE, b.26 Mar 1935
Sallie Raylene AGEE, b.-- May 1937
MARRIAGES
Benjamin Franklin AGEE to Bertha ATKINS, 20 Oct 1934
Vivian Marie AGEE to Dewey BROWN, 3 Jul 1939
Olive Clarinda AGEE to James Elmer DUFF of Charleston, WV; 7 Sep 1940
Eula Delema AGEE to Stanley Lavene PIERSON, 10 Jan 1942
Mamie Jenerene AGEE to Kenneth WOOD, 26 Jun 1943
Eleanor Francis AGEE to Lawrence Jr DUFF, 11 Sep 1943
(Matthieu Agee File #2)

THE JOHN WILLIAM MITCHELL BIBLE

No Title Page or Date

BIRTHS
John William MITCHELL, b.7 Feb 1856
Alto May MANLOVE MITCHELL, b.22 Oct 1871
Roy Clyde MITCHELL, b.17 Sep 1892
Greta Mable MITCHELL, b.13 Feb 1897
Guy Silby MITCHELL, b.3 Jul 1899
Flora Belle MITCHELL, b.11 Sep 1907
W.B. MANLOVE, Father, b.31 May 1846
Rose MANLOVE, b.14 Feb 1848
Park Everett MANLOVE, brother, b.21 May 1869
Floyd FURGASON, brother, b.19 Dec 1869
Grandchildren of J.W. & Alto M. MITCHELL
Roy Clyde MITCHELL, b.5 Oct 1915
William Silby MITCHELL, 18 Mar 1924
John Manlove MITCHELL, b.9 Nov 1925

Alto Pauline MITCHELL, b.28 Dec 1925
Kenneth Eugene MITCHELL, b.22 Apr 1929
Richard Silby MITCHELL, b.19 Sep 1932
Frances Patricia DURBECK, b.12 Jul 1930
Edward III DURBECK, b.3 Mar 1935
Sandra DURBECK, b.11 Sep 1937
MARRIAGES
John William MITCHELL to Alto May MANLOVE, [--] Sep 1889 at Elmer, MO
CHILDREN
Roy Clyde MITCHELL to Helen May D[----], 2 Jan 1918
Guy Sibley MITCHELL to Velma LEWIS, 23 Apr 1925 at Tulsa, OK
Edward F. DURBECK, Jr to Flora Belle MITCHELL, 30 Jun 1929 at Salem, NJ
Guy Sibley MITCHELL to Jessamine FUGATE, 24 Jun 1946 at Wichita, KS
(Matthieu Agee File)

WILLIAM A. MITCHELL BIBLE
No Title Page or Date
BIRTHS
William A. MITCHELL, b.8 Jun 1821
Nancy J. MITCHELL, his wife, b.27 Mar 1830
Mary E.V. MITCHELL, b.10 Jun 1854
John W. MITCHELL, b.7 Feb 1850
Laura E. MITCHELL, b.29 Aug 1857
second son, d. 26 Jun 1859
Thomas Allen MITCHELL, b.26 Aug 1860
James Robert MITCHELL, 28 Jan 1862
Anna Jenkins MITCHELL, b.20 Dec 1864
Sara Jane L. MITCHELL, b.12 Sep 1866

Ida Lee MITCHELL, b.28 Feb 1868
Lula [-]abrell MITCHELL, b.11 Feb 1873
Minnie Price MITCHELL, b.21 Jan 1875
Edwin Marvin MITCHELL, 18 Apr 1877
MARRIAGE
Wm A. MITCHELL and Nancy J. PRICE, 23 Sep 1852
(Matthieu Agee File #2)

DAVIS BIBLE

HOLY BIBLE published by American and Foreign Bible Society, New York, 1844
FAMILY RECORDS
BIRTHS
Albert DAVIS b.25 Jan 1831
S.E. DAVIS, b.2 Apr 1841
Emily F. DAVIS, dau of the above, b.25 May 1860
Elizabeth Riding DAVIS, b.25 Jan. ----
Albert DAVIS, b.28 Jan 1831
S. E. DAVIS, b.2 Apr 1840
E. F. DAVIS, dau of the above, b.25 May 1860
L. [-] DAVIS, dau, b.26 Apr 1864
J.B. DAVIS, son b. 23 Dec 1856
John H. FLECK, b.17 Dec 1837
Mariah F. FLECK, b. 4 Feb 1844
John M. FLECK, son of the above, b.9 May 1866
Burtha A. FLECK, dau of the above, b.26 Jan 1869
Julia Ann LAMPHRE, b.8 Jun 1865
Ralph LAMPHRE, son of the above b. [-] Aug 1881
(Matthieu Agee File)

ACKENEY BIBLE

No Title Page or Date
FAMILY RECORDS
BIRTHS
Nelson ANKENEY, b.15 Sep 1825
Elizabeth S. ANKENEY, b.8 Dec 1832
Emma Lusena ANKENEY, b. 19 May 1852
Charles Edwin ANKENEY, b. 6 Dec 1853
Lewis Warren ANKENEY, b.13 Jan 1856
Daniel Howard ANKENEY, b.25 Feb 1858
Clara Jane ANKENEY, b.26 Apr 1859
MARRIAGES
Nelson ANKENEY to Elizabeth S. COFFELT, his wife, 22 May 1856
DEATHS
Daniel Howard ANKENEY, d. 19 Apr 1858
Nelson ANKENEY, d. 7 Oct 1902
Elizabeth Sydney ANKENEY, d.12 Apr 1921
(Abel Auquenat/ Ankeney File)

ALLEE BIBLE
No Title Page or Date
BIRTHS
Albert Marion ALLEE, b.Henry Co, IN, 22 Aug 1855
Nancy [-] MERCHANT, b.Allen Co, OH, 3 Apr 1858
Etta M. ALLEE, b.Caldwell Co, MO, 25 Jan 1879
Ola May ALLEE, b.Caldwell Co, MO, 14 Sep 1880
Elsie Mert ALLEE, b.Custer Co, NE, 9 Feb 1884
Lalla Rook ALLEE, b.Custer Co, NE, 1 Jun 1886
Fora Morrison ALLEE, b. Custer Co, NE, 17 Sep 1889
(Jan Aliee/ Alyea File)

WILLIAM M. ALLEE FAMILY BIBLE
No Title Page or Date
PARENTS' RECORD

Father Wm M. ALLEE, b. 17 Mar 1814; d.20 Feb 1883
Mother Ann ALLEE, b.18 Mar 1813; d.20 Sep 1881
MARRIAGE
Wm M. ALLEE to Ann ALLEE, 9 May 1839
BIRTHS
Wm Clark ALLEE, b.29 Mar 1840
Rizpah Ann ALLEE, b.16 Dec 1841
Sarah Elizabeth ALLEE, b.21 Jul 1843
Enoch ALLEE, b.29 Jan 1846
Laura Jane ALLEE, b.22 Sep 1847
Robert Jonathan ALLEE, b.10 Jun 1850
Rhoda Becca ALLEE, b.18 Apr 1853
Henry Barzilla ALLEE, b.31 Jan 1856
Charles Oscar ALLEE, b.24 May 1858
Millard S. ALLEE, b. 14 Sep 1861
DEATHS
Enoch ALLEE, d.6 Dec 1846
Sarah Elizabeth ALLEE, d.24 Feb 1849
Laura Jane ALLEE, d.4 Mar 1849
William Clark ALLEE, d.12 Feb 1864
Rhoda Rebecca MORRIS, d.29 Mar 1898
(Jan Aliee/Alyea File)

JOSHUA CARPENTER BIBLE

The NEW TESTAMENT, printed by Sage and Clough, New York 1803

Joshua CARPENTER married Agness SIMS 27 Nov 1825
Martin Sims CARPENTER, b.28 Aug 1826
Hester Ann, b.12 Oct 1827
Joshua CARPENTER d.24 Sep 1843
Martha C. CARPENTER b.7 Apr 1847
seperate sheet of paper
Martin Sims CARPENTER married in Franklin Co, GA to Sarah C. CHEEK, 9 Apr 1846
Sarah C. CHEEK, b.15 May 1825
Martha C. CARPENTER b. in GA, 7 Apr 1847
Mary A. CARPENTER, b.in GA, 20 Sep 1848
Flavius J. CARPENTER b. in GA 24 Mar 1851
Sallie C. CARPENTER b. Clarke Co, AR, 4 Aug 1858
Sarah C. CHEEK CARPENTER d. Clark Co, AR, 29 Aug 1858
(Theodore D'Aubigne / Dabney File)

DONALDSON FAMILY BIBLE

No Title Page or Date, original in the possession of Flo D. Taylor about 1966, No Title Page attached

J. T. DONALDSON, b.Fox Spring, 2 Aug 1865; d.12 Jan 1914
married 17 Jan 1897 to
Emma BROWN, b.Celina, TN, 25 Mar 1874; d.20 Aug 1908

Elise T. DONALDSON, b.Celina, TN, 13 Nov 1897; m.25 Sep 1912
Ben Allen DONALSON, b.Celina, TN, 10 Jan 1900; d.8 Sep 1901
Carbell DONALDSON, b.Celina, TN, 24 Jan 1902, d. 23 Mar 1956; m.30 Jun 1941

Ava B. DONALDSON, b. Celina, TN, 28 Jan 1905; d. Oct 1909
Flo E. DONALDSON, b.Celina, TN, 28 Jan 1905; m. 15 May 1932
(Theodore D'Aubigne / Dabney)

JOHNSON / HEYWOOD FAMILY BIBLE

HOLY BIBLE published by Oxford University Press; no date

REGISTER OF BIRTHS

Flora Millie JOHNSON, b.26 Mar 1859
John Wicks HEYWOOD, b.14 Aug 1854
Johnson HEYWOOD, b.25 Feb 1885
Mary Elizabeth COLMAN, b.12 Sep 1925
Flora Jeannette HEYWOOD, b.7 Feb 1894
Virginia Heywod COLMAN, b.30 Oct 1917
Mary Anne RUBIDGE, wife of Johnson HEYWOOD, b.5 Sep 1891
Sally WILLIAMS, b.4 Jun 1952, dau. of Mary E. COLMAN and Richard S. WILLIAMS
Anne HEYWOOD, b.6 Dec 1913
Myron Homer COLEMAN, b.11 Oct 1887, husband of Jeanette HEYWARD
Martha Jane HEYWOOD, b.11 Aug 1915
John Edward BECKER, b.11 Apr 1945

REGISTER OF MARRIAGES

John W. HEYWOOD to Flora M. JOHNSON,14 Apr 1884, Minneapolis, MN
Johnson HEYWARD to Mary Ann RUBIDGE, 21 Dec 1912, at Keckuk, IA
Flora Jeannette HEYWOOD to Myron Homer COLMAN, 14 Apr 1915, at Chicago, IL

Virginia Heywood COLMAN to George Charles BECKER, 25 Apr 1941, St Pauls by the Lake, Chicago, IL
Mary Elizabeth COLMAN to Richard Settle WILLIAMS, 4 Nov 1944, St Marks Church, Evanston, IL
REGISTER OF DEATHS
Flora M. JOHNSON, wife of John W. HEYWOOD, d.7 Apr 1894
John W. HEYWOOD, d. 5 Sep 1910, Boston, MA
Ida Russell HEYWOOD PAGE, wife of W.R. PAGE, d.5 Sep 1922, Minneapolis, MN
Mary HEYWOOD, wife of Johnson HEYWOOD, d.6 Apr 1950
Johnson HEYWOOD, son of John Wicks HEYWOOD, d.6 Apr 1950
Ella Corrine COLMAN, d.28 Oct 1931, b.18 Mar 1849, Mother of Myron H. COLMAN
Cousin Florence LEE, grandaughter of Auntie DHUMWAY - (HEYWOOD), 4 Aug 1961
(Robert Bascom file)

BASS BIBLE

No Title Page or Date

MARRIAGES
L.S. BASS to Asthena PHILLIPS, 1 Mar 1865
D.S. BASS to Julie A. BARUM, 12 Jan 1871
John N. CLARK to N--- A. BASS, 4 Oct 1884
A.D. BASS to M-- ANGEL, 27 Sep 1891
J.H. GLEAVES to Minnie BASS, 30 Dec 1896
W.W. PHILLIPS to Julia BASS, 25 Sep 1897
Simson MORGAN to Olia BASS, 2 Nov ____
Simpson MORGAN to Ocia BASS, 22 Nov 1900

William BULLINGTON to Flossie BASS, 9 Apr 1913
BIRTHS
M---- BASS, b.24 Jan 1866
Cornelus BASS, b.12 Mar 1868
Adolphus BASS, b.2 Dec 1871
Minnie BASS, b.15 Jun 1873
Herman BASS, b.9 May 1875
Robert Hugh BASS, b.6 May 1877
Ocha N. BASS, b.15 Jan 1880
Nellie D. BASS, b.14 Mar 1882
(Humphrey Basse File)

BASS BIBLE II

Title page missing, Xeroxed original by Mrs Betty B. Cleere of Hattiesburg, MS

BIRTHS
Richard BASS, b.22 Jul 1805
Emily E. DUKE, b.8 Jan 1810
Alfred J. BASS, b.29 May 1826
Robert C. BASS, b.5 Aug 1828
Terecy M. BASS, b.4 Jun 1830
Hixy C. BASS, b.14 Sep 1831
Anna J. BASS, b.23 May 1833
Elizabeth BASS, b.5 May 1834
Poly BASS, b.21 Jun 1835
Sion D. BASS, b.21 Apr 1841
Daniel S. BASS, b.2 May 1843
Richard M. BASS, b.25 Jul 1846
Parthena P. BASS, b.28 Jan 1851
Rockcilany G. BASS, b.18 Mar 1858
Ozias D. BASS, b.15 Apr 1845
MARRIAGES
Richard BASS to Emily E. DUKE, 28 Dec 1824

Alfred J. BASS to Elizabeth ANDREWS, 16 Sep 1847
Robert C. BASS to Malisa PHILIPS, 23 Aug 1848
Bethel PHILIPS to Hixy C. BASS, 23 Sep 1849
Daniel S. BASS to Atheney PHILIPS, 1 Mar 1865
S.D. BASS to Lucinda JONES, 23 Jul 1868
Nancy Jane born 26 Jun 1869
George W. JONES to Partheney P. BASS, 13 Oct 1870
Richard M. BASS to Salley [TAILOR], [--] March 1869
M. C. JONES to Emeley E. BASS, 28 Mar 1871
Turner G. BORUM to Roxie L. BASS, 20 Apr 1881

DEATHS

Teresy M. BASS, d.16 Jun 1830
Anna J. BASS, d. [--] Aug 1833
Polly BASS, d.25 Sep 1836
ELizabeth BASS, d.12 Jul 1834
Ozias D. BASS, d.20 Aug 1845
Ozias D. BASS, d.12 Aug 1845
Richard BASS, d.16 Oct 1860
Meral C. JONES, d.8 Nov 1881
Emily E. JONES, d.26 Apr 1883, age 74yrs
(Humphrey Basse File)

BASSE BIBLE III

also as the John BASS BIBLE. original in 1979 owned by Lwarence Beard of Lebanon, TN. HOLY BIBLE, printed by M. Carey & Sons, Philadelphia, 1817

MARRIAGES

John BASS to Anna BASS, his wife, 9 Sep 1801
John x BASS 9 June
Anna BASS 1820
James GADDY to Elizabeth GADDY, his wife, 14 Jun 1821
James W. BELL to M.M. BASS, 7 Oct 1855

Sion BASS to Sally BASS, his wife, 21 Aug 1823
Josiah PHILIPS to Polly PHILIPS, his wife, 18 Mar 1824
Richard BASS to his wife Emily BASS, 28 Dec 1824
John BASS to his wife Mary BASS, 27 Oct 1841
Sion B. BASS to his wife Emir [Emma], 10 Jan 1871
Sarah BASS wife to Sion BASS, b.7 Jul 1803
Eliza BELL, b.12 Jun 1814
<u>BIRTHS</u>
Their CHILDREN
Sion BASS, b.11 Aug 1802
Elizabeth BASS, b.4 Feb 1804
Richard BASS, b.22 Jul 1805
Polly BASS, b.15 Oct 1807
Luiza Ann BASS, b.25 Jul 1812
Leacy BASS, b.1 Mar 1814
Linna BASS, b.15 May 1816
Terressy BASS, b.16 May 1818
Asenah BASS, b.26 Nov 1809
Terressa BASS, b.16 May 1818
(in pencil over the above: M.M. BELL, b.14 Jul--)
Ann[a] BASS, b.24 Aug 1784
John GADDY, b.20 Feb 1822 A son of James GADDY & Eliz GADDY
Anna GADDY, b.19 Apr 1823
John D. BASS, b.4 Apr 1824
Milly b. in Oct 1812
James a nigro, b.21 May 1819
Liza Jane BASS, b.18 Sep 1824
Thomas Wherry BASS, b.3 Nov 1825
Edward PHILIPS, b.24 Mar 1827
William W. BASS, b.24 Jul 1827
Simeon WHERRY, b.21 Sep 1786
Milleys Childrens age

Lewis a nigro, b.26 Mar 1830
Tilford, b.11 Jul 1832
Leacy Gaddy, d.8 Jan 1851
Sion B. BASS, b.15 Mar 1846
[in pencil] Eliza BELL, wife of Allen BELL, b.12 Oct 1814
DEATHS
Asenah BASS, d.25 Jun 1811
Anna GADDY, d.21 Dec 1823
Rachel BASS, d.11 Apr 1824
Polly PHILIPS, d.22 Sep 1824
Theophilus BASS, d.24 Feb 1826
Thomas Wherry BASS, d.16 Mar 1828
--------- BASS, d.6 Apr 1857
Mary BASS, d.-----
William Wherry BASS, d.16 Apr 1829
Anna BASS, d.27 Mar 1841;age 56yrs, 8mos, lacking of 3 days
John E. BASS, b.5 Dec 1846
Reubin I. BASS, b.7 Oct 1845
Pollyan BASS, b.19 Nov 1848
Elizabeth ___ BASS, b.7 Sep 1850
Daniel BASS, b.11 Aug 1852
Sarah BASS, d.17 Nov 1874

My Uncles
John Thomas BELL, b.31 Jul 1858
Edward Price BELL, b.31 Aug 1861
J.W. BELL, b.8 Jun 1836
J.W. Bell & M.M. BASS married 7 Nov 1856
Margaret Malissa BELL, b.24 Nov 1836

From a loose paper in the Bible on which the edge bearing year dates had partially crumbled away:

James William BELL, b.18 Jun 18[--]
Margaret M. BELL, b.14 Jul 1837
John Thomas BELL, b.31 Jul 185[-]
Edward Price BELL, b.31 Aug [----]
Eliza BELL, b.12 Jun 1814
Milly, a negro, b.16 [--] 18[--]
(Humphrey Bass File)

WHITE BIBLE
No Title Page or Date
FAMILY RECORDS
BIRTHS
Frank Elipha WHITE, b.25 Mar 1863
Fannie May WHITE, b.23 Mar 1866
Charles Luther WHITE, b.27 Apr 1868
Fred Walter WHITE, b.24 Aug 1870
Elleanor WHITE, b.7 Jul 1880
Francis Wallace WHITE, b.19 Dec 1883
Lizzie Eva WHITE, b.10 Aug 1873
DEATHS
Frank Elipha WHITE. d.27 Apr 1864
Sissan Frances WHITE, d.27 Jan 1883
Elipha WHITE, d.29 Mar 1902
Fannie May WHITE, 15 May 1896
Cecil Norman AVERY, d.5 Sep 1902
Francis Cornelia AVERY EXUM, d.23 Apr 1945
Fred Walter WHITE, d.23 Jan 1947
Eleanor White LUTZ, d.28 Jul 1959
Charles Luther WHITE, d.20 May 1947
Jack Aubrey AVERY, d.24 Nov 1948
Katymae Avery HAYES, d.26 May 19[--]
Fred Harmon AVERY, d.26 Oct 1965

(Theodore D'Aubigne / Dabney File)

BALDRIDGE BIBLE

No Title Page or date

<Parents Record>

FATHER

David BALDRIDGE, b. 13 Jun 1804, Westmoreland Co, PA

William Todd BALDRIDGE, b.16 Dec 1831, Westmoreland Co, PA

MOTHER

Phebe St Clair JERVIS, b.1 Sep 1802, Cincinnati, OH

Margaret E. HILLS, b.19 Jun 1833, in Indiana Co, PA

MARRIAGES

David BALDRIGE to Phebe St Clair JARVIS, 11 Sep 1827 by William Spees in Westmoreland Co, PA

W. Todd BALDRIGE to Margaret E. HILL, 18 Mar 1856 by Rev George Hills in Indiana Co, PA

BIRTHS

Margaret StC. BALDRIGE, b.28 Nov 1857, Knox Co, IL

Franklin Hill BALDRIGE, b.9 Sep 1859, Knox Co, IL

John Edger BALDRIGE, b.28 Apr 1864, Indiana Co, PA

Thomas Jefferson BALDRIGE, b.7 May 1866, Burrell Twp, Indiana Co, PA

James Okar BALDRIDGE, b.23 Jan 1868, Burrell Twp, Indiana Co, PA

Ida May BALDRIGE, b.28 Mar 1870, Perry Twp,Westmoreland Co, PA

William Clark BALDRIGE, b.3 Jul 1874, Derry Twp, Westmoreland Co, PA

DEATHS

David BALDRIGE, d.22 Aug 1857, Falls City, age 52yrs

Phebe St Clair BALDRIGE, d. at Blairsville, Indiana Co, PA

Margaret E, BALDRIGE, d.27 Oct 1891, at Cokeville, Westmoreland Co, PA , age58yrs 4 mos 8dys
John Edgar BALDRIGE, d.28 Nov 1877, age 14yrs, Cokeville, Westmoreland Co, PA
(Pierre Boudouin File)

BERTOLETTE BIBLE RECORDS

No Title Page or date

David A. BERTOLETTE married to Ann BOONE, dau of George BOONE, 9 March 1812
David A. BERTOLETTE, d.24 Sep 1837
Ann, wife of Daniel A. BERTOLETTE, d.
Their Children;
Maybury Augustus BERTOLETTE, b.16 Feb 1813
Amelia Douglass BERTOLETTE, b.3 Mar 1814
Elizabeth BERTOLETTE, b.1 Jan 1816
Wellington BERTOLETTE, b.17 Feb 1818
Beuveville BERTOLETTE, b.3 Jul 1819
(Jean Berlolet File)

KLINE BIBLE

No Title Page or date

MARRIAGES
Geo KLINE, Jr to Amelia Douglass BERTOLET, dau of Daniel A. BERTOLET and Ann BERTOLET, m.10 Feb 1835
BIRTHS
George KLINE, JR, b.22 Feb 1808
Amelia D. KLINE, b.23 Mar 1814
Miranda KLINE, b.11 Dec 1837
Wellington B. KLINE, b.3 Feb 1840
Irvin KLINE, b.4 Oct 1841

Luther KLINE, b.31 Jan 1844
Maybury B. KLINE, b.29 Mar 1846
(Jean Berlolet File)

HAWXHURST BIBLE

No Title Page or date

MARRIAGES

Solomon HAWXHURST to Ann JACKSON, 27 Sep 1834
Jackson HAWXHURST to Ratchel McNEEL, 18 Feb 1863
Robert WILLIARD to Susan HAWXHURST, 7 May 1863
Jackson HAWXHURST to Afaline WEEKS, 5 Jan 1865
Maybury B. KLINE to Anna Maria HAWXHURST, 4 March 1875

BIRTHS

Soloman HAWXHURST, b.24 Sep 1814
Ann JACKSON, his wife, b.11 Oct 1816
Jackson HAWXHURST, their first child, b.9 Jun 1836
Charles E. HAWXHURST, 23 Apr 1839
William Henry Simonson HAWXHURST, b.1 Jan 1841
Susannah HAWXHURST, b.10 Jan 1843
Mary E. HAWXHURST, b.18 Sep 1844
Ann Maria HAWXHURST, b.18 Nov 1849
(Jean Bertolet File)

KIMS BIBLE

No Title Page or Date

BIRTHS

C.D. KIMS, b.20 Jul 1851
Nancy KIMS, b.21 Jun 1847
Emily Viola KIMS, b.16 Mar 1871
Charles William KIMS, b.25 May 1873
James Alven KIMS, b.25 Mar 1877
George Otto KIMS, b.16 Mar 1883

Forest O Key KIMS, b.23 Feb 1885
Richard Thorn KIMES, b. Apr 1904
Gertrude KIMES, b. Jan 1908
Ivan KIMES, b. Jun 1900
Elva KIMES, b. Jun 1913
Gerald POSTLEWAITE, b. 1930
Madelan Margaret KIMS, b. Jan 1915
(John Bertrand File)

JEWELL / BEATTY BIBLE

NEW TESTAMENT published by M. Carey & Son, Philadelphia, 1817

Original was in the posession of Ramer Beatty Jewell, Clinton, KY

FAMILY RECORD

<u>BIRTHS</u>

DAVID JEWELL, SR, b.31 Jul 1771
Ruthy BEATTY, b.1 Apr 1782
Births of David and Ruthy JEWELL's Children
Eliza JEWELL, b.18 Jul 1799
James JEWELL, b.27 Apr 1801
Lewis JEWELL, b.7 Nov 1802
Christopher Greenup JEWELL, b.7 Jul 1806
David JEWELL, Jr, b.15 Oct 1808
Ruthy JEWELL, b.3 Oct 1810
Susan JEWELL, b.5 May 1812
Malinda JEWELL, b.13 Aug 1814
Lucinda JEWELL, b.4 Dec 1815
Ann Neill JEWELL, b.23 Feb 1819
Samuel Wart JEWELL, b.31 May 1821

<u>MARRIAGES</u>

David JEWELL, Sr to Ruthy BEATTY, 8 Jul 1798

Lewis JEWELL to Polly [-] POTTS, 4 Sep 1825
Christopher G. JEWELL to Clemenine BROWN, 20 Jan 1830
James R. SPURR to Susan JEWELL, 21 Jan 1830
James B. JEWELL to Rachel PATTERSON, 19 Sep 1833
David JEWELL to [---] BOVION(?), 10 Feb 1833
David D. JEWELL to Malinda B. JEWELL, 21 Jan 1835

BIRTHS

James BEATTY, b.16 Oct 1742 (old style)
Elizabeth BEATTY, his wife, b.25 Jul 1747 (old style)
Mary BEATTY, b.1 Nov 1766, NS
Michael BEATTY, b.9 Oct 1768
James BEATTY, Jr, b.30 Sep 1770
Elizabeth BEATTY, b.6 Aug 1772
Lidia BEATTY, b.5 Jul 1774
Edward BEATTY, b.1 Jun 1776
Nancy BEATTY, b.5 Mar 1780
Anna BEATTY, b.10 Dec 1784
Barbara BEATTY, b.20 Aug 1786; d.1 May 1879

DEATHS

Lucendea JEWELL, d.6 Dec 1816, age 12mos,2dys
Ann Neill JEWELL, d.15 Jun 1819, age 3mos,20dys
Samuel Wort JEWELL, d.5 Aug 1821; age 2mos, 5dys
Ruthy JEWELL, d. 21 Dec 1828
Eliza JEWELL, d. 1 Mar 1831
Ruthy JEWELL, consort of David JEWELL, and Mother of the above; d.6 Nov 1833
Jas B. JEWELL, d.30 Jun 184[-]
David Jewell, Sr, d.17 Dec 1848
Susan JEWELL, d.14 Jan 1866
Lewis JEWELL, d.1 Jun 1873
(Matthew Blanchan File II)

SPURR FAMILY BIBLE

HOLY BIBLE, published in London by Mark Baskett, dated MDCCLXVII
Original was in the possession of George Etta Emerson of Oklahoma City, OK

Frances SPURR, Sr , d.9 Jan 1819
Eliza F. DELPH, d.25 Oct 1831
Daniel SPURR, Sr, d.14 Oct 1832
Ramer SPURR, Sr, d.5 Mar 1820
Elizabeth BEATTY, d.13 Aug 1841
Ramer (?) DELPH, son of John M & Eliza F. DELPH, d.4 May 1844, age 15yrs
Barbara SPURR, wife of Daniel SPURR, d.1 May 1879, age 93yrs
Lydia B. BLINCOE, d.3 May 1889
Beatty Ramer SPURR, d.4 Nov 1915
William Harold SPUR, d.24 Jul 1919
BIRTHS
Children of Richard SPURR and Frances, his wife
James SPURR, b.25 Mar 1773
William SPURR, b.10 Apr 1775
Mary SPURR, b.30 Jul 1776
Richard SPURR, b.27 Feb 1778
Frances SPURR, b.10 Dec 1779
Judith SPURR, b.15 Apr 1781
John SPURR, b.3 Nov 1783
Daniel SPURR, b.28 Aug 1785

James BEATTY, Sr, b.16 Oct 1742
Elizabeth RAMER, b.25 July 1747
James BEATTY and Eliz RAMER married 18 Jun 1765
Births of their Children

Mary BEATTY, b.1 Nov 1766
Michael BEATTY, b.9 Oct 1768
James BEATTY, b.30 Sep 1770
Elizabeth BEATTY, b.6 Aug 1772
Lydia BEATTY, b.5 Jul 1774
Edward BEATTY, b.1 Jun 1776
Johnathan BEATTY, b.22 Jul 1778
Nancy BEATTY, b.5 Mar 1780
Ruth BEATTY, b.1 Apr 1782
Anna BEATTY, b.10 Dec 1784
Barbara BEATTY, b.20 Aug 1786

Barbara BEATTY, daughter of James Beatty and Elizabeth his wife, b.20 Aug 1786
Daniel SPURR and Barbara BEATTY married 1 Apr 1807
Their Children;
Richard James SPURR, b.5 Mar 1808
Eliza Frances SPURR, b.24 Feb 1810
Lydia Beatty SPURR, b.21 Jan 1813
Mary Ann SPURR, b.30 Jun 1815
William Potts SPURR, b.13 Nov 1817
Martha Ann SPURR, b. 6 Jan 1820
Daniel Junior SPURR, b.17 Aug 1822
Beatty Ramer SPURR, b.16 Aug 1825
(Matthew Blanchan File II)

RELLY HARRIS BIBLE

No Title page or date

FAMILY RECORDS

MARRIAGES

Relly HARRIS b. 20 Jun 1809
Maria HARRIS, b.20 Jul 1814

married 20 Feb 1834
Phebe HARRIS m. 21 Mar 1858
Fanny A. HARRIS m. 12 Oct 1866
Mariam HARRIS, m.25 Aug 1859
Emily HARRIS, m.17 Jan 1861
Emerson E. HARRIS, m.28 Sep 1870
Ida Josephine HARRIS, m.10 Dec 1874 to William Henry CONOVER

BIRTHS

Phebe HARRIS, b.5 Aug 1835
Fanny A. HARRIS, b.10 Apr 1837
Marium HARRIS, b.6 Apr 1839
Emily HARRIS, b.6 Jun 1841
Milford G. HARRIS, b.13 Oct 1843
Bemane P. HARRIS, b.31 May 1846
Emerson E. HARRIS, b.11 Jan 1848

DEATHS

Phebe GIBBS, d. Sep 1882
Ida CONVERS, d.27 Jan 1941
William Henry CONVERS, b.14 Jul 1853; d.14 Mar 1929
Beaman P. HARRIS, d.23 Mar 1847
Emerson E. HARRIS, d.9 Feb 1901

BIRTHS

Ida P. HARRIS, b.25 Dec 1855

DEATHS

Maria HARRIS, d.6 Aug 1872
Relly HARRIS, d.16 Sep 1877
(Thomas Bonnell File)

HUNLET BIBLE

No Title Page or Date

MARRIAGES

John W. HUNLEY to Maria R. BOUDINOT,22 Feb 1844
John B. HUNLEY to Mary B. Van SLYKE, 17 Nov 1874
George N. OGLEBAY to Mary Francis HUNLEY, 30 [---] 1879
Robert [-] YOUNG to Louisa Marie HUNLEY, 10 Apr 1901
John W. NELSON to Katherine L. HUNLEY, 26 Dec 1907
John Boudinot HUNLEY, Jr to Margaret Jane GRAY, 5 Jun 1909
Jane Gray HUNLEY to Andrew Jackson CLEARE, 29 Mar 1944
Adelaude Katherine WEISS to John Boundinot HUNLEY, III, 31 Jan 1953

BIRTHS

John W. HUNLEY, b.20 Nov 1820
Maria B. BOUDINOT, b.18 Feb 1825
Mary Francis HUNLEY, b.10 Jan 1845
John B. HUNLEY, b.18 Nov 1849
Charlotte T. HUNLEY, b.13 Jun 1852
Mary B. VanSLYKE, b.21 Jul 1854
Kate L. HUNLEY, b.28 Jul 1877
Louisa Marie HUNLEY, b.22 Feb 1879
John B. HUNLEY, Jr, b.12 Aug 1881
Mary HUNLEY, b.20 Apr 1883
Francis HUNLEY, b.1 Sep 1884
Elias Bradford HUNLEY, b.23 Jul 1886
Frances L. YOUNG, b.22 Oct 1902
Cornelus YOUNG, b.22 May 1905
Mary VanSlyke NELSON, b.29 Jan 1910
Jane Gray HUNLEY, b.20 May 1910
John Boudinot HUNLEY, III, b.12 Sep 1911

(Elie Boudinot File)

BONDURANT BIBLE

THE HOLY BIBLE published by McCarty & Davis, Philadelphia, 1832

The original seems to be in the Virginia State Library (69-767)

<u>FAMILY RECORDS</u>

<u>BIRTHS</u>

Robert M. BONDURANT, b.9 Apr 1801

Pamelia H. BONDURANT, b.13 Apr 1801

Mary H. J. BONDURANT, dau of Robert and Pamelia H. BONDURANT, b.3 Nov 1825

Edward BONDURANT, son of Robert and Pamelia H. BONDURANT, b.10 Oct 1826

Peter M. BONDURANT, son of Robert and Pamelia H. BONDURANT, b.29 May 1829

<u>DEATHS</u>

Robert M. BONDURANT, d.16 Apr 1865

Pamelia H. BONDURANT, d.26 Feb 1845, age 44yrs

Mary H. J. MURRELL, d.26 Jan 1855, age 30yrs

Edward BONDURANT, d.16 Jul 1827

<u>MARRIAGES</u>

Robert M. BONDURANT to Pamelia MOSELEY, Dau of Peter MOSELEY, 11 Nov 1824

Mary H. J. BONDURANT to B. F. MURRELL, 8 Jun 1840

P. M. BONDURANT to L. B. WILLIARD, 5 Apr 1854

John M. BONDURANT to Rebecca R. OWEN, 30 Aug 1857

Ida May BONDURANT to A. G. SMITH, 1 Apr 1880

Bessie BONDURANT SMITH to T. E. CAMPBELL, 26 Apr 1904

(Jean Pierre Bondurant File)

WOOLFOLK BIBLE

No Tile Page or Date

FAMILY RECORD

BIRTHS

Richard WOOLFOLK, b.24 Mar 1753
Sarah TAYLOR, b.13 Apr 1775 and married to Richard WOOLFOLK, 2 Sep 1792
Betsy [--] WOOLFOLK, 23 Sep 1793
[-----]
Alice T. WOOLFOLK, [-] Feb 1798
Alexander WOOLFOLK, b.9 Jan 1799
[----] H. WOOLFOLK, b. 16 [---] 1801
Zachary T. WOOLFOLK, b.10 May 1803
Richard A. WOOLFOLK, b.4 Mar 1805
Martha E.[--] WOOLFOLK, b.10 Feb 1808
Henry Coleman WOOLFOLK, b.16 [---] 1812
Charles Richard EUBANK, b.7 Jul 1827
Nicholas Alexander WOOLFOLK, b.25 [---] 1828
[------] son of [---], b.4 Jul 1828
Charlotte Elizabeth LONGEST, b.5 Feb 1832

Hugh F. LUCKER, b.15 Jun 1783, married to Elizabeth WOOLFOLK, dau of R. WOOLFOLK, 19 Jul 1800
Wm. LUCKER, son of Hugh LUCKER, b.25 [--] 1810
[---] Isaac, b.20 Apr [---]
Richard Alex, b.3 Sep 1815, d. the same day
John Alex, b.[-----] 1817; d.11 Oct 18[--]
Robert Elliot, b.3 Nov 1822
I[---] E[---], b.22 Jan 1824
Charles R. EUBANK, d.22 Aug 1828

DEATHS

Alexander WOOLFOLK, d.4 Dec 1805
[-----]
Sarah WOOLFOLK, wife of Richard WOOLFOLK, d. [----] 1833 at 5 o'clock

P.R. EUBANK, d.18 Nov 1838, age 37
Mary C. LONGEST, d.24 Dec 1839
Clarborne LONGEST, d.10 May 1842
Charles M. LONGEST, d. [-] May 18[--]
MARRIAGES
Claiborne LONGEST to Mary C. WOOLFOLK, 19 Apr 1831
Samuel H. WOOLFOLK to [-----] 7 Feb 1832
Isaac Philips to Alice L. WOOLFOLK, 23 Apr 1825 Alice died 16 Mar 1826
Philip Roger EUBANK to Martha Elliot WOOLFOLK, 1 Jan 1826
[--------] Son of Richard WOOLFOLK to Cornelia M. TAYLOR, 8 Feb 1827
daughter of Francis TAYLOR
Richard WOOLFOLK, son of Richard WOOLFOLK to Sarah SUTTON, dau of John SUTTON of Louisville, on [--] Mar 1828
DEATHS
Henry TAYLOR, d.18 Jan 1815, age 80yrs 3mos 18dys
Charoltte Elizabeth LONGEST, d.19 Oct 1833, age 1yrs, 8mos, 14dys
[--] Clairborne LONGEST, born 22 Jul 1834
[------] LONGEST, b. [--] March 1836
R. B[--] WOOLFOLK, son of [----] [---] 1837, age [--] yrs 11mos 14dys

BIRTHS
Jeffrey W. BONDURANT, b. 22 [--] 1798
[---------] b. 11 Dec 1808
Lucinda L. BONDURANT, alias Lucinda L. COLEMAN, b.1 Feb 1799
James Coleman BONDURANT, son of Jeffrey and Lucinda BONDURANT, b.19 Jan 1829

Joseph David BONDURANT, son of Jeffrey and Lucinda BONDURANT, b.5 Jun 1830
[-----] Taylor BONDURANT, b.15 Dec 1831
Sarah Elizabeth BONDURANT, first dau of Jeffery and Lucinda BONDURANT, b.12 Apr 1834
Mary Jane BONDURANT, alias Mary Jane GREEN, alias Mary Jane MORRIS, b.8 Sept 1823
Lucinda C. BONDURANT, dau of J. H. & C. P. BONDURANT, b.20 Feb 1852
Sallie B. G. BONDURANT, dau of J.C. & M.C. BONDURANT, b.4 Nov 1855
Annie {?} Jeffrey BONDURANT, dau of J.C. & M.C. BONDURANT, b.5 Dec 1858
[---] BONDURANT, {Father}
Jeffery was born [--] Jun 1756
Elizabeth BONDURANT [-] Elizabeth DAVIS , b.3 Mar 1757
they were married 17 May 1778

MARRIAGES

Jeffrey William BONDURANT to Martha T. MILLER [--] Oct 1825
Jeffrey W. BONDURANT to Lucinda L. COLEMAN, [-] Feb 1828
Jeffrey W. BONDURANT to Mary Jane GREEN, 17 Aug 1854
J.C. BONDURANT to S.P. TALIAFERRO, 8 Apr 1851
J. C. BONDURANT to M.C. WOOLFOLK, 9 May 1854

DEATHS

Martha F. BONDURANT, first wife of Jeffrey W. BONDURANT, d.25 Aug 1826
Sailathiel Taylor BONDURANT, d.9 Jun 1838
Lucinda L. BONDURANT, second wife of Jeffrey W. BONDURANT, d.5 Oct 1850
Jeffrey W. BONDURANT, d.23 May 1859

Catherine P. BONDURANT, wife of J.C. BONDURANT, d.8 Aug 1852

[-------]
Mary BONDURANT, dau of M.C. & J.C. BONDURANT, d.4 Oct 1865
Alice Force BONDURANT, dau of M.C. & J.C. BONDURANT, b.24 Jul 1862
(Jean Pierre Bondurant File / 21-234)

MURRELL BIBLE

THE HOLY BIBLE, published by Oxford University Press. no date but newer edition
Record of Ben. F. MURRELL and Evelyn Horton RIDDICK MURRELL's Family
{copied from our Family Bible Jan 1945}
Ben F. MURRELL, b.20 Dec 1852; d.5 Oct 1916
Evelyn Horton R. MURRELL, b.8 Dec 1854; d.12 Jan 1896
Born to this union were
Mary Evelyn MURRELL, 7 May 1876
Harriet Ann MURRELL, 12 Mar 1878
Sallie Adeline MURRELL, 27 Apr 1880
Benjamin Horton MURRELL, 5 Sep 1882
Mittie Riddick MURRELL, 21 Feb 1884
Nona Bondurant MURRELL, 4 Nov 1885
Edward Garrett MURRELL, 2 Oct 1887
Lucy Mayo MURRELL, 25 Aug 1889
Walter Jeffrey MURRELL, 14 Jul 1891
Thomas Kader MURRELL, 22 Jun 1893
Infant son. 11 Jan 1896
<u>MARRIAGES</u>
David Henry NELMES to Mittie Riddies MURRELL, 20 Apr

1905 at Somerville, TN
Ralph Howard MAXSON, Jr to Margaret Evelyn NELMES, 6 Oct 1926, at Oakland, TN
<u>BIRTHS</u>
David Henry NELMES, b.31 Jul 1875
Mittie Riddick MURRELL, b.21 Feb 1884
Children born to this union
Margaret Evelyn NELMS, b.15 Aug 1906
Mittie Evelyn NELMS, b.10 Dec 1908
Lucy Boone NELMS, b.11 Jan 1911
Benjamin David NELMS, b. 21 Jan 1917
Patrick Edward NELMS, b.3 Mar 1919
Murrell Abner NELMS, b.29 Mar 1921
Harriet Ann NELMS, b.22 Dec 1923
(Jean Pierre Bondurant File)

BRUCE BIBLE

THE NEW TESTAMENT Published by Luther Roby, Concord, NH, 1843
original book found and copied by Mrs Mary Bruce Woodbury about 27 Apr 1980
<u>MARRIAGES</u>
Wm N. BRUCE to Sarah Ann WILLIAMS, 23 Mar 1850
WM N. BRUCE married at [---] Caroline Co, VA by Rev W. Trice to Mary Susan, dau of W. D. BRUCE, 24 Jul 1857
Wm A. GAINES to Sallie, youngest dau of Dr Wm N. & Mary S. BRUCE, at Bambridge, Decater Co, GA by Rev John Jester on 13 Nov 1902
Wm A. GAINES, b.14 Dec 1842; d.8/7 Jan 1926 age 83yrs
<u>BIRTHS</u>
William N. BRUCE, b.15 Oct 1811; 6 miles north of C[----],

SC
Sarah Ann WILLIAMS, b.25 Sep 1832 at Tired Creek, Decater Co, GA
Mary Susan BATES, b.4 Dec 1831, in Caroline Co, VA
Louisa POWELL was born
Sarah, eight child of Wm & Mary S. BRUCE, b.26 Oct 1872, at Bainbridge

BIRTHS

James SHIPARD, b.20 Mar 1850, first son of Wm N. & Sarah Ann BRUCE, at Foresttown,, Decater Co, GA
Lucy Estelle, first child of Wm N. & M.S. BRUCE, b.4 May 1858, Tuesday morn
Mary Susan Leonard, child of Wm N. & M.S. BRUCE, b.25 Apr 1868
George Williamson, third child of W.N. & M.S. BRUCE, b.3 Aug 1862
Robert Lee, fourth son of Wm N. & M.S. BRUCE, b.24 Apr 1864, at the plantation 6 miles NE of Bainbridge
John Potter, fifth child of Wm N. & M.S. BRUCE, b.9 Jun 1866 in Bainbridge
6th Female child born still 13 Jan 1868
Charles BRUCE, b.5 Feb 1869

DEATHS

Sarah Ann BRUCE, d. 18 [---] 1853, age 20yrs, 8mos, 24dys, second dau of Mrs C. Williams, third dau of W.W. WILLIAMS
John Potter BRUCE, d.10 Jul 1884
James Shipherd BRUCE, only child of Wm N. and Sarah A. BRUCE; d.4 May ----
Wm N. BRUCE, d.25 Oct 86 in the 75th year of his age
George William BRUCE, d.1 Jul ---, age 34yrs at Bainbridge

Mary Susan, 2nd dau of Wm N. & M.S. BRUCE married14

Mar 1881 to [------]
Lucy Estelle, oldest dau of Wm N. & M.S. BRUCE, married 12 Feb 1885
Mrs Mary Susan BRUCE d. 29 Dec 1916, Bainbridge, GA, age 85yrs 25dys
[--]llis M. CRAWFORD d. 3 Oct 1888 at Bainbridge
Lucy Bruce GRIFFIN, d. 22 Oct 1935
Eunice GRIFFIN d. 29 Aug 1961
Sallie Bruce GAINES, d. 1 May 1962
(Jean Bonnell File)

LANGSTAFF BIBLE

No Title Page or Date

MISCELLANEOUS
Henry H. LANGSTAFF married Frances A. CAFFEE, 31 Mar 1870 at Springville, IA
Henry H. LANGSTAFF married Emma E. LEE, 15 Sep 1876 at Sigourney, IA

BIRTHS
Corena Mary, dau of Henry & Emma LANGSTAFF, b.22 Dec 1877 at West Branch, IA
Vera Frances LANGSTAFF, b.18 May 1879 at West Branch, IA
Hanna Ellan LANGSTAFF, b.23 Sep 1880 at Barclay, KS
Lina Anna LANGSTAFF, b.28 Aug 1881 at Barclay, KS

DEATHS
Alva W., son of Henry and Frances LANGSTAFF, d.1st Month 16th aged 26 Years 1899
Ruben J., son of Henry & Emma LANGSTAFF, d.6 / 1st age 5yrs 8mo 15dys 1900
(Robert Brasseur, Sr File)

STEEL BIBLE

The NEW TESTAMENT published by American Bible Society, New York, 1848

FAMILY RECORDS

Ferdinard Laurence STEEL, b.17 Sep 1813 in Fayetteville, NC
Amanda Fitz-Gerald HANKINS, b.5 Apr 1827, in Henry Co, TN
Samuel Augustus Hankins STEEL, 1st son of F.L. & A.F. STEEL, b.5 Oct 1849, Springhill, Carroll Co, MS; Baptized 3 Jul 1850, by Rev R.L. Andrews, PE Grenada, MS
Mary Eliza Julia STEEL, 1st dau of F.L. & A.F. STEEL, b.26 Jul 185[2], at Ironwood Bluff, 14 miles South east of Fulton, MS; Baptized 29 May 1853 by Rev Joseph M. Blackwell at Pleasant Grove Church, 4 miles south west of Holly Springs, Marshall Co, MS
Christine Tips Crub STEEL, b.10 May 1882, Columbus, MS; d. May 1896
Miriam STEEL, b.18 Sep 1886, Memphis, TN
Thomas Brevard STEEL, b.12 Feb 1894, Union City, TN
Edith Fitzgarld STEEL, b.6 Mar 1896, Union City, TN
Virginia Battle STEEL, b.28 Jan 1900, Richmond, VA
Ella Lee STEEL, b.15 Jul 1903, Lumberton, MS
Chloe Malone STEEL, b.25 Jun 1906, Union City, TN
Samuel A. STEEL & Miss Ella Battle BREVARD married at Union City, TN 4 Jan 1893
Ella Battle BREVARD, b.5 Dec 1873, Union City, TN
Samuel Augustus STEEL, d.18 Feb 1934, Mansfield, LA
Ella B. STEEL, wife of Samuel Augustus STEEL, d.20 Nov 1962 at Laurel, MS
(Jean Brevard File)

BREVARD BIBLE

No Title Page or Date

BIRTHS

John BREVARD Sr, b.18 Feb 1751
Hannah Thompson BREVARD, his wife, b.23 Aug 1765
Alfred Alexander BREVARD, b.10 Jan 1796
Mary Brandon BREVARD, b.14 Mar 1805
Susan Allen BREVARD, b.24 Oct 1825
Hannah Stone BREVARD, b.14 Apr 1825
John Bowen BREVARD, b.19 Jan 1827
William Alexander BREVARD, b.17 Oct 1828
Mary Jane BREVARD, b.3 Oct 1830
Tabitha Grant BREVARD, b.14 Oct 1832
Clarissa Harris BREVARD, b.4 May 1834
Cynthia Ann BREVARD, b.29 Apr 1836
Richard Brandon BREVARD, b.8 Mar 1837
Polyxena White BREVARD, b.19 May 1840
Alfred Lee BREVARD, b.10 Feb 1842
John Marshall Thompson BREVARD, b.3 Dec 1843
Cyrus Windom BREVARD, b.24 Nov 1847
Archibald Debow BREVARD, b.14 Feb 1850
Nancy Debow BREVARD, b.14 Feb 1850, still born
Mary Jane KNOX, b.7 Aug 1853
Ella Bell BREVARD, b.5 Dec 1873
Mary Loretta CRENSHAW, b.17 Aug 1867
Adria BREVARD, b.7 Mar 1883

MARRIAGES

Alfred A. BREVARD to Mary B. ALEXANDER, 18 Jul 1822
W.C. JOHNSON to Mary Jane BREVARD, 26 Jul 1849
Spencer S. THOMPSON to Hannah S. BREVARD, 28 Nov 1849
A.J. KNOX to Tabitha G. BREVARD, 20 Oct 1852
James C. CRENSHAW to C.H. BREVARD Feb 1959

S. DEBOW to Polexana BREVARD, 16 Dec 1869
Alfred L. BREVARD to Sallie L. MALONE, 13 Feb 1873
C.W. BREVARD to M.L. BRENSHAW, 15 Mar 1882
DEATHS
John BREVARD, Sr, d.9 Nov 1826
Hannah BREVARD, his wife d. 1 Jun 1833
Alfred A. BREVARD, d.17 Oct 1865
Mary B. BREVARD, d.3 Aug 1887
John Bowen BREVARD, d.9 Apr 1829
Susan Allen BREVARD, d.1 Sep 1851; age 27yrs 10mos 7dys
Arch. Debow BREVARD, d.21 [--] 1851, age 1yr 7mo 7dys
John M.G. BREVARD, d.12 Apr 1862 at Corrinth, MS from wounds received at the battle of 7 Apr 1862
Wiliam A. BREVARD, d.16 Sep 1878
Cynthia A. BREVARD, d.11 Aug 18[--]
(Jean Brevard File)

KNOX BIBLE
No Title Page or Date
Family Records
MARRIAGES
A.J. KNOX to Tabitha G. BREVARD 24 Oct 1852
D.R. BOUDURANT to M.L. KNOX, 12 Jul 1874
J.F. RICE to M.J. KNOX, 14 Dec 1876
S.H. LEYTHOUR to S.A. KNOX 1[-] Jul 1879
Edward D. WOODBURN to Emma KNOX, 22 Feb 1899
BIRTHS
A. J. KNOX, b.21 Sep 1825
Tabitha G. KNOX, b.14 Oct 1832
Mary J. KNOX, b.7 Aug 1853
Robert M. KNOX, b.19 Nov 1854

Martha L. KNOX, b.25 Mar 1856
Clara Bell KNOX, b.2 Oct 1857
Alfred A. KNOX, b.23 Oct 1859
Susan A. KNOX, b.17 Dec 1861
Margaret V. KNOX, b.23 Jul 1864
John B. KNOX, b.26 Mar 1866
Bennota KNOX, b.28 Jul 1868
Emma KNOX 2 Oct 1870
William E. KNOX,b.27 Dec 1872
Polyxnia KNOX, b.2 Jun 1875
T.G. KNOX, b.8 Feb 1879
E.K. BONDERANT,b. Nov 1878
Knox SUTTON, b.7 Jun 1884
Clara Belle [---] b.5 Oct 1887
Iona BONDERANT, b.10 May 1875
Mary Lee BOUNDERANT, b.13 Mar 1877
Edna RICE, b.19 Sep 1877
F. G. RICE, b.17 Jul 1879
Nora SUTTON, b.20 Jun 1880
W.A. RICE,b.6 Jan 1881
Besse RICE, b.29 Oct 1882
DEATHS
Alfred A. KNOX, d. 12 May 1932
Benola KNOX, d.17 Jan 1941
Robert M. KNOX, d.21 Nov 1863
John B. KNOX, d.20 Apr 1869
William E. KNOX, d.17 Nov 1878
M.L. BOUNDERANT, d.24 Mar 1879
L[---] C. KNOX, d.6 Jul 1890
Tabitha SUTTON, d. Feb 1891
Mary B. BREVARD, d.3 Aug 1887
Cynthia BREVARD, d.11 Aug 1887
Susan D. SUTTON, d.6 Mar 1891

C.B. KNOX, d.16 Nov 1891
Clara B. SYTTON, d.22 Jul 1901
Tabitha Grant KNOX, d.5 Jun 1913
Anbdrew Jackson KNOX, d.12 Feb 1918
Knox SYTTON, d.5 Feb 1924
Pabithat Grant KNOX, d.16 Jun 1928
(JEAN Brevard File)

ALLEN BIBLE

No Title Page or date, owned by Mary Asenath King Allen until 1923, copied by Lamar Allen Grace about 1982.
No Title Page or Date
FAMILY RECORDS
MARRIAGES
J.B. ALLEN to Sarah P. RUSSELL, 30 Jul 1889
S.E. ALLEN to M.R. WOODSON, 20 Nov 1867
J.R. ALLEN to Sallie YOUNGER, 25 Nov 1868
S.C. ALLEN to M.A. KING, 1 Dec 1870
F.R. WOODSON to D.P. KING, 31 Dec 1867
T.L. BEARD to S.J. KING, 6 Sep 1877
Lamar GRACE to Willie C. ALLEN, 11 May 1898
Roderick ALLEN to Mary HALL, 24 Nov 1900
BIRTHS
Walter P. ALLEN, b.18 Nov 1872
Roderick ALLEN, b.30 Mar 1875
Willie Crozier ALLEN, b.14 Oct 1877
DEATHS
Walter P. ALLEN, d.6 Jul 1888
S.C. ALLEN, d.19 Oct 1902
On a loose sheet attached
FAMIY RECORD
Elisha B. KING, b.21 Mar 1816 in Iredell Co, NC

Jane ALLISON, b.31 Aug 1816, Iredell Co, NC
E.B. KING and Jane ALLISON married 16 Nov 1839
Eleanor KING, b.26 Jan 1843
Delia P. KING, b.21 Dec 1848
Mary A. KING, b.21 Dec 1848
Stanhope H. KING, b.15 Sep 1852
Sarah J. KING, b.16 Jan 1857
Samuel C. ALLEN, b.12 May 1845
M.A. KING, b.21 Dec 1848
S.C. ALLEN and M.A. KING married 1 Dec 1870
Walter P. ALLEN, b.18 Nov 1872
Roderick ALLEN, b.30 Mar 1875
Willie C. ALLEN b.14 Oct 1877
Walter P. ALLEN, d.6 Jul 1888
Samuel C. ALLEN, d.19 Oct 1902
Willie C. ALLEN and Lamar GRACE married 11 May 1898
Roderick ALLEN and Mary HALL married 24 Nov 1900
Stanhope H. KING, d.27 Apr 1855
Elisha B. KING d.20 Nov 1860
Jane KING, d.21 Nov 1865
Eleanor KING, d.24 Dec 1870
Delia P. WOODSON, d.10 Jan 1914
Beulah Allen , dau of D.P. WOODSON, d.24 Jun 1914
Delia P. KING married F.R. WOODSON, 31 Dec 1867
M.A. KING married S.C. ALLEN, 1 Dec 1870
S.J. KING married T.L. BEARD, 6 Sep 1877
Jean Brevard File)

MACKIE BIBLE

HOLY BIBLE published by American Bible Society, New York 1849

C.B. WICKER'S book presented by Clovis BROOKS 14 Jun

1851

Leola G. JAQUES, b.29 Oct 1868 Chillicothe, IA
W.A. MACKIE, b.10 May 1864 Saqinaw, MI
William Willard MACKIE, b.9 Apr 1888
Pearl Leota MACKIE, b.26 Dec 1889
Eddie & Georgie MACKIE, b.18 Sep 1892, in Alameda, CA
Pearl in Boulder Creek, CA
George E. JAMES, b.26 Apr 1917
Jane Ann JAMES, 11 May 1922
Patricia Ann MACKIE, b.23 Oct 1931
Edwina Leota MACKIE, b.18 Jan 1935
(Pierre Butin File)

SALISBURY BIBLE

NEW TESTAMENT printed by the American Bible Society, New York, 1845

BIRTHS

Tobias SALISBURY, 30 Sep 1817
Mary Jane SALISBURY {crossed out} WILHELM, b.23 Jul 1823
Charles Andrew SALISBURY, b.25 Jan 1844
Elizabeth J. SALISBURY, b.1 Feb 1846
John B. SALISBURY, b.25 May 1848
Jacob W. SALISBURY, b. 28 [---] 1850
Charlott Ann SALISBURY, b.14 Dec 1852
George T. SALISBURY, b.21 May 1860
Mary Angeline SALISBURY, b.4 Oct 1864

MARRIAGES

Tobias SALISBURY to Mary Jane WILHELM, 2 Mar 1843
Children
John B. SALISBURY to Louisa BROWN, 21 Oct 1868

Charles SYMONDS to Lebbie SALISBURY, 4 Nov 1868
Jacob W. SALISBURY to Mary E. CUMMINS, 23 Nov 1870
Georg T. SALISBURY to S.M. BROWN, 4 Dec 1882
E.T. GATES to Mary A. SALISBURY, 24 Mar 1885
DEATHS
Charles Andrew SALISBURY, d.26 Feb 1850, age 6yrs 1mo
Libbie SYMONDS, d.7 Mar 1878, aged 32yrs 1mo 7dys
Charlotte A. SALISBURY, d.2 May 1880, age 27yrs 4mos 18dys
Louisa SALISBURY, d.28 Oct 1891, age 39yrs
Tobias SALISBURY, d.29 Oct 1895, age 76yrs 1mo
Mary J. SALISBURY, d.4 Jan 1896, age 72yrs 5mo,11dys
{on Title page}
Mary Eva SALISBURY, d.14 Jul 1932, age 79yrs
Jacob W. SALISBURY, d.4 May 1933, age 83yrs 3mos 6dys
John B. SALISBURY, d.3 Jun 1911, age 63yrs 9dys
May SALISBURY GATES, d.12 Aug 1939
(JAN Broucard File)

CARLEY BIBLE

HOLY BIBLE, published by William W. Harding, Philadelphia 1865
only the page for marriages is in the file.
MARRIAGES
John CARLEY to Mary A. UPDYKE, 11 Jan 1865
Children
Cheslon R. GALLUP to Frankie E. CARLEY, 23 Oct 1889
Newton M. BEACH to Carrie M. CARLEY, 17 Mar 1893
M.R. LEFLER to Hattie G. CARLEY, 22 Aug 1901
Clarence J. CARLEY to Bertha SEDINGER, 23 Dec 1902

(Jan Broucard File)

DeCAMP FAMILY

A Lithograph by E.C. Kellogg of New York City. A Family Chart framed, original at one time in the home of Elsie DeCamp Crow of Watertown, SD

PARENTS

Henry DeCAMP, b.15 Mar 1810, d.2 Aug 1859
married 15 Jul 1849 at Dubuque County, IA to
Ann Maria DeCAMP, b.16 Sep 1827, d.7 May 1885

CHILDREN:

Emma Jane DeCAMP, b.3 Jul 1850, d.4 Jan 1917, m.17 Feb 1867
Amaretta DeCAMP, b.23 Jan 1853, d.15 Jan 1875
Mary DeCAMP, b.8 Sep 1855, d.15 Jun 1897, m.29 Mar 1874
Merritt DeCAMP, b.30 Aug 1857, d.30 Apr 1900, m.25 Nov 1885
Henry DeCAMP, b.2 Mar 1860, d.15 Nov 1934, m.25 Nov 1891

(Lauret de Camp file)

GARRISON BIBLE

THE HOLY BIBLE, published by Wesleyan Methodist Publishing House, D.S. Kinney, Agent; no date

<u>BIRTHS</u>

William S. GARRISON, b.5 Sep 1846
Emma J. De CAMP, b. 3 Jul 1850
Henry L. GARRISON, b.22 May 1868
Hattie A. GARRISON, b.27 Feb 1870

Milo M. GARRISON, 3 Jul 1876
William D. C. GARRISON, b.18 Jan 1884
Elsie Fern GARRISON, b.20 Apr 1887
DEATHS
Emma J. DeCAMP GARRISON, d.4 Jan 1917
Henry L. GARRISON, d.10 Mar 1920
William D.C. GARRISON, d.16 Jul 1930
William S. GARRISON, d.13 Feb 1935
Milo M. GARRISON, d.10 Apr 1945
Elsie, d.16 Oct 1952
Hattie, d.16 Mar 1956
MEMORANDA
marriage certificate pasted in:
William S. GARRISON age 20yrs to Emma J. DeCAMP age 17yrs married by J.G. Wilson, Justice of the Peace 17 Feb 1867, Dubuque Co, IA
(Lauret de Camp File)

VAN NESS BIBLE

THE HOLY BIBLE published by Thomas Mason & George Lane for the Methodist Episcopal Church, 1837
BIRTHS
Edward Palmer ROSBOUGH, the son of Alex W. and Nartha J, ROSOROUGH, b. 29 Jan 1859
William J.VAN NESS, son of James U. and Martha J. Van Ness b, 14 Feb,1868
Mary Jane VAN NESS, b.6 Oct 1870
John Rosbough VAN NESS b. 4 Sep 1873
Laura Maria VAN NESS, b. 23 Mar 1876
James Henry VAN NESS, b.2 Apr 1878
Charles Albert VAN NESS, b.4 Oct 1881
Rufus Bullock OATES, son of Jas C. & Mary E. OATES, b.4

Apr 1865
Mattie Rosbrough OATES, dau of Jas C. & Mary E. OATES, b.25 Feb 1868
Mary E. ROSBOROUGH, first born of B.C. & R.E. ROSBOROUGH, b.10 May 186[-]
Jane Bell ROSBOROUGH, b.1 Apr 1872
(Marquis Calmas file)

GOCKEY BIBLE

No Title Page or Date

Parents
Jacob W. GOCKEY, son of Bemjamin and Ann GOCKEY, daughter of Abraham WINGER, b. 12 Aug 1845, West C[---] Lancaster Co, PA
Eliza Ann GOCKEY, daughter of Aaron and Elizabeth PULLER , a daughter of Philip H[____], b. 16 Mar 1848 in Heidelberg TWP, Lebanon Co, PA
CHILDREN:
Henry P. GOCKEY, b.15 Nov 1866
Benjamin GOCKEY, b. 7 Aug 1868
Jacob P. GOCKEY, b. 22 Jul 1869
Cyrus P. GOCKEY, 10 Apr 1871
I[___] P. GCGKEY, b.29 Jan 1873

Jacob W. GOCKEY to Eliza Ann PULLER married 14 Jun 1866

also attached are photographes of four tombstones:
Samuel GOCKEY, b.23 June 17[-]5; d.7 Jun [--]73; ages 89yrs 11mos 9dys
Benjamin GOCKEY, ist Geboden 11 Oct 1811; d. 4 Aug 1877; age 63 jahr 9 mo 28 doge

Susanna wife of Samuel GOCKEY, b.5 Nov 1780; d.12 Jun 1871, aged 81yrs 7mos 7dys
Anna, the wife of Benjamin GOCKEY; b.[-] Aug 1811, d.9 Jul 1876; age 64jahr 11mo [-] dogs
(Sebastian Caquelin File)

JOHN BLANCHARD BIBLE

No Title Page or date, original in the posession of the Second Congregational Church Palmer, MA. Originally published in Philadelphia, PA; 1807

BIRTHS
John B. BLANCHARD b.2 Mar 1780
Siley BARTON, b.24 Dec 1780
Alanzo V. BLANCHARD, b.2 Dec 1805
William J. BLANCHARD, b.19 Dec 1808
Emily BLANCHARD, b.12 May 1812
John D. BLANCHARD, 15 Jul 1815
Franklin BLANCHARD, b.20 May 1818

MARRIAGES
John B. BLANCHARD to Siley BARTON, 7 Feb 1805
Alonzo V. BLANCHARD to Elvira A. SHEARER, 25 Oct 1827
William J. BLANCHARD to Jane Maria SHEARER, 23 Aug 1831
Thomas BELL to Emily BLANCHARD, 5 Nov 1838
John D. BLANCHARD to Dolly M. PHELPS, 4 Sep 1838
Franklin BLANCHARD to Sarah L., BLANCHARD, 19 Sep 1843

BIRTHS
Mary [__]ing, b.15 Jun 1830
Jane BREWER, b.13 Dec 1834
(Peter Chamois File)

BLYTHE FAMILY BIBLE

No Title Page or Date, copied from the bible "currently" owned by Mrs Bliss Ham of Iuka, MS

MARRIAGE

John Jefferson BLYTHE, Sr of Iuka, MS to Cleopatra USSERY of Iuka, MS on 7 Mar 1850

PARENTS

John Jefferson BLYTHE, Sr, b.22 Jul 1820, eldest son of Elijah and Jane BLYTHE

Cleopatra USSARY, b.27 Jun 1832, eldest dau of Shelby and Malethia USSERY

Their Issue

William Franklin BLYTHE, b.1 Mar 1851 at Ripley, MS
Thomas Shelby BLYTHE, b.9 Nov 1852, at Jesinte, MS
Elijah Daniel Wright BLYTHE, b.11 Oct 1854, at Daulton, MS
James Howard BLYTHE, b.1 Aug 1856, at Fulton, MS
Ida Jane BLYTHE, b.9 Aug 1858, at Iuka, MS
John Jefferson BLYTHE, Jr, b.12 Jun 1866, at Iuka, MS
Andrew Knox BLYTHE, b.9 Jan 1868, at Iuka, MS
Robert Edwin Lee BLYTHE, b.20 Sep 1870, at Iuka, MS
Jordon Craven BLYTHE, b.23 Oct 1878, at Iuka, MS

Children's Marriages

W. F. BLYTHE to Miss Linnah BARNES at Waldron, AR
T.S. BLYTHE to Miss Bridget GANLEY, at Smithdale, AR; married second to Miss Fannie NANCE in Palastine, TX
E.D. BLYTHE to Miss Lizzie ROBINSEN at Clarksville, AR, 23 Dec.
Ida Jane BLYTHE to Clairborne WHITWORTH, 21 Feb 1892
John Jefferson BLYTHE, Jr to Miss Anne FULLWOOD in Crittenden, AR
Robert Edwin Lee BLYTHE to Clara FULLWOOD in

Crittenden, AR

DEATHS

J.J. BLYTHE, Sr d.3 Aug 1895, Iuka, MS
Cleopatra BLYTHE, d.4 Jan 1899, Iuka, MS
Elijah Daniel Wright BLYTHE, d.20 Feb 1891, at Crawfordville, AR
Jordan Graven BLYTHE, d.15 Dec 1898, Boonville. MS
John Jefferson BLYTHE, d.18 Aug 1901, Marion, AR
Wm Franklin BLYTHE, d.15 Oct 1903, Jonesboro, AR
Thomas Shelby BLYTHE, d.22 Mar 1916, Wynne, AR
James Howard BLYTHE, d.7 Feb 1928, Warren, AR
(Pierre Chastain File)

HACK FAMILY BIBLE

No Title Page or Date, the original in the Maryland Historical Society, Baltimore. Noted from "Scherer Bible Record" Filing Case A.

FAMILY RECORDS

BIRTHS

Peter HACK, son of Peter & Metilda, was b. 9 Jul 1715
George HACK, son of Peter & Ann, b.9 Dec 1743
Ann HACK, dau of Peter & Ann, b.10 Apr 1740
Metilda HACK, dau of Peter & Ann, b.1 Nov 1741
Frances HACK, dau of Peter & Ann, b.17 Nov 1745
Elizabeth HACK, dau of Peter & Ann, b.13 Jul 1752
Peter HACK, son of Peter & Ann, b.11 Apr 1754
Margaret Lawes SCHERER, dau of G.W. H. SCHERER & Henrietta, his wife, b.30 Sep 1851
George HACK, son of Peter & Ann, b.9 Dec 1743
Margaret HACK, wife of George HACK, b.9 Apr 1749
Ann HACK, dau of George & Margaret, b.29 Jul 1766
Elizabeth HACK, dau of George & Margaret, b.5 Sep 1768

George Nicholas HACK, son of George & Margaret, b.26 Jan 1771
Margaret HACK, dau of George & Margaret, b.17 Jan 1774
Peter HACK, son of George & Margaret, b.9 Sep 1776
Leah HACK, dau of George & Margaret, b.8 Apr 1779
Sarah HACK, dau of George & Margaret, b.8 May 1782
Charlotte HACK, dau of George & Margaret, b.23 Oct 1784
Molly HACK, day of George & Margaret, b.16 Aug 1787
Frances HACK, dau of George & Margaret, b.29 Aug 1790
(Jacques de Chiel File)

BOGGS / RODGERS BIBLE

POLYGLOTT BIBLE, published in 1843, belonged to Elizabeth S. Boggs

MARRIAGES

William W. RODGERS to Rachel BOGGS, 8 Mar 1820
Henry J. BOGGS to Elizabeth S. RODGERS, 29 Jan 1843
Littleton T. BOGGS to Emily T. BOGGS, 16 Dec 1863

BIRTHS

William W. RODGERS, b.25 Jan 1785
Rachel RODGERS, his wife, b.22 Oct 1784
Henry J. BOGGS, son of Arthur & Susan BOGGS, b.26 Jan 1814
Elizabeth S. ROGERS, his wife, b.14 May 1821, the dau of William W. RODGERS and Rachel
Arthur W. BOGGS, son of Henry & Elizabeth S. BOGGS. b.26 Nov 1843
Emily T. BOGGS, dau of Henry J. and Elizabeth S. BOGGS, b.30 Jan 1847
Littleton T. BOGGS, b.2 Sep 1838, son of William & Elizabeth BOGGS
Emily T. BOGGS, b.30 Jan 1847

Henry W. BOGGS, son of L.T. & Emily T. BOGGS, b.19 Jul 1865
Elizabeth P. BOGGS, day of L.T. & Emily T,. BOGGS, b.28 Oct 1868
<u>DEATHS</u>
William W. RODGERS, d.19 Mar 1856 [57]
Rachel RODGERS, his wife, d.13 Dec 1858
Henry J. BOGGS, d.20 Aug 1858
Arthur W. BOGGS, d.22 Sep 1853
(Jacques de Chiel File)

FINNELL - SNYDER PRAYER BOOK

The Book of Common Prayer for the Episcopal Church, Published by Joseph Robinson, Baltimore 1820. Owned by Mrs Mary Finnell Marshall of Ghent, MN until 1970, obtained from her estate by Arthur Louis Finnell, 1973

Henry W. SNYDER
Presented to Him Balter [Baltimore] 23 Sep 1821 by the Rev H.H. PFEIFFER
W.H.F. (under this is written several words too faint to make out)
Presented to H.W. SNYDER, Dothr 23 Sep 1821 by his Cousin The Rev H.H. PFEIFFER of Philadelphia
Doctor H.W. SNYDER Reisterstown or Baltimore
Geo H. EVANS 1841
In The year of our lord 1842 James GAREINER His Book on page 360
William H. FINNELL, b.3 Sep 1843
John W. FINNELL, b.25 Mar 1848
Cornelia FINNELL, b.9 Jul 1849
Thomas J. FINNELL, b.29 Aug 1850

(Jacques Cossart File)

FINNELL FAMILY BIBLE

HOLY BIBLE published by John E. Potter & Co, Philadelphia, PA 1873. Original owned by Kathleen J. Finnell of Seattle, copied in 1968.

MARRIAGE CERTIFICATE

Thomas FINNELL to Malinda WOLF m.25 Sep 1873 by John A. Burns, Pastor of U.P. Cong N.E. Poweshiek Co, IA

Grandfather b. 11 Jul 1791 [Chrsitopher WOLFE]
John D, WOLFE, b.13 Nov 1818
Margaret E. WOLFE, b.6 May 1823
Thomas J. FINNELL, b.29 Aug 1850
Malinda A. WOLFE, b.21 Dec 1851
Mary R. FINNELL, b.13 Jul 1874
John M. FINNELL, b.4 Mar 1876
Wheeler J. A. FINNELL, b.19 Mar 1880
Jesse E. FINNELL, b.16 May 1887
Jane E. FINNELL, b.6 Jan 1890

on a loose paper a contract for a tombstone
Johnnie M. son of T.J. & M.A. FINNELL, d.22 Mar 1877, age 1yr & 18dys
(Jacques Cossart File)

MOSS BIBLE

HOLY BIBLE, published by American Bible Society, New York, 1866

FAMILY RECORDS

Helen Imogene MOSS, b.4 Jul 1882
Mary Edith MOSS, b.3 Jun 1885

Ethel Maude MOSS, b.17 Jan 1888
Raymond Leroy MOSS, b.20 Oct 1895
(Jacques Cossart File)

CHAPMAN BIBLE

No Title Page or Date

MARRIAGES

Harry M. CHAPMAN to Lizzie C. BARDWELL on 14 Nov [--] by Rev J.P. BARDWELL of Oberlin, Lorian Co, OH
Henry Bardwell CHAPMAN to Edith PERRY, 30 Jun 1896
William Bardwell CHAPMAN to Elsie Violet PARSONS, 29 Oct 1896
Ralph Whitney REYNOLDS to Harriet Bardwell CHAPMAN, 14 Jun 1905
Ralph Arthur BROCKELS to Margaret E. CHAPMAN, 26 Dec 1925

BIRTHS

Henry Bardwell CHAPMAN, b.21 Dec 1864
Harriet Bardwell CHAPMAN, b.4 Jan 1869
William Bardwell CHAPMAN, 3 Jul 1872
Margaret Elizabeth CHAPMAN, b.3 Nov 1900; dau of William Bardwell CHAPMAN & Elsie Violet PARSON CHAPMAN
Marian Elizabeth REYNOLDS, dau of R.W. REYNOLDS & Harriet B. CHAPMAN REYNOLDS, b.19 Jul 1906
Virginia Margaret BROCKELSBY, b.1 May 1928, dau of Ralph A. & Margaret E. BROCKELSBY
Mary Bliss BROCKELSBY, b.27 Oct 1933
Alice Jane BROCKELSBY, b.8 Mar 1936
William Ralph BROCKELSBY, b.29 Mar 1939

DEATHS

Henry Martin CHAPMAN, d.13 Jan 1910 in Pasadena, CA;

funeral at E. Cleveland, OH 25 Jan 1910; bur.Lake View Cemetery, b.26 Jul 1830
Cornelia E. (Lizzie C.) CHAPMAN, d.17 Apr 1916 in Pasadena, CA, bur next to Husband
Henry Bradwell CHAPMAN, d.6 Aug 1918, age 53yrs, bur Lake View Cemetery
Elsie Parsons CHAPMAN, d.22 Mar 1933, East Cleveland, OH
Ralph Whitney REYNOLDS, d.19 Apr 1934, age 64yrs 10mos, at Pasadena, bur. Forest Lawn Memorial Park, Glendale, CA; b.21 May 1869
Marian Elizabeth REYNOLDS, d.8 Feb 1935, Denver, CO, bur. Forest Lawn Memorial Park
Edith Perry CHAPMAN, d.8 Sep 1939 at Elmira, NY, bur Lake View Cemetery
Edwin Wermore CHAPMAN, b.1842 at Euclid, son of W.S. CHAPMAN, d. 13 Feb 1862
William Bardwell CHAPMAN, 2 Jul 1949 at Pasadena, CA; bur. Lake View Cemetery
(Jacques Cossart File)

COUTANT BIBLE

HOLY BIBLE printed by John Archaeacon, Cambridge, London, 1769
Copied from original book in Whitlock's Bookstore, New Haven, CT 1950. Copy in the Connecticut State Library.
<u>FAMILY RECORD</u>
To Peter COUTANT by his Mother
John COUTANT, b.22 Mar 1757
Jean RENOUD, b.26 Nov 1763; they were married 15 Dec 1781
Polly COUTANT, their Daughter, b.1 Feb 1784

Elizabeth COUTANT, their Daughter, b.4 Oct 1786
Sufanna COUTANT, their Daughter, b.28 Oct [---], d. age 9 days
John Pruth COUTANT, their son, b.7 Jan 1791
Peter COUTANT, their son, b.26, Feb 1724
Sufanna COUTANT, their Daughter, b.4 Aug 1796
Girhard T. COUTANT, their son, b.4 Mar [___]
BIRTHS
Peter COUTANT, b.3 Feb 1794
Sarah C. WINSHIP, b.10 Oct 1799
Mary Ann COUTANT, their daughter, b.19 Mar 1819
Ann COUTANT, their daughter, b.20 Jul 1820
John Edgar COUTANT, their son, b.5 Feb 1822
Emily Theresa COUTANT, their daughter, b.4 Apr 1824
Thomas Jefferson COUTANT, their son, b.2 Apr 1831
Mary Eliza COUTANT, their daughter, b.14 Dec 1832
Sarah Emily Blanche CHAPPELL, their grandaughter, b.10 Dec 1855
__ry Ida Coutant CHAPPEL, their grandaughter, b.25 Feb 1857
Elia Wheaton D. CHAPPELL, their grandaughter, b.21 Sep 1858
MARRIAGES
[Parents of Peter COUTANT]
John COUTANT, b.22 Mar 1757
Jean RENOUD, b.26 Nov 1763
They were married 15 Dec 1761
(Parents of Sarah C, WINSHIP)
Daniel WINSHIP, b.4 Jun 1765
Mary SEABURY, b.6 Apr 1776
Peter COUTANT to Sarah C. WINSHIP, m.1 Jan 1818 by Bishop Soule
John Edgar COUTANT to Harriet MILES, on 8 Sep 1844, by

Rev Lot Jones
Bartholomew B. CHAPPELL to Mary E. COUTANT, on 29 Aug 1853, by Rev C.R. Dubble,, if the Church of St John the Baptist
Harriet MILES, their Daughter in law, b.14 Feb 1828 [Interment at Mamaroneck Episcopal Churchyard near Depot]
Mary Elizabeth COUTANT, their grandaughter, b.11 Jul 1845
Peter William COUTANT, their grandson, b.31 Mar 1847
<u>DEATHS</u>
Ann COUTANT, d.20 Jul 1820 [St Paul Church yard, NYC]
Mary Ann COUTANT, d.1 Sep 1820
Peter COUTANT, d.18 Dec 1874, age 80yrs, 10mos 9dys [Interment at St Paul Churchyard, Eastchester]
Sarah C. COUTANT, d.2 Jan 1882, age 82yrs 2mos 23dys, [Intered at St Paul churchyard, Eastchester]
(Jean Coutant File)

SMITH - GOODWIN BIBLE
No Title Page or Date
<u>MARRIAGES</u>
Josiah GOODWIN, son of Morris GOODWIN and Sarah his wife, b.27 day 6th month 1831
Morris GOODWIN, son of Morris GOODWIN and Sarah his wife, b.20 day, 10 month, 1833
Dorothy GOODWIN, daughter of Morris GOODWIN and Sarah his wife, b. 8 day, 8 month 1837; d.18 day same month, age 10 days
Marmaduke SMITH, d.16 day, 12 month 1828
Martha GOODWIN, daughter of Morris and Sarah GOODWIN, d.7 day 10 month 1826
Mark SMITH, d.8 day, 4 month, 1842, age 55yrs
page 678

BIRTHS
Robert SMITH, b.10 day, 10 month, 1752
Dorothy SMITH, b. 30 day, 7 month, 1756
Rebecca SMITH, b.21 day, 1 month, 1775
Marmaduke SMITH, b.21 day, 7 month, 1778
Mark SMITH, b.21 day, 3 month, 1788
Letitia SMITH, b.21 day, 6 month, 1790
Sarah SMITH, b.29 day, 7 month, 1792
Daniel SMITH, b.23 day, 4 month, 1795
Josiah SMITH, b.29 day, 9 month, 1797
page 679
BIRTHS
Dorothy SMITH, d. 29 day, 11 month, 1823, age 67 yrs
Daniel SMITH, son of Robert & Dorothy SMITH, d.3 day, 2 month, 1824, age 29 yrs
Rachel GOODWIN, daughter of Morris and Sarah GOODWIN, b.1 day, 5 month, 1826
Sarah Ann GOODWIN, daughter of Morris & Sarah GOODWIN, b.21 dys, 4 month, 1829
DEATHS
Robert SMITH, d.17 day, 2 month, 1802, his remains interred the 19th of the Inst in the Friends Burying at Egg harbor; Aged 49 yrs
Rebecca SMITH, d.21 day, 11 Month, 1798, remains intrred in Friends Burying Grounds at Eggharbor on 22 day Inst, 1798, age 23 yrs
Letitia SMITH, d.10 day, 8 month, 1790; age 1 month, 3 weeks
page 680
DEATHS
John GOODWIN, son of Morris & Sarah GOODWIN, b.23 day, 8 month 1817; d. 21 day, 9 month, 1817
Mary D. SMITH, daughter of Daniel L. SMITH & Abigail

SMITH, b.17 day, 12 Month, 1818
Morris GOODWIN, son of Morris & Sarah GOODWIN, b.17 day, 11 month, 1820; d.31 day, 7 month, 1821, age 8 months, 14 days
Mary GOODWIN, daughter of Morris and Sarah GOODWIN, b.19 day, 3 month, 1822; d.2 day, 11 Month, 1822; age 7 months, 15 days
(Pierre Cresson File, 2-357)

WILLIAM R. MORTON BIBLE

No Title Page or Date

BIRTHS

William R. MORTON, b.13 May 1808
Abagail F. MONROE, b.23 Dec 1809
Albert Henry MORTON, b.23 Jan 1833
Adelaide R. MORTON, b.14 Mar 1834
Josephine M. MORTON, 2 Feb 1837
Samuel R. MORTON, b.19 Feb 1840
Isaac N. MORTON, b.20 Nov 1842
Ellen Eliza MORTON, b.13 Mar 184[-]
Francis Asbury MORTON, b.29 Sep 1849
Charles G. BARTO, b.25 Mar 1832
Charles Alfred BARTO, b.26 Aug 18[--]

DEATHS

Albert Henry MORTON, d.31 May 1833
Abigail M. MORTON, d.12 Oct 1856
Lydia E. MORTON, d.23 Jun 1887
William R. MORTON, d.2 Jan 1894

MARRIAGES

William R. MORTON to Abagail F. MONROE, 14 Oct 1830
Charles G. BARTO to Adelaide R. MORTON, 6 Nov 1857
William R. MORTON to Lydia E. BUTCHER, 2 Dec 1857

(Pierre Cresson File, 2-357)

MORTON - ROBERTS BIBLE RECORDS

No Title Page, original last in the possession of Mrs Charles Loveland, Salem, NJ. Copied 16 Dec 1887.

Children of Benjamion and Susannah R. MORTON
Benjamin MORTON, b.14 Aug 1783; d.20 Nov 1860
Susannah R. MORTON, b.6 Sep 1789; d.31 Aug 1875
William R. MORTON, b.13 May 1808
Joshua R. MORTON, b.7 Apr 1810; d.25 Jun 1885
Jacob E. MORTON, b.14 May 1812; d.7 May 1875
Mary A.B. PAGE, b.14 Feb 1814
Abram M. MORTON, b.8 Feb 1816
Susannah A. MORTON, b.31 Mar 1818
Sarah R. MORTON, b.27 Jan 1820; d.18 Jan 1862
Rachell A. BENNETT, b.1 Mar 1822
Benjamin A. MORTON, b.7 Jun 1824
Samantha MORTON, b.19 Sep 1826
John R. MORTON, b.16 Jan 1828
Emeline COOPER, b.8 Jan 1830
(Pierre Cresson; 2-357)

HOLDCRAFT BIBLE

The PICTORIAL HOME BIBLE; Published by William Flint & Co, J.B. Stewart, New Castle, PA; 1872

<u>BIRTHS</u>

Joseph S. HOLDCRAFT, b.28 Mar 1855
Sarah S. RUCHER, b.13 Apr 1857
Harry S. HOLDCRAFT, son of Joseph S. & Sarah S. HOLDCRAFT, b.28 Jun 1876
Lizzie J. HOLDCRAFT, daughter of Joseph & Sarah

HOLDCRAFT, b.27 Apr 1879
Ida F. HOLDCRAFT, daughter of Joseph & Sarah HOLDCRAFT, b.10 Jan 1885
Warner R. HOLDCRAFT, son of Joseph S & Sarah S. HOLDCRAFT, b.21 Oct 1889
(Pierre Cresson File)

CORSON BIBLE
THE IllUSTRATED POLYGLOT FAMILY BIBLE, Published by William Flint,
Philadelphia, no date on title page
Marriage Certificate
John CORSON of Pedrichtown, NJ to Louisa MOULFORD of the same place married 9 Apr 1864 at Weedstown, NJ by A. Y. Hires
BIRTHS
John CORSON, son of Joel S. & Mary CORSON, b.7 Dec 1836
Mary FIRESTONE, daughter of Noah & Matilda FIRESTONE, b.---
Louisa MOULFORD, daughter of Samuel and Ann Maria MOULFORD, b.10 Apr 1840
Clara CORSON, daughter of John & Mary CORSON, b.24 Mar 1861
Walter CORSON, son of John & Mary CORSON, b.20 Feb 1863
David M. CORSON, son of John & Louisa CORSON, b.15 Dec 1864
Sharon CORSON, son of John & Louisa CORSON, b.8 Apr 1866
Arabella CORSON, daughter of John & Louisa CORSON, b.16 Oct 1867
John L. CORSON, son of John & Louisa CORSON, b.11 Jul

1871
Jennie CORSON, daughter of John & Louisa CORSON, b.21 Oct 1874
Louisa M. CORSON, daughter of John & Louisa CORSON, b.22 May 1878
Mariam Louisa HOLDCRAFT EARLEY, daughter of Louisa and Harry S. HOLDCRASFT, b.23 May 1901
Isabelle Springer HOLDCRAFT , daughter of Louisa & Harry HOLDCRAFT, b.5 Sep [---]

MARRIAGES

John CORSON to Mary FIRESTONE at Swedebore, 24 Feb 1861
Joel S. CORSON to Mary TAILORMORE, Sep 1827; Joel S. CORSON the son of Joel
Louisa Mulford CORSON to Harry Shoemaker HOLDCRAFT, 29 Dec 1897
John [-] CORSON to Rebecca L. PLUMMER at Pedricktown, 18 Jan 1893
Miriam Louisa HOLDCRAFT to Russell Everett EARLEY, 19 Oct 1920 at Tacoma, WA
Isabella Springer HOLDCRAFT to Joseph M. HAWBETT, Jr 7 Oct 1944 at Philadelphia, PA

DEATHS

Mary CORSON, wife of John CORSON, d.12 [--] 1863, age 23 yrs
Walter CORSON, son of John & Mary CORSON, d.3 Sep 1863, age 6 mos, 14 days
David M. CORSON, son of John & Louisa CORSON, d.5 Jan 1865, aged 21 days
Emma W. CORSON, daughter of [---] & Ella, d.10 May 1889
Joel S. CORSON, d.18 Mar 18[--]
Daisy B. SPRINGER, d.18 Jul [----] age 7 [--]
Clinton SPRINGER, d. [-] Dec 1894

John L. CORSON, d.24 Jan 1943
Harry S. HOLDCRAFT, d.17 Feb 1935
Mrs Louisa CORSON, nee MULFROD, d.11 Oct 1916, age 77yrs
Sharon CORSON, d.28 Jan 1947, age 81yrs
Mrs Arcbella CORSON SPRINGER, d.22 Oct 1947, age 80yrs
Mrs Louisa Mulford HOLDCRAFT, nee CORAN, d. 24 Jan 1967, age 89yrs
(Pierre Cresson File)

MULFORD BIBLE

THE HOLY BIBLE, Published by Hogan & Thompson, Philadelphia, 1839

MARRIAGES

Samuel MULFORD to Louisa RUCEREWS, 10 Jan 1835
Samuel MULFORD to Ann Maria DARE, 21 Feb 1838
Edward URION to Jane Ella MULFORD, 19 Dec 1860
Samuel H. URION to Sallie E. CRISPIN, 20 Jan 1884
newspaper clippings pasted on page:
JONES - MULFORD, Salem: Thomas B. JONES to Prudence MULFORD, 27 Oct 1875
BROWN - MULFORD, At South Amboy, NJ Thomas BROWN to Mrs Mary Jane MULFORD, both of Salem, 7 Oct [---]

BIRTHS

Samuel MULFORD, son of David & Sarah {crossed out} Margaret MULFORD, b.30 Nov 1809
Louisa RUDDEROWS, daughter of William & Hannah RUDDEROWS, b.6 Jan 1808
Ann Maria DARE, daughter of Charles & Sarah DARE, b.16 Jan 1810 [?]

Henry MULFORD, son of Saml & Ann Maria MULFORD, b.1 Dec 1835
Charles MULFORD, son of Samuel & Ann Maria MULFORD, b.21 May 1837
Maria Louisa MULFORD, daughter of Samuel & Ann Maria MULFORD, b.10 Apr 1840
Jane Ella MULFORD, b. Salem, Salem Co, NJ 31 May 1842
Edward Thomas URION, son of Joseph & Lydia URION, b.26 Dec 1837
Samuel Mulford URION, son of Edward T. & Jane Ella URION, b.8 Mar 18[-]2
Edward Alden URION, son of Edward T. & Jane Ella URION, b.31 Aug 1868
Joseph Wilbert URION, son of Edward & Jane Ella URION, b. 20 Mar 1870
Harvey Dare URION, son of Edward T. & Jane Ella URION, b.12 Aug 1878
Charles Henry G[---] URION, son of Edward & Jane URION, b.7 Jan 1881

DEATHS

Louisa MULFORD, the wife of Samuel MULFORD, d.4 Dec 1835, age 24yrs, 10mos, 28dys
Samuel MULFORD, d.8 Feb 1844, age 35yrs, 2mos,8dys
Ann Maria MULFORD, wife of Samuel MULFORD, d.7 Feb 1848, age 31yrs, 22dys
Henry N. MULFORD, d.9 Mar 1871, age 35yrs, 3mos, 9dys
William DARE, d.18 Jun 1839, age 70yrs (newspaper clipping)
(Pierre Cresson File)

STEPHEN GARRISON FAMILY BIBLE

No Title Page or Date

Stephen GARRISON, b.31 Jul 1747
Elizabeth AIRS, wife of Stephen GARRISON, b.19 Dec 1760
Ruth, daughter of Stephen & Elizabeth GARRISON, b.14 Jan 1798
Samuel, son of Stephen & Elizabeth GARRISON, b.18 Oct 1799
Susannah, daughter of Stephen & Elizabeth GARRISON, b.22 Nov 1801
Stephen GARRISON, son of Stephen & Elizabeth GARRISON, b.24 Jun 1806

Samuel GARRISON to Mariah MILLER married 20 May 1824
Ruth GARRISON to William PORCH, married 1 Mar 1825
Stephen A. GARRISON to Elizabeth COOMBS, married 1 Mar 1830
Susannah GARRISON to William C. WALLACE, married 25 Aug 1830
(Pierre Cresson File)

SAMUEL GARRISON BIBLE

No Title Page or date

Children of Samuel and Annie Maria (Miller) GARRISON
Charles GARRISON, b.2 Jun 1825; d.4 Jan 1854
Joseph Miller GARRISON, b.16 Jul 1827; d.13 Aug 1901
Elizabeth GARRISON, b.26 Jul 1829
Phebe Miller GARRISON, b.12 Oct 1831
Harriet Miller GARRISON, b.16 Jan 1834
Stephen Ayars GARRISON, b.19 Nov 1835
Moses Tullis Miller GARRISON, b.28 Oct 1837
Samuel GARRISON, b.10 Apr 1840
Susanna GARRISON, b.6 May 1842

Francis GARRISON, b.26 Jul 1844; d.same day
Mary Atkinson GARRISON, b.25 Aug 1845
Annie Maria GARRISON, b.10 Oct 1848
(Pierre Cresson File)

LANGHORNE BIBLE

No Title Page or Date

MARRIAGE

Daniel A. LANGHORNE to Virginia Preston KENT, 15 Feb 1852[crossed out] 3 added; at Edge Hill, Montgomery Co, VA, by Rev Jacob D. Mitchell
Eliza Meem PAYNE to Alexander Parker ESKRIDGE, 10 Jun 1908 at Ascension Church, Amherst, VA
Ellen Edmundson ESKRIDGE to Walter Lee SANDERS, Jr, 26 Jun 1937 at Ascension Church, Amherst, VA
Elizabeth Langhorne ESKRIDGE to Lewis Carter AMBLER, 26 Nov 1955 at Emmanuel Episcopal Church, Alexandria, VA
John Meem PAYNE to Elizabeth Allen LONGHORNE, 2 Dec 1863 at Walnut Grove, Montgomery Co, VA

DEATHS

Maurice Kent LANGHORNE, d.10 Apr 1864, Lynchburg
Daniel Allen LANGHORNE, d. 10 Feb 1908, Lynchburg, VA; age 82yrs, 7mos
Virginia Preston LANGHORNE, d.22 Oct 1909, Lynchburg, VA; age 76yrs, 2mos, 9dys
John Meem PAYNE, Jr, d.10 Feb 1897,at Iron Gate, VA
Archer Langhorne PAYNE, d.16 Sep 1901, Amherst, VA
Robert Spotswood PAYNE, d.1 Dec 1920
John Meem PAYNE, d.16 May 1934, Amherst, VA
Elizabeth Allen Langhorne PAYNE, d.17 Jan 1936, Amherst, VA
Daniel Allen PAYNE, d.19 Jan 1938, Lynchburg, VA

Eliza Payne ESKRIDGE, d.16 Jun 1957, Amherst, VA; bur. Amherst Cemetery
Alexander Parker ESKRIDGE, d.7 Dec 1965, Lynchburg, VA
Margaret Payne GATLING, d.17 Jan 1967, Amherst, VA
BIRTHS
Ellen Edmundson ESKRIDGE, b.17 Mar 1910, Keelona, Amherst, VA
Elizabeth Langhorne ESKRIDGE, b.13 May 1912, Keelone, Amherst, VA
(Antoine Crocketagne / Crockett File)

GEORGE BERRY CHAMNESS BIBLE

No Title Page or Date, copy of Bible page taken from the Book owned by George Berry CHAMNESS and Martha Jane Turnage CHAMNESS
George Berry CHAMNESS, b.26 May 1831; d.12 May 1915
Martha Jane TURNAGE CHAMNESS, b. 25 [Oct] 1840; d.25 [Nov] 19[14]
George D. CHAMNESS, b.16 [-] 1863
Charlie T.CHAMNESS, b.19 Jun 196[-]; d.12 Jun 1872
Mary Eveline CHAMNESS, b.14 Jun 1868; d.[-] Jul, 187[-]
Laura CHAMNESS, b.13 Nov 1869
Ambrose CHAMNESS, b.7 Jul 1871
Maudda CHAMNESS, b.24 Aug 1873; d.6 Sep 1874
Daughter (not named), b.& d. 17 Dec 1876
Frank CHAMNESS, b.[-] Ja[-] 1878
Martha CHAMNESS, b.[---]; d.[---]
Lallie Lucille CHAMNESS, b.[-] Jun [----]

NOTE: attached transcripts of tombstomes in the Creal Springs City Cemetery, Creal Springs, IL.
George B. CHAMESS, b.26 May 1831, d.12 May 1915
Martha J. CHAMNESS, b.25 Oct 1840, d.25 Nov 1914

George D. CHAMNESS, b.16 Feb 1863, d.1 Feb 19540
Elizabeth CHAMNESS, b.6 Jul 1865; d.2 Feb 1948
Antoine Crocketagne / Crockett File)

HARRISON BIBLE

No Title Page or Date

MARRIAGES

James M. HARRISON to Jane E. SAYER, [-] May 1855, by Rev [-] W. Crockett
[---] V. HARRISON to [----] BROWN, 11 Mar 1885
[---] LINSLEY to [---] HARRISON, [-] May 1886
[-] Crockett HARRISON to [--]ive Hallun WERN, 6 Mar 1901
Albert Sidney Johnson HARRISON to Marie JONES, 30 May 1906, by Rev Dr Cowan
James Samuel HARRISON to Morlie Lee McKIM, 27 Nov 1907, by Rev J.B. Jones
Martha Draper PINSLET to Homer MARSHALL, 20 Aug 1912
James Harrison BROWN to Catherine BERNICE, 15 Oct 1920
John Franklin HARRISON, son of Crockett & Olive HARRISON, married to Dorothy PACKARD, 2 Oct 1956
Crockett Allen HARRISON to Fannie Elizabeth COLLINS, 28 Aug 1930
(Antoine Crocketagne / Crockett File)

BRYANT FAMILY BIBLE

WILMORE'S ANALYTICAL REFERENCE BIBLE; Published New York, 1907

FAMILY RECORDS

<Grand Parents>

William Avery BRYANT, Sr, b.16 Feb 1830; d.21 Aug 1905,

Lexington., GA
Martha C. MOORE BRYANT, b.7 Aug 1834; d.10 Feb 1916, Lexington, GA
Josiah HEWELL, b.28 Sep 1824; d.21 Dec 1896, Lexington, GA
Mary Caroline VAUGHN, b.18 Jan 1830; d.8 Feb 1914, Carlton, GA
<Parents>
William Avery BRYANT, Jr., b.4 Oct 1862; d.8 Feb 1916, Lexington, GA
Martha Lissie HEWELL, b.21 Feb 1865; d.10 May 1925, Rayle, GA
married 22 Dec 1887
<Children>
Willie Mae BRYANT, b.25 Nov 1888, Lexington, GA
O'Neal BRYANT, b.15 Aug 1890; m.26 Dec 1923 to Mattie Lou EDWARDS; d.23 Feb 1966
Charlie Alvin BRYANT, b.27 Mar 1893; m.9 Dec 1920 to Addie Neal JACKSON; d.30 Dec
Fred Gilbert BRYANT, b.16 Apr 1897; m.9 Feb 1926 to Ophelia ADKINS
Lydia Victoria BRYANT, b.23 Sep 1904; m.8 Aug 1927 to Steward SISK; d.7-3-54
<Grandchildren>
Winifred Agnes BRYANT, b.6 Jan 1924, Rayle, GA
William A. BRYAN, b. 22 Sep [--]
Mary Frances BRYANT, b. 26 Oct 1927
William Marvin SISK, b.5 Jun 1928
Lydia Virginia SISK, b.10 Sep 1937; m. to Pat S. SHACKELFORD

Agnes BRYANT b.6 Jan 1924

Bolin E. BRYANT, b.28 Jan 1856
Lula BRYANT, b.24 Feb 1857
Charles W. BRYANT, b.26 Jan 1860
William A. BRYANT, b.4 Oct 1862; d.8 Feb 1916
Katie B. BRYANT, b.18 Dec 1867
Jeff C. BRYANT, b.7 Aug 1770; d.22 May 1911

Iaham H. G. HEWELL, b.2 Oct 1853
Mary Elizabeth HEWELL, b.21 Jul 1856; d.18 Feb 1863
William Alex HEWELL, b.5 May 1859
Martha Lissie HEWELL, b.21 Feb 1865; d.10 May 1925
Perlinia C. HEWELL, b.11 Apr 1869
(Jean David File)

MARY C. VAUGHANS BIBLE

HOLY BIBLE; Published by the American Bible Society, New York, 1847
Bible in 1978 was owned by Carolyn Virginia Bryuant Faz.
Entries from inside cover page. Entries very faded.
Mary C. VAUGHANS, book a present to her by B[----] DAVID
Mary C. VAUGHAN, b.18 Jan 1830
Writen by Alexander VAUGHAN her father 21 Mar 1852
(Jean David File)

HEWELL FAMILY BIBLE

THE PEOPLES' STANDARD EDITION OF THE HOLY BIBLE; Published by Ziegler & McCurdy, no date on title page
<u>CERTIFICATE</u>

Josiah HEWELL to Mary C. VAUGHAN [---] 1852; by J.H. Goss

BIRTHS

Wm K. HEWELL, b.12 Apr 1790
Elizabeth VAUGHAN, b. Jul 1788
Josiah HEWELL, b.28 Sep 1824
Mary C. HEWELL, b.18 Jan 1830
J.H.G. HEWELL, b.29 Oct 1853
Mary E. HEWELL, b.21 Jul 1856
William A. HEWELL, b.5 May 1859
Martha L. HEWELL, b.21 Feb 1865
Perlinia C. HEWELL, b.11 Apr 1869

MARRIAGES

J.H.G. HEWELL to Minnie E. PATTON, 23 Dec 1885
Martha L. HEWELL to Wm BRYANT, 22 Dec 1884
W.A. HEWELL to Lider WADSON, 20 Dec 189[-]

DEATHS

Wm W. HEWELL, d.21 Aug 1874
Elizabeth VAUGHAN, d.7 Oct 1873
Mary E. HEWELL, d.18 Feb 1863
Thomas H. HEWELL, b&d 15 Nov 1863
Alexander VAUGHAN, d.28 May 1880
Josiah HEWELL, d.21 Dec 1896
(Jean David File)

RYKER FAMILY BIBLE

No Title Page or Date

BIRTHS

Joseph H. RYKER, b.8 Oct 1826
John F. RYKER, b.25 Sep 1828
Mary E. RYKER, b.22 Mar 1831
William H. RYKER, b.15 Oct 1833

Sarah [---] RYKER, b.10 Feb 1836
Amanda S. RYKER, b.12 Jan 1839
Margaret C. RYKER, b.1 Aug 1841
DEATHS
Samuel [-] RYKER, d.16 Jun 1843
William H. RYKER, d.20 Mar 1880
Sarah A. RYKER, d.16 Mar 1880
Joseph H. RYKER, d.13 Jul 1880
Margaret RYKER, d.6 Sep 1887
MARRIAGES
Samuel RYKER to Margaret K. HOLTON; 15 Sep 1825
Joseph H. RYKER to Eliza S. McCLOUD; 2 Nov 1848
John F. RYKER to Ann Rebecca MICHELL; 17 Oct 1849
George M. VAUGHAN to Mary E. RYKER; 17 Jan 1850
John W. BENEFIEL to Sarah A. RYKER; d.4 Dec 1856
William H. BENEFIEL to Amanda J. RYKER; 18 Feb 1858
Samuel McCLOUD to Margaret C. RYKER; 24 Jan 1860
William H. RYKER to Margaret SNYDER; 19 Dec 1861
(David des Morets / Demarest File)

HAMMER FAMILY BIBLE

NO Title Page or Date

BIRTHS
J.B. HAMMER, b.21 Aug 1846, Wrightsville, York Co, PA
Martha A. SHIRK, b.24 Jul 1843, Pittsburgh, PA
Uaniue (?) Bell HAMMER, b.29 Aug 1870, Pittsburgh, PA
Alfred Shirk HAMMER, b.27 Feb 1873, Allegheney City
Philander Hammer BETTS, b.17 Nov 1897, Washington, DC, son of Nannie HAMMER & Philander BETTS
MARRIAGES
J.B. HAMMER to Mattie A. SHIRK, 14 Apr 1869, by Rev W.M. Young

Nannie Bell HAMMER to Philander BETTS, 19 Nov 1896 by Rev W.A. Kuiter, Providence Presbyteriam Church, Allegheny City, PA

DEATHS

Jacob B. HAMMER, d.16 Feb 1911, Pittsburgh, PA, age 64yrs

Martha A. SHIRK HAMMER, d.13 Oct 1911, Pittsburgh, PA, age 67yrs

Alfred Shirk HAMMER, son of J.B. & Martha Anne SHIRK HAMMER, d.6 Dec 1924, Bethlehem, PA, age 51yrs

Nannie Belle HAMMER BETTS, dau of J.B. HAMMER and Martha Ann SHIRK HAMMER

(David des Marets / Demarest File ; 2-249)

BETTS FAMILY BIBLE

No Title Page or Date

BIRTHS

Philander BETTS, 3rd, b.28 May 1868, Nyack, NY

Eugene BETTS, b.19 Oct 1870, Hackensack, NJ

Fanny BETTS, b.18 Oct 1872, Hackensack, NJ

Percy BETTS, b.30 May 1874, Hackensack, NJ

Guy BETTS, b.13 Dec 1875, Hackensack, NJ

Irvin W. BETTS, b.16 Aug 1880

Philander Hammer BETTS, b.17 Nov 1897, Washington DC

Sarah Louise BETTS, b.26 Mar 1900, Hackensack, NJ

Lewis Chafer HUBBARD, son of Frances BETTS, b.25 Dec 1902, Princeton, NJ

John Robert HUBBARD, b.13 Jun 1905, Boydton, VA

Helen Frances HUBBARD, b.13 Feb 1909, Honeoye Falls,

NY
Gordon Palmer HUBBARD, b.17 Mar 1914, Gainsville, GA
Sherman Wilcox BETTS, son of Irving BETTS, b.6 Oct 1909, Westwood, NJ
Austin Worthan BETTS, son of Irving, b.22 Nov 1912, Westwood, NJ
Earl Forrest BETTS, son of Irving, b.23 Jun 1915
MARRIAGES
Philander BETTS, Jr to Sarah DEMAREST, dau of John & Isabella DEMAREST, married by the Rev John Y. Demarest, at Nyack, [NY], 4 Jun 1867
Philander BETTS, 3rd to Nanny Bell HAMMER at Pittsburgh, PA, 19 Nov 1896
Gary BETTS to Grace M. ACKERMAN (?)
Frances Sarah BETTS to John Aljoe HUBBARD at Rochester, NY, 8 Oct 1901
Percy De Mareta BETTS to Emma Narie (Ferguson) SAMPTURE at New York, 26 Sep 1905
Irving Wilcox BETTS to Bessie Harris BOARDMAN at Yonkers, NY, 1 Nov 1905
Eugene BETTS to Anna Eldridge KENAH at New York City, [-] Nov 1917
Percy DeM. BETTS to Winifred A. HALL
DEATHS
Sarah Louise BETTS, d.3 Oct 1900, Hackensack; dau of Guy & Grace ACKERMAN BETTS
Infant Dau of Irving & Bessie H.B. BETTS, 1911
Sarah D. BETTS, d.13 Aug 1901, Hackensack, NJ, wife of Philander BETTS, JR
Philander BETTS, Jr, d.11 Aug 1919, Englewood, NJ
(David desMorets / Demarest file)

ACKERMAN BIBLE

HOLY BIBLE, Published by the American Bible Society, New York, 1854

Original in 1961 in the possession of Mrs C. Edward Scott of Warren, OH

On Flyleaf

Mr David C. ACKERMAN

Book bought of Wm W. Stiger, Morris County Bible Agent - 2 Nov 1854

MARRIAGES

David C. ACKERMAN to Sarah Ann TOLMAN [TALLMAN], 1 Apr 1848 by Rev H.B. Beegle

William WIGGINS to Clara ACKERMAN, 7 Aug 1878, by Rev Biscoe

Charles C. STEIGMANN to Flossie E. WIGGINS, 28 Nov 1906, by Rev F. Hock

Chas Edward SCOTT, Jr to Hilda Amelia STEIGMAN, 20 Oct 1928, by Rev Beattie

BIRTHS

David C. ACKERMAN, b.23 Oct 1825

Sarah Ann TOLMAN [TALLMAN], b.11 Nov 1832

Children:

Levi ACKERMAN, b.15 Feb 1849

Eliza Ann ACKERMAN, b.25 Apr 1853

Clara ACKERMAN, b.31 Dec 1860

Mary Elizabeth ACKERMAN, b.3 Jun 1866

BIRTHS

William WIGGINS, b.30 Jun 1853

Clara ACKERMAN, b.31 Dec 1860

Children:

Flossie E. WIGGINS, b.26 Aug 1883

Charles C. STEIGMANN, b.12 Mar 1882

Children:

Clara Louise STEIGMANN, b.14 Nov 1907
Hilda Amelia STEIGMANN, b.18 Mar 1909
Albertina Frieda STEIGMANN, b.29 Aug 1913

Charles Edwrad SCOTT, b.9 Jul 1907
Richard Edward SCOTT, b.8 Mar 1932
Gloria June SCOTT, b.22 Jun 1937
DEATHS
Eliza Ann ACKERSON, d.20 Nov 1853
Levi ACKERSON, d.16 Feb 1854
Mary E. ACKERSON, d. age few months
David C. ACKERSON, d.31 Jul 1887
Sarah Ann ACKERSON, d.20 Sep 1915
Clara WIGGINS, d.22 Jun 1934
William WIGGINS, d.8 Sep 1935
Albertina Frieda STEIGMANN, d.16 Jun 1914
Charles C. STEIGMAN, d.12 Oct 1947
Gloria June SCOTT, d.22 Jun 1927
Flossie (WIGGINS) STEIGMAN MILLER, d.6 Jun 1961
(David desMorets / Demarest)

SHULTZ BIBLE

No Title Page or date, the original bible in 1948 was in the possession of Mrs E. Donald Dietrich of College Park, MD.

MARRIAGE
Geeorge R. SHULTZ to Laura HENDRIX at Paris, IL on 22 Sep 1873, by Wm Wordth, J.P.
Charles R. SHULTZ to Florence McINTIRE, 12 Nov 1899
BIRTHS
George R. SHULTZ, b.15 Oct 1848, Fountain Co, IN
Laura HENDRIX, b.25 Aug 1855

Maud M. SHULTZ, b.22 Nov 1874
Charles R. SHULTZ, b.11 Nov 1876, Vigo Co, IN
Lone SHULTZ, b.14 Oct 1878
Martha Jane SHULTZ, b.30 Aug 1886
Oral T. SHULTZ, b.28 Mar 1888
Earl Wain SHULTZ, b.22 Dec 1890
Abbot G. SHULTZ, Father of G.R. SHULTZ, b.21 May 1818
Martha J. SHULTZ, Mother of G.R. SHULTZ, b.1 Apr 1828
DEATHS
Maud M. SHULTZ, d.25 Jan 1875
Oral SHULTZ, d.20 Feb 1893
Martha J. SERRIN, d.4 Dec 1908
George R. SHULTZ, d.8 May 1914
Abbot G. SHULTZ, Father of G.R. SHULTZ, d.7 Sep 1866
Martha J. SHULTZ, Mother of G.R. SHULTZ, d.23 Mar 1899
(David desMarets / Demarest)

McINTIRE BIBLE
No Title Page or Date
FAMILY RECORD
Parents' Names
Husband - Harbon McINTIRE, b.16 Nov 1857
Wife - Alice Whiteneck McINTIRE, b.20 Jan 1860
they married 1 Sep 1880
Children's Names
Lemuel McINTIRE, b.29 May 1881
Clara E. McINTIRE, b.24 Jan 1883
Florence D. McINTIRE, b.28 Jul 1884
Ophelia McINTIRE, b.24 Jan 1887
Nona E. McINTIRE, b.24 Jul 1889
Hugh McINTIRE, b.29 Jun 1891

Forest E. McINTIRE, b.14 Dec 1893
<u>MARRIAGES</u>
Florence D. McINTIRE to Chas R. SHULTZ, 12 Nov 1899
Clara E. McINTIRE to W.B. THOMPSON, 4 Jun 1907
Nona E. McINTIRE to A.Q. DICKSON, 31 Oct 1913
Hugh McINTIRE to Natalie KOCHER, 15 Dec 1914
Forest E. McINTIRE to Lela B. PEE, 25 Dec 1919
Lemuel McINTIRE to Caney BOXLEY, 30 Jul 1922
<u>DEATHS</u>
Ophelia McINTIRE, d.11 Mar 1887
Harbon McINTIRE, d.28 Oct 1916
(David deMarets / Desmarest)

PETER D. DEMAREST RECORDS

These Records seem to have been copied from a earlier unidentified BIble source, copied by N. S. Demarest
<u>DEATHS</u>
Peter D. DEMAREST, d.10 Oct 1842
Hannah COOPER, his wife, d.3 Apr 1860
David D. DEMAREST, d.10 Jul 1844, age 75yrs 1mo 5dys
Maria DEMAREST, d.10 Nov 1847, aged 76yrs 3mos 15dys
<u>BIRTHS</u>
Peter D. DEMAREST, b.2 Oct 1804
Hannah COOPER, his wife, b.7 Mar 1804
Sons
Henry P. DEMAREST, b.23 Jun 1827
James DEMAREST, b.19 Oct 1840 [15 May 1903]
David DEMAREST, b.10 Oct 1862; d.27 Dec 1912
(David desMarets / Demarest File)

DEMAREST BIBLE

No Title Page or Date

BIRTHS
Aletty DEMAREST, b.13 Jul 1818
Mary Catherine DEMAREST, b.24 Jun 1822
Leah DEMAREST, b.19 Feb 1828
MARRIAGES
Samuel DEMAREST to Elizabeth TERHUNE, 24 Feb 1816
John VANDERBEEK to Aletty DEMAREST, Nov 1835
John MANDIGO to Leah DEMAREST, 22 Jul 1846
John J. WINTER to Mary Catherine DEMAREST, 28 Oct 1846
(David desMarets / Desmarest File)

RAMSEY BIBLE
No Title Page or Date
BIRTHS
John RAMSEY b.12 Oct 1850
Elizabeth M. MANDIGO, b.21 Apr 1848
John W. REMSEY, b.16 Jun 1669
Alonzo RAMSEY, b.18 Feb 1871
Ida M. RAMSEY, b.27 Jul 1872
Infant Dau, b.27 Apr 1874
Infant Dau, b.16 Jul 1875
Garret Peter RAMSEY, b.1 Aug 1876
Floyd E. RAMSEY, b.24 Feb 1879
Charles W. RAMSEY, b.29 Apr 1881
Matilda RAMSEY, b.22 Sep 1882
Walter A. RAMSEY, b.7 Sep 1885
Gracie RAMSEY, b.19 Dec 1891
Kittie McKinley RAMSEY, b.12 Oct 1896
MARRIAGES
John RAMSEY to Elizabeth M. MANDIGO, 23 Apr 1868
Ida M. RAMSEY to Charles SNYDER, 24 Feb 1891

John W. RAMSEY to Belle WHITE, 27 Aug 1891
Alanzo W. RAMSEY to Susan SNYDER, 16 Jul 1892
Floyd RAMSEY to Fannie TILDEN, 23 Apr 1901
Matilda RAMSEY to J. Roe COX, 21 Oct 1905
Grace RAMSEY to Walter Estabrook SMITH, 22 Nov 1913
Floyd RAMSEY to Margaret [-] CAHILL, 26 Nov 1913[?]
Charles W. RAMSEY to Evalyn THORNE, 27 Sep 1927

DEATHS

Infant dau, d.27 Apr 1874
Infant dua, d.26 Sep 1875
Walter A. RAMSEY, d.23 Sep 1889
Garret Peter RAMSEY, d.22 Feb 1898
Kitty McKinley RAMSEY, d.8 Nov 1920
Elizabeth M. RAMSEY, d.27 Nov 1921
John RAMSEY, d.17 Dec 1922
Ida M. SNYDER, d.9 Aug 1923, Fresno, CA
John W. RAMSEY, d.7 Oct 1938
Belle White RAMSEY, d.29 Sep 1933
Charles SNYDER, d.16 Mar 1946
Charles W. RAMSEY, d.13 Jan 1953
Alonzo W. RAMSEY, d.7 Aug 1954
J. Roe COX, d.7 Jun 1955
Susan Jane Synder RAMSEY, d.21 Jan 1956
(David desMarets / Desmarest File)

HARR BIBLE

No Title Page or Date

BIRTHS

Milford Cookman HARR, b.4 Mar 1873
Emma Currey HARR, b.15 Mar 1876
Jesse Irvine HARR, b.23 Jun 1880
Annie Virginia HARR, b.18 Dec 1882

John Herbert HARR, b.15 Jun 1886
Edith May HARR, b.9 Sep 1893
Herbert Wm COOPER, b.14 May 1910
Family of Milford C. HARR
Florence V. HARR, b.17 Sep 1895
Selby C. HARR, b.24 Dec 1896
Geo. Calvert HARR, b.12 Nov 1897
Ruth HARR, b.23 Mar 1900
Frances Mildred HARR, b.17 Nov 1901
Marian Estelle HARR, b.16 Dec 1903
Samuel Morton HARR, b.24 Feb 1908
Robt Russell HARR, b.14 May 1912
Herbert Randolf HARR, b. 1915
Milton
David

<u>DEATHS</u>

Mrs Eliza Ann UNDERWOOD, [nee GRANT], d.16 Dec 1870, aged 52yrs, Mother of Annie E. HARR, nee WOOD
William E. HARR, d.19 Dec 1871, aged 69yrs, father of Jesse M. HARR
John Herbert HARR, d.7 Nov 1889, aged 3yrs 4mos 24dys, third son of Jesse M. & Annie E. HARR
Emma C. COOPER, [nee HARR], d.24 Jun 1911, aged 35yrs 3mos
Emma HODGSON, d.10 Jan 1883, sister of Annie E. HARR, dau of Mrs Eliza Ann UNDERWOOD
Susannah STARR, d.23 Feb 1896, aged 88yrs
Marian Selby HARR, wife of Milford HARR,d.16 Dec 1903
Jna T. WOOD- brother of Annie E. HARR, wife of J. M. HARR, d.23 Apr 1905
Annie Virginia HARR, d.11 Nov 1912, age 29yrs, 10mos, 22dys
On seperate sheet of paper:

Albert Whitfield HARR, d.15 Sep 1845, aged 7yrs 7mos 15dys

Charles W. HARR, d.27 Mar 1854, aged 15yrs, 8mos 16dys
Carrie V. BEACH, d.16 Apr 1868, aged 32yrs 6mos
William Evans HARR, d.19 Dec 1871, aged 68yrs
Susannah Ferree HARR, d.23 Feb 1896, age 88yrs
Isabelle Emma HODGSON, twin sister of Annis E, HARR, d.10 Jan 1883, aged 33yrs
Annie E. HARR, (nee WOODS), married Jesse M. HARR, the son of W.E. & Susannah Ferre HARR, 6 Jun 1872
Stephen HARR,native of Ennis, Ireland, married Mary EVANS, a native of Virginia and dau of John Evans of England, granddaughter of Daniel & Ann C[---]oley, natives of Scotland
James FERREE, native of Pennsylvania, whose Ancestors were of France was married to Catherine LaFEVER, originally of France, and granddaughter of Isac PEEK, a Native of Germany
Wm E. HARR, son of Stephen and Mary HARR, a native of [----] married 2 Aug 1832 to Susannah FERREE, native of Pennsylvainia, dau of James and Catherine FERREE
Wm E. HARR b. 2 Mar 1804
Susannah FERREE, b.21 Nov 1808
Catherine LaFEVER, dau of Daniel LaFEVER, of France
James Wm HERR, son of Wm E. & Susannah HARR, b.9 Nov 1833
Caroline Virginia HARR, dau of W, E. & Susannah HARR, b.19 Sep 183[6]
Charles Worthington HARR, son of Wm E. & Susannah HARR, b.10 Jul 1838
Oliver Randolph HARR, son of Wm E. & Susannah HARR, b.10 Jan 1842
Albert Whitfield HARR, son of W, E. & Susannah HARR, b.1

Apr 1844
Jessiah Morgan HARR, son of Wm E. & Susannah HARR, b.19 Dec 1846

William E. HARR, d.19 Dec. --, aged 68yrs 9mos 15dys
Susannah HARR, d.23 Feb 1896, aged 88yrs
James Wm HARR, d.29 Aug 1911, aged 78yrs
Oliver R. HARR, d.28 Feb 1917, aged 76yrs
(Christian Deyo File)

DANIEL FEGAN BIBLE

THE HOLY BIBLE, Published by Kimber and Sharpless, Philadelphia; 1824

MARRIAGES

Daniel FEGAN to Magadeline KILLINGER, 9 Nov 1817

BIRTHS

Elisa, b.8 Nov 1818
Susanna, b.26 Jan 1820
Polly, b.14 Nov 1821
George, b.13 May 1823
Catherine, b.20 Aug 1826
Fanny, b.20 Aug 1826
John, b.31 Mar 1829
Rosannah, b.11 Jun 1831
Peter, b.17 Feb 1833
Daniel, b.30 Dec 1836
infant, b.30 Dec 1836
Henry Marian, b.21 Nov 1839
Joseph Killinger, b.21 Nov 1839

DEATHS

Catherine, d.16 May 1829

Rscan[?] d. 26 Dec 1856
FATHER, d.22 Feb 1864, aged 71yrs
MOTHER, d.26 Dec 1866, aged 68yrs
Eliza, d.24 Jun 1883 at Harrisburg, aged 65yrs
Susannah, d.19 Aug 1894, aged 74yrs 6mos 20dys
Polly, d.17 Mar 1895, Union TWP, aged 73yrs 4mos 3mos
George, d.23 Feb 1896, Burlington, IA, aged 72yrs 9mos 10dys
Fanny, d.21 May 1897, Amesville, PA, aged 70yrs 8mos 2dys
Peter, d.29 Dec 1895, North Lebanon TWP, PA, aged 65yrs 10mos 12dys
Henry Harrison FAGEN, d.8 Oct 1906, aged 64yrs 10mos 18dys
John, d.27 May 1905, Aville, PA, aged 76yrs 1mo 27dys
Joseph Killinger, d.21 Feb 1907, Annville, PA, aged 67yrs 3mos
Daniel FEGAN, d.5 Sep 1914, Annville, PA, aged 77yrs 8mos 5dys
(Casper Diller File)

JOHN FEGAN BIBLE

HOLY BIBLE, Published by John B. Perry, Philadelphia, 1855

MARRIAGES

John FEGAN to Lucella SHIFFLER, 30 Oct 1855

BIRTHS

John FEGAN, b.27 Mar 1829
Lucella FEGAN, b.23 Jan 1832
John Daniel FEGAN b,26 Oct 1856
Mary Magdalene FEGAN, b.1 Aug 1858

[several entries too faint to read]
George Henry FEGAN, b.31 Jan 1862
Benjamin Franklin FEGAN, b.22 Apr 1864
Simon Peter FEGAN, b.[--] Jan 1867
David [-----] FAGEN, b.[--] Mar 1869
Charles Silas FEGAN, b.7 Oct 1870
[-----------] Aug 1873
Carry [---] FEGAN b. [--] Oct 1874
Lizzie Gertrude FEGAN, b.31 Jan 1878
Walter BOLTZ, son of Mary F. BOLTZ, b.25 Sep 1885
S. Mark FEGAN, b.3 Jun 1900
Mary Eliza FEGAN, b.20 Jul 1902
Jennie Phillipe FEGAN, wife of S. Mark
Mary FEGAN m. to Richard SNYDER, 26 Jul 1933
Mark FEGAN married to Mary FEGAN SNYDER are the children of Simon FEGAN

DEATHS

Kate Shiffler FEGAN, d.6 Feb 1862
George Henry FEGAN, d.10 Aug 1863
Charles Silas FEGAN, d.5 Sep 1872
David Killinger FEGAN, d.5 Oct 1875
Lizzie Gertrude FEGAN, d.6 Feb 1875
Allen Shiffler FEGAN, d.13 Feb 1875
John W. FEGAN, d.27 May 1905
Simon P. FEGAN, d. Sep 1932
his wife Tacie, d. 29 Apr 19[-]1
Mary F. BOLTZ, d.6 Dec 1931
son Walter F. BOLTZ, d.[--] Dec 1965
(Casper Diller File)

HARDENBURGH BIBLE

No Title Page or Dates

BIRTHS
D.D. BRINK, b.21 Mar 1848
Cornelia BRINK, b.5 May 1849
Clair BRINK, b.24 Oct 1875
Ida BRINK, b.14 Feb 1877
Ira BRINK, b.19 Apr 1879
Jesse BRINK, b.13 Feb 1883
Mary BRINK, b.17 Nov 1885
DEATHS
Dennis D. BRINK, d.27 Mar 1886
MARRIAGES
Dennis D. BRINK to Cornelia HARDENBERG, m.14 Jan 1874
(Chretien DuBois File)

COONS FAMILY BIBLE

THE NEW TESTAMENT, Published by Samuel Bagster & Sons, Limited. London ; James DOTT, New York, No date

BIRTHS
Foster A. COONS, b.16 Dec 1870
Ida B. COONS, b.14 Feb 1877
Sheldon F. COONS, b.5 Mar 1909
Shelby Ann COONS, b.12 Jul 1935
Audrey Ellen COONS, b.9 Jan 1838
Aaron COONS, b.3 Apr 1833
Emma Sheldon COONS, b.22 Sep 1841
Ella COON GRIFFIN, b.26 May 1860
William S. COONS, b.3 Oct 1865
Richard B. COONS, b.7 Oct 1874
Whitney SHELDON, b.7 Jun 1812
Catherine Van Tossel SHELDON, b.14 Jun 1812

MARRIAGES
Foster A. COONS to Ida BRINK, m.9 Apr 1901
Sheldon F. COONS to Thyson J. LASSY, m.29 Nov 1933
Aaron COONS to Emma SHELDON, m.24 Feb 1859
DEATHS
Emma Sheldon COONS, d.15 Jan 1900
Aaron COONS, d.2 Feb 1910
Alice GAYNOR COONS, d.29 Nov 1935
William Sheldon COONS, d.17 Jan 1936
Ella COONS GRIFFIN, d.17 Apr 1903
Hiram GRIFFIN, d.2 Mar 1892
Whiting SHELDON, d.19 Feb 1900
Catherine Van Tassel SHELDON, d.7 Oct 1900
Foster A. COONS, d.1 Dec 1954
Ida B. COONS, d.4 Apr 1960
(Chretien DuBois File)

HAYCRAFT FAMILY BIBLE

THE HOLY BIBLE; Published by J.A. Wilmore & Co; New York, Sept 1891
FAMILY RECORD
<GRANDPARENTS>
Samuel M. Haycraft, b.18 Jan 1822, Harden Co, KY; d.14 Oct 1886 Lewis Co, MO
Mary Jane BUISCA, b.18 Mar 1827, Hardin Co KY; d.21 Apr 1905
John FACKLER, b.1816, Hagerstown, MD; d.Apr 1886, Clark Co, MO
Mary MOONY, b.1819, Elizabethtown, KY; d.1895, Winchester, MO
<PARENTS>
Samuel Nevil HAYCRAFT, b.12 Nov 1854, Grundy Co, MO;

d.11 Aug 1934, Wichita, KS
Annie Pleasant FACKLER, b.8 Sep 1852, Clark Co, MO; d.27 May 1927, Wichita, KS
married 17 Jun 1877, Winchester, MO
<CHILDREN>
Samuel Hugh, b.6 Apr 1878, Lewis Co, MO; m.18 Jun 1909 to Effie PAYNE; d.5 Apr 1929
Mamie Annette, b.5 Sep 1879, Lewis Co, MO; m.15 Mar 1903 to Alfred L. CHASE, d.2 Jan 19[--] Alfred b.31 Mar 1875; d.2 Feb 1956
Charles William, b.18 Aug 1881, Lewis Co, MO; d.30 May 1915
Edith Elsie; b.7 Jul 1884, Lewis Co, MO; m. Cas A. BULL (b.16 Apr 1879); d.3 Dec 1962.
<Grandchildren>
Edith Nadine CHASE, b.16 Mar 1906, Tawkawa, OK; m.12 Oct 1941 to Charles Wilber WALTS (b.13 Oct 1897)
June Frances CHASE, b.31 Aug 1911, Dunxcan, OK; m. 16 Oct 1936 to Jess Walter ELLIOTT; d.12 May 1967, (b.3 Jun 1907; d.2 Oct 1957)
(Chretien Dubois File)

BUTT FAMILY BIBLE

HOLY BIBLE, published by the American Bible Society, New York, 1894
FAMILY RECORDS
<u>MARRIAGES</u>
Rev Leonidas BUTT to Sarah Elizabeth PARKER, m.1 Mar 1870
Charles L. STERN to Mary Catherine BUTT, m.7 Sep 1898
Arthur P. BUTT to Bessie May [JUTA?], m.5 Apr 1899

Richard Bosworth TALBOTT to Birtha Thelma BUTT, m.16 Oct 1926
Chas Robt STEVENS to Thelma WOOD, m.19 Aug 1933
Kenneth Lee BUTT to Bettie HARWOOD, m.4 Jun [---]
Richard Butt TALBOTT to Mavis Ann Morris JACKSON, m.8 Sep 1957
DEATHS
Daisie BUTT, d.1 Nov 1908
Leonidas BUTT, d.9 Jul 1912
Sarah Elizabeth BUTT, d.7 Dec 1931
Bessie May BUTT, d.1[-] Mar 1939
Arthur Parker BUTT, d.5 Aug 1936
Roberta Susan BUTT, d.13 Oct 1941
Mary Catherine B. STEVENS, d.26 Sep 1945
Arthur Parker BUTT, Jr, d.16 Dec 1953, Melburne, FL
BIRTHS
Leonidas BUTT, b.5 Jul 1841
Sarah E. PARKER, b.3 Dec 1847
Arthur P. BUTT, b.16 Jan 1871
Mary G. BUTT, b.9 May 1873
Roberta S. BUTT, b.6 Apr 1875
Bessie BUTT, b.5 Aug 1877
Daisie BUTT, b.4 Feb 1880
Bessie May SUTOR BUTT, b.2 Mar 1872
Chas L. STEVENS, d.4 Jan 1974
Bertha Thelma BUTT, b.11 Sep 1900
Charles Robert STEVENS, b.22 Oct 1901
Arthur Parker BUTT, Jr, b.12 Jul 1902
Kenneth Lee BUTT, b.22 Feb 1906
Richard Butt TALBOTT, b.21 Apr 1928
Thelma May TALBOTT, b.24 Oct 1933
Chas David STEVENS, b.8 Feb 1935
Flora Elizabeth BUTT, b.11 Sep 1935

Thelma Wood STEVENS, b.22 Feb 1903
Betty Lee BUTT, b.30 Apr 1947
Susan Kenlee BUTT, b.24 Jul 1956
Richard Norris TALBOTT, b.26 Jun 1958
(Louis Du Bois File)

BUTT FAMILY BIBLE II

NEW TESTAMENT, Published by the American Bible Society, New York, 1873
FAMILY RECORDS
DEATHS
Mary Jane BUTT, d.10 Jan 1853
Shannon BUTT, d.16 Nov 1863
Mary M. BUTT, d.28 Jun 1860
Josephine BUTT, d.25 Mar 1863
F.M. MURPHY, d.7 Jan 1884
S.F. BUTT, d. 1903
A.H. BUTT, d.8 Feb 1906
Ann E. BUTT, now PECK, d.22 Jul 1906
Martha Josephine BUTT, d.1910
Daisy BUTT, d.1 Nov 1908
Rev Leonidas BUTT, d.8 Jul 1912
Dr Shennon P. PECK, d. Sep 1914
Dr Charles BUTT, d.
Sarah Elizabeth Parker BUTT, d.10 Dec 1931
Susan BUTT, d.13 Oct 1941
Dr Arthur P. BUTT, d.5 May 1936
MARRIAGES
Rev Leonidas BUTT to Sarah E. PARKER, m.14 Mar 1870 by Rev S. G. BUTT
BIRTHS
Arthur Parker BUTT, b.16 Jan 1871

Mary Catherine BUTT, b.9 May 1873
Roberta Susan BUTT, b.6 Apr 1875
Bessie BUTT, b.5 Aug 1877
Daisy BUTT, b.4 Feb 188[-]
Sarah Elizabeth PARKER, now BUTT, b.3 Dec 1847
Clara Elizabeth BUTT, dau of Arthur P. BUTT and Flora KNUTH BUTT, b.11 Sep 1935
Shannon BUTT, b.4 Jan 1806
Mary J. REESE, b.13 Aug 1804
Henry C. BUTT, b.22 Jan 1832
Arvn(?) E. BUTT, b.5 Jan 1834
A.F. BUTT, b.10 Dec 1835
Richard L. BUTT, b.20 Oct 1837
Shannon F. BUTT, b.19 Apr 1839
Leonidas BUTT, b.5 Jul 1841
Jane E. BUTT, b.30 Sep 1843
Francis MURPHY, b.7 Jan 1824
Virginia W. BUTT, b.11 Mar 1850
Mary M. BUTT, b.18 Jul 1854
Josephine BUTT, b.16 Dec 1857
Eugenia BUTT, b.28 Feb 1860
Martha Josephine BUTT, b.15 Apr 1860
(Louis Du Bois File)

FRY FAMILY BIBLE

BIRTHS

John H. FRY, b.21 Feb 1828, d.28 Sep 1907
Eliza FRY, b.30 Sep 1832, d.23 Oct 1894
Sarah Jane FRY, dau of John & Eliza, b.10 Mar 1853
Mary Alice FRY, dau of John & Eliza, b.20 Jul 1854
James Harvey FRY, son of John & Eliza, b.20 [--] 1859

Virgiania May FRY, dau of John H. & Eliza, b.18 May 1864
Lillie Leota FRY, dau of Joh & Eliza, b.23 Mar 1868
Marriett Evelyn HARMAN, dau of R.A. & Lellia L. HERMAN, b.15 Aug 1894, Terre Haute, IN
Reuben St John HERMAN, son of R.A. & Lillie L. HERMAN, b.26 Apr 1897, Chicago, IL
MARRIAGES
John K. FRY to Eliza St JOHN, m.15 Dec 1850
George NIPPER to Alice M. FRY, m.25 Mar 1875
George E. GRAFT to Viggie M. FRY, m. 23 Sep 1882
Russell A. HERMAN to Lillie L. FRY, m.20 Oct 1892
James H. FRY to Josephine E. SCHERMERHORN, m. Nov 1895
BIRTHS
Samuel C. GRAFT, son of George & Virgie GRAFT, b.30 Sep 1883, Lafayette, IN
Katherine Schermerhorn FRY, dau of James H. & Josephine FRY, b. in Ft Wayne, IN
DEATHS
Sarah Jane FRY, d.18 Aug 1853
George [BURTON] ?? d. [---]1879
John K. FRY, d.28 Sep 1907
Eliza FRY, d.23 Oct 1894
(Louis De Bois File)

EOFF BIBLE

THE HOLY BIBLE, Published by the American Bible Society, New York, 1874
FAMILY RECORD
MARRIAGES
Charles W. EOFF to Henrietta H. ROEMER, m.27 Apr 1875

by Rev James D. Wright at Wheeling, WV
Maude R. EOFF to Robert Morgan WILLIAMS, m.22 Aug 1898, by Rev J.M. Cromer, Kansas City, MO
BIRTHS
Helen Woods EOFF, b.4 Sep 1877
Maude Roemer EOFF, b.24 Sep 1878
(Louis Du Bois File)

WICKS FAMILY BIBLE

No Title Page or Dates, copied from the Family Bible by Aunt Ida Thomas 15 Sep 1952
BIRTHS
James S. WICKS, b.10 Jan 1821
Sarah J. SNEE, b.4 Mar 1824
Sarah Anette WICKS, b.4 Dec 1862
Infant Dau, b./ d. 16 May 1865
Rhoda Jane WICKS, b.28 Jan 1849
Elizabeth WICKS, b.11 Sep 1850
Silas Monroe WICKS, b.18 Apr 1852
John WICKS, b.2 Feb 1854
Charles Wesley WICKS, b.14 Jul 1856
Jesse Lee & James Axley WICKS, b.29 Oct 1858
Amanda B. WICKS, b.10 Jan 1861
DEATHS
Amanda WICKS, d. 27 Apr 1861, age 4mos
Sarah Anette WICKS, d.14 Oct 1872, aged 10yrs
Jesse Lee WICKS, d.1 Jun 1888, aged 30yrs
Elizabeth WICKS, consort of Silas WICKS, d.10 Nov 1828, aged 28yrs
Silas WICKS, d.5 Jun 1833, aged 50yrs
Nancy WICKS, dau of Elizabeth & Silas WICKS, d.20 Sep 1829, aged 15mos

John SNEE, d.27 Jul 1842, aged 49yrs
Thomas SNEE, d. Jul 1828, aged 18mos
F. SNEE, d.23 Dec 1845, aged 16yrs
Salley SNEE, concort of John SNEE, d.3 Jan 1875, aged 76yrs
James A. WICKS, d.15 Feb 1908, aged 50yrs
Elizabeth Wicks BARKLEY,
James S. WICKS, d. 3 Dec 1890, aged 69
Sarah J. WICKS, d.29 Jul 1889, aged 65
MARRIAGES
James S. WICKS to Sarah Jane SNEE,m.27 Apr 1848
George W. BOYER to Rhoda Jane WICKS, m.17 Sep 1871
Robert BARKLEY to Elizabeth WICKS, m.25 Sep 1873
John S. WICKS to Luzerne LYTLE, m.24 Dec 1874
Silas Monroe WICKS to Annie SCOTT, m.21 Jun 1877
Charles Wesley WICKS to Mollie Jane RALSTON, m.1 Aug 1881
Charles Wesley WICKS to Nancy Jane TOWNSEND, m.14 Feb 1895
(Louis Du Bois File)

HENDRICKSON FAMILY BIBLE

No Title Page or Dates

FAMILY RECORD
BIRTHS
Isaac HENDRICKSON, b.17 Apr 1808
Mariah HENDRICKSON, wife of Isaac HENDRICKSON, b.20 Jun 1812
Isaac HENDRICKSON, son of Isaac & Maria HENDRIKSON, b.16 Apr 1835
William H. HENDRICKSON, son of Isaac & Maria D. HENDRICKSON, b.8 Nov 1836
Richard H. HENDRICKSON, son of Isaac & Maria

HENDRICKSON, b.24 Nov 1838

DEATHS

Isaac HENDRICKSON, Sr, d.5 Apr 1860

Prudence HENDRICKSON, wife of I. HENDRICKSON,Sr, d.14 Apr 1850

Isaac HENDRICKSON, Jr, d.11 Sep 1880, aged 73yrs

BIRTHS

Edwin, son of Isaac & Jane HENDRICKSON, b.20 Jul 1862

Lilly M. HENDRICKSON, dau of Isaac & Jane HENDRICKSON, b.28 Sep 1864

Children of Wm & Miranda HENDRICKSON

Lizzie G. HENDRICKSON, b.5 Dec 1864

James G. T. HENDRICKSON, b.2 Dec 1867

Maria HENDRICKSON, b.20 May 1870

Isaac HENDRICKSON, b.16 Nov 1871

Florine B. HENDRICKSON, b.2 Nov 1877

DEATHS

Edwin M. HENDRICKSON, d.24 Feb 1868, aged 5yrs 7mos 3dys

Maria HENDRICKSON, dau of William & Miranda HENDRICKSON, d.21 Aug 1870

MARRIAGES

Isaac HENDRICKSON to Maria D. HOLSTON, m.28 Nov 1833

Marriages of the Sons of Isaac and Mariah HENDRICKSON

Isaac, 1st son to Jane MORRISON, m.11 Dec 1861

Wm, 2nd son, to Maranda FORD, m.29 Aug 1861

Richd, 3rd son to Juliet R. GRIFFITHS, m.27 Mar 1862

[next entry to faint to read]

(Louis Du Bois File; 1-2877)

DU BOIS BIBLE

No Title Page or Date

FAMILY RECORDS

DEATHS

Lafe E. DuBOIS, d.8 Jan 1904
Christina C. DuBOIS, d.18 May 1921
Oscar Scott DuBOIS, d.9 Jul 1926
married 31 Dec 1863
Rose Celina DuBOIS d.9 Oct 1964
Mary Heard DuBOIS, d.25 Oct 1963

BIRTHS

Lafe E. DuBOIS, b.5 Feb 1877
Walter S. DuBOIS, b.21 Mar 1877
Donald M. DuBOIS, b.27 Apr 1900
Mary Edna DuBOIS, b.5 Oct 1885
Harold Heard DuBOIS, b.29 Jan 1910
Donald Murphy DuBOIS, b.27 Apr 1900
Rose Selina DuBOIS, b.12 Feb 1901
Patsy Lou DuBOIS, b.30 Apr 1932
Harold Heard DuBOIS, b.29 Jan 1910
Dorothy Jane DuBOIS, b.22 May 1912
Richard Heard DuBOIS, b.8 Jun 1936
Sally Ann DuBOIS, b.8 Jun 1936

BIRTHS

Grandparents
Oscar Scott DuBOIS, b.25 Apr 1841
Christinia C. DuBOIS, b.27 Dec 1839
Walter Scott DuBOIS, b.21 Mar 1877
Mary Edna DuBOIS, b.5 Oct 1885

MARRIAGES

Walter S. DuBOIS to Lafe E. HAYWARD, m.4 Aug 1898
Walter S. DuBOIS to Mary Edna [can't read], m.27 Feb 1908
Donald Murphy DuBOIS to Rose S. MURPHY, m.26 Nov

1930
Harold Heard DuBOIS to Dorothy Jane GRANSEE, m.3 Aug 1935
(Louis DuBois File; 4-236)

MAGEE BIBLE
No Title Page or dates
CERTIFICATE
James E. WARREN of Sthelena, PA married to Nancy Jane WAMACK of Sthelena, PA on 13 Jan 1870 by Judge George Wittess: Pierce Phillips and W.Z. Wamock
BIRTHS
Leon Lula MAGEE, b.25 Feb 1862
James Edger WARREN, b.2 Nov 1849
Nancy Jane WARREN, b.8 Jul 1846
Leon Luke MAGEE, b.22 Feb 1862
Addie Emlalie WARREN, dau of James Edgar and Nancy Jane WARREN, b.9 Aug 1871
Adde May MAGEE, b.13 Dec 1892
[---] Beatrice Henderson b. [----]
DEATHS
James Edgar Warren, d.7 Mar 1905
Leon Luke MAGEE, d.11 Mar 1912
MARRIAGES
Leon L. MAGEE to Addie E, WARREN, 22 Dec 1891, by Rev J.W. Ellison
Addie Mae MAGEE to Hugh Evins WARDLAW, 8 Jun 1913
Nannie Maude MAGEE to Edmund Franklin BARNES,, 7 Mar 1917
Fannie Warren MAGEE to Edwin Nelson WENNERLUND, 27 Jun 1922
CERTIFICATE

W.E. WARDLOW to Mae Addie MAGEE, 3 Jan 1913, Pike Co, MS
(Louis Dubose File)

LUCAS FAMILY BIBLE

NEW TESTAMENT; Published by the American Bible Society, New York, 1891
FAMILY RECORD
MARRIAGE
Edw P. LUCAS to Sarah J. BROWN , Charleston, SC, 23 Oct 1863
Eddie R. LUCAS to W.L. BASS, 16 Jun 1886, KIngston, SC
Ennie V. LUCAS to Dr J.L. BASS, 23 May 1887, Kingston, SC
Gretchen Emmie BASS to Lowell M. RIVERRE, 2 Dec 1919, Lake City, SC
Sallie Georgie BASS to E. Henrdix ROBVELL, 14 Jul 1926, Palm Harbor, FL
DEATHS
Emmie BASS, dau of Dr J.L. & Emmie V. BASS, d.4 May 1888, Willacomshell {?}, GA
Emmie Inez BASS, dau of W.L. & E.R. BASS, d.29 Aug 1887, Kingston. SC
Natalie BASS, dau of W. L. & E.R. BASS, d.2 Jan 1891, Adel, GA
Eddie R. BASS, wife of W.L. BASS, d.13 Aug 1919, Tampa, FL
William Levnidas BASS, d.31 Jan 1920, Lake City, SC
Mrs S.J. LUCAS, d.3 Oct 1902, Lake City, SC
Mrs Emma P. BROWN, Grandmother of Mrs E.R. & E.V. BASS, d.12 Aug 1900, Lake City, SC
Dr J.L. BASS, d. at Lake City, SC

BIRTHS
Emmie V. LUCAS, dau of Edw P. & Sarah J. LUCAS, b.7 Dec 1865
Eddie R. LUCAS, dau of Edw P. & Sarah J. LUCAS, b.25 Aug 1869
Emmie V. BASS, dau of Dr J.L. & Emmie V. BASS, b.4 May 1888, Willcrocker {?}, GA
Emmie Inez BASS, dau of W.L. & E.R. BASS, b.23 Mar 1887, Kingston, SC
Natalie BASS, dau of W.L. & E.R. BASS, b.27 Nov 1890, Lake City, SC
Sallie G. BASS, dau of W.L. & E.R. BASS, b.8 Mar 1892, Lake City, SC
Gretchen BASS, dau of W.L. & E.L. BASS, b.3 Mar 1896, Lake City, SC
(Louis Dubose File)

DuBOSE BIBLE

HOLY BIBLE, published by E.H. Bulter & Co, Philadelphia, 1852

BIRTHS
John E. G. DuBOSE, b.2 Sep 1809, Williamsburg Dist, SC
Caroline R. DuBOSE, b.13 May 1825, Colleton Dist, SC
Julius L. DuBOSE, b.30 Mar 1845, Darlington, SC
Ella Amanda DuBOSE, b.18 Aug 1846, Santee, SC
John Edwin DuBOSE, b.20 Jul 1848, Cossville, GA
Caroline Rebecca DuBOSE, b.5 Aug 1850, Canton, GA
William Thompson DuBOSE, 14 Apr 1853, Canton, GA
Pratt Cassels DuBOSE, b.4 Sep 1855, Atlanta, GA
Francis Camilla DuBOSE, b.20 Mar 1858, Atlanta, GA
Laura Grace DuBOSE, b.29 Aug 1860, Tallahasse
J [--] DuBose FEATHERSTON b.25 Oct 1888, Newnan, GA

MEMORANDA

L [--] FEATHERSTON, b. 4 Nov 1892, Atlanta
Annie Carolyn FEATHERSTON, b.19 Dec 1894, Atlanta, GA
Lucile DuBOSE, b.21 Jun 1887, Spring Hill, TN, dau of W.T. DuBOSE
Ethel DuBOSE, b.21 Dec 189[-], Spring Hill, TN, dau of W.T. DuBOSE
Samuel Wilds DuBOSE, b. 8 Jul 1907, son of Samuel W. & Maud, born DuBOSE
Joseph Harlan GILMORE, Jr, b.3 Dec 1916, Gallaton, TN, son of Joseph Harlan GILMARE & Anne Carolyn FEATHERSTON
William Featherston GILMORE, b.17 Sep 1918, Gallatin, TN, son of Joseph Harlan GILMORE & Anne FEATHERSTON GILMORE

DEATHS

Pratt Capels DuBOSE, d.23 Jun 1862, Tallahasse, FL
Caroline R. DuBOSE, wife of Rev G.E. DuBOSE d.3 May 1863, Tallahasse, FL
Ella Amanda DuBOSE, d.21 Dec 1863, Tallahasse, FL
Julius Harlon DuBOSE, d.27 Jul 1886, Decatur, GA
Julius DuBose FEATHERSTON, d.22 Apr 1895, Decatur, GA

Mary Hollen DuBOSE, wife of Rev John E. DuBOSE, d.15 Apr 1908, Decatur, GA
John E. DuBOSE, son of Rev J.E. d.10 Jan 1910, Bowling Green,
Hampden C. DuBOSE, son of Rev Julius and Margaret DuBOSE, d.22 Mar 1910, Loochow, China
Carolina Rebecca DuBOSE, dau of Rev J.E. & Caroline Rebecca DuBOSE, d.14 Dec 1911, Atlanta, GA
Fannie C. DuBOSE, dau of J.E. & Caroline Rebecca DuBOSE, d.6 Oct 1940, Atlanta, GA

William Thompson DuBOSE, son of J. E. & Caroline Rebecca DuBOSE, d.6 Jun 1936, Nashville, TN
Samuel Wiers DuBOSE, son of J.E. & Mary H. Holland DUBOSE, d.1926, Pocomake City, MD
Louise Moore DuBOSE, dau of J.E. & Mary Holland DuBOSE, d.28 Nov ---, Moultie, GA
Laura Grant DuBOSE FEATHERSTON, Dau of J.E. & Caroline Rebecca THOMPSON DuBOSE, d.29 Jan 1944, Atlanta, GA
William S. FEATHERSTON, son of Judge Lucius Horace and Maria Thompson, d.[--] Jun 1932, Atlanta, GA
<u>MARRIAGES</u>
John E. DuBOSE to Carline R. THOMPSON, 25 Jan 1843, By Rev Julius J. DuBOSE, Columbia, SC
John E. DuBOSE to Mary H. HOLLAND, formarly Mary H. GUTHRIE, 25 Apr 1866, by Rev F.H. Ruthladge, Tallahassee, FL
John E. DuBOSE, Jr to Ru[--] BINGHAM, 5 Nov 1878, by Rev John E. DuBOSE, Bowling Green, KY
[entry too bloched to read clearly] Wm DuBOSE to L -- m. 26 Oct 1881 {??}
Wm S. FEATHERSTON to Laura G. DuBOSE, 22 Nov 1887
(Louis DuBose File)

DuBOSE BIBLE II

The New Testament, Self Pronouncing Edition, no publisher or dates on Title page
<u>BIRTHS</u>
Samuel B. DuBOSE, b.29 Aug 1861
Florence May BRECKENRIDGE, b.31 May [--]
Lala Gray DuBOSE, dau of S.B. & Florence M. DuBASE, b.15 Nov 1896

Mivtie Lucile DuBOSE, dau of S.B. & Florence M. DuBOSE, b.25 Sep 1899
Mammie Belle DuBOSE, b.9 Jul 1902
DEATHS
Lenour DuBOSE, d.15 Mar 1924, age 10yrs 11mos
Florence May DuBOSE, d.1 Feb 1926, age 50yrs
Maggie DuBOSE, d.8 Apr 1929
S.B. DuBOSE, d.12 May 1929
Florence May DuBOSE, d.1 Feb 1926, age 50yrs
Mirtie Lucile DuBOSE McDUFFIE, d.22 Feb 1936
MARRIAGES
Samuel B. DuBOSE to Florence May BRICKENRIDGE, 19 Feb 1896
Vidmore Lenora DuBOSE, b.15 Apr 1913
Bessie Vermelle DuBOSE, b.13 Aug 1904
Willie George DuBOSE, b.6 Mar 1906
Henry M. DuBOSE, b.26 Apr 1908
Little S.B. DuBOSE, b.5 Nov 1910
(Louis DuBOSE FILE)

MOORE / FLOOD BIBLE

WILMORE'S NEW ANALYTICAL REFERENCE BIBLE, Published by J. A. Wilmore & Co, New York 1898
FAMILY RECORD
<GRAND PARENTS>
Geo F. MOORE, b.2 Jun 1832; d.2 Mar 1911, E[---], KY
Margaret MOORE, b.9 Jun 1835; d.2 Sep 1924, E[--], KY
J. Monroe FLOOD, b.25 Mar 1825; d.12 Oct 1911, Cropper, KY
Sue Katherine BRYANT, b.11 Mar 1841, d.28 Dec 1906, Cropper, KY
<PARENTS>

A.T. MOORE, b.25 Aug 1855, Henry Co, KY; d.11 Jul 1942, E[--], KY
Sallie Lee FLOOD, b.23 Oct 1864, Shelby Co, KY; d.6 Aug 1932, Em[--], KY
they married 5 Nov 1885, Cropper, KY by Rev B.M. Vaughan
<CHILDREN>
Mary Aline MOORE, b.11 Dec 1889, Shelby Co, KY; m.21 a Willcou MAYDWELL; d.9 Oct 1970
A. William MAYDWELL, b.5 Apr 1895, Louisville, KY; d.21 Aug 1962
Sara Louise MAYDWELL, b.7 Jan 1918, Louisville, m.7 Nov 1948 to Lois Lambert NOE at Floydsburg, KY
Lois Lambert NOE, b.7 Nov 1919; d. 1964
<u><FAMILY RECORDS> MISCELLANEOUS</u>
"Copied from Grandfather Floods Bible"
Monroe FLOOD m. to Sue SINGLETON 17 Dec 1863
Lucy FLOOD to Walker B. SNEED m.15 Jun 1898
Sallie Lee FLOOD, to A.T. MOORE, m.5 Nov 1885
Robert P. FLOOD to Mary B. UNDERWOOD, m.19 Nov 1908
Elestin F. BRYANT to Francis EASTER, m.8 Dec 1835
Francis Bryant FLOOD to James R. RADCLIFFE, m.4 Oct 1923
Mary E. FLOOD to J. Bradck SMITH, m.13 Feb 1890
<u>FAMILY RECORD</u>
<GRAND PARENTS>
Elistra F. BRYANT, b.26 Feb 1812; d.27 Mar 1880
Frankie EASTES, b.20 Aug 1814; d.7 May 1886
<PARENTS>
James Monroe FLOOD, b.25 Mar 1825; d.12 Oct 1911, Cropper, KY
Sue Katherine FLOOD, b.11 Mar 1841; d.28 Dec 1906, Cropper, KY

they married 17 Dec 1863, Campbellsburg, KY, by Rev T.M. Daniel

<CHILDREN>

Sallie Lee FLOOD, b.23 Oct 1864, Shelby Co; m.5 Nov 1885 to Allan Thomas MOORE; d.11 Jul 1942

Mary Elizabeth FLOOD, b.28 Jan 1866, Shelby Co; m.13 Feb 1890 to J. Brock SMITH, d.11 Oct 1895

Robert Price FLOOD, b.5 Nov 1869; m.19 Nov 1908 to Mary UNDERWOOD

Lucy H. FLOOD, b.26 Jul 1872; m.15 Jun 1898 to Walker B. SNOOK

Frankie B. FLOOD, b.1 Dec 1876; m.14 Oct 1923 to James RADCLIFFE

GRANDCHILDREN

M. Aline MOORE, b.17 Dec 1889, Shelby Co; m.21 Mar 1917 to A. Willson MAYDWELL

Effie Lee SMITH, b.11 Mar 1891, Shelby Co; m. to Gayle THOMAS

Katherine Roberta SMITH, b.21 Oct 1893, m. to Theodore JACKSON

James Van SNOOK, b.15 Apr 1899, m. to Irene PAYTOR

Bryant SNOOK

Robert SNOOK, m. to Esrelle [---]

Helen SNOOK, m. to Marv BOWMAN

Harold SNOOK, m. Inaz THROOP

Mary Anne BOWMAN m. to Bobbie WILLARD

FAMILY RECORD, MISCELLANEOUS

births copies from Flood Bible

Monroe FLOOD, b.25 Mar 1825

Sue FLOOD, b.11 Mar 1841

Sallie Lee FLOOD, b.23 Oct 1864

Mary E. FLOOD, b.28 Jan 1866

Robert Price FLOOD, b.5 Nov 1869

Lucy Ann FLOOD, b.26 Jul 1872
Francis Bryant FLOOD, b.1 Dec 1876
Mary Aline MOORE, b.17 Dec 1889
Salaltiel H. BRYANT b.9 Dec 1861
Effie Lee SMITH, b.11 Mar 1891
Katherine Roberta SMITH, b.21 Oct 1893
E.F. BRYANT, 26 Feb 1812
Frankie BRYTANT, b.20 Aug 1814
Amanda E. BRYANT, b.21 Jan 1837
Lucy Ann BRYANT, b.12 Oct 1838
Susan K. BRYANT, b.11 Mar 1841
Sarah F. BRYANT, b.1 Mar 1843
Mary Jane BRYANT, b.25 Oct 1845
Samuel J. BRYANT, b.7 Aug 1849
Louisa E. BRYANT, b.17 Nov 1854
deaths copied from Grandpa Floods Bible
Mary E. SMITH, d.11 Oct 1895
Walker Bryant SNOOK, Jr, d.10 May 1905
Susan K. FLOOD, d.28 Dec 1906
Monroe FLOOD, d.12 Oct 1911
Walker B. SNOOK, Sr; d.10 Nov 1918
James R. RADCLIFF, d.19 Sep 1927
Sallie Lee MOORE, d.6 Aug 1932
Lucy A. SNOOK, d.17 Apr 1942
Robert P. FLOOD, d.14 Oct 1961
Fannie B. RADCLIFFE, d.10 Oct 1964
A.T. MOORE, d. Jul 1942
<FAMILY RECORD> MISCELLANEOUS
William FLOOD, Sr; b.12 Jan 1777
Mary JAMES FLOOD, b.18 Sep 1784
Katherine Roberta SMITH, b.21 Oct 1893
James Van SNOOK, b.15 Apr 1899
Walker Bryant SNOOK, Jr, b.31 Jan 1902

Robert Allen SNOOK,b.6 Aug 1906
Helen Lucille SNOOK, b.4 Mar 1904
Harold Lee SNOOK, b.29 Jan 1916
William FLOOD, Sr, d.5 Dec 1845
Mary Janes FLOOD, d.4 Oct 1846
Elishia BRYANT, d.2 Mar 1883
Francis BRYANT, d.7 May 1886
Louise E. BRYANT, d.19 Oct 1861
Lucy Ann OREM, d.23, Jan 1872
Salathiel H. BRYANT, d.30 Sep 1882
FAMILY RECORD <Gr GRAND PARENTS>
Joel EASTES (capt War 1812) b.7 Nov 1779, Culperer Co, Va; d.1856, Christianburg, KY
Lucy Sanders EASTES, b.5 Feb 1790, Bradford Co, VA; d.5 Mar 1874
(Christopher DuBreuil File)

WALKER BIBLE

No Title Page or Date

BIRTHS
Samuel Scott WALKER, b.18 Mar 1847
Chrisa Ellen DUHAMELL, b.5 Aug 1853
Nancy Elizabeth WALKER, b.7 Jan 1874
Santford Daniel WALKER, b.28 Nov 1877
Franklin James WALKER, b.6 Apr 1882
Effie Lurena WALKER, b.11 Apr -----
Vernon Howard WALKER, b.21 Jan 1890
Harley Baker WALKER, b.20 May 1892
(Isaac DuHamel File)

HERNDON BIBLE

No Title Page or Date

FAMILY RECORD

BIRTHS

Elijah HERNDON, b.27 Nov 1774
Catherine HERNDON, b.3 Oct 1791
John T. HERNDON, b.5 Mar 1800
James HERNDON, b.30 Aug 1801
Isabella HERNDON, b.12 Sep 1803
George R. HERNDON, b.22 Jan 1806
Elisa HERNDON, b.22 Jul 1808
Francis HENDRON, b.15 Apr 1810
Susan R. HERNDON, 20 Apr 1820
Evaline HERNDON, b.16 Jun 1822

DEATHS

Elijah HENDON, d.26 Jul 1849
Benjamin, colored man servent of the above d.14 Jun 1849
Catherine HERNDON, d.21 Apr 1851
Helen M. HERNDON, d.5 Oct 1869
Emma HERNDON, d.26 Oct 1869
James HERNDON, d.20 Oct 1882
Clifford HERNDON, d.2 Feb 1890
Mary J. HERNDON, d.7 Mar 1920
Fletcher HERNDON, d.21 May 1920
Otto E. HERNDON, d.15 Jan 1940
Edith D.HERNDON, (nee TARIEN), d.14 Oct 1949 (wife of Otto E. HERNDON)
Holden R. HERNDON, son of Robert W. & Wilma E. HERNDON, d.22 Aug 1948
Flora Herndon McARTHUR, b.15 Aug 1875; d.17 Jan 1971, widow of James Madison McARTHUR +1960 son Madison +25 May 1957
Daughter Catherine (Mrs Robert NUNN of Greenwood, Sud

(Louis Dumas / De Moss File)

JOHN DEMOSS BIBLE

No Title Page or Date. Original in the National Archives, Washington, DC

John DEMOSS, b. 16 Sep 1756; m. 25 Jan 17[8]7 to Lucy CHAPEL, she b.24 Sep 1765
Peter DEMOSS, son of John & Lucy, b.15 Dec 1788
Dorothy DEMOSS, dau of John & Lucy, b.25 Sep 1790
Susanna DEMOSS, dau of John & Lucy, b.28 Feb 1793
Sarah DEMOSS, dau of John & Lucy, b.8 Feb 1796
John DEMOSS, son of John & Lucy, b.10 Dec 1798
Charley DEMOSS, son of John & Lucy, b.4 Feb 1800
Lucy DEMOSS, dau of John & Lucy, b.6 Sep 1803
Mary DEMOSS, dau of John & Lucy, b.6 Jul 1807

Lucy 24 Sep 1765
Peter 15 Dec 1788
D[--], 23 Sep 1790
Susan, 20 Feb 1793
Sarah 8 Feb 1796
(Louis Dumas / De Moss File)

BARKER BIBLE

PICTORIAL FAMILY BIBLE, Published by Walden & Stowe, no date on title page

MARRIAGE CERTIFICATE

Jno H. BARKER of Falmouth, KY to Ella N. FEE of Mascord, OH, m.13 May 1880 at residence of J.W. FEE, by Rev W.B. Molen. Witness: J.B. BARKER; W.E. Fisher

BIRTHS

John Hamilton BARKER, son of Joseph & Sallie BARKER,

b.1 May 1854, Campbell Co, KY
Ella Maria FEE, dau of John W. & Alice FEE, b.23 Aug 1856
Lida Louise BARKER, dau of Hamilton & Ella Maria BARKER, b.31 Jul 1881, Falmouth, KY
Mary Ella BARKER, dau of Hamilton & Ella Maria BARTON, b.25 Mar 1885
John Hamilton BISHOP, son of Mary E. & H.W. BISHOP, b.15 Sep [--]
Ella Lonier BISHOP, Dau of Mary E. & H.W. BISHOP
[two entries too poor to read]
John Hamilton BARKER, son of Joseph & Sallie BARKER, married to Ella Maria FEE, dau of John W. & Alice FEE at the latters residence in Mascow, OH, 13 May 1880
John Hamilton BARKER, son of Joseph & Sallie BARKER and Lizzie L. SEETENY, dau of Dr W.W. SEUTEUY, married in Louisville, KY 20 Nov 1893 by Rev W.G. Miller
Lida Leneoa BARKER, dau of John & E;lla Marie , married Dr [-----]
[entry too faint to read]
DEATHS
Ella Maria BARKER, d.8 Sep 1891, Falmouth, KY
Joseph BARKER, d.25 Nov 1895, Falmouth, KY
Sallie BARKER, d.5 Nov 1896, Falmouth
John Hamilton BARKER, d.18 Mar 1914, Falmouth, KY
(Louis Dumas / DeMoss File)

REYNOLDS BIBLE

No Title Page or Date

FAMILY RECORD
MARRIAGES
Sacket REYNOLDS to Mary Ann GUESS 21 [--] 1819

W. John [---] m. to Lydia [---], 9 Mar [---]
W. Ben REYNOLDS to [---] GUESS, 9 Mar [---]
BIRTHS
Sacket REYNOLDS, b.8 Nov 2794
Mary Ann GUESS, b.1 Feb 1797
Mary Bathurst, their first child, b.12 Apr 1821, Cincinnati, OH
,their second dau, b.22 Jun 1824
Julia, their third dau b. 15 Apr 1826, Cincinnati,OH
, fourth dau, b.19 May 1827
Caroline, fifth dau, b.4 Apr 1829
Amanda, sixth dau, b.14 Jul 1831
Andrew Jackson, a son b.
MARRIAGES
Andrew Jackson REYNOLDS to Miss Charity [--] Hunter, dau of Paul H. m. 16 Dec 1858, Hamilton Co
BIRTHS
Clarence Guest REYNOLDS, son b.18 Apr 1859
Mary Elizabeth REYNOLDS, b.2 Oct 1861
Walter Hunter REYNOLDS, b.7 Nov 1864
Grace Anna, b.25 Jun 1868
Caroline Cornelia, b.10 Sep 1871
Andrew Joseph, b.25 Aug 1874
(Wallerand Dumont File)

WALKER BIBLE

THE HOLY BIBLE. Published by Jesper Harding, Philadelphia, 1848
FAMILY RECORDS
MARRIAGES
William T. WALKER to Mary DUPUY, 7 Jun 1815
Sarah W. WALKER, dau of Wm T & Mary WALKER to Jno

DUPUY, 21 Dec 1842
Susan A. WALKER, dau of Wm T & Mary WALKER to Henry A. WATKINS, 1 Jan 1852
William T. WALKER, son of Wm T & Mary WALKER to S. Josephine SIMPSON, 26 Oct 1852
Judith T. WALKER, dau of Wm T. & Mary WALKER to Robert K. WATKINS, 13 May 1857
Mary D. WALKER, dau of Wm T & Mary WALKER to Saml T. CLARK, 1 Nov 1859

BIRTHS

William T. WALKER, b. 1756
Mary WALKER, wife of Wm T. WALKER, b.20 Nov 1792
Frances Jane WALKER, dau of Wm T. & Mary WALKER, b.1 Apr 1816
Sarah Aatham WALKER, dau, b.14 Apr 1818
Elizabeth Harriet WALKER, dau, b.31 Jan 1821
Judith Towns WALKER, dau, b.27 Apr 1822
Mary Dupuy WALKER, dau, b.12 Nov 1823
William Towns WALKER, son, b.22 Aug 1825
Susan Agnes WALKER, dau, b.22 Jun 1827
John Edmund WALKER, son, b.12 Apr 1830
Martha Ann WALKER, dau, b.30 Nov 1832

DEATHS

Frances Jane WALKER, dau of Wm T. & Mary WALKER, d.24 Jul 1816
Elizabeth H. WALKER, dau d. [1830]
John E. WALKER, son, d.[1830]
William T. WALKER, Sr, d.28 Sep 1833
Martha Ann WALKER, dau, d. [1834]
Judith T. WATKINS, dau. d.13 Nov 1857
Mary WALKER, wife of Wm T. WALKER, d.12 Feb 1861, age 68yrs
Sarah W. DUPUY, dau of Wm T & Mary Walker, wife of K.

Jno DUPUY, d.8 Aug 1864, age 46yrs 3mos 22dys
(Bertholomew Dupuy File)

CROUCH / WALKINS BIBLE

THE HOLY BIBLE, Published by G.W. Borland & Co, Peoria, IL, 1876

MARRIAGE CERTIFICATE

W.A. CROUCH of Plattsburg, MO to M. Alice WALKINS of Clay Co, MO m. 3 Apr 1877 by Eld. W. P. Fleeuor

BIRTHS

Martha Amy CROUCH, b.16 Jan 1878
Annie Judson CROUCH, b.19 Jul 1879
William Anderson CROUCH, b.11 Jan 1881
Mary Leone CROUCH, b.6 Nov 1882
Beulah Edith CROUCH, b.15 Aug 1884
Alice Amelia CROUCH, b.9 Oct 1886
Ann Browning CROUCH, b.15 Sep 1888
Jesse Walkins CROUCH, b.24 Dec 1890
Charles Spurgeon CROUCH, b.29 Jan 1894
(Bartholomew Dupuy File)

WALKER BIBLE

THE COMPREHENSIVE BIBLE, Published byJ.B. Lippincott & Co, Philadelphia; 1848

FAMILY RECORD

MARRIAGES

William Townes WALKER to Susan Josephine SAMPSON, 26 Oct 1852 at Dover, Goochland Co, VA by Rev Francis S. Sampson, DD

William Townes WALKER to Mrs Fanny H[---] BUGBY, 25 May 1873 (?)

Richard Sampson WALKER to Maud M. MILLER 19 Dec 1883, Lynchburg, 2nd Presbyterian Church
John WALKER to Laura May STEBBINS, 29 Nov 1905, South Boston, VA, Presbyterian Church
Gulielems WALKER to Richard Lee SIMPSON in the 1st Presbyterian Church
Mary S. WALKER to Nicholas Hill ROBERTSON in first Presbyterian Church, Lynchburg, VA
Rose Vivian BAYLY child of Fanny Holladay WALKER, married 2 Oct 1889 to Howard Douglass JOHNSON of Lynchburg, VA
William Townes WALKER to Mary K[---] STOKES, 29 Oct 1891 at Prince Edwards Co.
Mary Kenna Stokes d. in SC
[entry too faint to read]
William Townes WALKER to Lottie Reynor AREY of NC; Jun 1904 died 1920
William Townes WALKER to Miss Janie McEACHIN, Oct 192-

BIRTHS

Lilia WALKER, b.17 Dec 1853, Dover, VA
Frank WALKER, b.28 Nov 1854, Dover
Richard S. WALKER, b.8 Feb 1858, Matanzas, CUBA
Josephine Sampson WALKER, b.29 Oct 1861, Dover
Mary Susan WALKER, b.20 Oct 1862, Dover
William Townes WALKER, 7 Oct 1865, Dover
John WALKER, b.1 Jul 1867, Dover
Robert WALKER, b.8 May 1869
Rosa Vivian BAYLY, child of Mrs Fanny Holladay BAYLY, b.23 Jul 1867
Henrietta Oakley BAYLY, b.Cherry Grove, Spottsyvania,28 Jul 1869
Gulillma WALKER, dau of W.T. WALKER & Fanny, his

wife, b.25 Jan 1880, Dover, Goochland Co, VA
Maud Miller WALKER, child of R.S. WALKER & Maud, his wife, b.[-] Oct 1885, Lynchburg
Josephine Sampson WALKER, child of R.S. & Maud WALKER, b. 1887, Lynchburg
[-----], child of Richard & Maud WALKER, b.12 Jul 1888, Lynchburg
[--] WALKER, son of R.S. & Maud, b.1890
DEATHS
Robert WALKER, d.11 Jul 1869
Josephine Sampson WALKER, wife of W.T. WALKER, d. 23 Sep 1870, Dover, aged 42yrs 9mos
William Townes WALKER, husband of Josephine Sampson WALKER, d.13 May 1898, Lynchburg, VA
Richard S. WALKER, d. Dec 1907, Lynchburg
Frank WALKER, d. Oakland, CA no children
Maria J. WALKER, wife of Frank, d. Oakland, CA
Lelia WALKER, d. 19 [-too faint to read]
Mary S. WALKER ROBERTSON, d.8 Jun 1939, Lynchburg
Jsephine Sampson WALKER, d.30 Nov 1941, Lynchburg, VA, bur. Presbyterian Cem
Richard SAMPSON, father of Josephine WALKER, d.18 Mar 1814, aged 90yrs
(Bartholomew Dupuy File)

WALKER BIBLE II

No Title Page or Date

FAMILY RECORD
<GRANDPARENTS>
Wm T. WALKER, M.D., b.22 Aug 1825, Prince Edward Co, VA; d.13 May 1898, Lynchburg, VA
Josephine SIMPSON, b. 1827, Dover, Goochland Co, VA;

d.23 Sep 1870, Goochland Co, VA
Edwin E. AREY, b.31 Dec 1845,Iredell Co, NC; d.14 Jan 1902, Iredell Co, NC
Alice E. CORNELIUS, b.14 Jan 1851, Iredell Co, NC; d.26 Oct 1930, Wayram, NC.
<PARENTS>
Rev W.T. WALKER, b. 7 Oct 1865, Goochland Co, VA; d.28 Nov 1946, Lynchburg, VA
Lottie Raynor AREY, b.3 Aug 1877, Iredell Co, NC; d.14 Feb 1920, Iredell Co, NC
married 22 Jun 1904 near Elmwood, NC
<CHILDREN>
Lottie Arey, b.11 Apr 1905, Rowland, NC
Alice Dupuy, b.5 Aug 1906, Elmwood, NC
William Townes, b.10 Aug 1908, Antioch, NC, m.8 Oct 1933 to Elizabeth R. MURFF
John Edwin, b.28 Apr 1910, Barium Springs; d.21 May 1910
Josephine Sampson, b.14 Jun 1911, Barium Springs, m.28 Aug 1937 to H. Boyd HEALY, Jr
Ruth Raynor, b.29 Dec 1913, Barium Springs; m.4 Dec 1938 to Claude P. DUNN; d.31 Jul 1970, Fredericksburg, VA
Lois, b.7 Jan 1916, Barium Springs; d.14 Jan 1916
Jean Adams, b.9 May 1917; m.24 Jul 1940 to Jas Riley WEEKS
Frank Richard, b.8 Feb 1920; m.15 Jun 1942 to Marjorie Ann WALKER
<MISCELLANEOUS>
The father of Wm T. WALKER, MD a colonel in the Revolutionary War, his name was also Wm Townes WALKER

Copies from an old BIBLE which belonged to Polly Dupuy WALKER and which was printed by William Bentley, London Anno Domini 1646

William T. WALKER m. to Polly DUPUY, 7 Jun 1815
Frances Jane WALKER, b.1 Apr 1816; d.2 Jul 1816
Sarah Watkins WALKER, b.14 Apr 1818
Elizabeth Hariot WALKER, b.31 Jan 1821
Judith Townes WALKER, b.27 Apr 1822
Mary Dupuy WALKER, b.12 Nov 1823
William T. WALKER, b.22 Aug 1825
Susan Agnes WALKER, b.22 Jun 1827
John Edmund WALKER, b.12 Apr 1830
Martha Ann WALKER, b.30 Nov 1832
(Bartholomew Dupuy File)

OWENS BIBLE

THE HOLY BIBLE, Printed by the American Bible Society, New York, 1892
owned by John Ray Moss, Eminence, KY in 1974
on the front page: Presented to Mrs Lou Owens, by her Husband as a New Year's gift 1901

MARRIAGES

William T. OWENS to Harriet Lucretia BRUCE, 12 Feb 1852
Florence Viola, dau of W.T. & Lucretia OWENS to Charles William MOSS, 27 Oct 1873
Lizzie O. OWENS, dau of W.T. & Lucretia OWENS to Robert O. MIDDLETON, 24 Feb 1879

BIRTHS

William T. OWENS, son of Robert L. OWENS, b.6 Nov 1826
Harriet Lucretia BRUCE, dau of Thomas V. & Elizabeth BRUCE, b.26 May 1830
Florence V. OWENS, dau of William T. & Lucretia OWENS, b.26 Jul 1855
Lizzie O. OWENS, dau of William T & Lucredia OWENS, b.3 Oct 1861

Lou Willie, dau of W.J. & Lucretia OWENS, b.10 Sep 1873
<u>DEATHS</u>
Lou Willie OWENS, Dau of William T. & Lucretia OWENS, d.10 Sep 1873
Harriet Lucretia OWENS, wife of William T. OWENS, d.2 Nov 1901
William Thomas OWENS, d.16 Jul 1903, Kansas City
(Bartholomew Dupuy File / 17-267)

BRUCE BIBLE

HOLY BIBLE, printed by the Sealfield Publishing Co, Chicago, Akron, OH, New York, no date
owned by Mrs Charles Oldham BRUCE, Louisville, KY, 1973

<u>BIRTHS</u>
Thomas V. BRUCE, b.30 Jul 1802
Elizabeth BRUCE, b.29 Jun 1807
William Henry BRUCE, son of Thos V. & Elizabeth BRUCE, b.20 Feb 1826; d.8 Sep 1851, aged 25yrs 7mos 18dys
John Owens BRUCE, son of Thos V. & Elizabeth BRUCE, b.8 Feb 1828
Harriet Lucretia BRUCE, dau of Thos V. & Elizabeth BRUCE, b.26 May 1830
Thomas Madison (Middleton -crossed out) BRUCE, son of Thos V. & Elizabeth BRUCE, b.3 Dec [page torn]
(Bartholomew Dupuy File / 17-267)

MOSS BIBLE

HOLY BIBLE, Printed by A.J. JOHNSON, Pittsburg, PA, 1870; also known as the Hitchcock's Holy Bible. Original owned by Lewis Arnold Moss, Annadale, VA.

MARRIAGES

Charles William MOSS to Florence Viola OWENS, 27 Oct 1873

Rev J.W. CRATES to Lillie Viola MOSS, 25 Oct 1894

Charles Ray MOSS, son of Wm & Florence MOSS to Martha Coleman HERNDON, 23 Oct 1901

Robert Owens MOSS, son of William & Florence MOSS to Mary Elizabeth HAGGARD, 18 Dec 1907

Rev John Edwin MOSS, son of William & Florence MOSS to Lillian Riggen DAUGHERTY,24 Dec 1907

Lewis Samuel MOSS, son of William & Florence MOSS to Rosalind Rowland ARNOLD, 4 Mar 1914

Mary CRATES., dau of Lillian H. CRATES to Eska Kennedy WATKINS, 30 Mar 1919

BIRTHS

Mary Moss CRATES, dau of Rev John Wright & Lillie CRATES, b.20 May 1898

Florence Phyllis CRATES, dau of Rev J.W. & Lillie Moss CRATES, b.19 Mar 1902

Anna Bright CRATES, dau of Rev J.W. & Lillie Moss CRATES, b.12 Nov 1903

Rosalina Louise MOSS, dau of Louis S. & Rosalind Arnold MOSS, b.30 Nov 1914

William Hardon MOSS, son of Charles & Martha Moss, b.21 Oct 19[--]

Elizabeth Haggard MOSS, dau of Robert O. & Mary MOSS, b.26 Mar 1910

Nancy Belle MOSS, dau of Rev J.E. & Lillian MOSS, b.18 Jun 1911

Ralph Crates MOSS, son of Robert O. & Mary MOSS, b.21 Jan 1916

Lewis Arnold MOSS, son of Lewis & Rosalind MOSS, b.8 Feb 1917

Robert Owens MOSS, Jr, son of Robert Owens & Mary Haggard Moss, b.22 Sep 1916
(Bartholomew Dupuy File / 17-267)

DAUGHDRILL BIBLE

No Title Page or Date (July 1901)

BIRTHS

children of J.H. and Kate DANGHDRILL
Kathryn Ella DAUGHRILL, TWIN and
Lyda Ennes DAUGHRILL, TWIN, b.4 Jun 1904
Dorothy Henry DAUGHRILL, b.13 May 1906
Charlotta May DAUGHRILL, b.2 Apr 1909
Helen Elizabeth DAUGHRILL, b.27 Oct 1907
Dau of A.H. & A.E. DAUGHRILL
(Nicholas Dupuis / Dupuy

MANDEVILLE FAMILY BIBLE

HOLY BIBLE, Published by Daniel D. Smith, New York, 1823
Original owned by Mr H.K. Manderville, Norwich, NY, about 1936

MARRIAGES

Rev Garrett MANDEVILLE to Margaret DeWITT, 10 Jan 1799
Reuben D.W. MANDEVILLE to Margaret JACKSON, 19 May 1825
James H. MANDEVILLE to Jane CANTINE, 20 Nov 1830
George MANDERVILLE, Jr to Almira HITCHINSON, 27 Feb 1834
Thomas DIMOCK to Elizabeth MANDEVILLE, 12 Oct 1836
William Garret MANDEVILLE to Mercy Jane KNAPP, 4 Jan

1857
William Garret MANDEVILLE to Bertha Abigail DAVIS, 27 Jul 1886
Mary Imogene MANDEVILLE to W.D. VAN DUSEN, 25 Dec 1891
Henry K. MANDEVILLE to Pearl E. DYER, 16 Jul 1903
<u>BIRTHS</u>
Garret MANDEVILLE, b.19 Mar 1775
Margaret DeWITT, b.11 Oct 1775
Reuben D.W. MANDEVILLE, b.8 Jul 1800
Margaret JACKSON, wife of Reuben, b.19 Feb 1803
Maria J. MANDEVILLE, b.10 Feb 1802
James Henry MANDEVILLE, b.3 Oct 1804
John MANDEVILLE, b.13 Jan 1807
Gerard MANDEVILLE, b.28 Aug 1808
Elizabeth MANDEVILLE, b.9 Aug 1810
Simeon D.W. MANDEVILLE, b.6 Jun 1813
Henry MANDEVILLE, b.21 Jul 1815
Margaret MANDEVILLE, b.5 Jan 1819
Elsie Ann MANDEVILLE, b.16 Oct 1821
William Garret MANDEVILLE, b.20 Apr 1826
Mercy Jane KNAPP, wife of Wm Garret MANDEVILLE, b.2 Feb 1831
Their Children:
George DeWitt MANDEVILLE, b.10 Oct 1857
Daisy Jane MANDEVILLE, b.16 Jan 1859
Mary Imogene MANDEVILLE, b.28 May 1860
William Garret MANDEVILLE, b.28 Jun 1864
Henry Knapp MANDEVILLE, b.18 May 1869
<u>DEATHS</u>
Maria J. MANDEVILLE, d.7 Jun 1828, aged 26yrs
Margaret DeWITT, wife of Garret MANDEVILLE, d.22 May 1829, aged 53yrs 7mos

Jane CANTINE, wife of James H. MANDEVILLE, d.10 Jul 1834, aged 28yrs 3dys
Henry MANDEVILLE, d.9 Nov 1839, aged 25yrs
Elsie Ann MANDEVILLE, d.23 Nov 1853, aged 32yrs
Rev. Garret MANDEVILLE, d.13 Dec 1853, aged 78yrs 8 mos
Elizabeth Mandeville DIMOCK, d.21 Feb 1878, Syracuse, aged 67yrs
Margaret Jackson MANDEVILLE, d.26 Mar 1887, aged 84yrs
Reuben D.W. MANDEVILLE, d.31 Aug 1887, aged 87yrs
James Henry MANDEVILLE, d.18 Jul 1889, aged 85yrs
Daisy Jane, dau of Wm Garret & Mercy Jane MANDEVILLE, d.2 Mar 1859
Wm G, MANDERVILLE, d.4 Nov 1897, aged 71yrs
Mercy Jane (KNAPP) MANDERVILLE, d.13 Jun 1907, aged 76yrs
(Nicholas Dupuis / Dupuy; William Witt file)

MARTINDALE BIBLE

HOLY BIBLE, Published by A.J. Holman & Co, Philadelphia, PA, 1880
The original Bible in 1973 in the posession of Charles James Schjott
<u>BIRTHS</u>
Charles C. MARTINDALE, b.5 Aug 1840, Dryden, NY
Lida Madora ENNES, b.21 Mar 1852, Birmingham , Erie Co, OH
Eliza Mary MARTINDALE, b.29 Jun 1874, South Saginaw, MI
Catherine Madore MARTINDALE, b.17 Mar 1876, South Saginaw
Emily MARTINDALE, b.19 Aug 1877

Willie C. MARTINDALE, b.22 Nov 1878, South Saginaw, MI
Charles James MARTINDALE, b.10 Apr 1881, South Saginaw, MI
Lida E. MARTINDALE, b.16 Feb 1884, South Saginaw
Marian MARTINDALE, b.17 May 1891, Kalkaska, MI
<u>DEATHS</u>
Emily MARTINDALE, d.19 Aug 1877
Willie C. MARTINDALE, d.2 Dec 1878
Charles J. MARTINDALE, d.8 Aug 1881
Lida E. MARTINDALE, d.16 Feb 1884
Lida Ennes MARTINDALE, d.4 Dec 1894, Saginaw, MI
Charles Clay MARTINDALE, d.23 Sep 1917, Hattiesburg, MS
(Nicholas Dupuis / Dupuy)

GUNSAUL BIBLE

THE HOLY BIBLE, Published by William W. HARDING, Philadelphia, 1866
<u>BIRTHS</u>
Gilbert GUNSAUL, b.26 May 1829
Fannie A. PEASE, b.21 Mar 1835
Seward GUNSAUL, first child of Gilbert & Fannie GUNSAUL, b.3 Feb 1860
Freddie GUNSAUL, second child of Gilbert & Fannie GUNSAUL, b.23 Sep 1861
Frank Jos GUNSAUL, third child of Gilbert & Fannie GUNSAUL, b.21 Nov 1863
Hubert & Florence GUNSAUL (TWINS), fourth & Fifth children of Gilbert & Fannie GUNSAUL, b.27 Feb 1866

Nellie GUNSAUL, sixth child of Gilbert & Fannie GUNSAUL, b.19 May 1868

BIRTHS

Lelia Lenore GUNSAUL, first child of Seward & Minnie GUNSAUL, b.30 Mar 1887

Fannie White GUNSAUL, second child of Seward & Minnie GUNSAUL, b.17 Aug 1889

Mary Louise GUNSAUL, third child of Seward & Minnie GUNSAUL, b.18 Mar 1891

Ora May GUNSAUL, b.4 Jun 1894, fourth child of Seward & Minnie GUNSAUL

Ruth Lucille GUNSAUL, fisth child of Seward & Minnie GUNSAUL, b.8 Aug 1897

Tyler Sandus STILLWATER, first child of Fannie W. GUNSAUL & Tyler STILLWATER, b.18 Apr 1917

John Gunsaul WIEDMAN, first child of Mary L. GUNSAUL & Earl Vernon WIEDMAN, b.1 Jul 1920

Russell Gunsaul STILLWATER, second child of Fannie & Tyler Sanders STILLWATER, b.14 Apr 1923

Wilbur Gunsaul WIEDMAN, second child of Mary L & Earl Vernon WIEDMAN, b.11 Mar 1924

Mary Louise Gunsaul WIEDMAN, third child of Mary L. & Earl Vernon Wiedman, b.19 Apr 1927

Janette Camron STILLWATER, first child of Tyler Chandus STILLWATER & Frances Malden Doffemyer, b.30 Jul 1943

David STILLWATER, second Child of Tyler Chandus & Frances Malden Doffemyer STILLWATER, b.17 Oct 1947

Laurence York WIEDMAN, b.10 Jul 1941, Lincoln, NE, son of Wilbur & Jean WIEDMAN

MARRIAGES

Gilbert GUNSAUL to Fannie A. PEASE, 3 Feb 1859

Seward M. GUNSAUL to Minnie A. WHITE, 13 Oct 1885

Fannie White GUNSAUL to Tyler Sanders STILLWATER, 5

Jun 1912
Lelia Lenore GUNSAUL to Russell Edson WAITT
Ruth Lucille GUNSAUL to Arthur MUCHARD
Mary Louise GUNSAUL to Earl Vernon WIEDMAN, 28 Aug 1919
Ruth Lucille GUNSAUL to Francis SHOEMAKER
Tyler Sanders STILLWATER, II to Francis Malden DOFFEMYER, 5 Sep 1942
John Gunsaul WIEDMAN to Margaret KENNER at Hebron, NE

DEATHS

Freddie GUNSAUL, d.28 Dec 1864
Gilbert GUNSAUL, d. 1871
Fannie A. PEASE GUNSAUL, d.21 Aug 1879, Rockford, IL
Seward M. GUNSAUL, d.7 Jun 1923, Greeley, CO
Frank J. GUNSAUL, bur Rockford, IL unmarried
Herbert GUNSAUL, bur Rockford, IL, unmarried
Florence GUNSAUL LUMM, d.Apr 1946, Duluth, MN
Nellie Gunsaul VIERCK, d.1944, Rockford, IL
Ora May GUNSAUL, d.31 Dec 1910, aged 16yrs
Lelia Lenore GUNSAUL WAITT, d. Apr 1931, Syracuse, NY
Auther MUCHOW, bur 1919, Denver, CO
Minnie White GUNSAUL, d.17 Dec 1926, Greeley, CO
Tyler Chandus STILLWELL, d.22 Jan 1951
(Philip De Trieux / 12-28)

VAN PATTEN BIBLE

THE HOLY BIBLE, Published by W.A. Burnham, Syracuse, NY, 1868

BIRTHS

Jacob VAN PATTEN, b.2 Dec 1834
Minerva A. CHAPPELL, b.31 Dec 1844

MARRIAGES
Jacob VAN PATTEN to Minerva A. CHAPPELL, 3 Nov 1860
BIRTHS
Warren E., b.24 Jul 1861
Wilfred L., b.20 May 1863
Grace W., b.13 Dec 1865
Edith F., b.6 Sep 1868
Ira Betts, b.21 Dec 1869
Tracy P., b.13 Sep 1871
Charles E., b.15 Mar 1873
Peter J., b.3 Mar 1878
Jacob L., b.2 Oct 1879
Archibald D., b.17 Mar 1884
(Philip Du Trieux)

STUM BIBLE

THE HOLY BIBLE, Published by Edward W. MILLER, Philadelphia, 1849
BIRTHS
Emma Jane STUM, b.23 Apr 1855
John Alexander STUM, b.25 Apr 1857
Isabella STUM, b.4 Aug 1858
William Lincoln STUM, b.11 Nov 1860 [61]
Anna Laura WELCHANS, b.19 May 1860
Mr William STUM married to Miss Anna WELCHAMS, 22 May 1883
Sallie Margaret STUM married to Archibald Douglass VAN PATTEN, 15 Sep 1914
Sallie Margaret STUM, b.13 Jan 1885 [Maytown, PA]
Maxin Ann VAN PATTEN, b.20 Jan 1916, Spirit Lake, IA
William Douglass, b.12 Sep 1917, Bruce, WI
Allyn Foster VAN PATTEN, b.8 Jul 1921, Salen, OR

Archibald Douglas VAN PATTEN, b.17 Mar 1884
(Philip Du Trieux)

STOCUM BIBLE

THE HOLY BIBLE, Bulter's Edition; Published by E.H. Butler & Co, Philadelphia, 1851

Julia Margaret DENNIS, dau of Zachariah G. & Margaret Ann DENNIS, b.3 Nov 1850

Ida Louise, Dau of Zachariah G. & Margaret Ann DENNIS, b. 18 Dec 1853

Eber M. ANDERSON, son of A. Jefferson & Julia M. ANDERSON, b.18 Nov 1875

Martha B. DENNIS, dau of Zachariah G. & Margaret E. DENNIS, b.18 Feb 1869, at Princess Anne, Somerset Co, MD

George Howard STOCUM, son of James D. & Ida K. STOCUM, b.18 Jan 1880, Philadelphia, PA

William B. STOCUM, son of James D. & Ida K. STOCUM, b.2 May 1882, Bath, NY

Thomas A, STOCUM, son of James D. & Ida K. STOCUM, b.20 Mar 1885, Bath, NY

Clarence M. STOCUM, son of James D. & Ida K. STOCUM, b.25 May 1889, Phila, PA

Melvin H. STOCUM, son of James D. & Ida K. STOCUM, b.22 Jan 1892, Phila, PA

Helen N. STOCUM, dau of James D. & Ida K. STOCUM, b.1 Aug 1894, Phila, PA

James D. STOCUM, Jr, son of James D. & Ida K. STOCUM, b.1 Nov 1898, Phila, PA

Jane H. STOCUM, dau of Clarence & Abigail H. STOCUM, b.31 Aug 1914, Phila, PA

Louise Ida STOCUM, dau of James D. & Hazel Tullis STOCUM, b.21 Sep 1917, Phila

William Tullis STOCUM, son of James D. & Hazel Tullis

STOCUM, b.25 Mar 1933, Phila
David Stephen CABLE, son of Jane STOCUM CABLE & George R. CABLE, b.24 Jan 1953, Phila
William Joseph STOCUM, son of W. Tullis & Terry Wood STOCUM, b.3 Dec 1953
James Dennis STOCUM, son of Wm Tullis & Terry Wood STOCUM, b.19 Jun 1955
Albert James GESSNER, son of Albert & Louise Stocum GESSNER, b.7 Jan 1954, Phila

DEATHS

Ida K. STOCUM, d.4 May 1932, aged 78yrs 7mos 16dys, b.18 Sep 1883
bur. Brandywine, Wilmington, DE
Thomas Anderson STOCUM, d.21 Jan 1944, aged 57yrs; b.20 Mar 1885
Clarence Metcalf STOCUM, d.22 Nov 1952; aged 63yrs 6mos 5dys, b.25 May 1889
James D. STOCUM, husband of Ida K. STOCUM, d.3 Dec 1919, aged 69yrs
Eber M. ANDERSON, son of A. Jefferson & Julia M. ANDERSON, d. bur CA
Jane Seward STOCUM, wife of Geo Howard STOCUM, d.3 Dec 1960
Wm Beeks STOCUM, b.2 May 1882, Bath, NY; d.19 Apr 1962, age 79ys, Philadelphia, PA
(Philip Du Trieux)

BASKETTE BIBLE

No Title Page or Dates

BIRTHS

John H. BASKETTE, b.15 Jun 1829
Matilda K. DUVAL, b.7 Oct 1834

William H., son of John H. & Matilda K. BASKETTE, b.25 Oct 1855
Claiborne A., son of John H. & Matilda K. BASKETTE, b.12 Jun 1858, Shelbyvile
Margaret Gwen, dau of John H. & Matilda K. BASKETTE, b.26 Apr 1860, Issaquena Co, MS
John H. BASKETTE, b.27 Sep 1862, Issaquena Co, MS
Robert Lee BASKETTE, b. 1 Jul 1865, Logan Co, KY
Ernest Duval BASKETTE, b.13 Jun 1869, Nashville, TN
Marvin Young BASKETTE, b.28 Apr 1871, Nashville, TN
Alvin Kelley BASKETTE, b.21 Nov 1873, Nashville, TN
Tilla Grace BASKETTE, b.25 Nov 1875, Nashville
Walter Lambuth BASKETTE, b.31 Jan 1878, Nashville
MARRIAGES
John H. BASKETTE to Matilda K., dau of A.D. & M. DUVAL, 14 Nov 1854
W.H. BASKETTE to Lena R. COPELAND, 11 Apr 1878
C.A. BASKETTE to Madeline SAND, 12 Jun 1881
Margaret G. BASKETTE to Rev G.H. BUCHANAN, 20 Oct 1885
R.L. BASKETTE to Alice EARLY, 10 Oct 1886
Ernest D. BASKETTE to Belle BOQUSKI
John H. BASKETTE
Alvin K. BASKETTE to Mabel Grace FLISHER, 2 Jan 1895
Walter L. BASKETTE to Kitty STROUD
Ernest D. BASKETTE to
Alvin K.BASKETTE to Nellie WILDER,1 May 1905 [27 Apr]
A.D. DUVAL to Margaret GUIN, 12 Mar 1818
Elizabeth P. DUVAL to W.H.M. WAIN, 8 Aug 1838
Caroline A. DUVAL to Inof COOK, 14 Oct 1841
Margaret A. DUVAL to W.L. LOWERY, 8 Feb 1844
Manjle C. DUVAL to Jos A. KELLY, 8 Jan 1852
Claiborne A. DUVAL to Miss Julia A. EASTON, Feb 1860

Matilda K. DUVAL to Jno H. BASKETTE, 4 Nov 1854
Gwinnette S. DUVAL to L.S. EASTON, 14 Nov 1865
9 Daniel Duval File)

JAMESON BIBLE

No Title Page or Date

FAMILY RECORDS

DEATHS
Eddie Lee JAMESON, d.18 Aug 1864
Jessie JAMESON, d.22 Jul 1866
B.H. JAMESON, d.5 Sep 1870

BIRTHS
B.H. JAMESON, b.22 Feb 1835
Martha J. JAMESON, b.6 Apr 1842
Lucy Emily JAMESON, b.30 Oct 1860
Eddie Lee JAMESON, b.25 Sep 1863
Jessie JAMESON, b.9 Sep 1865

MARRIAGES
Ing R. COLLIER to Martha COVINGTON, 24 Dec 1817
Wm LANE to Martha S. COLLIER, 1 Nov 1843
Jas M. COLLIER to E.L. McFADDEN, 6 Nov 1845
Jno A. COLLIER to Sarah F. BREWER, 21 Aug 1851
N.C. COLLIER to Joe A. ROWE, 11 Jun 1858
Jesse A, COLLIER to Martha C. McKNIGHT, 14 Feb 1860
B.H. JAMESON to Martha J. COX, 7 Feb 1860
(Daniel Duval)

ELLN BIBLE

HOLY BIBLE, published by Butler Brothers, New York & Chicago, no date

J.H. ELLN married to Bertha ATHEY at Clay Center, 1 Jul

1888
BIRTHS
Jacob H. ELLN, b.27 Aug 1861, Wafselle Co, IA
Bertha A. ATHEY, b.18 Feb 1867, Lincoln, Burton Co, MO
Mary Merle ELLN, 21 Mar 1889, Clay Center, NE
Mabel Ruth ELLN, b.29 Oct 1890, Clay Center
Florence ELLN, b.15 Oct 1892, Clay Center
Frances ELLN, b.19 Sep 1896, Clay Center
Infant son, b.28 Sep 1898
Raymond ELLN, b.23 Feb 1900, Clay Center
(Daniel Duval File / 18-116)

ASHCRAFT BIBLE

No Title page or date cover missing

MARRIAGES
Elijah B. ASHCRAFT to Nancy C. ASHCRAFT, 4 Feb 1857
Allen S. ASHCRAFT married Oct 1882
James W. ASHCRAFT married 1 Mar 1892
Joseph ASHCRAFT married 24 Jan 1900
Amelia ASHCRAFT married 5 Sep 1892
Christopher A. ASHCRAFT married 27 Jan 1903
Elijah B. ASHCRAFT married 15 Feb 1905
Effie MILLER to William SIMMONS 4 Jan 1905, she d.17 Jul 1906
William D. ASHCRAFT married 4 Dec 1906
BIRTHS
Elijah B. ASHCRAFT, b.11 Mar 1836
Nancy C. ASHCRAFT, b.3 Jul 1842
Allen S. ASHCRAFT, b.15 Sep 1860
James W. ASHCRAFT, b.9 Apr 1863
George T. ASHCRAFT, b.18 Sep 1865
William D. ASHCRAFT, b.9 Mar 1867

Christopher A. ASHCRAFT, b.14 Sep 1869
Joseph ASHCRAFT, b.5 Jan 1872
Elijah Blant ASHCRAFT, b.12 Jan 1875
Nancy Catherine ASHCRAFT, b.3 Sep 1906
DEATHS
Elijah B. ASHCRAFT, d.7 Oct 1874
Joseph ASHCRAFT, d.17 Jul 1906
James W. ASHCRAFT, d.19 Mar 1891
Allen S. ASHCRAFT, d.6 Sep 1900
Allen SIMMONS, d.15 Feb 1882
Permelia SIMMONS, d.6 Mar 1882
Sallie ANDERSON, d.1 Jan 1892
Annie ANDERSON, d.8 Aug 1900
(Mareen Duvall File)

WARFIELD BIBLE

HOLY BIBLE Holman's Edition, Published by A.J. Holman & Co, Philadelphia, 1876
MARRIAGE
John Ogle WARFIELD, b.12 May 1871 of Baltimore to Louyse Duvall SPRAGINS, b.19 Nov 1869 of Baltimore, MD; married 26 Oct 1898 at Grace Church, Baltimore, MD by Rev Arthur Chilton Powell
John Ogle WARFIELD, son of Cecilius Edwin WARFIELD & Laura Winters THOMAS
Louyse Duvall SPRAGNIS, dau of Stith Bolling SPRAGINS & Elizabeth Ann HAMILTON
BIRTHS
John Ogle WARFIELD, Jr, b.3 Apr 1900, Baltimore, MD
Edwin Spragins WARFIELD, b.26 Jun 1901, Phila, PA
Louyse Spargins WARFIELD, b.23 Dec 1902, Phil, PA
Elizabeth Hamilton WARFIELD, b.25 Apr 1905, Chestnut

Hill, PA
Cecilius Edwin WARFIELD, Jr, b.17 Sep 1906, Chestnut Hill, PA
Stith Bolling WARFIELD, b.17 Sep 1906, Chestnut Hill, PA
Diana Louyse, dau of Geo B. & Louyse S.W. BARCLAY, b.2 Sep 1926, Phila
Elizabeth Baldwin, dau of Dr J. Ogle & Rachel Eliz B. WARFIELD, b.11 Oct 1926, Balto.
John Ogle, III, son of J. Ogle, Jr and Eliz B. , b.8 Apr 1930, Wash, DC
Georgia Anne, dau of Geo G. & Louyse S.W. BARCLAY,b.18 Aug 1930, Phila.
John Kennedy WARFIELD, son of Geo G. & Louyse S.W. BARCLAY. b.11 Jan 1933, Bryn Mawr, PA
John Ogle WARFIELD, IV, son of J. Ogle III and Jimmie K. WARFIELD,b.13 Oct 1954, Wash, DC

MARRIAGES

John Ogle WARFIELD, Jr MD to Rachel Elizabeth BALDWIN, 16 Dec 1924 The dau of John Rush and Cora BALDWIN
Louyse Spagins WARFIELD to George Goodard BARCLAY, 16 Jun 1925, the son of William K. & Florence Brunner BARCLAY
Edwin Spragins WARFIELD, to Euphemia Ann HODGEN, 30 Dec 1932, dau of Robert Allen & Alice Mae FRY HODGEN
Elizabeth Hamilton WARFIELD to Charles Henry BALDWIN, 4 Aug 1945 at Cynwyd, PA. He born 19 May 1902, son of John Rush & Cora BALDWIN
John Ogle WARFIELD, III to Jimmie Lou KIRKLAND, 14 Jul 1953, at Panama City, FL. She b.23 Jun 1933, dau of James Cliatt & Martha Blanche CLARK KIRKLAND

DEATHS

Stith Bolling WARFIELD, d.15 Apr 1908

Laura Winters (THOMAS) WARFIELD, d.19 Jan 1912, Balto, MD; b.1 Dec 1844
Cecilius Edwin WARFIELD, Sr, d.8 Sep 1915, Balto, MD; b.15 Aug 1841
Stith Bolling SPRAGINS, b.3 Oct 1829; d.5 Jul 1904, m.29 May 1866 to Elizabeth Ann Hamilton
Elizabeth Ann (HAMILTON) SPRAGINS, b.20 Feb 1837; d.31 Jan 1912
Frederick Howard WARFIELD, b.28 Aug 1874; d.5 Apr 1928
Louyse Duvall (SPRAGINS) WARFIELD, b.19 Nov 1869, d.6 Jul 1948
John Ogle WARFIELD, b.12 May 1871; d.16 Mar 1950
(Mareen Duvall File)

SPRAGINS BIBLE

HOLY BIBLE, Published by William W. Harding, Philadelphia, 1866

MARRIAGES

Stith B. SPRAGINS to Elizabeth Anne HAMILTON, 29 May 1866
Rev J. Ogle WARFIELD to Louyse Duvall SPARGINS, 26 Oct 1898
Samuel Hamilton SPARGINS to Martha Govan TAPPAN, 17 Jun 1903

BIRTHS

Lizzie Hamilton SPARGINS, b.26 Jul 1867
Louisa Duvall SPRAGINS, b.19 Nov 1869
Stith Bolling SPARGINS, Jr, b.2 Jun 1872
Samuel Hamilton SPARGINS, b.23 Aug 1875
Melchijah SPARGINS, b.10 Dec 1877

DEATHS

Lizzie Hamilton SPARGINS, d.15 Sep 1878

Stith Bolling SPRAGINS, Jr, d.23 Mar 1882
Stith Bolling SPRAGINS, b.3 Oct 1829; d.5 Jul 1904
Elizabeth Anne HAMILTON, b.20 Feb 1837; d.31 Jan 1912
Melchijah SPRAGINS, d.5 Oct 1907
Louyse Duvall SPRAGINS, d.6 Jul 1948
Samuel H. SPRAGINS, d.15 Nov 1950

Obituary pasted on page:
Mrs Eliza Aperson SPRAGINS, d.19 Dec 1889 at her dau, Mrs Rebecca S. KING, Mecklenburg, VA. Age 90yrs. The dau of Col Grief GREEN & Miss Rebecca MAYO
(Mareen Duvall File)

GARDNER BIBLE

No Title Page or Date. Original appears to be in the National Archives, Washington, DC Andrew J. GARDNER Civil War Pension file

BIRTHS

Mary Ellen GARDNER, b.4 Aug 1851
Marthey GARDNER, b.16 Aug 1858
Stephen Anthony GARDNER, b.23 Sep 1855, dead
Evan GARDNER, b.24 Sep 1857
Volina GARDNER, b.13 Oct 1857
Myrtla GARDNER, b.31 Dec 1862
M.S.G. PETERS. son of Emily & William PETERS, b.6 Sep 1864

BIRTHS

A.J. GARDNER, b.30 Nov 1830
Charlotte, [DAVIS] his wife, b.26 Jan 1834

Emily, [CHEEVER] wife of A.J., b.12 Nov 1837
<u>MARRIAGES</u>
Andrew J. GARDNER to Charlotte DAVIS, 12 Sep 1850
Andrew J. GARDNER to Emily CHEEVER, 19 Jun 1856
William PETERS to Emily GARDNER, 1 Nov 1863
<u>DEATHS</u>
Charlotte GARDNER, d.5 Mar 1856, aged 22yrs 1mo 10dys
Stephen A. GARDNER, d.12 Mar 1856, aged 5mos 18dys
A.J. GARDNER, d.19 Mar 1863, at Milican Bend, MS in service of the United Sates of America
(Mareen Duvall File / 18-204)

McKINLAY BIBLE

THE NEW PICTORIAL ROYAL QUARTO BIBLE, Published by N.D. Thompson & Co, New York & St Louis, Mo; 1882
<u>BIRTHS</u>
Angus McKINLAY, b.17 May 1812
Sarah A. MURRAY, b.30 Nov 1822
Fanny FORBES, b.12 Sep 1825
CHILDREN
Sarah Ann, b.23 Mar 1846
George Angus, b.14 Dec 1847
William Olmsted, b.3 Jun 1850
Melandhon, b.13 Jul 1852
James Forbes, b.13 Jan 1854
Harriet, b.11 Jul 1856
John Jotham, b.9 Nov 1858
Lincoln, b.31 Oct 1860
Fanny Maria, b.8 Mar 1863
Gertrude Eva, b.28 Mar 1866
Mary, b.2 Sep 1868

Donald [Cameron], b.13 Sep 1872

MARRIAGE

Angus McKINLAY to Fanny FORBES, 23 Feb 1847 at Clyde, OH by Rev L.M. Pounds

MARRIAGES

Angus McKINLAY to Sarah Ann MURRAY, 4 Nov 1844
George A. McKINLAY to Julia Bruce PATCH, 25 Dec 1868
William O. McKINLAY to Carrie W. HIGGINS, 21 Jun 1873
Hattie McKINLAY to George E. KNICKERBACKER, 11 Aug 1880
Lincoln McKINLAY to Jennie KNICKENBOCKER, 23 May 1884
Gertrude E. McKINLAY to Dr A.H. LACKEY, 19 Jun 1888
Fannie M. McKINLEY to Burton H. WOODFORD, 14 Apr 1897
Donald C. McKINLAY to Grace B. KIMBALL, 22 Jul 1903

DEATHS

Sarah Ann, d.17 Apr 1846
Sarah A. McKINLAY, d.20 Apr 1846
James FORBES, d.1 Feb 1858
Melanther, d.28 Feb 1863
John Jotham, d.21 Feb 1861
Mary, d.29 Apr 1887
Angus McKINLAY, d.28 Jan 1896
Frances McKINLAY, d.25 Jul 1910
George Angus, d.15 Jul 1928
Lincoln, d.17 Jul 1930
William Olmsted, d.23 Sep 1931
Harriet McKINLEY KNICKERBOCKER, 1 Oct 1939
Fannie Maria McKINLAY WOODFORD, d.20 Dec 1942
Gertrude Eva McKINLAY LACKEY
Jennie KNICKERBOCKER McKINLEY, d.27 Oct 1936
Donald Cameron McKINLAY, d.10 Mar 1948

Grace B. KIMBALL McKINLAY, d.1 Jun 1953
(Mareen Duvall File)

McKINLAY BIBLE II

THE PRONOUNCING EDITION HOLY BIBLE, Published by A.J. Holman & Co, Philadelphia, 1893

BIRTHS

Donald Cameron McKINLAY, b.13 Sep 1872
Grace B. KIMBALL, b.4 Oct 1870

CHILDREN

Elizabeth Lois, b.8 Nov 1907
Frances Muriel, b.23 Aug 1914

GRANDCHILDREN

Margaret Grace CARPENTER, b.19 Jul 1944
Muriel Elizabeth CARPENTER, b.21 Dec 1947

MARRIAGES

Donald C. McKINLAY to Grace B. KIMBALL, 22 Jul 1903
Elizabeth Lois McKINLAY to Herbert Preston CARPENTER, 26 Jun 1937
Elizabeth Lois McKINLAY CARPENTER to Robert Manley PURDY, 22 Jun 1960

DEATHS

Donald Cameron McKINLAY, d.10 Mar 1948
Grace B. KIMBALL, d.1 Jun 1953
Herbert P. CARPENTER, d.18 Sep 1959
Robert Manley PURDY, d.13 Mar 1967
Frances Muriel, d.28 Aug 1914
(Mareen Duvall File / 18-208)

SIMMONS BIBLE

No Title Page or date. The original was copied prior to

1974 near Irvington or Brandenburg, KY. The original may have been destroyed in a tornade 3 Apr 1974

Allen SIMMONS, b.24 Mar 1822
Permelia SIMMONS, b.19 Oct 1824
Nancy Catherine SIMMONS, b.3 Jul 1842
Sarah Jane Elizabeth SIMMONS, b.19 Jul 1844
Sashwell Jordan SIMMONS, b.18 Feb 1846
William Joseph SIMMONS, b.4 Mar 1848
Mary Allen SIMMONS, b.25 Apr 1851
Judith Ann SIMMONS, b.24 Apr 1854
John Walter SIMMONS, b.22 Jul 1858
Charles Thomas SIMMONS, b.1 May 1861
Allen HENDRICK, b.15 Mar 1868
Sarah J.E. ANDERSON, d.2 Jan 1883
Allen SIMMONS, d.15 Feb 1883
Permelia SIMMONS, d.6 Mar 1883

John W. SIMMONS, b.22 Jul 1859
Thomas Allen SIMMONS, b.21 Jan 1881
Emma P. dau of Sash & Sarah SIMMONS, b.28 Dec 1867
Julia Bell SIMMONS, dau of Sash & Sarah SIMMONS, b.7 Apr 1873
Lelie Mary SIMMONS, b.17 Mar 1875
Annie Larie SIMMONS, b.31 May 1877
Wm Allen SIMMONS, b.14 Mar 1880
Floid SIMMONS, b.20 Jan 1882

Mary A. SIMMONS married 14 Mar 1867
Nancy C. SIMMONS married 4 Feb 1858
Walter SIMMONS married 28 Oct 1878
John Walter SIMMONS, b.12 Feb 1885
Clide Vernon SIMMONS, b.23 Jan 1887

Nella Blanch SIMMONS, b.15 Nov 1889
Floyd Ernest SIMMONS, b.14 Mar 1880
Sash J. SIMMONS, b.18 Feb 1846
Emma E. SIMMONS, b.17 Dec 1851
Emma P. SIMMONS, b.28 Dec 1867
Eunice Beatrice SIMMONS, b.24 May 1893
Nannie Lee SIMMONS, b.20 Oct 1896

DEATHS
Nannie Lee SIMMONS, d.18 Jul 1898
Annie Laure SIMMONS, d.1 Jan 1901
Emma SIMMONS, d.29 Nov 1903
Effie Jane SIMMONS, d.17 Jul 1906
MARRIAGES
Mary Lillie SIMMONS married 2 Feb 1892
Julia Bill SIMMONS married 24 Jan 1894
Willia SIMMONS married 4 Jan 1905
(Mareen Duvall File)

FORE BIBLE

No Title Page or Date. Original seems to be in the Virginia State Library Bible Records Box 15

DEATHS
John FORE, Sr, d.29 Sep 1800
John FORE, Jr, d.12 Nov 1808
Thomas FORE, d.20 Feb 1809
William FORE, d.1 Mar 1812
Sarah FORE, d.19 Oct 1819
James FORE, d.19 Oct 1823
Judith FORE, wife of John FORE, d.4 Jul 1877
William FORE, d.1 Feb 1889, aged 87yrs
Emily E. BURTON, wife of John H. BURTON, & youngest

dau of Wm & Elizabeth FORE, d.25 Apr 1881
Charoltte SLEDD, eldest dau of Wm & Elizabeth FORE, d.19 Feb 1893
(Daniel Foure / Fore File)

HARRIS BIBLE

No Title Page or Date

FAMILY RECORD

Thos J. HARRIS,b.12 Aug 1854, Howard Co, MO; d.24 Oct 1909,
m.14 Feb 1883 to
Mary E. HARRIS, b.8 Jul 1863, Grundy Co, MO
Infant dau, b.24 Nov 1883, Grundy Co, MO; d.24 Nov 1883
Orville Philip , b.6 Jun 1888, Grundy Co, MO; m. 15 Jun 1910
Wm Maxie HARRIS, b.17 Dec 1895, Grundy, Co, MO; m. 30 Jun 1918
Thom J. HARRIS,
(Pierre Foure / Ford File)

RUTH BIBLE

HOLY BIBLE, published by T. Carlton & Z. Phillips, New York, 1851

Family Record

<u>BIRTHS</u>

Job Stillman RUTH, b.6 Jan 1830
Elizabeth E. RUTH, b.29 Nov 1836
Charles Vaughn RUTH, b.19 Mar 1855
William Ashley RUTH, b.20 Jun 1857
Clara Ashley RUTH, b.7 May 1878
Ralph Stillman RUTH, b.6 Dec 1880

Herbert Vaughn RUTH, b.28 Jun 1893
MARRIAGES
Job S. RUTH to Elizabeth E. STONE, 30 Nov 1853
Chas V. RUTH to Alice S. PARKER, 28 Jun 1877, by Rev J.L. Durrant, Ohio Annual Conference
DEATHS
Job S. RUTH, d.22 Mar 1879
Elizabeth E. RUTH, d.10 Mar 1924
both buried at Hockingport, OH
C.V. RUTH d.15 Apr 1934
William Ashley RUTH, d.9 Nov 1941
Clara Ashley BASLEY, d.13 Jun 1950
Herbert Vaughn RUTH, d.25 Oct 1952

Record of the Family of Enoch & Elinda STONE
Enoch H. STONE, b.11 Jun 1811, Surry Co, NC
Elinda STONE, b.22 Nov 1816, Athens, OH
Elizabeth E. STONE, b.29 Nov 1836, Coolville, OH
Mary E. Stone, b.19 Sep 1838, Coolville, OH
Martha Ann STONE, b.22 Dec 1840, Coolville, OH
Delmar F. STONE, b.12 May 1843, Hockingport, OH
Charles H. STONE, b.9 Oct 1845, Hoskingport, OH
Jasper S. STONE, b.20 Dec 1846, Hockingport, OH
Howell [-] STONE, b.29 Sep 1850
Addie A. STONE, b.5 Aug [crossed out] 1852
Alice L. STONE, b.22 Aug 1855, Hockingport, OH
Fannie STONE, b.8 Nov 1857, Hockingport, OH
Chester A. STONE, b.1 Mar 1860, Hosckingport, OH
Elmer E. STONE, b.13 Sep 1861, Hockingport, OH
Enoch STONE and Elinder FOSTER married 22 Sep 1835, in Athens Co, OH
Enoch STONE d.15 Jan 1879
Elinda FROST STONE, d.12 Mar 1896

(Christopher Ferret / Ferry File)

BLEDSOE BIBLE

No Title Page or Date

M.M. BLEDSOE, dau of John A. BLEDSOE, b.10 Aug 1860
M.S. BLEDSOE, b.17 Aug 1862; d.12 May 1879 at Pratwell, Sartanga, AL
John A. BLEDSOE, b.1 Jan 1879
Victoria A. BLEDSOE, Jul 1865
Thomas P[--], b.6 Jul 1854
Victoria A. BLEDSOE, b.4 Jul 1865
(Christopher Ferret / Ferry File)

HAINES BIBLE

No Title Page or Date. was in the possession of Jean Grambling Noel, Jackson, MS
FAMILY RECORD
<u>BIRTHS</u>
James HAINES, b.1 Sep 1785
Temperance HAINES, b.7 Mar 1788
Roberson GOODWIN, b.5 Feb 1766
Mary HAINES, b.30 Apr 1819, married 5 May 1835 to Daniel A. HAINES
Samuel GREGORY, Jr b.2 Jan 1843
Adalphus CASPER married to Mary LINGERFELD, 5 May 1866
Franklin Asbury HUBBARD, b. [---]
<u>DEATHS</u>
James HAINES, d. 11 Jun 1842, aged 56yrs 9mos 10dys
Robert GOODWIN, d.26 Jun 1843

Temperance HAINES, d.29 Jan 1868
Albert HAINES, d. 1825
Daniel Asbury HAYES, d.26 Apr 1897
MARRIAGES
Robert HAYNES to Elizabeth CARPENTER, 30 Nov 1830
Sophia B. HAYES to Robert MCASLIN
Samuel S. GREGORY, Jr married 21 Apr 1866
Daniel A. HAYNES to Mary CANSHEN, 5 May 1836
Hilliard M. HAYNES to Jane GAULE, 13 May 1840
Newton A. HAYNES to Susan CLEEK
Sophia B. McASTON to Wyatt GOULT
Hilliard M. HAYNES to Sarah LEE, 15 May 1844
Susan C. HAYNES to Stewart L. PRYOR, 8 Aug 1844
Eleander STONE to Belzoy HAINES, 18 Jul 1847
G.M. HAYNES to R.R. GROSS, 28 Jan 1861
BIRTHS
Robert Goodwin HAINES, b.1 Nov 1808
Sophia BARNES HAINES, b.1 Jul 1812
Daniel Asbury HAINES, b.18 Dec 1814
Eva Forney HAINES, b. Oct 1817
Hilliard McKindner HAINES, b.16 --- 1820
Newton Norman HAINES, b.29 Oct 1822
Albert HAINES, b.1825
Susan Catherine HAINES, b.11 Aug 1827
Belzora HAINES, b.13 Jun 1832
George Macon, son of D.A. & Mary HAYNES, b.23 Dec 1840
Melvina Sophia Isabell, dau of S.L. & S.C, PRYOR, b.24 Oct 1845

G.M. HAYNES married to Miss Salli GROSS, 1 Jan 1861
Ruth McCAFFEY, b.11 Aug 1800
Sarah Rosannah Barbor GROSS, b.23 Mar 1841

Harriet Ann Elizabeth GROSS, b.16 Apr 1843
George Macon HAYNES, b.23 Dec 1840
Maryetta HAYNES, b.16 Oct 1861
William Boston HAYNES, b.12 Apr 1866
MARRIAGES
R.W. HINTON to M.E. HAYNES, 31 May 1880
W.P. HAYNES to F. HENTON, 25 Dec ---
Clarence Luther RICE to Beulah [-] HAYNES, 9 Oct 1895
Daniel Burgner HAYNES to Miss Florence TISCURT, 22 Jan 1903 (?)
Sarah Elizabeth HINTON to Warren Hall GAY, 31 Aug 1929
BIRTHS
R.W. HINTON, b.28 Dec 1854
Marietta HAYNES, b.16 Oct 1861
Hammond Haynes HINTON, b.6 Apr 1881
Robert Wood HINTON, Jr, 16 Jun 1883
Dale HINTON, b.3 May 1886
Ruth HINTON, b.[----] 1889
James HINTON, b. 1 Feb 1892
David [--] HINTON, b.7 Aug 1894
(Pierre Chivalier de Ferney File)

ROPER BIBLE

No Title Page or date

MARRIAGES
Dewitt C. ROPER to Mary A. MITCHELL, 5 Dec 1869
BIRTHS
Dewitt C. ROPER, b.13 Mar 1846
Mary A. MITCHELL, b.14 Nov 1850
William H. ROPER, b. 1 Apr 187[-]
Mary T. ROPER, b.10 Feb 1873
Sarah Maggie ROPER, b.30 Mar 1874

Frank H. ROPER, b.1 Oct 1876
Ollie D. ROPER, b.3 Sep 1879
Lulu L. ROPER, b.8 Sep 1881
George Wiley ROPER, b.5 Jul 1884
Fred L. ROPER, b.8 Jul 1886
Grace G. ROPER, b.19 Sep 1890
Clay M. ROPER, b.27 Feb 1895
DEATHS
Sarah Maggie ROPER, d.24 Sep 1875
Ollie D. ROPER, d.28 Jul 1880
George Wiley ROPER, d.21 Aug 1885
Minerva ROPER, Mother, d.7 Dec 1887
W.B. ROPER, Father, d.24 Nov 1897
Lulu L. ROPER CONOVER, d.14 May 1921
Dewitt C. ROPER, d.17 Mar 1924
Mary Ann ROPER, d.19 Apr 1937
(Pierre Chivalier du Ferney File)

GIBBONEY BIBLE

No Title Page or Date
FAMILY RECORDS
BIRTHS
Benjamin, son of Joel & Susannah GIBBONEY, b.10 May 1826
Elizabeth, wife of Benjamin GIBBONEY, b.18 Dec 1831
Daniel, son of Benjamin & Elizabeth GIBBONEY, b.19 Feb 1851
Henry, son of Benjamin & Elizabeth GIBBONEY, b.19 Oct 1852
Jacob, son of Benjamin & Elizabeth GIBBONEY, b.11 Oct 1854
Suzanna, dau of Benjamin & Elizabeth GIBBONEY, b.29 Dec

1856
Mary, dau of Benjamin & Elizabeth GIBBONEY, b.9 Feb 1859
Frances, dau of Benjamin & Elizabeth GIBBONEY, b.4 Nov 1860
MARRAIGES
Benjamin & Elizabeth GIBBONEY married 20 Dec 1849
Jacob GIBBONEY to Hulada DUNCAN, 30 Nov 1873
Benjamin GIBBONEY to Elizabeth BOYER, 15 Mar 1877
(Daniel FERREE File / 4-227)

KIRKWOOD BIBLE

No Title Page or Date. The original Bible in possession of T. Wade Kirkwood, Akron, OH.

MARRIAGE
John KIRKWOOD to Elizabeth FOWLER, 17 May 1831
Wm F. KIRKWOOD, son of the above and --
John KIRKWOOD to Lydia FERREE, 11 Jun 1836
Mary C. KIRKWOOD, dau of John & Lydia, to C.H. MATTOCK, 21 Nov 1855
John B. KIRKWOOD, son of John & Lydia KIRKWOOD to Elizabeth Neome SLOTTS, 22 Sep 1874.
Thos C. KIRKWOOD, son of John & Lydia KIRKWOOD to Hattie E. RUNDLE, 26 Oct 1870
BIRTHS
John KIRKWOOD, b.18 Jan 1811
Elizabeth FOWLER, b. ----
William KIRKWOOD, son of John & Elizabeth KIRKWOOD, b.7 Apr 1833
Lydia FERREE, b.1 Mar 1810 (1809)
Mary Catherine KIRKWOOD, dau of John & Lydia KIRKWOOD, b.24 May 1837

Henry Clay KIRKWOOD, son of John & Lydia KIRKWOOD, b.6 Mar 1839
John KIRKWOOD, son of John & Lydia KIRKWOOD, b.29 Jan 1843
Thomas Cody KIRKWOOD, son of John & Lydia KIRKWOOD, b.25 Sep 1845
Allen Ferree KIRKWOOD, son of John & Lydia KIRKWOOD, b.8 Jul 1848
George Freeman KIRKWOOD, son of John & Lydia KIRKWOOD, b.16 Jul 1850
<u>BIRTHS</u>
Andrew K. MATLOCK, son of Mary Catherine & Chas H. MATLOCK, b.29 Jul 1856
<u>DEATHS</u>
Elizabeth KIRKWOOD,consort of John KIRKWOOD, d.12 Sep 1834
Lydia KIRKWOOD, wife of John KIRKWOOD, d.10 Oct 1878
Dr John KIRKWOOD, d.31 Aug 1882
Allen Ferree KIRKWOOD, son of John & Lydia KIRKWOOD, d.19 Mar 1849
Kate KIRKWOOD, dau of John & Lydia KIRKWOOD, d.23 Mar 1857
H.C. KIRKWOOD, son of John & Lydia KIRKWOOD, d.2 Jun 1859
Thomas C. KIRKWOOD, son of John & Lydia KIRKWOOD, d.9 Aug 1907
(Daniel Ferree File)

WALKER VITAL RECORDS

From a small handmade book, with covers of heavy paper marbled with white pages. The cover and pages sewed together with white and blue thread. Last in the possession of

Mrs Winnifred Carroll and Kathryn E. William, Wilmington, OH.

Mordecai WALKER, b.17day 8th month 1742, d.1st day, 4th month 1830
Rachel BARRETT, wife of Mordecai WALKER, b.22day, 2nd month 1746/47; d.23day 4th month 1834
David FAULKNER, b.26day 6th month 1749; d.30day 1st month 1821
Judith THORNBURG, wife of David FAULKNER, b.3day 10th month 1760; d.23day 4th month 1843
William WALKER, son of Mordecai & Rachel WALKER, b.16day 6th month 1776
Martha WALKER, dau of David & Judith FAULKNER, b.23day 6th month 1780
William WALKER and Martha married 5day 3rd month 1800
William Walker d.19day 2nd month 1846
Martha, wife of William WALKER, d.3day 11th month 1850
Azel WALKER, d.8day 5th month 1861
Mordecai WALKER, son of William & Martha WALKER, b.13day 1st month 1801
Azel WALKER, son of Willaim & Martha WALKER, b.21day 11th month 1802
David F. WALKER, son of William & Martha WALKER, b.20day 12th month 1804
Moredicai WALKER and Mary GREE married 3day 9th month 1823
Mary WALKER d.18day 9th month 1834
Mordecai WALKER and Mary OSBORN married 25day 9th month 1836
Mary WALKLER, d.11day 8th month 1848
Azel WALKER and Elizabeth ROBINSON married 28day 3rd month 1825

Phebe F. WALKER, dau of William & Martha WALKER, b.21day 4th month 1807
Eli WALKER, son of William & Martha WALKER, b.22day 10th month 1809
Asa WALKER, son of William & Martha WALKER, b.6day 7th month 1812
David F. WALKER and Rebecca WALL married 1day 10th month 1829
John HUNT and Phebe F. WALKER married 21day 11th month 1832
Eli WALKER and Hannah BROOMHALL married 8day 9th month 1831
Asa WALKLER and Sally ROBINSON married 4day 9th month 1834
John S. WALKER and Ruth HAWKINS married 30day 3rd Month 1837
John S. WALKER, son of William & Martha WALKER, b.13day 8th month 1815
Lewis WALKER, son of William & Martha WALKER, b.11day 8th month 1819
Rachel WALKER, dau of William & Martha WALKER, b.9day 11th month 1821
Rachel and Samuel SPRAY married 9day 9th month 1841
Joshua R. WALKER, son of Asa & Maria WALKER, b.26day 7th month 1835
Joshua R. WALKER and Eliza J. BANKSON married 27day 8th month 1861
Eliza J. WALKER, b.29day 10th month 1838
Wm H. WALKER, son of Asa & Maria WALKER, b.31day 12th month 1839
Wm H. WALKER and Sarah Jane OSBORN married 23day 10th month 1862
Sarah J. WALKER, b.20day 4th month 1840

Phebe H. WALKER, dau of Lewis & Dinah WALKER, b.2day 5th month 1840
Sarah S. WALKER,dau of Lewis & Dinah WALKER, b.29day 1st month 1842
Asa WALKER, d.11 Aug 1881 (in pencil)
Bruce Mc WALKER, son of Asa & Maria WALKER, b.22day 8th month 1855
Bruce Mc WALKER and Kate HIXSON married 31 Jan 1878
Katie HIXSON, b.30day 1st month 1857
Lasura M. WALKER, b.9 Jul 1860
Hattie S. WALKER, b.31 Jul 1864
Charles A. WALKER, b.25day 9th month 1867
Dinah SPRAY, wife of Lewis WALKER, b.22day 2nd month 1819; d.18day 5th month 1843
Lewis WALKER, d.1day 1st month 1844

Copied from the family records of Phebe H. Walker for her uncle Asa Walker 2day 17month 1863

Sally Maria WALKER, day of Joshua & Ann ROBINSON, b.10day 2nd month 1814 (in pencil)
(Daniel Ferree File / 4-271)

WALKER BIBLE

HOLY BIBLE, Published by U.S.B. Publishing Co, Toledo, OH, no date

Last in the possession of Mrs Winnifred Carroll and Kathryn E. Williams, Wilmington, OH

On the flyleaf the inscription "Presented to Katie WALKER by Mother 1885"

Bruce Mc WALKER marriage to Katie HIXSON 31 Jan 1878 at Lexington, OH in presence of J.E. Smith, D.D. Signed J.R. WALKER, Joe HIXSON

<u>MARRIAGES</u>

Fred Glenn WILLIAMS to Genia M. WALKER, 6 Oct 1897, by Rev N.E. BENNETT
Marx A. MASON to Winnifred Nelson WILLIAMS, 30 Oct 1926 at El Paso, TX. Marx Mason d.22 Nov 1929
Winnifred Williams MASON to Fred U. CARROLL, 24 Jun 1943, Russell, Ky by Rev Harold Deitch
Genia Walker WILLIAMS, d.5 Oct 1918
Fred Glenn WILLIAMS, d.8 Mar 1935
BIRTHS
Genietta WALKER, dau of Bruce Mc & Katie WALKER, b.5 Aug 1879
Kathryn Ellen WILLIAMS, dau of Dr & Mrs Fred Glenn WILLIAMS, b.23 Aug 1898, Wilmington, OH
Winnifred Nelson WILLIAMS, dau of Fred G. & Genia WILLIAMS, b.30 Jan 1901
DEATHS
Asa WALKER, b.6 Jul 1812; d.11 Aug 1881
MEMORANDA
Bruce McL WALKER, son of Asa & Maria Robinson WALKER, b.22 Aug 1855; d.11 Nov 1936, bur Wilmington, OH
Katie HIXSON, dau of William & Ruth Antram HIXSON, b.30 Jan 1857; d.19 Nov '936
(Daniel Ferree File / 4-271)

RYAN BIBLE

No Title Page or Date

FAMILY REGISTER BIRTHS
James Alberic RYAN, b.28 May 1879
Marjorie Rose RYAN, b.2 Mar 1881
James Alberic RYAN, Jr. b.6 Mar 1910
William Brown RYAN, b.8 Mar 1911

Roger RYAN, b.6 Sep 1912
Catherine Alina RYAN, b.15 Dec 1913
Philip RYAN, b.9 Jul 1916
(Jesse deForest File)

SERGEANT BIBLE

A typed notorized transcript, No Title page or date listed. Copied 1897 in Boston
TITLE PAGE
Erastus Sergeant's Bible A gift from his Uncle, Josiah Williams and Elizabeth Sergeant Williams

The RECORD
Erastus SERGEANT, b.27 Jul 1742, O.S.
Elizabeth PARTRIDGE, b.15 Mar 1744, O.S. they married 19 Oct 1769, N.S.
Their CHILDREN
John, d.26 Mar 1781
Erastus, b.18 Mar 1772; d.30 May 1832; m. 17 Jun 1802 to Miss Margaret KEELER
Martha, d.26 Mar 1821, m.8 Jun 1797 to Doc. James B. ROOT
Betsy d. 26 May 1837
Sophia, d.24 Jan 1846
Nancy, d.1 Mar 1797
Oliver Partridge, d.1 Oct 1849
Eunice SERGEANT, b.15 Jan 1782; m.16 Jul 1812, Middlebury, VT to Peter STARR
John SERGEANT, d.24 May 1839; m.6 Dec 1824 to Miss Cynthia WEST
Emily, d.25 Apr 1814
Sewall, d. Aug 1858; m.27 Feb 1816 to Clarissa PARTRIDGE

George, d.15 May 1825
Doc. Erastus SERGEANT, d.14 Nov 1814, aged 72yrs 3mos 7dys
Mrs Elizabeth Partridge SEARGEANT, d.18 Dec 1815, aged 71yrs 8mos 22dys
Mrs Margaret Keeler SERGEANT, d.31 Oct 1837, Peru, IN
Dr Erastus SERGEANT m. to Elizabeth PARTRIDGE, 19 Oct 1769
John, son of Erastus & Elizabeth SERGEANT, b.29 Aug 1770
Dr Erastus, Jr, b.18 Mar 1772; d.30 May 1832, Lee, MA; m. 17 Jun 1802 to Margaret KEELER
Martha, b.7 Dec 1773; m.8 Jun 1797 to Dr James B. ROOT
Elizabeth & Sophie, b.17 Dec 1775
Anna, b.10 Sep 1777; d.1 Mar 1797; aged 20yrs
Oliver PARTRIDGE, b.7 Aug 1779
Eunice, b.15 Jan 1782; m. 16 Jul 1812 to Peter STARR
John, b.12 Feb 1784
Emily, b.13 Jun 1787; d.25 Apr 1814, Aged 23yrs
Sewell, b.20 Sep 1789
George, b.19 Mar 1792, d.15 May 1825

Stephen W. WILLIAMS, b.30 Jun 1769; d.12 Jan 1790
Mrs Abigail WILLIAMS SERGEANT DWIGHT; d.15 Feb 1791, aged 70 wanting 2 months
Mrs Judith THAYER, sister of Abigail Williams S. DWIGHT, d.5 Apr 1801, aged 80yrs 1mo
Mrs Anna Williams PARTRIDGE, wife of Col Oliver PARTRIDGE, d.21 Dec 1802, aged 85yrs 3mos 4dys
Mrs Eunice STODDARD, wife of Maj Israel STODDARD, d.27 Mar 1807, aged 65yrs
Mrs Elizabeth JAMES, d.20 Oct 1809, aged 95yrs
Mrs Sarah GRAY, d.27 Oct 1809, aged 73yrs
Doc. James B. ROOT, d.28 Feb 1813

Sewall SERGEANT of Stockbridge married to Clarissa PARTRIDGE of Hatfield on 27 Feb 1816
Their CHILDREN
Catherine Sedwick, b.10 Apr 1817; d.2 Apr 1896, Lakewood, NJ; m. 6 Aug 1840 to Henry A. De FOREST
an anonymous son, b.30 Jan 1819; d.within half an hour
George, b.19 Feb 1820; d.3 Feb 1875, Northampton, MA; m. 24 Aug 1847 to Lydia A. CLARK of Northampton, MA
Mrs Lydia SERGEANT, d.17 Dec 1862
Caroline Elizabeth, b.26 Jun 1822; m.29 Jul 1846 to George F. De FOREST
Susan, b.3 Feb 1825; d.22 May 1827; aged 2yrs 3mos
Sewall, b.21 May 1827; d.22 Nov 1890, m. to Alma MERCIEN
Clarissa Partridge, b.24 Sep 1829; d.1 Oct 1846; aged 17yrs
Susan Emily, b.29 Mar 1832; m.17 Jun 1857 to Alfred H. DASHIELL, Jr
John Elliot, b.18 Aug 1835; d.26 Jan 1895; m.10 Jun 1872 to Caroline H. MATTHEWS
Anna Williams, b.15 Aug 1838; m. to George F. De FOREST
Sewall SERGEANT, b.20 Sep 1789; d.3 Aug 1858
Clarissa PARTRIDGE, b.15 Jan 1793, d.31 Jan 1860
(Jesse de Forest File)

PARSLY BIBLE

The HOLY BIBLE; published by Henry Altemus, Philadelohia, 1884
MARRIAGE CERTIFICATE
John H. PARSLY to Corris A SEARCH on 5 Feb 1885
FAMILY RECORD BIRTHS
John H. PARSLY, b.29 Nov 1851
Cornelia A. SEARCH, b.7 Feb 1858

Elmer Griffith PARSLY, b.13 Apr 1886
Mary Louise PARSLY, b.6 Nov 1887
Lewis Fuller PARSLY, b.12 Dec 1889
Isabell Jackson PARSLY, b.2 Dec 1891
Alice Search PARSLY, b.17 Mar 1894

MARRIAGES

Elmer Griffieth PARSLY to Stella Wren BANES, 25 Aug 1917
Mary Louise PARSLY to Renest Clyde FISHBOUGH, July ---
Lewis Fuller PARSLY to Hester Carroll ANDERSON, 21 Apr 1917
Isabel Jackson PARSLY to Lee Clagett WARFIELD, 1 Apr 1915
Alice Search PARSLY to Rpane Alexander CLAY, 17 Aug 1922
George Melvin PARSLY to Mariam RIPPY,17 Aug 1927
Elmer Griffith PARSLY to Frances Rhodes HAWKINS, 27 Oct 1969

DEATHS

John Henry PARSLY, d.14 Dec 1927
Cornelia Search PARSLY, d.24 Jan 1936
Lewis Fuller PARSLY, d.14 Jan 1965
Elmer Griffieth PARSLY, d.12 Mar 1972
Griffieth Mielen SEARCH, d.5 Jun 1901
Maria Louisa SEARCH, d.2 May 1863
Henry Clara SEARCH, d.2 May 1862
Margarest Louisa SEARCH, d.16 Jul 1862
Mary Meiler SEARCH, d.2 Aug 1862
Alice Rex SEARCH, d.23 Mar 1912

(Jesse de Forest File)

DUESLER BIBLE

Typed Transcript Holy Bible 1847

MARRIAGES

Simeon DUESLER to Catherine GODWIN, 12 Oct 1831
Stephen DUESLER to Eleanor DUESLER, 15 Dec 1853
Chauncey SMITH to Betsey DUESLER, 13 Apr 1854
Martin DUESLER to Harriet DUESLER, 7 Jun 1855
Stephen DUESLER to Emeline DUESLER, 31 Dec 1862
Edward S. DUESLER to Magdalen Ann ALLEN, 29 Jan 1864

BIRTHS

Simeon DUESLER, b.7 Oct 1810
Catherine GODWIN, b.1 May 1810
Betsy Ann DUESLER, b.15 Nov 1832
Eleanor DUESLER, b.27 Feb 1836
Harriet DUESLER, b.22 May 1837
Edward DUESLER, b.27 Jan 1839
Emeline DUESLER, b.31 Jul 1844

DEATHS

Betsy Ann SMITH, d.30 May 1881
Simeon DUESLER, d.5 May 1892
Edward S. DUESLER, d.24 Nov 1895
Catherine DUESLER, d.4 Apr 1901
Magdalen A. DUESLER, d.1 Nov 1905
(Jesse de Forest File)

DYGERT BIBLE

No Title Page or date [1882]

BIRTHS

George W. DYGERT, b.12 Mar 1857
Wesley L. DYGERT, b.29 May 1879
Clyde L. DYGERT, b.23 [--] 1884
George S. DYGERT, b.2 Oct 1886

Libie Elen SMITH, b.26 May 1860
Emma A. DYGERT, b.18 Sep 1881
(Jesse de Forest File)

HUNTLEY BIBLE

No Title Page or date

DEATHS

Sarah, the Mother of William HUNTLEY, d.22 Dec 1842, aged 54yrs
William HUNTLEY, d.19 Aug 1875, aged 67yrs, son of Sarah HUNTLEY and Grandson of John DeFOREST of Sheffield, MA
on attached page typescript:
William HUNTLEY married to Mariette KLINE, 8 Jan 1834
William HUNTLEY b.20 Dec 1814
Mariette HUNTLEY, wife of William HUNTLEY, b.28 Dec 1816
Harriet Eliza HUNTLEY, b.19 Feb 1849
Mariette HUNTLEY, d.6 Jan 1903, Elizabeth, NJ, bur. Mill River, MA
Harriet Eliza Huntley PFAU, d.29 May 1897
Alfred PFAU, d.18 Aug 1892
(Jesse de Forest File)

SMITH BIBLE

Copied from bible of Louis Smith in 1939, No Title Page or Date

DEATHS

Betsey Ann SMITH, d.30 May 1881
Chancey SMITH, d.12 Feb 1901
Mary C. SMITH, d.11 Nov 1907

Asenath KRING, d.2 Dec 1909
Jane L. SMITH, d.30 Jan 1913
Jane Ann KRING, d.11 Apr 1925
Laura BELGEN, d.22 Jun 1932
Peter BELGEN, d.3 Oct 1931
Hattie E. JEWELL, d.25 Dec 1838
<u>BIRTHS</u>
Betsy Ann DUESLER, b.10 Nov 1832
Chancey SMITH, b.11 Sep 1834
Jane L. DEMPSTER, b.3 Jan 1840
Mary C. SMITH, b.10 Feb 1856
Jane A. SMITH, 10 Oct 1857
Elizabeth E. SMITH, b.26 May 1860
Harriet E. SMITH, b.13 May 1864
Emma L. SMITH, b.10 Feb 1867
Laura SMITH, b.17 Feb 1871
Lewis C. SMITH, b.7 Oct 1872
Jennie KRING, b.29 Apr 1875
Amas SHAVER, b.21 Feb 1876; note son of Mary C. SMITH
Wesley C. DYGERT, b.29 May 1879
Mary E. SMITH, b.29 Nov 1895
Asenath KRING, b.13 Apr 1879
Raymond KRING, b.4 Oct 1889
Ernest C. SMITH, b.9 Jun 1898
Chancey W. SMITH, b.22 Aug 1901
Jane Ann BELGEN, b.7 Nov 1911
Ronald Howard KRUTZ, b.26 Feb 1939
(Jesse de Forest file)

SCHNEE / ROBSON BIBLE

The HOLY BIBLE, Published by American Bible

Society, New York, 1867
FAMILY RECORDS MARRIAGES
David M. SCHNEE to Nancy W. TRAVER, 5 Nov 1845
Richard P. ROBSON to Louisa Ann SCHNEE, 7 Oct 1869
Dr Lewis W. HIGHMAN to Eleanor SCHNEE, 9 Dec 1877
Harry T. SCHNEE to Minnie E. WILSON, 26 Dec 1882
Louis RELHAM to Eleanor HIGHMAN, 4 May 1884
Edward E. HIGHMAN to Kate May SCHNEE, 25 Dec 1884
DEATHS
Louisa A. ROBSON, d.13 Aug 1877
Dr Lewis W. HIGHMAN, d.22 Jan 1879
Infant son of Louis & Eleanor PELHAM, d.7 May 1885, aged 4dys
Charles Wilson, son of Harry T. & Minnie SCHNEE, d.26 Jul 1885, aged 20mos 19dys
Helen HIGHMAN, d.30 Apr 1895
Nancy W. SCHNEE, d.22 Nov 1900
David M. SCHNEE, d.25 Sep 1908
William T. ROBSON, d.13 Apr 1912
H.T. SCHNEE, d.21 Apr 1941
Mrs Minnie SCHNEE, d.18 Apr 1942
Eloise SCHNEE SCHESTIGER, d.20 Jul 1942
Lt Alfred Harry CONRAD, killed in action in Holland 19 Sep 1944
BIRTHS
Nellie SCHNEE, dau of H.T. & Minnie SCHNEE, b.11 Mar 1886
Eloise SCHNEE, dau of H.T. & Minnie SCHNEE, b.8 Jan 1888
Wilbur PELHAM, son of Louis & Elenora PELHAM, b.21 Nov 1887
Mary Helen HIGHMAN, dau of Edward & Kate HIGHMAN, b.24 Dec 1892

Anna Belle HIGHMAN, dau of Edward & Kate HIGHMAN, b.12 Sep 1894
Edith HIGHMAN, dau of Edward & Kate HIGHMAN, b.12 Aug 1896
Henry Ward CONRAD and Harry Alfred CONRAD, twin sons of Henry W, & Nellie Schnee CONRAD, b.13 Nov 1921
Alfred Ward CONRAD, son of Henry Ward & Marjorie Bartholomew CONRAD, b.6 Dec 1944, Terre Hunte, IN
(Jean Henri Fortineux File)

FUQUA BIBLES

Copies of pages from two Bibles ie: Thomas Fuqua Bible and the Washington L. Fuqua Bible The NEW TESTAMENT, no publisher or date.

MARRIAGES

Thomas FUQUA to Nancy Heart McLAUGHLIN m.4 Nov 1841
Washington L. FUQUA to Melsura M. FUQUA, m.8 Oct 1871

BIRTHS

Adelbert L. FUQUA, b.8 Oct 1842
William H. FUQUA, b.24 Sep 1844
Ephraim [-] FUQUA, b.4 Sep 1846
Washington L. FUQUA, b.3 Jul 1849
Melsura M. [-] FUQUA, b.17 May 1857
Theophilus L. FUQUA, b.17 Mar 1873
Adolphus A. FUQUA, b.2 Feb 1875
Sadie [-] FUQUA, b.13 May 1878
Nane C. FUQUA, b.27 May 1882
Thomas Washington FUQUA, b.27 Aug 1884

BIRTHS

Thomas FUQUA, b.7 Feb 1813

Nancy H. FUQUA, b.18 [--] 1823
Thomas N. FUQUA, b.1 Apr 1833
Sallie A. FUQUA, b.19 Jan 1835
Peter FUQUA, b.12 Feb 1778
William FUQUA, b.17 Dec 1779
Elizabeth FUQUA, b.8 Dec 1782
Joshua FUQUA, b.17 Feb 1787
Thomas FUQUA, b.[--] Nov 1788
Nathan FUQUA, b.6 Feb 1790
Jesse FUQUA, b.[--] May 1793
Joel FUQUA, 27 Mar 1797
Polly FUQUA, b.22 Feb 1799
DEATHS
Nancy Heart FUQUA, d.7 Aug 1853
Thomas FUQUA, d.26 Aug 1861
Thomas N. FUQUA, d.9 Oct 1875
Sallie Ann FUQUA, d.2 Dec 1894
DEATHS
Nancy H. FUQUA, d.7 Aug 1853
Thomas FUQUA, d.26 Aug 1861
Thomas N. FUQUA, d.9 Oct 1875
Sallie A. FUQUA, d.2 Dec 1894
Sadie G. SMITH, d.10 Jan 1904
Homer WERRELL, d.30 Dec 1920
W.L. FUQUA, d.12 Jul 1924
Sadie L. SMITH, b.1 Oct 1902
Bessie G. SMITH, b.8 Nov 1903
Willie SMITH ----
BIRTHS
A.L. FUQUA, b.8 Oct 1842
William H. FUQUA, b.24 Sep 1844
Ephraim M. FUQUA, b.4 Sep 1846
Washington L. FUQUA, b.3 Jul 1849

Melsune M. FUQUA, b.17 May 1857
Theophilus L. FUQUA, b.17 Mar 1873
Adolphus A. FUQUA, b.2 Feb 1875
Clarence FUQUA, b.3 Jan 1911
Sadie G. FUQUA, b.13 May 1879
Nannie C. FUQUA, b.28 May 1882
Thomas W. FUQUA, b.27 Aug 1884
Willie J. SMITH, b.6 Jan 1900
Elmer C. WARRELL, b.4 May 1904
Never WORRELL, b.31 May 1906
Robbie Well WORRELL, b.11 Oct 1908
Nonia WORRELL, b.20 Jul 1930
Thomas [---], b.26 Jul 1914

MARRIAGES

Thomas FUQUA to Nancy Heart McLAUGHLIN, 4 Nov 1841
T. LeRoy FUQUA to Susie CARVER, 5 Nov 1899
J.R. SMITH to Sadie FUQUA, 22 Dec 1878
Char FUQUA to Hermon WORRELL, 31 May 1903
A.A. FUQUA to Annie WAGGONER, 27 Mar 1904
Y.W. FUQUA to Lucile R[---], [-] 1910
Paul WASHER to Nonia WORRELL, 16 Jun 1929
(Guillaume Fouquet / Fuqua File)

STREETER BIBLE

HARDING'S ROYAL EDITION HOLY BIBLE, Publishers William W. Harding, Philadelphia, PA; 1870. Original owned by Mrs Elma V. Shaffer

BIRTHS

PARENTS

William F. STREETER, b.28 Dec 1834, Lexington, Greene Co, NY
Mary Elma FREER, b.1 Jul 1838, Eaton, Wyoming Co, PA

CHILDREN:
Nine STREETER, b.12 Dec 1860
Leonora STREETER, b.24 Mar 1862
Sarah Ellen STREETER, b.5 Dec 1864
Clara STREETER, b.6 Mar 1867
Ruth Marian STREETER, b.27 Aug 1869
Elma STREETER, b.17 Mar 1871
Marjorie C. STREETER, b.14 Jan 1873
Allyn Anson STREETER, b.30 Jul 1874
Wm Freer STREETER, b.24 Jul 1877
Robert Leroy STREETER, b.18 Mar 1880
<u>MARRIAGES</u>
William F. STREETER to Mary Elma FREAR, 25 Jan 1860
Rev George M. REMLEY to Elma M. STREETER, 28 Dec 1897
John L. KOHL to Leonora STREETER, 20 May 1880
Allyn A. STREETER to Annie M. STOVER, 14 Jun 1899
Ernest M. PORTER to Sarah Ellen STREETER, 3 Oct 1884
Dr Herbert H. GLOSSER to Ruth M. STREETER, 8 Aug 1900
William C. STEERE to Nina STREETER, 29 Jul 1885
Robert L. STREETER to Helen Louise RAPALJE, 12 Nov 1907
Jacob HEGETSCHWEILER to Clara STREETER, 28 Sep 1888
William F. STREETER to Margaret YOST, 7 Apr 1910
W. Walter SMITH to Margery C. STREETER, 12 Feb 1916
<u>DEATHS</u>
Clara HEGETSCHWEILER, d.12 Feb 1912
William F. STREETER, Sr, d.7 Feb 1914
Mrs Wm F. STREETER, Sr, d.23 Feb 1918
Mrs Nina STEERE, d.15 Sep 1939
Mrs Nora KOHL, d.17 Jun 1925

Mrs Ruth GLOSSER, d.11 Apr 1941
Mrs Sadie PORTER, d.10 Apr 1949
Mrs Margery SMITH, d.20 May 1939
Mrs Elma REMLEY, d.9 Mar 1935
Robert L. STREETER, d.10 Dec 1932
Wm Frear STREETER, d.20 Nov 1959

Allyn A. STREETER, d.18 Dec 1961, aged 87yrs 4mos 18dys
(Hugo Freer File)

MASE BIBLE

No Title Page or Dates

BIRTHS

Starr D. MASE, b.22 Feb 1877, Prattsville, NY
Parents Theodore M. MASE & Emily FRAYER MASE
Charlotte May MASE, his wife, b.25 Apr 1880, Prattsville, NY
Parents W.B. CHATFIELD & Ida TURK CHATFIELD
Freda Florence MASE, b.11 Jun 1899, Prattsville, NY
Theodore Starr MASE, b.23 Apr 1907, Prattsville, NY
Stanley Wilson MASE, b.27 Mar 1918, Prattsville, NY

MARRIAGES

Starr D. MASE to Charlotte May CHATFIELD, married at Windham, NY 28 Mar 1898 by Rev W.H. Vaughn
(Hugo Freer File)

SCOTT BIBLE

THE HOLY BIBLE, Published by G.& C. Merrian, Springfield, MA; 1846

BIRTHS

Abram SCOTT b. 14 Mar 1795

Electa CURTIS, b.22 Aug 1800
Harriet SCOTT, b. [blurred can't read]
Eliza SCOTT, b.14 Sep 1823
Walter W. SCOTT, b.31 May 1825
El[--] W. SCOTT, b.25 Jan 1828
Amanda SCOTT, b.18 Jul 1830
Fanny M. SCOTT, b.30 [--] 1832
[----] C. SCOTT, b.[--] Apr 1835
Charles O. SCOTT, b.2 Apr 1838
MARRIAGES
Abram SCOTT to Electa CURTIS, 31 Mar 1819
21 Mar 1851 Gilbert STRIKER and family moved from Jackson Co to Baltimore, B[--] Co
DEATHS
Electa SCOTT, d.8 Jul 1845
Electa A. CLOSE, d.9 Nov 1852
Chas O SCOTT, d.[--] Apr 1863
Eliza SCOTT, d.15 Oct 1865
Abram SCOTT, d.30 Apr 1882
Walter SCOTT, d. [----]
Harriet CARLTON, d.6 Jan 1892/3
Fanny M. TOLLETT, d.7 Aug 1897
Ala M. SCOTT, d.[--] Jun 1899
Amanda MIXER, d. 1913
George C. SCOTT, d.8 Apr 1820
Abran CARLTON. d.13 Jan 1930
(Hugo Freer File)

SCHRYVER BIBLE

THE HOLY BIBLE and NEW TESTAMENT, Published by H.& E. Phinney, Cooperstown, NY; 1834 / 1835
BIRTHS

Philip SCHRYVER, b.16 Oct 1823
Julian SCHRYVER, b.4 Dec 1824
Benjamin Albert SCHRYVER, b.31 Mar 1826
Catherine Eliza SCHRYVER, b.8 Jan 1827
Levi Stephen SCHRYVER, b.24 Nov 1831
Charles Edwards SCHRYVER, b.24 Apr 1834
John Henry SCHRYVER, b.26 Oct 1841
Henry B. SCHRYVER, b.29 Apr 1798
Mary Ann VANDYKE, b.4 Sep 1802

BIRTHS

Edmond SCHRYVER, b.8 Oct 1829; d.5 Apr 1830; aged 5mos, 7dys

DEATHS

Elizabeth VAN DYKE, d.2 Feb 1846; aged 70yrs, 6mos 15dys
Mary Ann SCHRYVER, d.18 Apr 1853, aged 50yrs 7mos 14dys
Henry B. SCHRYVER, d.29 Aug 1861, aged 63 yrs, 4mos

MARRIAGES

Henry B. SCHRYVER to Mary Ann VAN DYK, 7 Dec 1822
Philip A. SCHRYVER to Jane Eliza HOUGHTALING, 11 Jan 1846 by Rev Abraham Fort
Albert B. SCHRYVER to Lola Ann HADDEN, 9 Dec 1847, by John Hinchman

David PHILLIPS to Julia Ann SCHRYVER, 23 Dec 1847, by Rev C. Bolster
Henry CORKE to Catherine E. SCHRYVER, 29 Mar 1847, by Rev C. Bolster
Charles E. SCHRYVER to Louisa A. KIPPEL, 7 Jul 1855 at No.9 Christpher Street, NY by Rev W.C. SMITH
(Hugo Freer File)

VIELE BIBLE

No Title page or Dates

FAMILY RECORDS

BIRTHS

Charles Hanson VIELE, b.19 Oct 1787
Margaret PUTMAN, b.2 Jul 1793
Peter Maber VIELE, b.4 Oct 1816, first son
Sephen Flenny VIELE, b.9 Feb 1819, second son
William Putmam VIELE, b.28 Jun 1821. third son

DEATHS

Second son d. 18 Oct 1827; aged 2yrs 7nos 25dys
Charles H. VIELE, d.5 Nov 1857
Margaret VIELE, d.22 May 1868
Peter M. VIELE, d.20 Oct 1894

MARRIAGES

Charles Hanson VIELE to Margaret PUTMAN, 7 Jan 1816
(Hugo Freer File)

McGEE BIBLE

THE HOLY BIBLE, Published by Jasper Harding, Philadelphia, PA, 1844

The bible last in the possession of William Charles McGee of Jackson, TN.

FAMILY RECORDS

BIRTHS

Richard McGEE, b.18 Sep 1775
Elizabeth McGEE, wife & Consort of Richard McGEE, b.20 Jul 1787
Callaway Low McGEE, son of Rich & Elizabeth, b.6 Jun 1806
James Gentry McGEE, b.18 Nov 1808
William Carrol McGEE, b.4 Jul 1814
Richard Bartley McGEE, b.4 Jul 1819

Sarah Ann McGEE, b.2 Apr 1823
Martha Coteney McGEE, b.28 Jun 1826
John Preston McGEE, b.7 Mar 1833
DEATHS
Richard McGEE, d.17 Apr 1845,aged 89yrs 6mos 14dys
Elizabeth McGEE, d.31 Aug 1834
Callaway Low McGEE, d. in Texas
James Gentry McGEE, d.17 Dec 1851, his wife Mary Ann d. on the same day
William Carrol McGEE, d.27 Jun 1874
Richard Bartly McGEE, d.27 May 1880
Sarah Ann McGEE, d.13 Jan 1824
John Preston McGEE, d.22 Feb 1890
MARRIAGES
Richard McGEE to Elizabeth GENTRY, 19 Jun 1804
James G. McGEE to Mrs Mary Ann BARNES, nee Mary Ann FORDA, 29 Jun 1837
Richard B. McGEE to Eliza E. TORAFE, 19 Feb 1846
Callaway L. McGEE to Mrs Linna NELSON, nee Linna PARKER, 6 Feb 1850 (Holmes City, MS)
William C. McGEE to Mary G. BAINS, 26 Jun 1850 (Holmes City, MS)
(Nicholas Gaillard / Gaylord File)

HADDEN BIBLE

No Title Page or Date

FAMILY RECORDS
BIRTHS
Robert HADDEN, b.11 May 1822, Mentz, Cayuga Co, NY
Esther M. RUMSEY, b.30 Sep 1822, Victory, Cayuga Co, NY
Frank R. HADDEN, b.27 Jul 1848, Mentz, Cayuga Co, NY

Delos D. HADDEN, b.20 Nov 1849, Mentz, Cayuga Co, NY
DEATHS
Frank R. HADDEN, d.11 Sep 1848, Mentz, Cayuga Co, NY
Robert HADDEN, d.23 Jul 1896, Port Bryon, NY
Esther M. HADDEN, d.28 Aug 1902, Port Byran, NY
MARRIAGES
Robert HADDEN to Esther M. RUMSEY, 1 Jan 1846
Delos D. HADDEN to Helen E. SMITH, 6 Dec 1871
Clarence A. HADDEN to Elizabeth KENYON, 8 Nov 1906
Raymond D. HADDEN to Elizabeth A. STUART, 16 Oct 1948
BIRTHS
Clarence A. HADDEN, b.11 Oct 1877, Mentz, NY
Elizabeth KENYON, b.14 Jan 1878
Helen Louise HADDEN, b.27 Apr 1912
Raymond Delve HADDEN, b.26 Aug 1914
Sharon Roberta HADDEN, b.7 Jan 1950
Robert Joseph HADDEN, b.20 Feb 1952
Stuart Raymond HADDEN, b.12 May 1953
Elizabeth A. STUART, b.8 Sep 1924
DEATHS
Delos D. HADDEN, d.12 Jun 1911, Port Bryan, NY
Helen E. HADDEN, d.12 Jun 1913, Port Bryan, NY
Clarence A. HADDEN, d.29 Apr 1955
Elizabeth P. HADDEN, d.6 Dec 1966
(Nicholas Gaillard / Gaylord File)

STOCKING BIBLE

THE HOLY BIBLE, Published by the American Bible Society, New York, 1868. The Bible in 1966 was in the possession of William Gubb, Batavia, NY
FAMILY RECORDS

MARRIAGES

Joseph STOCKING to Betsey ROBBINS, 9 Jan 1806, Pittsfield, MA

Abner BIDWELL to Sylvia CURTIS, 4 Oct 1812, Farmington, CT

Thos R. STOCKING to Julia Ann BIDWELL, 6 May 1835, Farmington, CT

Miles Isaac BULL to Maria Curtis STOCKING, 2 Jun 1863, Buffalo, NY

Howard M. MILLARD to Alice G. BULL, 2 Jun 1886, Batavia, NY

John Edward GUBB to Lula Bidwell BULL, 4 Jun 1891, Batavia, NY

Louis Adelbert PRENTICE to Helen Miles BULL, 5 Sep 1894, Batavia, NY

Edward Carrington BULL to Nancy WARREN, 19 Oct 1898, Buffalo, NY

Edward Lawrence GUBB to Helen Lydia PARKER, 11 Oct 1915 [1916]

Karl G. KAFFENBERGER to Helen D. MILLARD, 24 Jun 1915 [1916], Buffalo

Wm Miles GUBB to Marie Beatrice MEAD, 7 Nov 1923, Elmira, NY

Douglass Willard McGLIVE to Emily Warren BULL, 21 Apr 1924, Buffalo, NY

Julie Hinsdale BULL to John Warwick FAWCETT, 23 Jun 1928, [-----]

Edgar P. CHENEY to Nancy Henrietta BULL, 27 Dec 1930, Buffalo, NY

BIRTHS

Joseph STOCKING, b.18 Nov 1774, Middle Haddam, CT

Betsey ROBBINS, b.9 May 1786, Pittsfield, MA

Sarah B. SHELDON, b.27 Nov 1788, Williamstown, MA

Abner BIDWELL, b.8 Jul 1785
Sylvia CURTIS, b.20 Sep 1790, Farmington, CT
Thos Robbins STOCKING, son of Joseph & Betsey, b.24 Jul 1809, Utica, NY
Julia Ann BIDWELL, dau of Abner & Sylvia, b.31 Jan 1815, Farmington, CT
Jane Bidwell STOCKING, dau of T.R. & J.A., b.20 Aug 1836, Buffalo, NY
Maria Curtis STOCKING, dau of T.R. & J.A., b.6 Oct 1837, Buffalo, NY
Jos Addison STOCKING, son of T.R. & J.A., b.7 Jan 1840, Buffalo, NY
Eliza Robbins STOCKING, dau of T.R. & J.A.; b.3 Feb 1842, Buffalo, NY
Miles Isaac BULL, b.26 Jul 1838, Orwell, PA
Alice Gardner BULL, dau of M.& M.C., b.14 Apr 1864, Buffalo, NY
Julie Bidwell BULL, dau of M.I.& M.C.; b.22 Feb 1868, Olean, NY
Edw'd Carrington BULL, son of Miles & M.C.; b.12 Mar 1871, Olean, NY
Helen Miles BULL, dau of M.I. & M.C.; b.11 Jun 1872, Olean, NY
Raymond Hincent MILLARD, son of H.M. & Alice B.; b.14 Apr 1887, Buffalo, NY
Edward Norman. b.18 Aug 1889, Bradford, PA
Helen Dorethea MILLARD, b.18 Aug 1892, Brooklyn, NY
Edward Lawrence GUBB, son of Edward & Julie B.; b.[-] Nov 1892, Batavia, NY
Edward Carrington BULL, Jr, son of E.C. & Nancy Warren BULL, b.20 Aug 1899, Buffalo, NY
Emily Warren BULL, dau of E.C.& Nancy BULL; b.26 Mar 1902, Buffalo,, NY

William Miles GUBB, son of J.E. & Julia B. GUBB; b.9 May 1901, Batavia, NY
Julia Hinsdale BULL, dau of Edward C. & Nancy Warren BULL; b.20 Apr 1905, Buffalo, NY
Nancy BULL, dau of E.C.& Nancy BULL; b.29 Oct 1907, Buffalo, NY
Karl G. KAUFFENBERGER, son of Karl & Helen KAUFFENBERGER, b.3 Feb 1918, Spartanburg, SC
Alice Julia GUBB, dau of E.C. & Helen L. GUBB, b.18 Oct 1917, Batavia, NY
Mary Alice KAUFFENBERGER, dau of Karl W. & Helen M.; b.1 Jun 1920, Buffalo, NY

DEATHS

Betsey R. STOCKING, wife of Joseph; d.30 Apr 1810, Utica, NY
Sylvia C. BIDWELL, wife of Abner; d.20 Sep 1817, Farmington, CT
Joseph STOCKING, d.4 Sep 1835, Buffalo, NY
Eliza Robbins STOCKING, d.21 Jul 1843, Buffalo, NY; dau of T.R. & J.A.
Julia A. [Anne Bidwell] STOCKING, wife of Thos R., d.5 Nov 1859, Buffalo, NY
Miles Isaac BULL, husband of Maria; d.28 Sep 1872, Oleans, NY
Abner BIDWELL, d.31 Aug 1885, Farmington, CT, aged 95yrs
Raymond Vincent BULL, son of H.M. & Alice; d.20 Oct 1887
Thomas Robbins STOCKING, husband of Julia Ann BIDWELL; d.6 Mar 1895, Buffalo, NY
Jane B. STOCKING, dau of Thomas R. & Julia A.; d.3 Mar 1907, Batavia, NY
Maria C. BULL, d.11 May 1916, Buffalo, NY
John Edward GUBB, husband of Julia BULL, d.22 Feb 1927,

Batavia, NY
Louis Adlebert PRENTICE, husband of Helen M. BULL; d. 1934, Batavia, NY
Julia Bidwell Bull GUBB, wife of John Edward GUBB, d.23 Sep 1944, Batavia, NY, age 76yrs
Mrs Alice Bull MILLARD, d.14 Jan 1950, Buffalo, NY
Mrs Louis PRENTICE, d.21 Jun 1956, Batavia, NY, wife of Louis A. PRENTICE
Lawrence Edward GUBB, son of John Edward & Julia Bull GUBB; d.10 Nov 1966, Rydal, PA
(Nicholas Gaillard / Gaylard File)

DEMING BIBLE

No Title Page or Dates. Original Bible in 1976 in the possession of Louise Deming Smith. Hardman Co, TN.
FAMILY RECORDS
MARRIAGES
Fisher DEMING to Elizabeth A. DEMING, 6 Oct 1818
James M. BURK to Sally M. DEMING, 3 [--] 1834
William DIXON to Eliza J. DEMING, 23 Jul 1935
James W. DEMING to Nancy JONES [no dates]
Wiley J. DEMING to Harriet JONES, 1853
Charles W. DEMING to Harriet E. RUFFIN, 30 Sep 1866
Henry A. DEMING to Nancy SAVAGE, 2 Oct 1864
BIRTHS
Mrs Elizabeth DEMING, b.5 Nov 1801
Fisher DEMING, b.9 Oct 1789
Sally Merrick DEMING, b.21 Aug 1819
Eliza Jones DEMING, b.2 Apr 1821
James W. DEMING, b.11 Dec 1823
Charles W. DEMING, b.8 Mar 1841
Henry A. DEMING, b.24 Feb 1844

Ammi Kirby DEMING, b.1 Oct 1827
Wiley Jones DEMING, b.13 Sep 1835
Levena Rebecca DEMING, b.22 Jun 1837
DEATHS
James JONES, d.30 Oct 1832; aged 60yrs, Father of Elizabeth DEMING
Fisher DEMING, d.19 Sep 1844
Mrs Elizabeth A. Coton DEMING, d.26 Nov 1873, aged 73yrs
Ammi Kirby DEMING, d.14 Jul 1828
Levina DEMING, d. [no dates]
(Nicholas Gaillard / Gaylord File)

BALDWIN BIBLE

THE HOLY BIBLE, Published by William W. Harding, Philadelphia, PA, 1860
DEATHS
Gerorgianna BALDWIN, d.16 Sep 185[-]
Mary L. BALDWIN, d.22 Dec 186[-]
Eveanna E. WILLSON, d.3 Jan 1867
E.E. BALDWIN,Sr, d.30 Oct 1880
Brucker BALDWIN, d.13 Nov 188[-]
John A. BALDWIN, d.8 Feb 1891
Mary E. BALDWIN, d. Jun 1891
Edith W. BALDWIN, d. Sep 1906
MARRIAGES
Edward E. BALDWIN to Mary E. BLUCKER, 1 Apr 1840
Eveanna E. BALDWIN to William R. WILLSON, 20 Jun 1866
Blucker BALDWIN to Addie BATES, 9 Dec 1874
Edward J. BALDWIN to Mamie J. HOWELL, 17 Jun 1875
John A. BALDWIN to Edith A. WRIGHT, 19 Mar 1884
John V. BALDWIN to Edna BOWMAN, 25 Oct 1911

BIRTHS
E.E. BALDWIN, b.3 Jan 1817
Mary E. BLUCKER, b.27 Mar 1821
Blucker BALDWIN, b.14 Jan 1842
Eveanna E. BALDWIN, b.2 Feb 1843
Edward E. BALDWIN, Jr, b.25 Mar 1845
Georgianna BALDWIN, b.11 Jul 1854
John A. BALDWIN, b.25 Apr 1856
Mary L. BALDWIN, b.11 Nov 1864
BIRTHS
John A. BALDWIN, b.25 Apr 1855
Edith A. WRIGHT, b.17 Dec 1860
Frank E. BALDWIN, b.20 Jan 1885
John V. BALDWIN, b.12 Jul 1886
Evalena BALDWIN, b.3 Jan 1889
Edna BOWMAN, b.20 Jul 1889
Dorothy Edna BALDWIN, b.25 Apr 1915
(Nicholas Gaillard / Gaylord File; 46-13)

BEARDSLEY BIBLE

THE HOLY BIBLE, Published by Mark Bassett, London, England, 1766
Last known in the possession of Dr David Elijah Beardsley, Cedar Rapids, IA

Elijah Hubbel BEARDSLEY, b.10 Sep 1807, New York State
Matilda LEHMAN, b.18 Oct 1812, OHIO
They were married 5 Jan 1830, Montgomery Co, OH
David Elijah BEARDSLEY, b.8 Dec 1830
infant son, b.4 Jan 1833; d. same day
Laura Ann BEARDSLEY, b.12 Mar 1834
Solomon Lehman BEARDSLEY, b.23 Apr 1836

William Granville BEARDSLEY, b.28 Apr 1836
Henry Harrison BEARDSLEY, b.7 Sep 1840
Edward Cristie BEARDSLEY, b.16 Sep 1842
An Matilda BEARDSLEY, b.15 Jun 1846
(Nicholas Gaillard / Gaylord File; 8-150)

GLENNEY BIBLE I

No Title Page or Date.

Presented to Eunice Glenney by Walter 21 Jun 1865. New York

<u>BIRTHS</u>
Samuel Clark GLENNEY, b.8 Jan 1817
Eunice CAMP, b.25 Mar 1817
Walter La Clare GLENNEY, b.25 Jan 1850

<u>MARRIAGES</u>
Samuel Clark GLENNEY to Eunice CAMP, 8 Jan 1838 by Rev B. PINNEO

Also bound in this Bible are pages from a older Bible:

<u>BIRTHS</u>
David CAMP, b. May 1779
Eunice FORD, b.10 May 1792
Anna CAMP, b.2 Feb 1814
Fidelia CAMP, b.26 Jul 1815
Eunice CAMP, b.25 Mar 1817

<u>DEATHS</u>
David CAMP, d.16 May 1821, aged 42yrs
Eunice FORD, d.30 Aug 1838, aged 46yrs

GLENNEY BIBLE II

No Title page or Dates

<u>BIRTHS</u>
Samuel Clark GLENNEY, b.8 Jan 1817

Eunice CAMP, b.25 Mar 1817
Walter La Clair GLENNEY, b.25 Jan 1850
MARRIAGES
Samuel C. GLENNEY to Eunice CAMP, 8 Jan 1838, by Rev Bezaleel PINEO
Walter L.C. GLENNEY to Eva L. GREGG, 30 Jan 1873, by Rev J. Clements French
1838 114 Brooklyn Ave Brooklyn, NY 1888
8 Jan 1888 Mr & Mrs Samuel C. GLENNEY celebrated the fifieth Anniversary of their marriage
Walter Lester GLENNEY to Elizabeth Marsh LIBBEY, 22 Jan 1916, at Princeton, NJ by Rev M.W. Jacobus & S.W. Beach
DEATHS
Samuel Clark GLENNEY, d.7 Jul 1892, Plainfield, NJ; aged 75yrs 6mos
Eunice Camp GLENNEY, d.8 Oct 1901, Plainfield, NJ; aged 84yrs 5mos
Eva L. GLENNEY, d.4 Dec 1913; aged 64yrs 4mos
Walter L.C. GLENNEY, d.2, Mar 1923,Plainfield, NJ, aged 73yrs 2mos
(Nicholas Gaillard / Gaylord File; 2-247)

MILLER BIBLE

THE NEW TESTAMENT, Published by Samuel Wood & Sons, New York, 1822
FAMILY RECORDS
BIRTHS
Zedidiah MILLER, b.25 Nov 1775
Hannah MILLER, his wife, b.14 Aug 1774
Levi, their son b. 10 Dec 1798
Rhoda, b.7 Sep 1800
Daniel, b.21 May 1802

John, b.10 Oct 1803
Mary, b.12 Sep 1805
Betsey, b.18 Aug 1807
Andrew B.,b.28 Jan 1809
Hannah, b.21 Dec 1810
Jane, b.20 Dec 1812
Zedidiah, b.5 Dec 1814
Charles, b.1 Jan 1817

died 16 Jan 1889
Aunt Ann OSBORN, d.6 Feb 1889
Mary HOLLENBECK, d.7 Jan 1892
A.E. W[---]d, d. 1899
<u>DEATHS</u>
Births of Mr Jacob VELIE, b.13 Feb 1796; d.31 Mar 1847
born
first son 1 Mar 1826, d.26 Mar 1826
Martha Ann, b.14 Feb 1827, d.22 Sep 1882
John W., b.18 Mar 1829
Hannah M., b.1 Jun 1831
Alvina Jane, b.25 Apr 1833
William, b.24 Feb 1835
Mary Louise, b.26 Oct 1836, d.7 Jan 1892
Franklin, b.5 Sep 1838, d.12 Nov 1913
Alma C., b.31 May 1840, d.22 Apr 1903
Abram J., b.16 Jun 1842
George W., b.13 Jun 1844, d.29 Apr 1865
Emma A., b.31 Dec 1846, d.12 Jul 1899
Miss Mary B. MILLER, b.12 Sep 1806, d.16 Jan 1889; married 18 Jan 1825

Joshua B. HOLLENBECK, b.5 Nov 1801, d.10 Apr 1872, m.24 Nov 1825 to

Clarissa MARSH HOLLENBECK, b.9 Mar 1803, d.16 Nov 1878
David C. HOLLENBECK, b.26 Sep 1826, d.5 Feb 1865, m.23 Apr 1857
Abram HOLLENBECK, b.8 Jan 1828, d.7 Sep 1892, m.4 Mar 1859
Ann Eliza HOLLENBECK, b.13 Aug 1831, d.2 Mar 1889, m.26 Apr 1865
Maritta HOLLENBECK, b.6 Dec 1833, d.14 Feb 1834
George A. HOLLENBECK, b.14 Apr 1836; d.14 Feb 1838
Margaret HOLLENBECK, b.30 [--] 1839, d.26 Feb 1894
Emily HOLLENBECK, b.12 Jan 1843, d.16 Sep 1907, m.19 Oct 1861
Sadie Leonia VELIE, b.22 Jul 1886; m.3 Aug 1905
Franklin VELIE, b.5 Sep 1838, d.12 Nov 1913, m.19 Oct 1861
Emily HOLLENBECK VELIE, b.12 Jan 1843, d.16 Sep 1907, m.19 Oct 1861
Hattie VELIE, b.29 Feb 1863; d.3 Mar 1863
George VELIE, b.24 Sep 1865, m.12 Mar 1890
Sherman Leroy VELIE, b.9 Feb 1868, m.25 Oct 18[--]
Mary Eliza VELIE, b.18 Dec 1868, m.1 Nov 1883
Martha Ann VELIE, b.23 Mar 1873, m.19 Feb 1902
Clara VELIE, b.25 Jan 1875, m.6 Dec 1893
Grace VELIE, b.27 Jan 1877,
Emma VELIE, b.10 May 1879
Arthur VELIE, b.19 Feb 1881
Jessie VELIE, b.17 Jan 1883
(Misc Bible Records File)

REED BIBLE

THE HOLY BIBLE, Published by William W.

Harding, Philadelphia, 1865

BIRTHS

Liberty REED, b.10 Feb 1832
Angeline REED, b.1 Jan 1834
Alfred REED, b.7 Feb 1835
Josiah REED, b.23 Oct 1836
Hannah J. REED, b.13 Jun 1838
Harriet REED, b.13 Oct 1841
Malissa REED, b.30 Mar 1844
Jacob M. REED, b.25 Mar 1849
Emma Adella REED, b.16 Jul 1852

MARRIAGES

Jacob REED to Maria JONES, 26 Jan 1828
Jacob Miles REED to Sarah Ann FIELDS, 4 Feb 1869
Jacob Orville REED to Carrie THOMPSON, 24 Jun 1908, by James Wolleston Kirk

BIRTHS

Jacob REED, great grandfather b. England married to Miss WOLFORD a native of Switzerland
Casper REED, grandfather b. Lebann PA married a Miss Mary E. BAUSLOCK of Maryland
Jacob REED, father b.1782, PA married a Miss Hannah R[---] of PA
Jacob REED b. 22 May 1806
Maria JONES, b.4 Aug 1808

Children of Jacon & Maria Jones REED

Mary REED, b.29 Oct 1828
William REED, b.13 Apr 1830
(Misc Bible Records File)

HEWLETT BIBLE

THE HOLY BIBLE, Published by Edward W. Miller,

Philadelphia, no date

MARRIAGES

Archibald HEWLETT to Rose CHEASLEY, 11 Oct 1855

Alexander WHITTINGHAM to Sallie D. HEWLETT, 25 Nov 1885

William David HEWLETT to Rebecca A. BIRD

Joseph Mitchell HEWLETT to Elizabeth SLOAN, 12 Dec 1900

Joseph M. HEWLETT, Jr, son of Joseph M. & Elizabeth Sloan HEWLETT to Isabelle Springer HOLDCROFT, dau of Harry Shoemaker & Louisa Mulford CORSON HOLDCRAFT, 7 Oct 1944, by Rev Robert R. Littell

BIRTHS

Joseph David HEWLETT, b.22 Sep 1856

William Davis HEWLETT, b.22 Jan 1858

Sarah Ann Davis HEWLETT, b.12 Dec 1859

Eliza Jane HEWLETT, b.17 Feb 1862

Joseph M. HEWLETT, b.18 Jan 1865

Robert John HEWLETT, b.22 Jan 1867

Archibald HEWLETT, Sr, b.19 Sep 1829, son of Joseph & Ann MITCHELL HEWLETT

Rose CHEATLEY, wife of Archibald HEWLETT, b.2 Feb 1825, dau of William & Sarah CHEATLEY

BIRTHS

William John HEWLETT, b.11 Jan 1885

Ella Louise HEWLETT, b.11 Jul 1884

Rose HEWLETT, b.22 Aug 1889

Archibald HEWLETT, b.17 Dec 1893

Annie Willing HEWLETT, b.22 Jan 1897

The above 5 children of William Davis & Rebecca HEWLETT

Archibald Hewlette WHITTINGHAM, b.13 Aug 1887

Rebecca Jamison WHITTINGHAM, b.12 Sep 1886

The above two children of Jamison & Sarah A. David WHITTINGHAM
Joseph Mitchell HEWLETT, Jr, b.21 Sep 1901, son of Joseph Mitchell & Elizabeth Sloan HEWLETT
Joseph Mitchell HEWLETT, 3rd, b.22 Mar 1946, son of Joseph Mitchell HEWLETT, Jr & Isabelle S. HOLDCRAFT
DEATHS
Joseph Davis HEWLETT, d.3 Apr 1857
Rose Cheatley HEWLETT, d.14 Mar 1886
Archie HEWLETT, son of Wm D. & Rebecca HEWLETT, d.4 Feb 1896, aged 2yrs 1mo 17dys
Rebecca Jamison WHITTINGHAM, d.12 Sep 1886
Archibald HEWLETT, d.8 Nov 1905, aged 77yrs
Sarah Davis WHITTINGHAM, dau of Archibald & Rose HEWLETT; wife of Alexander J. WHITTINGHAM, d.3 Sep 1918
William John HEWLETT, son of William & Rebecca HEWLETT, husband of Mary, d.2 May 1916
Sarah CHEATLEY, mother of Rose Cheatly HEWLETT, d.31 Mar 1869, aged 72yrs
Alexander WHITTINGHAM, husband of Sarah D., d.17 Aug 1921
Robert John HEWLETT, son of Archibald & Rose HEWLETT, d.25 Dec 1923
Joseph HEWLETT, son of James & Eliza Alexander HEWLETT, father of Archibald HEWLETT, d.26 Apr 1877, Ireland
Annie William HEWLETT, dau of Wm & Rebecca HEWLETT, d.4 Aug 1932
William Davis HEWLETT, son of Alexander & Rose HEWLETT, d.15 Nov 1935
Joseph Mitchell HEWLETT, son of Archibald & Rose HEWLETT, d.18 Oct 1954, aged 89yrs

Elizabeth SLOAN HEWLETT, dau of Wm & Isabella SLOAN, d.9 Jan 1960, aged 82yrs
(Misc Bible Records File)

WORK BIBLE

THE HOLY BIBLE, Published by Brattleboro Typographic Company; Brattleboro, VT, 1840. A transcript from the original in the possession of Mrs George Armistead Work, II, Santa Cruz, CA.

Samuel, WORK, Sr; b.25 Nov 1772; d.4 Mar 1818
Anna PIGMAN, b.14 Jan 1781; d. Oct [15 Oct 1846, Hinds Co, MS]
they married 13 Jan 1801
George WORK, b.12 Nov 1801; d. c.1876
Juliet WORK, b.11 Sep 1803; d.17 Nov 1805
John WORK, b.13 May 1805
Sally WORK, b.10 May 1807
Joseph WORK, b.28 Apr 1809
Anna WORK, b.15 Apr 1813
Thomas WORK, b.11 Oct 1815, d. Oct 1842
Saml WORK, Jr, b.5 Jun 1818; d.10 Jun 1819

MARRIAGES

Maria MOREHEAD to George WORK, 26 Oct 1831
Charles WORK to Octavia SMITH, c.1868
George A. WORK to Lydia HERRON, 18 Dec 1870
Andrew Jackson WORK, b.6 Apr 1833; d.20 Sep 1836
Geo. Holt WORK, b.31 Mar 1836; d.28 Sep 1836
Geo Armistead WORK, b.11 Apr 1838; d.2 Apr 1892
Charles Saml WORK, b.31 Dec 1840; d. c1875
James Clayton WORK, b.23 Feb 1844; d. 3 Nov 1846
Maria WORK, b.27 Oct 1799; d.16 Aug 1862
Lydia WORK, b.---; d.31 Jan 1894

Annie M. WORK, b.10 Oct 1871
Maria WORK, b.1 Sep 1874
Mattie Octavia WORK, b.30 Mar 1876; d.26 Aug 1895
Charlie A. WORK, b.28 Mar 1879; d.24 Jul 1884
Kate Clark WORK, b.12 Feb 1882
Lillie Belle WORK, b.2 Jul 1884
George Armistead WORK, Jr; b.16 Mar 1889
George Armistead WORK married to Geraldine GRAHAM, 16 Mar 1921
Geo Armistead WORK, b.10 Nov 1922
Sally Jane WORK, b.14 Mar 1926
Martha Graham WORK, b.31 Oct 1927
Katherine Ruth WORK, b.26 Oct 1936
(Misc Bible Records File)

JORDAN BIBLE

No Title page or Dates

BIRTHS

William JORDAN, son of John & Mary JORDAN; b.17 Dec 1776; and his brother a twin still born.
Josiah William JORDAN, son of William & Martha JORDAN, b.1 Sep 1801
William Francis JORDAN, son of Josiah William & Frances M. JORDAN, b.1 Feb 1849
Sarah Elizabeth JOHNSON, b.22 Sep 1859
Ella Imogene JORDAN, b.26 Feb 1887
Sarah Elizabeth JORDAN, b.13 Feb 1888

MARRIAGES

William JORDAN, son of John JORDAN to Martha BIDGOOD, m.23 Dec 1797
Josiah W. JORDAN, son of William JORDAN to Frances M.

DAWLEY, dau of Rev James DAWLEY, m.8 Feb 1827, by Rev Dr. Ducasha
William Francis JORDAN to Sarah Elizabeth JOHNSON. m.31 Mar 1886, St John's Episcopal Church, Nansemond Co, VA, by Rev Douglass Hooff.
DEATHS
Martha JORDAN, wife of William JORDAN, d.20 Oct 1805
William JORDAN, d.6 Jan 1814
Josiah W. JORDAN, son of William JORDAN, d.8 Jan 1852
Frances Dawley JORDAN, wife of Josiah W. JORDAN, d.12 Oct 1855
William Fancis JORDAN, son of Josiah W. & Frances M. JORDAN,d.28 Apr 1903
Sarah Elizabeth Johnson JORDAN, d.17 Oct 1938
(Mics Bible Record File)

PRICE BIBLE

HOLY BIBLE, Published by John E. Potter and Company, Philadelphia, no date
MARRIAGES
Geo W. PRICE to Alice M. M. HADDEN, 25 Apr 1866
Wm N. PRICE to Minnie SCHURMAN, 7 Mar 1888
Jennie E. PRICE to Nelson T. CUMMINGS, 7 Jun 1893
Frank L. PRICE to Edith L. FREELAND, 31 Dec 1902
Elsie F. PRICE to Thomas Robert ELLIOTT, 19 Sep 1927
Charles D. PRICE to Martha ROSE, 25 Dec 1940
Elaine Ruth ELLIOTT to Edsall Reilly JOHNSTON, 1 Sep 1956
Charles Douglas PRICE, Jr to Carolyn CAMOLLI, 4 Dec 1871
DEATHS
George W. PRICE, d.17 Sep 1877
Alice M.M. PRICE, d.3 May 1887

Jennie Price CUMMINGS, d.1926
Frank Leslie PRICE, d.15 Jul 1939
Charles Douglass PRICE, d.19 Mar 1943
BIRTHS
George W. PRICE, b.17 Sep 1843
William N. PRICE, b.24 Jan 1867
Frank Leslie PRICE, b.25 Oct 1874
Charles D. PRICE, b.29 Mar 1906
Charles Douglas PRICE,Jr, b.11 May 1942
Erik Kelly PRICE, b.7 Mar 1978
Alice M.M. HADDEN, b.22 Sep 1848
Jennie L. PRICE, b.16 Jul 1871
Elsie F. PRICE, b.22 Oct 1903
Elaine Ruth ELLIOTT, b.7 Aug 1934
Lauren Jean JOHNSTON, b.30 Jan 1958
Scott Richard JOHNSTON, b.3 Jul 1960
Gregg Elliott JOHNSTON, b.13 May 1962
(Etinne Gayneau / Gano File)

WOODARD BIBLE

No Title Page or dates The Bible in 1981 in possession of Mrs D. Gracelon Mitchell, New Harbor, ME.
FAMILY RECORDS
MARRIAGES
William WOODARD to Sarah WHITNEY, 1 Jan 1812
Cosea FULLER to Harriet W. WOODARD, 4 Jun 1840
Joseph [-] GRACELON to Jane [-] WOODARD, 28 Jan 1841
William WOODARD to Betsy CLOUCH, 19 Oct 1845
Gardner F. WOODARD to Mary D. GRAFFAM, 26 Oct 1858
Moses WOODARD to Almira MARICK, Jun 1837
Nathaniel C. WOODARD to Ann M. WASHBURN, 11 Dec 1844
Abram WOODARD to Jane FULLER, 15 Jun 1844

Frances G. GODFREY to Mary G. WOODARD, 8 Sep 1849
Daniel M. GRACELON to Susan E.W. WOODARD, 1 Jan 1866
DEATHS
William WOODARD, d.22 Oct 1822
Harriet W. FULLER, d.23 Feb 1843
Sarah WOODARD, d.20 Feb 1845
Mary E. GODFRY, d.11 Jan 1852
Abner WOODARD, d.18 Dec 1852
Nathan C. WOODARD, d.17 Jan 1868
Gardner F. WOODARD, 18 Dec 1868
Betsey WOODARD, d.17 Dec 1873
William WOODARD, d.28 Jan 1880
Abram WOODARD, d.24 May 1876
Jane S. GRACELON, d.20 Jul 1896
John WOODARD, d.1817; aged 72
Mary WOODARD, d. 1832; aged 80
Abram WHITNEY, d. 1831; aged 79
Apphia WHITNEY, d. 1833; aged 73
Willie W. GRACELON, d.10 Nov 1873
Dannie G. GRACELON, d.1 Nov 1873
Sadie GRACELON, d.18 May 1882
Daniel M. GRACELON, d.9 May 1912
(Pierre Gracelon File)

HALL BIBLE

No Title page or date, original owned by Frances Hall Kropp, Signal Mountain, TN
MARRIAGES
Wm M. HALL to Sarah J. SIMMONS, 1850
Andrew [-] MONTGOMERY to Susan L. DIXON, 21 May 1851
Guion Q. HALL to M. Kate MONTGOMERY, 27 Oct 1875,

Madison Co, MS
William M. HALL to Isabel U. HARRIS, 23 May 1900, Jackson, MS
Their Children:
Frances U. HALL, b.21 Jun 1901
William G. HALL, b.4 May 1903

Frances U. HALL to W. Kirth KRAPP, 10 May 1923
Wm Guion HALL to Martha FITSGERALD, 15 Oct 1928
BIRTHS
Wm M. HALL, b.17 Jul 1809, Gallatin, TN; d.9 Nov 1882, [----] MS
Sarah J. (Simmons) HALL, b.3 Nov 1831; d.2 Jun 1861
Andrew J. MONTGOMERY, b.5 Sep 1817, Jefferson Co, MS
Susan L. (Dixion) MONTGOMERY, b.16 Jul 1832, Jefferson Co, MS
Guion Q. HALL, b.23 Jan 1851, Leuke Co, MS
M. Kate (Montgomery) HALL, b.15 Feb 1852, Madison Co, TN
Wm Montgomery HALL, b.6 Aug 1876, Carthage, MS
Ethel Barksdale HALL, b.9 Feb 1880, Carthage, MS (Hugh Ethel - crossed out)
(Peter Garrard File)

SMITH / DIAMOND BIBLE

NEW TESTAMENT, Published by H. & E. Phinney, Cooperstown, NY, 1828
Original in possession of Martin Diamond, Frankenmuth, MI
FAMILY RECORDS
BIRTHS
Cornelius SMITH, the father of Darius SMITH, b.in Taunton, Massatucks [sic] Bay and my Mother, Dorcas LINCOLN, was

b. in the same place. Darius SMITH, the 3rd son of Cornelius SMITH, was b. 6 Jan 1762. Darius SMITH'S Children are:
Mercy SMITH, b.9 Apr 1789
Darius Champion SMITH, b.9 Sep 1794
Isaac SMITH, b.15 Mar 1796
Lydea SMITH, b.6 Sep 1798
Sarah SMITH, b.18 Jan 1800
child b.6 Aug 1802
Claudia SMITH, b.20 Jul 1804
Catherine SMITH, b.27 Mar 1809
[----] can not read DIAMOND, b.10 Nov 182-
Almny DIAMOND, b.19 Apr 1823
Ashford DIAMOND, b.15 Jan 1825
Mary Ann DIAMOND, b.12 Feb 1827
Hiram G. DIAMOND, b.27 Jan 1827
Elizabeth DIAMOND, b.15 Oct 1830
RoxSally DIAMOND, 9 Jun 1832
Emily Jane DIAMOND, b.15 Feb 1834
Clarry Marie DIAMOND, b.27 Dec 1835
William H. DIAMOND, b.31 Aug 1837
Drias C. DIAMOND, b.31 Jul 1839
Catherine DIAMOND, 20 Nov 1841

DEATHS

Drias SMITH, d. Nov 1843
Robert DIAMOND, d.2 Mar 1869
Howard O. DIAMOND, d.1 Sep 1939
Frank DIAMOND, d.22 May 1870
Darius C. DIAMOND, d.21 Oct 1906
Sophia SMITH, d.27 Mar 1823
Sophia DIAMOND, d.12 Dec 1856
[----] can not read
Hiram G. DIAMOND, d.22 Aug 186-

BIRTHS

Robert DIAMOND, b.[--] May 2800
Harriet Ann [---], b.4 Nov 1845
Alice M. DIAMOND, b. [-] Oct 1907
Martin A. DIAMOND, b.9 Dec 1908
Harry L. DIAMOND, b.24 Jul 1910
Walter E. DIAMOND, b.19 Mar 1913
Ulysses G. DIAMOND, b.31 Jan 1867
Frank DIAMOND, b.20 Mar 1864
Abigail DIAMOND, b.[--] Mar [----]
John W. DIAMOND, b.22 Aug 1870
Frederic M. DIAMOND, b.6 May 1875
William S. DIAMOND, b.12 Oct 1882
MARRIAGES
Lucinday DIAMOND to Jacob J. LOYD, 4 Feb 1845
Almny DIAMOND to Lulu F. FRY, 3 Jun 1845
Ashford DIAMOND to Clasa Ann MOON, 14 Sep 1847
Thomas CARR to Mary Ann DIAMOND, [-] Sep 1849
[----] GREEN to Elizabeth DIAMOND, 4 Nov 1849
(David Gaschet File)

GASTON BIBLE

No Title page or date

FAMILY RECORD
Arthur B. GASTON, b.7 Dec 1843, Belfast, Allegany Co, PA
Hannah Jane McMASTER, b.9 Apr 1844, E. Fallowfield, Crawford Co, PA; d.7 Jan 1911

They were married 6 Nov 1866 by Rev H.H. Hervey, at Hartstown, PA

CHILDREN:
Winnie GASTON, b.24 Feb 1868
Sarah Phylinda GASTON, b.10 Oct 1869
James Edward GASTON, b.7 Jul 1874, Greenville, PA

Donald Jean GASTON, b.18 Sep 1879, Atlantic, PA; d.9 Sep 1880
Arthur Harold GASTON, b.10 Jun 1882, d.13 Feb 1945
Mattie Gertrude GASTON, b.13 May 1884, Utica, PA
(Jean Gaston File)

MARTIN BIBLE

HOLY BIBLE, published by Alvin J. Johnson & Son, New York, 1868

BIRTHS
Marshall Presley MARTIN, b.31 Jul 1847
Cora Belle MARTIN, b.3 Jul 1852
Ray Wilson MARTIN, b.25 Aug 1875
William Herbert MARTIN, b.8 Nov 1877
Clogett M. MARTIN, b.14 Feb 1883
John Marshall MARTIN, b.25 Oct 1885
Lawrence Walker MARTIN, b.11 Oct 1887
Alberta MARTIN, b.9 Dec 1889
Annie S. MARTIN, b.15 Feb 1857

MARRIAGES
Marshall P. MARTIN to Cora B. WILSON, 10 Dec 1873
M.G. MARTIN to Annie S. CLOGETT, 14 Oct 1880, Centerville
M.P. MARTIN to Mrs Elma HAWKINS, b. Aug 1894
Alberta MARTIN to Kintow G. KITTRELL, Jr, 1 Jun 1910
Walker Lawrence MARTIN to Myra NASH, 14 Oct 191[-], Union City, TN
John Marahall MARTIN to Luella Simonton HEFLEY, 1 Sep 1915, Jackson, TN
Clagett M. MARTIN to Ruth LaVonia LONG, 10 Jun 1920, Nashville, TN
Ray W. MARTIN to Susan Ida CARPINTON (nee

THOMPSON), 27 Dec 1926, divorced Tampa, FL 10 Nov 1932

DEATHS

Cora Belle MARTIN, d.10 Sep 1878
William Herbert MARTIN, d.6 Apr 18[--]
Annie S. MARTIN, d.21 Sep 1892, bur Centerville, TN
Marshall P. MARTIN, d.22 Jul 1896
Roy Wilson MARTIN, d.7 Jan 1942, San Antonio, TX
Hinton Greene KITTRELL,Jr, d.10 Feb 1937
Virginia Mae KITTRELL, d.15 Mar 1925
Myrah Nash MARTIN, d.23 Apr 1949
Ruth Long MARTIN, d.15 Jun 1953
Clogett M. MARTIN, d.30 Aug 1963
Walter L. MARTIN, d. Nov 1971
Luella Hefley MARTIN, d.16 Jul 1973
(Jean Gaston File)

WINSLOW BIBLE

No Title Page or Dates, Transcript lists original in possession of Velma Werden Scott. The bible published in New York 1866

John WINSLOW, son of John WINSLOW & Esther, his wife, b.9 Jul 1808
Mary SMITHSON, dau of Malici SMITHSON & Penelopy, his wife, b.6 Mar 1808
John and Mary married 7 Oct 1828
CHILDREN:
Ellen WINSLOW, b.8 Sep 1829
Jordan WINSLOW, b.12 Mar 1831
Mary WINSLOW, b.3 Jan 1836
Esther WINSLOW, b.29May 1838
Elizabeth WINSLOW, b.12 Apr 1840
Doctrin WINSLOW, b.23 Aug 1843

Hariet WINSLOW, b.12 Dec 1845
Margaret WINSLOW, b.31 Mar 1848

Lydia Ann SWAN, dau of Thomas & Esther SWAN, b.9 Sep 1860
(Jean Gaston File)

GIBERT BIBLE

No Title Page or Dates

MARRIAGES

John Lewis GIBERT to Jane [----] m. 16 May 1810
William J. HOUSTON to Drusella GIBERT m. 24 Jan 1832
William A. GRIFFITH to Amelia GIBERT m. 9 Apr 1839
William J. D[---] to Caroline Jane GIBERT m.30 May 1841
Joseph NOBLE to Adeline Harriet GIBERT m.19 Jan 1843
Benjamin E. [---] to Sarah Jane R[--] m.26 May 1846

BIRTHS

John L. GIBERT, b.1 Dec 1781
Jane Moragen [?], b.9 Jun 1783
Susan Amelia GIBERT, b.[--] Sep 1811
Benjamin Elijah GIBERT, b.[--] Jan 1813
Elizabeth Drusella GIBERT, b.28 Sep 1814
Gidean John GIBERT, b.1 Dec 1816
Lucy Dorcus GIBERT, b.14 Mar 181[-]
Caroline Jane GIBERT, b.25 Jan 1821
Harriet Adeline GIBERT, b.18 Jan 1823

DEATHS

John L. GIBERT, d.13 Nov [----]
Lucy Dorcus GIBERT, d.5 Nov 1819
Joseph NOBLE, d.26 Nov 1843
Adaline H. NOBLE, d.6 Apr 1845
Gideon John GIBERT, d.5 Nov 1845
(Pierre Gibert File)

HOUSTON BIBLE

THE HOLY BIBLE, Published by American Bible Society, New York, 1843

MARRIAGES

William J. HOUSTON to Elizabeth Drusilla GIBERT, m.24 Jan 1832
Thomas F. HOUSTON to Lou Anna CARDES, m.18 Apr 1904
Robert J. LAWSON to Lucy Drusilla HOUSTON, 15 May 1930
Lou Anna CORDES HOUSTON, d.21 Jan 1955
Elizabeth HOUSTON, d.3 Mar 1937
Marshall L. HOUSTON, d.8 May 1944
Mrs P.N., HOUSTON, d. 3 Mar 1940
Mrs Lewis B. HOUSTON, d. Nov 1944

BIRTHS

Thomas F. HOUSTON, b.29 Mar 1853
Thams Francis HOUSTON, b.29 Mar 1853; d.15 Dec 1921
L.L. HOUSTON, d.1 Jan 1892
Mattie HOUSTON, d.17 May 189[-]
Tommie F,. HOUSTON, b.4 Mar 1907
Lucy D. HOURTON, b.20 Sep 1909
Lucius C. HOUSTON, b.16 Nov 1913
Anna F. HOUSTON, b.18 Aug 1920

BIRTHS

Susan Jane HOUSTON, b.7 Jan 1833
John Lowellen HOUSTON, b.12 Sep 1834
Mary Elizabeth HOUSTON, b.16 Jan 1836
William Henry HOUSTON, b.26 Nov 1837
Caroline Noble HOUSTON, b.27 Jun 1840
Cornelia A[---] HOUSTON, b.5 Mar 1842
James Lewis HOUSTON, b.22 Jun 1844

Alexander Clark HOUSTON, b.18 Jul 1846
George Pickens HOUSTON, b. Sep 1848
Sophia Lee HOUSTON, b.13 Apr 18[--]; d.1 Jan 1892
<u>DEATHS</u>
G.P. HOUSTON, d.[-] Jan 1923
Maurice HOUSTON, d.30 Apr 1937
Mrs G.P. HOUSTON, d.6 Sep 1927
Caroline N. HOUSTON, d.2 Sep 1851
William H. HOUSTON, d.27 Jul 1858
John L. HOUSTON, d.14 Jun 1862
William J. HOUSTON, d.24 Feb 1863
Mrs E.D. HOUSTON, d.20 Nov 1879
S.J. HOUSTON, d.16 Dec 1879
J.L. HOUSTON, d.27 Feb 18[-]6Alexander Clark, d. May 1907
Mary E. HOUSTON, d.11 Apr 1913
Thomas F. HOUSTON, d.15 Dec 1921
(Pierre Gibert File / 6-210)

SWEET BIBLE
No Title Page or Date
FAMILY RECORDS
<u>DEATHS</u>
Mary An SWEET, d.when 33 days old
DeBorah BENTON, wife of James BENTON, d.20 Feb 1858
David Kefavor LARMER, d.13 Sep 1862
Susan M. LARIMER, d.18 May 1889
Thomas SWEET, d.29 JUn 1862
Elizabeth SWEET, d.2 Feb 1875
J[---] SWEET, d.13 Oct 1870
Elizabeth [---]wife of [---] Sweet, [-------]
E.J. Sweet, wife / Henry SWEET, 15 Feb (page torm)

(Daniel Giraud)

GANONG BIBLE

No Title Page or Date

FAMILY RECORD

<u>BIRTHS</u>

Lewis C. GANONG, b.9 Dec 1809
Mary Z. KNIFFIN, b.23 Jul 1800
Belinda & Cmmalinda GANONG, b.8 Sep 1833; d.10 Oct
Kniffin J. GANONG, b.15 Sep 1836; d.10 Oct 1910
Newman C. GANONG, b.29 Sep 1840; d.20 Mar 1863
Irene WORDEN, b.27 Nov 1855
Laura A. SMITH, b.22 Dec 1834
Jane Ann REYNOLDS, b.16 Feb 1838; d.20 Oct 1919
Ely BAILEY, b.18 Aug 1838
George RUSCO, b.27 Jul 1831
Newman M. WORDEN, b.3 May 1832; d.16 Dec 1899
Francis J. GANONG, b.13 Nov 1858
Addison GANONG, b.3 Mar 1861
Mary E. KNIFFIN, b.5 Dec 1840
Sarah J. KNIFFIN, b.29 Jan 1842
Newman GANONG, 2nd, b.7 Mar 1863
Malvina GANONG, b.9 Jul 1865
John Franklin CROFT, b.14 Oct 1861; d.10 Oct 1925
Letha May CROFT, b.6 Oct 1895; d.30 May 1902
Lucille Jane CROFT, b.10 Jun 1898
Miriaum Elda CROFT, b.18 Sep 1900
Irnia Jean CROFT, b.18 Sep 1900

<u>MARRIAGES</u>

Lewis C. GANONG to Mary Z. KNIFFIN, 5 Jan 1831
George RUSCOE to Belinda GANONG, 31 Dec 1850
Newman M. WORDEN to Emmalinda GANONG, 1 Jun 1853

Kniffin J. GANONG to Jane Ann REYNOLDS, 24 Dec 1857
Ely BAILEY to Laura A. SMITH, 13 Jan 1859
Elizes H. GANONG to Helen PECK, 29 May 1882
John Franklin CROFT to Malvina Ann GANONG, 2 Sep 1891

BIRTHS

Jereniah GANONG, Sr, b.8 Mar 1779
Hannah CARVER, b.8 May 1785
Rachal GANONG, b.15 Apr 1813
Phebe M. GANONG, b.19 Apr 1815; d.25 [--] 1900
Addison [-] GANONG, b.15 Dec 1817; d. [-----]
Elezer H. GANONG, b.11 Dec 1821
Maranda J. GANONG, b.1 Feb 1828
Jeremiah GANONG, Sr, 15 Aug 1740
Zeviah KELLOGG, b.6 Sep 1737
Hellen PECK, b.15 Jul 1825
Belinda RUSCOE, b.10 Oct 1862
Timothy CARVER, b.30 Oct 1753
Phebe BALDWIN, b.3 Oct 1755
Hannah BALDWIN, b.22 Sep 1758
Jonatha CARVER, b.21 Jul 1777
Mary CARVER, b.3 Dec 1778
Rebecca CARVER, b.29 Jan 1780
James CARVER, b.26 Sep 1787
Eliza CARVER, b.18 Jan 1783
Mahitable CARVER, b.8 Dec 1786
Elezer CARVER, b.28 Nov 1788
Barabus CARVER, b.7 Mar 1790
Sally CARVER, b.9 Aug 1791
John CARVER, b.24 Oct 1792
Lewis CARVER, b.20 Nov 1794
Zilla CARVER, b.13 Dec 1795
Rachel CARVER, b.5 Feb 1797
Daniel CARVER, b.3 Aug 1799

Henry CARVER, b.15 Feb 1804
DEATHS
Hester KNIFFIN, wife of John KNIFFIN, d.12 Feb 1831
In Memory of the wife of Silvenus KNIFFIN, d.16 Jan 1837
Sylvernus KNIFFIN, d.24 Aug 1850
Rachel GANONG, d.11 Oct 1814
Maeanda A. GANONG, d.8 Aug 1838
Belinda, wife of George RUSCOE, d.11 Oct 1862
Newman C. GANONG, d.20 Mar 1863, at Harpers Ferry, aged 22yrs 5mos 20dys
Jeremiah GANONG, SR; d.15 May 1827
Zeviah GANONG, d.5 Jun 1827
Jeremiah GANONG, Jr, d.21 Aug 1863
Jonathan CARVER, d.22 Jan 1783
Phebe CARVER, d.14 Mar 1798
Mary CARVER, d.5 Aug 1799
Rachel CARVER, d.12 Jul 1810
Rebecca PINCKNEY, d.15 Mar 1821
Hannes CARVER, d.20 Aug 1825
Timothy CARVER, d.3 Nov 1825
James CARVER, d.2 Jul 1837
Sally LONGWELL, d.15 Jul 1848
Elijah CARVER, d.14 Jul 1854
Lewis CARVER, d.12 Sep 1861
Daniel CARVER, d.5 Oct 1866
Mahitable LONGWELL, d.27 Feb 1869
Hannah CARVER [-----]
Jeremiah GANONG, d.30 Aug 1869
John CARVER, d.11 Mar 1871
Henry CARVER, d.19 Aug 1872
Elezer CARVER, d.21 Oct 1873
Barnabus CARVER, d.16 Jun 1876
Mary Z., wife of Lewis C. GANONG, d.25 Aug 1876

Zilla LONGWELL, d.4 Mar 1880
Lewis C. GANONG, d.27 Aug 1883
Addison GANONG, d.25 Jun 1900
(Jean Guenon File / 12-21)

DELLIBER BIBLE

HOLY BIBLE / POLYGLOTT BIBLE; published by Case, Tiffany & Burnham, Hartford, 1844

FAMILY RECORDS

MARRIAGES

Joseph DELLIBER to Levinia RICHARDSON, 4 May 1820
Lavinia DELLIBER to Lorenzo HAMILTON, 14 Mar 1847
Joseph DELLIBER, Jr to Mary Jane HURLBURT, 9 May 1843; dau of Thomas HURLBURT, married at Holland Patant, NY
Jos DELLIBER, Jr to Caroline S. RUST, 29 Dec 1852
Chas H. DELLIBER to Martha J. HENNION, 24 Apr 1889
Emma Hurlburt DELLIBER to George Clifford PRIME, 12 Jan 1910
Liela Jane DELLIBER to Edward Brailsford MAXWELL, 21 Jul 1920, Atlanta, GA; div 1930
Leila DELLIBER to Thomas E. WARREN, 5 Aug 1932, Fort Landerdale, FL
Dorothy PRIME to Edward MAXWELL, 5 Nov 1931, Gretman, AL

BIRTHS

Joseph DELLIBER, b.4 Oct 1796
Levinia RICHARDSON, b.8 Dec 1797
Joseph DELLIBER, Jr, b.25 Feb 1821
Henry DELLIBER, b.9 Feb 1823
Levinia DELLIBER, b.15 Jan 1825
Henry DELLIBER, 2nd, b.8 Jun 1830

Charles Henry DELLIBER, b.19 Feb 1844
Lorenzo HAMILTON, b.12 Dec 1818
Caroline H. RUST, b.4 Apr 1830
infant son, 25 Oct 1853
Martha J. HENNION, b.4 Sep 1858 {1857}
Emma H. DELLIBER, b.18 Aug 1893
Loila W. DELLIBER, b.11 Oct 1898
Dorothy Jean PRIME, b.23 Feb 1911
Edw B. MAXWELL, b.2 Jul 1894 Bainbridge, GA; son of Edw H. & Martha DONALDSON MAXWELL
Edalee Anne MAXWELL, b.9 Sep 1929
Delliber Arnold MAXWELL, b.11 Mar 1936
Delliber Russell MAXWELL, b.22 Dec 1962

DEATHS

Henry DELLIBER, d.29 Dec 1825
Martha DELLIBER, wife of [---], d.10 May 1829
Henry DELLIBER, 2nd; d.10 Dec 1831
Mary Jane, 1st wife of Joseph, d.6 Oct 1851
Infant son, d.26 Oct 1853
David DELLIBER, d.15 Apr 1859
Lavinia DELLIBER, d.6 Jul 1860
Lorenzo HAMILTON, d.20 Jul 1868, Sacramento, CA; remains carried around Cape Horn burial in [--]
Joseph DELLIBER,Sr, d.27 Oct 1876, aged 74yrs
Joseph DELLIBER, Jr, d.26 Mar 1888, aged 67yrs
Caroline Rust DELLIBER, d.23 May 1898, aged 69yrs
Charles Henry DELLIBER, d.20 Apr 1921, aged 77yrs
Martha Hennion DELLIBER, d.6 Aug 1941, Miami, Fl; bur.Paterson NJ
Edalee Anne MAXWELL, d.5 Sep 1941, Paterson, NJ
Thomas WARREN, d.29 Jan 1939, Miami, Fl
Martha J. Hennion DELLIBER, d.6 Aug 1941
Edalee Anne MAXWELL, d.5 Sep 1941

Edward B. MAXWELL, d.17 Jul 1954
(Jean Guenon File / 9-178)

KING BIBLE

No Title Page or Date

DEATHS

Mary KING, wife of M.L. KING, d.6 Nov 1873, aged 65yrs, 9mos,23dys
Leroy C. KING, d.11 Jul 1882, aged 54yrs 8mos 3dys
Miles D. KING, d.5 Jul 1894, aged 95yrs 3mos 1dy
Margaret KING, dau of U.M. & Annie KING, d.24 Aug 1902, aged 1yr 6mos 8dys
Charles Marion KING, son of L.C. & E.C. DAVIS, d.18 Oct 1917, St Lukes Hospital, Richmond, VA; aged 63yrs 3mos Bur Buckingham Co Family Grave Yard
Ellen M. KING, wife of L.C. KING, d.9 Nov 1922, aged 77yrs 7mos
Mattie Lee DAVIS, widow of Edward Carter DAVIS, d.12 Jun 1943, Richmond, VA; bur Riverview Cemetery

MEMORANDA

Clayton KING, son of W.M. & Annie KING, b.22 Jul 1898
Mary Jane DAVIS, dau of E.A. & Mattie DAVIS, b.22 Jun 1899
James Miles KING, son of W.M. & Annie KING, b.17 Mar 1900
Margret KING, dau of W. M. & Annie KING, b.16 Feb 1901
William M. KING, son of W.M. & Annie KING, b. Jun
Leroy King DAVIS, son of E.C. & Mattie DAVIS, b.17 Apr 1905
Margret Lucile DAVIS, dau of E.C. & Mattie DAVIS, b.13 Apr 1911
(Daniel Guerrant File)

MOSLEY BIBLE

THE HOLY BIBLE, Published by Henry Altemus, Philadelphia, PA, 1888

MARRIAGE CERTIFICATE

Alex C. MOSLEY to Martha E. RITTENHOUSE, 11 Jan 1882 at Ostrander, by Jos W. Scott, Baptist Minister. (Delaware Co, OH)

MARRIAGES

John A. MOSELEY to Mary Jane WINGFIELD, 20 Jul 1836
Geo MOSELEY to Louisa J. SCOTT, 1 Jan 1863
Chas B. MOSELEY to Allice B. HEATH, 15 Aug 1884
Claude T. MOSELEY to Edna Hautine MOORE, Jun 1907
Orien B. MOSELEY to Joe B. THOMAS, 2 Nov 1909
Grandison Mc MOSELEY to Hilder C. STAIRS, 3 Nov 1910
Hamilton W. RITTENHOUSE to Sallie J. ELSOM, 3 Nov 1859, Albermarle Co, VA

DEATHS

Mary J. MOSELEY, wife of John A. MOSELEY, d.17 Mar 1857, Amhurst Co, VA
John A. MOSELEY, d.11 May 1879
Sallie S. RITTENHOUSE, wife of Hamilton W. RITTENHOUSE, d.24 Dec 1884, Delaware Co, OH
Hamilton W. RITTENHOUSE, d.20 Mar 1917, Delaware Co, OH

BIRTHS

John A. MOSELEY, b.17 Nov 1811
Mary J. WINGFIELD, b.26 Feb 1817
Hamilton W. RITTENHOUSE, b.23 Jan 1834, Albemarle Co, VA
Sallie J. ELSOM, b.8 Mar 1842, Albemarle Co, VA
Alexander C., son of John A & Mary J. MOSELEY, b.11

May 1856, Amhurst Co, VA
M. Eve, dau of Hamilton W. & Sallie J. RITTENHOUSE, b.7 Feb 1864, Delaware Co, OH
Infant son of Alex C. & M.Eva MOSELEY, b.11 Mar 1885
Mary Adna, b.28 Apr 1886
Frank Wrothwill, b.9 Jan 1889
Marion Lester, b.27 Mar 1891
Nina Lillian, b.20 Feb 1893
Paul J., b.26 Apr 1896, Delaware Co, OH
Cecil E., b.2 Apr 1898, Union Co, OH
John R., b.10 Sep 1900, Union Co
Ralph B., B. 18 Jan 1903, Union Co.
(Daniel Guerrant File)

GUERRANT BIBLE
No Title Page or Date

CERTIFICATE
Mr William Gibson GUERRANT of Montgomery Co, VA to Bettie Guerrant ROBINSON of Nicholas Co, WV, married 5 Sep 1867 at Pilot, Montgomery Co, VA by Rev Charles A. Mills
BIRTHS
Mary Louisa ROBINSON, 14 Feb 1860
Joseph Vrgle ROBINSON, 21 Nov 1861
Willie Miller GUERRANT, first dau of Wm G. & Bettie R. GUERRANT, b.8 Jun 1868, d.1 Feb 1956
Hugh Capet GUERRANT, b.22 Jan 1870
Constance Lucy GUERRANT, b.23 Feb 1871, d.16 Jul 1953
Edward Heath GUERRANT, b.17 Apr 1873
John Gibson GUERRANT, b.20 Jan 1875
Sallie Adaline GUERRANT, b.26 Sep 1876; d. Jan 1954
William Heath Jones MILLER, b.6 Jun 1806, Goochland Co,

VA
Mary Joanna MILLER, nee GUERRANT, b.17 Nov 1805, Goochland Co, VA
Constance Guerrant RIGBY, b.29 Sep 1898
Elizabeth Miller RIGBY, b.4 Mar 1900
Sarah Mansfield RIGBY, b.24 Apr 1901
James RIGBY,III, b.28 May 1902
William Guerrant RIGBY, b.18 Jul 1904
Mary Nuth BIGBY, b.26 Jun 1908
John Gibson GUERRANT, Jr, b. Mar 1903
Ellen Armistead GUERRANT, b.19 Aug 1905
<u>DEATHS</u>
Edward Heath GUERRANT, drowned 21 Mar 1875, Pilot, VA
William Heath Jones MILLER, d.18 Feb 1883, Pilot, VA
Mary Joanna MILLER, d.4 Jan 1886, Pilot, VA
John R. GUERRANT, b.2 Apr 1794 near New Canton, Buckingham Co, VA; d.30 Nov 1858, Ash Grove, Franklin Co, VA
Octavia A. GIBSON, b.16 Oct 1813, Pilot, VA; d.11 Oct 1858, Ash Grove, VA; she married John R. GUERRANT
Wm G.,(Gibson), b.19 Feb 1829
P.M.,(Peter Moss), b.4 Jul 1830
E.T., (Elizabeth Tallioferro), b.
married P.H. CALLAWAY at Ash Grove & had two daus:
Elis Virginia, b.1 Feb 1849; d.11 May 1861 at Montgomery Co, Va
(Daniel Guerrant File)

SHUTE BIBLE

THE HOLY BIBLE, published by Jesper Harding & Son, 1859
FAMILY RECORDS

BIRTHS

Peter SHUTE, husband of Harrietta H. BANTA, b.17 Feb 1816
Harrietta H. BANTA, wife of Peter SHUTE, b.14 Aug 1821
Peter W. SHUTE, b.24 Oct 1843
George Niles SHUTE, b.19 Feb 1845; d, young
Harriet Amelia SHUTE, b.29 Jan 1847
Elisha Morgan SHUTE, b.21 Jun 1849
Josephine SHUTE, b.23 Nov 1851
Washington Irving SHUTE, b.2 Oct 1853; d. young
Elvira Ann SHUTE, b.4 Oct 1855
Emma Louisa SHUTE, b.8 Mar 1858
Martha Washington SHUTE, b.2 Dec 1859
Ella [---] Shute, b.[--] Mar 1862
Ella Augusta SHUTE, b.14 Mar 1862

BIRTHS

Charles E. SHUTE, son of Elisah M. & Adelia Kolyer SHUTE, b.15 Oct 1876
Henry Clay SHUTE, b.23 Jul 1878
Clarence SHUTE, b.,7 Nov 1887
Florence L. SHUTE, b.14 Sep 1889
Elsa L. COBB, b.4 Apr 1882
Franklin E. COBB, b.25 Nov 1888
Laurie COBB, d. Infant
Children of Thomas & Emma L Shute COBB

Children born to Alfred & Ella A. Shute SIMPSON
Nellie SIMPSON, d, infant
Mauda H. SIMPSON, b.1 Nov 1887
Alfred W. SIMPSON, b.10 Jan 1889
Everett C. SIMPSON, b.23 Apr 1890
Harry W. SIMPSON, b.13 Jul 1893
Leslie SIMPSON, d. infant

Arthur G. SIMPSON, b.25 Apr 1898
Edward S. SIMPSON, b.29 Jun 1901
Robert DeM. SIMPSON, b.14 Aug 1904

Children of Charles E. & Emma J. Sheer SHUTE
Charles Adair SHUTE, b.27 Jan 1901; d.16 Apr 1901
Leslie Elisha Spear SHUTE, b.20 Mar 1902
Alice Nelda SHUTE, b.21 Jun 1903
Florence Louise SHUTE, b.13 Jun 1908
Child of Henry Clay & Caroline Meadelene Traudt SHUTE
Henry Clay SHUTE, Jr, b. ____
Children of Florence L. Shute TRAUDT & Stephen C. TRAUDT
Marion L. TRAUDT, b.5 Jul 1910; d.7 Jun 1926
Stephen TRAUDT, Jr, b.18 Apr 1913
Florence Hazel TRAUDT, b.28 Jan 1915
Jeannette Ethel TRAVDTm, b.27 Dec 1923
Harold Sinclair TRAUDT, b.26 Oct 1929

Children of Alfred William SIMPSON, Jr & Lilliam Hyatt SIMPSON
Van Cortlandt Hyatt SIMPSON, b.14 Apr 1918
Glenna Irene SIMPSON, b.4 Oct 1920

Children of Harry Wilmarth & Clara Emma FROST SIMPSON
Clara Evelyn SIMPSON, b.23 Apr 1914
Katherine Ella SIMPSON,b.30 Aug 1915
Harry Walmarth SIMPSON, b.2 May 1917
Dorotha Caroline SIMPSON, b.11 May 1920
Edith Helen SIMPSON, b.3 Feb 1925
MARRIAGES
Peter SHUTE of Eastchester to Miss Harrietta H. BANTA,

Youngest dau of late William BANTA of NY; 13 Nov 1842 by Rev C.G. Sommers
Peter W. SHUTE to Harriet VAN NOSTRAND, dau of Norman Von NOSTRAND, 4 Jun 1869
Elisha M. SHUTE to Adelia KOLYLER, dau of Theodore KOLYLER of Brooklyn, granddau of Johannes KOLYER, 3 Dec 1874
Thomas COBB to Emma SHUTE, 16 Jun 1881
Elisha M. SHUTE to Hester HOPKINS, 8 Nov 1900
Henry Clay SHUTE, son of Elisha M. SCHUT, to Caroline Magalene TRAUDT, 3 Aug 1912
Franklin E. COBB, son of Thomas & Emma L. COBB to Agnolia Bertha PEARSON, 14 Dec 1912
Grace A. SHUTE, dau of Peter W. & Clara P. SHUTE, to Roy WEAGLY
Harry Wilmarth SIMPSON, son of Alfred W. & Ella A. SIMPSON to Clara Emma FROST of Newark, NJ, 2 Jul 1913
Everett SIMPSON to Gertrude WETMORE, Windhaven L.I. NY
Alfred SIMPSON, Jr, son of Alfred & Ella SIMPSON to Lillian HYATT of Montclair, NJ, 1917
Robert DeMille SIMPSON to Evelyn KOSTER, 24 Jun 1927
Edward Sainthill SIMPSON to Ella Mae CONKLIN, 29 Jun 1927
Clarence J. SCHUT to ______
James DICKIE of Brooklyn, NY to Josephine SHUTE, dau of Peter SHUTE of Brooklyn, NY, 22 Apr 1885
Alfred W. SIMPSON of Brooklyn, NY to Ella Augusta SHUTE, dau of Peter Shute of Brooklyn, 13 May 1885
Henry PINCKNEY of Brooklyn, NY to Martha Washington SHUTE, dau of Peter SHUTE, 6 Oct 1886
George BAKER of Brooklyn, NY to Hattie A. SHUTE, dau of Peter SHUTE, 28 Jul 1887

Charles E. SHUTE, son of Elisha M. SHUTE to Emma J. SPEAR of Montclair, NJ, 30 May 1900
Florence L. SHUTE, dau of Elisha M. SHUTE to Stephen C. TRAUDT, 21 Jul 1909
<u>DEATHS</u>
George Wilke SHUTE, d.12 May 1846; aged 1yr 2mo 21dys
Washington Irving SHUTE, d.4 Feb 1854; aged 1yr 2mos 2dys
Peter SHUTE, d.13 Feb 1895; aged 78yrs 11mos 27dys
Harrietta H. BANTA, wife of Peter SHUTE, d.6 Dec 1912; aged 91yrs 3mos 22dys
Josephine Shute DICKIE, wife of James DICKIE, d.13 Feb 1921; aged 69yrs
Peter Wilkes SHUTE, son of Peter & Henrietta H. Banta SHUTE, d.20 Dec 1921; aged 78yrs
Henry D. PINCKNEY, husband of Martha Washington SHUTE, d.4 Aug 1901; aged 49yrs 3mos 14dys
Thomas COBB, husband of Emma Louise SHUTE COBB, d.[-] Jan 1907; aged 52yrs
James DICKIE, husband of Josephine SHUTE DICKIE, d.14 Jan 1924; aged 70yrs
George BAKER, husband of Hattie A. SHUTE BAKER, d.1 Oct 1924; aged 86yrs 9mos 13dys

Richard SHUTE, b.13 Jul 1776
Phebe SHUTE (GUION), wife of Richard SHUTE, b.17 Nov 1778/80
Benjamin SHUTE, their son, b.25 Apr 1801; d. single
Richard SHUTE, b.24 May 1803
Rebekah SHUTE, b.27 Jan 1805
Mary Ann SHUTE, b.31 May 1808
Thomas SHUTE, b.1 Feb 1810
Sarah SHUTE, b.4 Jan 1812
Gilbert SHUTE, b.6 Feb 1814

Peter SHUTE, b.17 Feb 1816
Phebe Ann SHUTE, b.22 Jun 1818
Elisha SHUTE, b.10 Feb 1821; d. infant

Descentants of Thomas SHUTE & Mary HAYES, his wife
Thomas SHUTE, b.1 Feb 1810
Mary Ann HAYES, wife of Thomas SHUTE, b.-----
Mary Ann SHUTE, their dau, b.7 Apr 1845
Thomas SHUTE, son, b.7 Aug 1847 Eastchester
Phebe Hannah SHUTE, dau, b.31 Aug 1850; d.18 Mar 1853
James Henry SHUTE, son, b.3 Aug 1853, Eastchester
Annie Louise SHUTE, dau, b.6 May 1855, Eastchester
John Edgar SHUTE, son, b.6 Sep 1855, Eastchester
Gilbert SHUTE, son, b.14 Oct 1860, Eastchester
William F. SHUTE, son, b.22 Oct 1862, Eastchester; d.18 Oct 1872

Descendants of Phebe SHUTE & John ANTHONY
Phebe SHUTE, b.22 Jun 1818
John W. ANTHONY, husband of Phebe SHUTE, b.20 Jan 1818
John Benjamin ANTHONY, son, b.5 Aug 1849
Sarah Ann ANTHONY, dau, b.27 Jan 1852; d. childhood
Irving ANTHONY, son, b.3 Mar 1854, d. childhood
Mary Jane ANTHONY, dau , b.29 Jan 1856

Descendants of Peter SHUTE & Harrietta BANTA, his wife
Peter SHUTE, b.17 Feb 1816, Eastchester, Westchester Co, NY
Harrietta H. BANTA, wife of Peter SHUTE, b.14 Aug 1821, New York City
Peter W. SHUTE, son, b.24 Oct 1843, NYC
George Wilkes SHUTE, son, b.

Harriet Amelia, dau, b.29 Jan 1847, NYC
Elisha Morgan SHUTE, son, b.21 Jun 1849
Josephine SHUTE, dau, b.23 Nov 1851
Washington Irving SHUTE, son, b.2 Oct 1853
Eliza Ann SHUTE, dau, b.4 Oct 1855, Eastchester, NY
Emma Louisa SHUTE, dau, b.8 Mar 1858
Martha Washington SHUTE, dau, b.2 Dec 1859
Ella Augusta SHUTE, dau, b.14 Mar 1862, NYC

Descendants of Elisha Morgan SHUTE & Adelia KOLYER, his wife
Elisha M. SHUTE, b.21 Jun 1849
Adelia KOLYER, wife of Elisha M. SHUTE, b.
Charles Elisha SHUTE, son, b.15 Oct 1876, Brooklyn
Conry Clay SHUTE, son, b.28 Jul 1878, Brooklyn
Hattie Adelia SHUTE, dau, b.28 Oct 1884
Clarence SHUTE, son, b. Oct 1887
Florence Louise SHUTE, dau, b.15 Sep 1889

Descendants of Emma Louisa SHUTE & Thomas J. COBB, her husband
Emma L. SHUTE, b.8 Mar 1858
Tomas J. COBB, her husband, b. Sep
Elas Louise COBB, dau, b.4 Apr 1882, Brooklyn, NY
<u>MARRIAGES</u>
Elisah SHUTE to Phebe MORGAN
Richard SHUTE, their son to Phebe GUION, 22 Aug 1800
Susan SHUTE, dau to _____COLES
Rebekah SHUTE, dau to Andrew PRUDY
Isabella SHUTE, dau, unmarried
Peter SHUTE, son of Richard & Phebe GUION SHUTE to Harrietta H. BANTA, dau of late William BANTA of NYC, 30 Nov 1842

Thomas SHUTE, son of Richard, to Mary Ann HAYES at Eastchester, 31 Mar 1844
Phebe Ann SHUTE, dau of Richard, to John W. ANTHONY of NYC, 27 Jan 1848
Gilbert SHUTE, son of Richard, to Mary PECK, only dau of Israel Peck of Pecks Land, CT, Oct 1860
Peter W. SHUTE, son of Peter W. SHUTE & Harrietta BANYTA to Harriet VAN NOSTRAND, dau of late Norman VAN NOSTRAND, 4 Jun 1869
Elisha M. SHUTE, son of Peter, to Adelia KOLYER, dau of Theodore KOLYER of Brooklyn, granddaughter of Johannus KOLYER of Ridgewood, LI, 3 Dec 1874
Emma Louise SHUTE, dau of Peter, to Thomas COBB Jr all of Brooklyn, 16 Jun 1881

DEATHS

Phebe his wife died
Richard SHUTE, son of Elisha, d.23 Nov 1841, aged 65yrs 4mos 10dys
Phebe SHUTE, wife of Richard SHUTE, d.17 Aug 1846; aged 67yrs 9mos
Rebekah SHUTE, dau of Richard, d.22 Feb 1822; aged 17yrs 26dys
Elisha SHUTE, son of Richard SHUTE, d.22 Feb 1822, aged 1yr 12dys
Richard SHUTE, son of Richard, d.17 Nov 1861; aged 58yrs 5mos 21dys
Phebe SHUTE, dau of Richard & Phebe SHUTE, d.11 Nov 1856, Janesville, WI; aged 38yrs 4mos 19dys
Thomas SHUTE, son of Richard & Phebe SHUTE, d.28 Nov 1862, [---]chester; aged52yrs 9mos 21dys
Benjamin SHUTE, son of Richard & Phebe SHUTE, d.17 Jul 1866; Eastchester; aged 65yrs 5mos 21dys
Gilbert SHUTE, son of Richard & Phebe SHUTE, d.21 Apr

1882; aged 68yrs 2mos 15dys
Mary PECK, his wife d. 1864, leaving no issue
George Wilkes SHUTE, son of Peter & Harrietta SHUTE, d.12 May 1846; aged 1yr 2mos 21dys
Washington Irving SHUTE, son of Peter & Harrietta SHUTE, d.4 Feb 1855; aged 1yrs 4mos 2dys
(Louis Guion File)

POTTS BIBLE

THE HOLY BIBLE, Published by J.B. Lippincott & Company, Philadelphia, 1856

BIRTHS
Jefferson M. POTTS, b.8 Mar 1812
Elizabeth POTTS, b.31 Jan 1814
John S. POTTS, b.12 Jun 1835
Sarah Ann POTTS, b.15 Jun 1839
Schuyler POTTS, b.12 Jul 1842
Artamusa F. POTTS, b.1 Oct 1844
Adaline D. POTTS, b.15 Jun 1847
Joseph H. GRIDER, b.5 Jan 1839
T.L. WOOD, b.15 Sep 1835, married 19 Jan 1859 to Sarah Ann POTTS, d.17 Jan 1862
John Robert WOOD, b.20 Jan 1860
Josephine Adel WOODS, b.22 Aug 1861
Charles Roe GRIDEN, b.23 Jul 1865

MARRIAGES
Jefferson M. POTTS m. 26 Jun 1834
John S. POTTS, m.4 Dec 1856
Joseph H.GRIDER to Sarah A. WOOD, 11 Oct 1864

DEATHS
Elissey POTTS, wife of Schuyler POTTS, d.3 Sep 1873
Schuyler POTTS, d.6 Mar 1876

Jefferson M. POTTS, d. 23 Sep 1876
Elizabeth POTTS, d.29 Feb 1892
(Mark Hardin File)

STOKES BIBLE

THE HOLY BIBLE, Published by A.J. Holman & Co., 1872. A copy also in the Filson Club, Louisville, KY

BIRTHS
W. N. STOKES, b.17 May 1840
Atra F. STOKES, b.1 Oct 1844
Mary E. STOKES, b.3 Oct 1863
E[--] L[--] STOKES, b.[-] Mar 1867
[----] b. 3 Jan 1870
Sarah [---] STOKES, b.[---] 1872
[----] STOKES, b.16 [---] 1874
[----] STOKES, b.[---] 1877
[-------] STOKES, b. [-] Oct 1879

MARRIAGES
W.N. STOKES to Arta F. STOKES, 23 Dec 1862
A.L. STOKES to Adde STOKES, 9 Jul 1899
W.L. LONGE to Sallie E. LONGE, 10 Mar 1889

DEATHS
W.N. STOKES, d.14 Dec 1909
Mary A. STOKES, d.29 Sep 1898
Joel A. STOKES, d.9 Mar 1885
Arty STOKES, d.22 Nov 1926
Joel Jefferson STOKES, d.28 Mar 1937
Aita Missa STOKES. d.8 Sep 1878
Zud Lu STOKES, drowned 7 Apr 1882
Elizabeth POTTS, d.29 Feb 1894
W.M. BRADSHAW, d.24 Jan 1904

BIRTHS
Josid May STOKES, b.6 May 1883

Wm [--] STOKES, b. Jan
Luther D. LANGE, b.27 Oct 1890
Sue STOKES, b. 1902
Marra A. BRADSHAW, b.13 Aug 1903
W.M. BRADSHAW, b.14 Oct 1872
(Mark Hardin File)

FIELD BIBLE

THE HOLY BIBLE, Published by American Bible Society, 1856
John H. FIELD 1856
John H. FIELD married to Fannie A. PROVINES, 2 Jul 1850, Columbia, MO
John H. FIELD, eldest son of Curtis & Rosanna HARDIN FIELD, b.8 Jul 1812, Richmond, KY
Fannie A. PROVINES, dau of Dr William & Mary BROOKIE PROVINES, b.28 Dec 1823, Shelbyville, KY

Funeral notice for Mrs Mary BOOKIE PROVINES, b.17 Apr 1805, near Louisville, KY, d.1 Jun 1883, St Louis, MO
John H. FIELD, bur 10 Jul 1869, Columbia Cemetery; d.8 Jul 1869, Audrain Co.
Frances Provines FIELD, d. 1886, Trinidad, Co, Bur Riverside Cem, Denver
(Mark Hardin File)

HARPUR BIBLE

THE HOLY BIBLE, Published by Hogan & Thompson, Philadelphia, 1839
FAMILY RECORD
<u>MARRIAGES</u>
John and Jane HARPUR, m. 24 Nov 1815

James McNICHEL to Catherine HARPUR,{16 Nov 1843} date added later
Peter LAMB to Rebecca HARPUR, 3 Dec 1845
John Gaw HARPUR to Mary J. PASSMORE, 30 Apr 1857
William D. SLOAN to Isabella HARPUR, 28 Oct 1869
<u>BIRTHS</u>
John HARPUR, b.30 Mar 1788
Jane HARPUR, b.27 Jul 1796
Their Children
Catherine HARPUR, b.8 Jul 1817
William HARPUR, b.10 Oct 1819
James HARPUR, b.7 Jun 1822
Rebecca HARPUR, b.8 Jan 1825
Mary Anne HARPUR, b.8 Mar 1828
John Gaw HARPUR, b.4 Jul 1831
Sarah Jane HARPUR, b.29 Oct 1834
Isabella HARPUR, 13 Aug 1837
<u>DEATHS</u>
John HARPUR, d.22 Apr 1857; aged 69yrs 1mo 2dys
James HARPUR, d.15 Aug 1853,; aged 31yrs 2mos 9dys
William HARPUR, d.13 Aug 1855
Jane HARPUR, d.10 Jul 1885
John Gaw HARPUR, d.24 Apr 1862
Sarah Jane HARPUR, d.29 Apr 1910
Isabella Harpur SLOAN, d.27 Jul 1923; aged 86yrs
(Thomas Harpur File)

REYNOLDS BIBLE I

THE OLD AND NEW TESTAMENT, Published by Collins & Co., New York, 1819
The original Bible owned by Dr Eugenia Briscoe, Corpus Christi, TX.
FAMILY RECORDS

MARRIAGES
Levi REYNOLDS married 13 Oct 1811
Sarah Ann REYNOLDS, married 23 Dec 185[-]
George W. REYNOLDS, married 6 Jan 1853
J.S.B. REYNOLDS married 1 Feb 1853
George W. SIMS married 22 Apr 1833
William D. REYNOLDS married 31 Dec 1836
Elizabeth Ann REYNOLDS to Isaac EASON, 10 May 1838
Serenea REYNOLDS to William FOSTER, 7 Mar 1844
BIRTHS
Levi REYNOLDS, b.10 Feb 1785
Elizabeth REYNOLDS, b.14 Sep 1790
Polly REYNOLDS, b.26 Feb 181[4]
William Dudley REYNOLDS, b.31 Dec 1815
Little Bary REYNOLDS, b.25 Jul 181[6]
Betsy REYNOLDS, b. [------] 18[17]
James B. REYNOLDS, b.18 Apr 1818
Serenea REYNOLDS, b.28 Apr 1823
Augustus A. Levi REYNOLDS, b.30 Mar 18[--]
Vincin E. REYNOLDS, b.22 Dec 18[--]
George Washington REYNOLDS, 27 Jan 1832
Sarah Ann Rebecca REYNOLDS, b.[--] OCt 1833
William Levi REYNOLDS, b.17 Aug 1854
Thomas Louis REYNOLDS, b.24 Nov 1856
Mary Louisa REYNOLDS, b.31 Mar 1858
Robert Cortez REYNOLDS, b.27 Aug 1865
James Monroe REYNOLDS, b.18 Jul 1875
George W. SIMS, b.(?) 25 Jan 1812
Lucindy SIMS, b.25 Apr 183[-]
Martha Ann Elizabeth SIMS, b.29 Aug 183[-]
William Augustus SIMS, b.26 Nov 1836
DEATHS
Augustus L. REYNOLDS, d.15 Nov 1826

Vincin E. REYNOLDS, d.16 Dec 1830
Little Bery REYNOLDS, d.30 Jul 1838
Elizabeth REYNOLDS, d.19 Mar 1865
Martha Ann Elizabeth SIMS, d.10 Dec 18[--]
[----] SIMS, d.20 Oct 1867
Levi REYNOLDS, d.24 Jul 1851
Sara [-------], wife of Benjamin [-----]; d.28 Jul 18[--]
W.A. MASSEY, d.18 Mar 185[-]
(Benjamin Hubert File)

REYNOLDS BIBLE II

No Title Page or Dates

Family Record of Geo W. REYNOLDS
William L. REYNOLDS, b.17 Aug 1854
THomas Louis REYNOLDS, b.24 Nov 1856
Mary Louis REYNOLDS, b.31 Mar 1858
Robert C. REYNOLDS, b.27 Aug 1865
Infant son b.autumn 1860
James Monroe REYNOLDS, b.18 Jul 1875

Family Record of J.M. REYNOLDS
Watson Eldridge REYNOLDS, b.21 Jul 1904
Edith Massey REYNOLDS, b.22 Oct 1906
Leila Eugenia REYNOLDS, b.8 Jun 1914
Mary Louisa REYNOLDS, b.5 Sep 1918
<u>DEATHS</u>
Geo W. REYNOLDS, d.29 Dec 1904
William L. REYNOLDS, d.   1933
Robert Cortez REYNOLDS, d.13 Jul 1932
James Monroe REYNOLDS, 2 Apr 1957
(Benjamin Hubert File)

DUVALL BIBLE

THE NEW TESTAMENT, Printed by T. Wright and W. Gill, Printers to the University, 1770. In May 1971 the original in possession of Harriet Powe Jackson of Bennettsville, SC

Susanah DUVALL, wife of Joseph, d.18 Aug 1797

Sister Ruth WELCH, d.10 Jan 1807

Mareen DUVALL, son of Joseph & Susan DUVALL, d.17 Mar 1827; aged 51yrs 7mos 5dys

Sarah DUVALL, wife of Mareen DUVALL, d.16 Jul 1843; aged 53yrs 6mos 14dys

David DUVALL, son of Joseph & Susan DUVALL, b.24 Nov 1755

Mary Stewart DUVALL, b.30 May 1758

Susannah DUVALL, b.14 Nov 1760

Joseph DUVALL, JR, b.28 Jun 1763

Henry Howard DUVALL, b.13 Sep 1767

Ruth DUVALL, b.11 Aug 1770

Elizabeth DUVALL, b.27 Sep 1773; d.11 Aug 1775

Mareen DUVALL, son of Joseph & Susanah, b.13 Jul 1776

[---] Frances Marreen and John the sons of Joseph & Susanah DUVALL b. [---] 1766 and d. within 24 hours as will as I can remember

My daughter Mary Stewart JONES d.[--] Oct 1795 and left a dau [______]

DEATHS

Caroline E. DUVALL, wife of Gideon Walker DUVALL, d.1 May 1842, aged 26yrs 5mos

Priscilla Walker DUVALL, wife of George HUMES, d.4 Dec 1862, Prince Georges Co, MD; aged 42yrs 4mos 18dys

Mareen Henry [___] DUVALL, son of Mareen & Sarah Walker DUVALL, d.7 Nov 1865 [----]; aged 40yrs 8mos 28dys

Caroline Ellerbe DUVALL, dau of Mareen Henry Howard

and Mary Jane Ellerbe DUVALL, d.13 Sep 1866; aged 6yrs 3wks 6dys
George Cuthorn HUMES [?], son of Geo HUMES & Priscilla W. DUVALL, his wife, d.9 Dec 1880, Prince George Co, MD; aged 29yrs 9mos 27dys
Elizabeth Ruth DUVALL, dau of Mareen & Sarah Walker DUVALL, d.8 Mar 1881, Prince George Co, MD
Mary Jane Ellerbe, wife of Mareen H.H. DUVALL, d.27 Oct 1881, Cheraw, SC; aged 4yrs 7mos 19dys
Gideon Walker DUVALL, son of Mareen & Sarah Walker DUVALL, d.27 Nov 1882, Cheraw
aged 70yrs 4mos 15dys
Susan Keith DUVALL, dau of Mareen & Sarah Walker DUVALL, d.20 Feb 1885, Prince George Co, MD; aged 74yrs 4mos
Elizabeth Walker DUVALL, wife of John Murchen JACKSON, d.27 Nov 1923, Charlotte, NC
Willie Mae STROMAN, wife of Rev Roberich Humes JACKSON, d.17 Feb 1965, Portsmouth, VA
MISCELLANEOUS
Madison Farr ELLERBE, son of Thomas G. & Caroline C. ROWE ELLERBE, b.17 Jan 1836
Alexander Washington ELLERBE, son of Thomas G. & Caroline C. Rowe ELLERBE, b.3 Dec 1837
Mary Jane ELLERBE, dau of Thomas G. & Caroline C. ROWE ELLERBE, b.8 Mar 1840
BIRTHS
Susan Keith & Elizabeth Ruth DUVALL, twin Children of Mareen & Sarah Walker DUVALL, b.20 Oct 1810
Gideon Walker DUVALL, son of Mareen & Sarah Walker DUVALL, b.12 Jul 1812
Priscilla Walker DUVALL, dau of Mareen & Sarah Walker DUVALL, b.16 Aug 1820

Mareen Henry Howard DUVALL, son of Mareen & Sarah DUVALL, b.10 Feb 1825

BIRTHS

Henry Powe DUVALL, first born of Gideon Walker & Sarah R. POWE DUVALL, b.20 Nov 1846

Sarah Elizabeth DUVALL, dau of Gideon Walker & Sarah R. POWE DUVALL, b.8 Mar 1849

Martha Eliza DUVALL, dau of Gideon Walker & Sarah R. POWE DUVALL, b.31 Mar 1852

Mareen Walker DUVALL, son of Gideon Walker & Sarah R. POWE, b.26 May 1856

Susan Rebecca DUVALL, dau of Gideon Walker & Sarah R. POWE DUVALL, b.29 Jan 1859

George Calhoun HUMES, son of George & Priscilla W. DUVALL HUMES, b.12 Feb 1851, Washington DC

Mareen Duvall HUMES, son of George & Priscilla W. DUVALL HUMES, b.5 Feb 1853, Prince George Co, MD

MISCELLANEOUS

Henry P. DUVALL, son of Gideon Walker & Sarah POWE DUVALL, d.12 Aug 1923, Cheraw, SC

Sarah Duvall PEGNES, dau of Gideon Walker & Sarah POWE DUVALL, wife of Richard H. PEGNES, d.23 Oct 1928, Cheraw, SC

Martha Eliza DUVALL, dau of Gideon Walker & Sarah POWE DUVALL, d.1 Apr 1930, Cheraw, SC

Susan Rebecca McIVER, dau of Gideon Walker & Sarah POWE DUVALL, wife of Thomas P. McIVER, d.10 Sep 1932, Cheraw, SC

MARRIAGES

Gideon Walker DUVALL to Caroline C. ELLABE, 9 Dec 1841, Chesterfield Dist, SC

Gideon Walker DUVALL to Sarah R. POWE, 6 Jun 1844, Chesterfield Dist, SC

George HUMES to Priscilla W. DUVALL, 5 Nov 1846, Washington, DC
Mareen Henry Howard DUVALL to Mary Jane ELLABE, 14 Jun 1859, Cheraw, SC
John Murchison JACKSON to Elizabeth Walker DUVALL, dau of Mareen Henry Howard DUVALL, 10 Nov 1887, Bennettsville, SC
John Murchison JACKSON, Jr to Rebecca Gray BEACE of Clarksville, GA, 4 Mar 1920 in Lancester, SC

William Hartwell JACKSON, second child of Mareen Duvall & Susie Calbert Johnson JACKSON, b.14 May 1928 Bennetsville, SC
Rederick Boyd NASH, first child of Boyd & Elizabeth Duvall JACKSON NASH, b.2 Apr 1936, Spartenburg, SC
Elizabeth Duvall NASH, second child of Boyd & Elizabeth Duvall JACKSON NASH, b.17 Jul 1940, Spartanburg, SC
John Murchison JACKSON, III, b.26 Jan 1947
MARRIAGES
Henry Powe DUVALL to Sallie J. WADDILL, 7 Dec 1869, Chesterfield Co, SC
Mareen Walker DUVALL to Margaret D. EVAND, 17 Oct 1877, Chesterfield Co, SC
Thomas Powe McIVER to Susan R, DUVALL, 13 Jan 1878, Chesterfield Co, SC
Mareen Duvall JACKSON to Susie Culhburt JOHNSON, dau of Wesley H. & Aixon Co, SC, 22 Jan 1923, Bexington, NC
Frank A. PROCTOR to Mary Eleanor JACKSON, dau of John M. & Bessie Duvall JACKSON, 26 Aug 1923, Bennettsville, SC
Rev Roderick Humes JACKSON to Caroline Holdsworth BENSON, dau of Mr & Mrs John Francis BENSON, 21 May 1966

Boyd NASH, of Spartanburg, SC to Elizabeth Duvall JACKSON, dau of John M. & Bessie Duvall JACKSON, 25 Jun 1932, Bennettsville, SC
Rev Roderick Humes JACKSON to Willie Mae STROHMAN, dau of Wm R & Nancy Lee Baumister STROHMAN, of Orangeburg, SC, 26 Apr 1934
Henry Theodore Northcott GRAVES of Luray, VA to Rebecca Beall JACKSON, dau of John M. JACKSON, Jr, 29 Nov 1944, St Stevens Episcopal Church, Miami, FL
BIRTHS
Caroline Ellerbe DUVALL, dau of Mareen Henry Howard & Mary Jane ELLERBE DUVALL, b.17 Aug 1860
Elizabeth Walker DUVALL, dau of Mereen Henry Howard & Mary Jane ELLERBE DUVALL, b.21 Oct 1862
Mareen Duvall JACKSON, son of John Murchison & Elizabeth Walker DUVALL JACKSON, b.25 Nov 1888
Margaret Murchison JACKSON, dau of John Murchison & Elizabeth Walker DUVALL JACKSON, b.16 Feb 1891
Mary Eleanor JACKSON, dau of John Murchison & Elizabeth Walker DUVALL JACKSON, b.14 Sep 1893
John Murchison JACKSON, son of John Murchison & Elizabeth Walker DUVALL JACKSON, b.30 Nov 1895, Bennettsville, SC
Roderick Humes JACKSON, son of John Murchison & Elizabeth Walker DUVALL JACKSON, b.12 Feb 1900
Elizabeth Duvall JACKSON, dau of John Murchison & Elizabeth Walker DUVALL JACKSON, 31 Jan 1902
Harriet Powe JACKSON, dau of John Murchison & Elizabeth Walker DUVALL JACKSON, b.26 Aug 1906, Bennettsville, SC
Rebecca Beall JACKSON, child of John Murchison Jr & Rebecca Gray BEALL JACKSON, b.27 Sep 1922
Mareen Duvall JACKSON, son of Mareen Duvall & Susie

Cuthbert JOHNSON JACKSON, b.14 Nov 1923
(Mareen Duvall File)

JACK BIBLE

No Title page, Transcript of records kept by Charles James Jack in the Bible.

Charles James JACK married to Leonna O'BRIEN, 27 Jan 1824, Carlisle
Their Children
Harriet Maria JACK, b.27 May 1825
James Mahony JACK, b.17 Sep 1826
Robert Arundel JACK, b.23 Mar 1828
Margaret Rodgers JACK, b.3 Sep 1829
Leonna O'Brien JACK, b.23 Oct 1830
Charles Edward Murray JACK, b.14 Dec 1831 (change his name to Charles Mansfield JACK)
William Pitt JACK, b.13 Jun 1833
Walter Scott JACK, b.7 Oct 1934

Charles James JACK married to Mary Marie RIELAND, 27 Oct 1848

still born son, b.20 Mar 1849, son of Mary Marie JACK
Lettis JACK, b.28 Dec ----, dau of Mary Marie JACK
[______] JACK dau of Marie JACK, b.29 Apr 1851
Louis Napoleon JACK, son of C.J. & Mary M. JACK, b.20 Apr 1852, Brooklyn, NY
St Clair (Sinclair) JACK, son of C.J. & Mary M. JACK, b.18 Sep 1853
Eugenia JACK, dau of C.J. & Mary Maria JACK, b.11 Nov 1855
(Jack / Jacques File)

GREEN BIBLE

No Title page or Dates.

FAMILY RECORDS

BIRTHS

Wm J. GREEN b.14 Feb 1815
Emily BARNETT, b.24 Mar 1829
Mary Crittenden GREEN, b.8 Jul 1848
Arthur Barnett GREEN, b.23 Sep 1850
John Wm GREEN, b.12 Mar 1852
Kate Ella GREEN, b.1 Jan 1854
George Henry GREEN, b.31 May 1857
Robert R.B. GREEN, b.5 Jul 1860
James Andy GREEN, b.15 Sep 1864
Dora Alice GREEN, b.30 May 186[-]
Lissie Barnett GREEN, b.16 Jan 18[--]
Wm Barnett OWEN, b.12 Mar 1880
Ray Buford OWEN, b.8 Sep 1885
Emily Vance OWEN, b.30 Sep 1911
Kitty Barnett OWEN, b.5 Oct 1915
Wm Barnett OWEN, Jr, b.9 Apr 1922
Kitty Marshall EDELEN, b.27 Aug 1938
Penelope Allis HARRISON, b.8 May 1939
Wm Barnett Owen EDELEN, b.6 Jun 1940
Winston Pope HARRISON, Jr, b.16 Jun 1941
Charles Vance EDELEN, b.12 Oct 1944

DEATHS

Arthur B. GREEN, d.23 Sep 1852
Mary C. GREEN, d.3 Oct 1879
Wm S. GREEN, d.3 Feb 1881
John William GREEN, d.6 Nov 1906
Harry GREEN, d.25 Apr 1949
Elizabeth Barnett GREEN, d. May 1951

Dora Alice GREEN, d.6 Oct 1952
Ray Buford OWEN, d.8 Nov 1887
Jordan OWEN, d.13 Jan 1924
Kate Green OWEN, d.21 Feb 1938
William Barnett OWEN, d.23 Feb 1947
MARRIAGES
William S. GREEN to Emily BARNETT, 22 Jul 1847
Harry GREEN to Sallie CRABB, 15 Nov 1879
Jordan OWEN to Kate E. GREEN, 11 Feb 1875
Wm Barnett OWEN to Emily Chew VANCE, 11 Dec 1911
Emily Vance OWEN to Charles Maurice EDELEN, 16 Oct 1937
Kitty Barnett OWEN to Wnston Pope HARRISON, 18 Sep 1937
(Jean de Jarnette File)

BARNETT BIBLE

No Title Page or Date. Original in possession of Lucie Weston Albrecht of Chicago.

MARRIAGES
Wm BARNETT to Mary COWHERD, 25 Mar 1823
Wm BARNETT to Lucy R. CABLE, 8 Nov 1842
A.C. CRABB to Sally A. BARNETT, Aug 1842
W.S. GREEN to Emily BARNETT, 23 Jul 1847
W.C. WEBSTER to Lucinda BARNETT, 22 Dec 1847
Andy BARNETT to Kate F. TYLER, 11 Dec 1856
Wm BARNETT, Jr to Martha COWHERD, 17 Mar 1859
John BARNETT to Susan E. BARNETT, 21 Mar 1878
Thos BARNETT to Mary Agnes WILSON, 13 Aug 1872
Lorin W. WESTON to Mary A. BARNETT, 20 Jan 1876
Lewis BARNETT to Loura TOMBLER, 16 Nov 1893
BIRTHS

Sarah Agnes BARNETT, b.16 Apr 1825
Andrew BARNETT, b.4 Mar 1827
Emily BARNETT, b.24 Mar 1829
Lucinda BARNETT, b.8 Nov 1830
Wm BARNETT, b.6 May 1833
John BARNETT, b.9 Feb 1835
James BARNETT, b.15 Feb 1837
Thos BARNETT, b.7 Feb 1844
Robt Walker BARNETT and Lewis Cass BARNETT, b.13 Jan 1848
George BARNETT, b.8 Feb 1850
Mary Apphia BARNETT, b.4 Apr 1852
DEATHS
Mary BARNETT, d.7 May 1839
Lucinda WEBSTER, d. Jul 1849
Sarah A. CRABB, d.3 Nov 1855
James BARNETT, d.6 Jun 1862
Wm BARNETT, d.18 Apr 1868
Wm BARNETT, Jr, 22 Feb 1904
Andrew BARNETT, d.11 Feb 1910
John BARNETT, d.16 Jan 1915
George BARNETT, d.9 Jun 1855
Lucy Read BARNETT, d.22 Jun 1894
Robert Walker BARNETT, d.12 Jan 1898
Thomas BARNETT, d.20 Jan 1905
Emily BARNETT, d.7 Aug 1916
Mary Barnett WESTON, d.12 Feb 1920
Lewis Cass BARNETT, d.18 May 1936
(Jean de Jarnette File)

GREEN BIBLE II

THE HOLY BIBLE, Published by American Bible

Society, New York, 1859
FAMILY RECORDS
BIRTHS
Sarah Agnes CRABB, b.17 Oct 1856
Harry GREEN, b.31 May 1857
CHILDREN
Mattie Barnett GREEN, b.13 Jul 1880
Robert Coumpton GREEN, b.11 Feb 1883
Lewis Owen GREEN, b.18 Mar 1884
Emily Leslie GREEN, b.15 Jul 1886
Haynes Vertrees GREEN, b.8 Oct 1887
Catherine Fenton GREEN, b.5 Jan 1892
Mary Louise GREEN, b.22 Nov 1893
Sara Crabb GREEN, b.13 Aug 1895
MARRIAGE
Harry GREEN to Sallie A. CRABB, 13 Nov 1879
DEATHS
Mrs P.S. YOUNG, d.13 Feb 1876
A.C. CRABB, d.6 Jul 1876
Robert Coumpton GREEN, d.14 May 1883
Sarah Crabb GREEN, d.24 Aug 1907
(Jean de Jarnette File / 9-106)

McGEHEE BIBLE
No Title page or Dates
BIRTHS
E.R. McGEHEE, b.21 Jul 1852
E.M. McGEHEE, b.18 Oct 1855
A.A. McGEHEE, b.31 Jan 1873
K.J. McGEHEE, b.4 Jan 1875
J.M. McGEHEE, b.27 Sep 1877
J.S. McGEHEE, b.12 Sep 1879

C.S. McGEHEE, b.14 May 1881
BIRTHS
R.J. McGEHEE, b.27 Feb 1883
C.J. McGEHEE, b.14 Feb 1885
E.R. McGEHEE, b.11 May 1887
J.B. McGEHEE, b.16 Feb 1890
P.C. McGEHEE, b.27 Sep 1891
H.W. McGEHEE, b.15 Nov 1894
DEATHS
E.R. McGEHEE, d.26 Aug 1895
Miss J. Arie McGEHEE, d.24 Sep 1896
Mrs E.M. MOAK, d.25 Jun 1917
H.W. McGEHEE, d.3 Nov 1915
MISCELLANEOUS
E.R. McGEHEE m. to E.M. WROTTEN, 18 Apr 1879
T.A. LARD m. to A.A. McGEHEE, 8 Dec 1888
J.N. WESTBROOK m. to K.J. McGEHEE, 17 Feb 1891
MISCELLANEOUS
J.M. McGEHEE, b.14 Mar 1826
R.A. McGEHEE, b.16 Oct 1827
J.M. McGEHEE m. to R.A. JONES, 10 Feb 1846
James Madison [Mat] McGEHEE, d.28 Mar 1893
Rebecca Ann [Becky] McGEHEE, d.29 Jun 1888
(Jean de Jarnette File / 26-59)

WINDHAM BIBLE

No Title Page or Dates

FAMILY RECORDS
Henry F. WINDHAM m. to Susan E. ROWE, 28 Nov 1865
H.H. WINDHAM m. to Lizzie [-] BRADHAM, 29 Jul 1891
J.N. STRANGE m. to Lillie E. WINDHAM, 21 Dec 1892
Henry Harman WINDHAM, son of Henry & Susan E.

WINDHAM, b.7 Sep 1865
John William WINDHAM, son of Henry & Susan E. WINDHAM, b.2 May 1868
James Mandly WINDHAM, son of Henry & Susan E. WINDHAM, b.16 Aug 1869
Lilly E. WINDHAM, b.18 Jul 1878, dau of H. H. & S.E. WINDHAM
(George Juin File)

PACK BIBLE

Dictionary of the BIBLE, Published by A.J. Holman & Co, 1872
Marriage Certificate
Charles Henry PACK, of Clarendan Co, SC to Ann Eliza WALKER of Manning, SC; 20 Jan 1880, by Rev J.W. Perry
BIRTHS
Charles Henry PACK, 25 Dec 1858, Cedar Lane Clarendan Co, SC
Ann Eliza WALKER, b.29 Dec 1856, Junesville, Clarendan Co, SC
Alice Maud PACK, b.21 Aug 1882
Charles Simanton PACK, b.13 Oct 1884
Francis Enelyn PACK, b.8 Aug 1888
Annie Belle PACK, b.31 May 1897, Lancaster Co, SC
Jesse Eugene PACK, b.18 Jan 1893
son [not named], b.20 May 1894
Grace Eugenia PACK, b.23 Mar 1896, Greenville, SC
DEATHS
Infant son d.19 Jul 1887
Jesse Eugene PACK, d.8 Jul 1893, aged 5mos, 20dys
Infant son, d.9 Jul 1894, Kershaw, SC
(George Juin File)

UHRICH BIBLE

Sie Banke Geilige Schrifft (German Language Bible) Piblished MDCCXCVIII (1798)

David UHRICH, son of Christian & Catherine HOFFMAN UHRICH, b.22 Dec 1808, bp 12 Jan 1809 Lebanon TWP, Dauphin Co, PA; d.22 Apr 1872
Catherine DUBS, dau of John & Eve SOUSER DUBS, b.5 May 1814, Lebanon, Lebanon Co, PA; d.30 Aug 1893
Die Beyden Ghegaffen als
David UHRICH married to Catharin DUBS, 30 Oct 1831
John Henry UHRICH, son of David & Catherine UHRICH, b.22 Apr 1832, Lebanon, Lebanon Co, PA; d.12 Aug 1833, aged 1yr 3mos 20dys
William UHRICH, son of David & Catherine UHRICH, b.26 Oct 1833. The sponser was Eva DUBS, his Grandmother
Henry Brandt UHRICH, son of David & Catherine UHRICH, b.22 Dec 1835
Sarah Eve UHRICH, dau of David & Catherine UHRICH, b.2 Dec 1837
David Porter UHRICH, son of David & Catherine UHRICH, b.13 Dec 1839
Hannah UHRICH, son of David & Catherine UHRICH, b.19 May 1841, Lebanon TWP, Lebanon Co, PA
Elizabeth UHRICH, dau of David & Catherine UHRICH, b.22 Apr 1843, North Lebanon TWP; d.5 Apr 1845, aged 1yr 1 mo 5dys
Amanda UHRICH, dau of David & Catherine UHRICH, b.25 Jan 1845; d.18 Feb 1848; aged 7yrs 3wks 3dys
Catrina [--] UHRICH, dau of David & Catherine UHRICH, b.13 Nov 1846
Anna Matilda UHRICH, dau of David & Catherine UHRICH,

b.25 May 1849; d.7 Sep 1856; aged 7yrs 3mos 27dys
George Frainlin UHRICH son of David & Catherine UHRICH, b.22 May 1851
Rolara {?} UHRICH, dau of David & Catherine UHRICH, b. & d. 1 May 1853
Mary Alice UHRICH, dau of David & Catherine UHRICH, b.14 Jan 1855
<u>MARRIAGE CERTIFICATE</u>
F.T. MILLER to Sarah E. UHRICH, both of Lebanon Co, PA, 17 Feb 1856
(Misc Bible Records / 2-899)

SHEADS / MILLER BIBLE

THE HOLY BIBLE Published by Jesper Harding, Philadelphia, 1847
FAMILY RECORDS
<u>MARRIAGES</u>
Peter SHEADS, Jr to Mary Jane MILLER, dau of Andrew MILLER, deceased, 5 Oct 1847
<u>BIRTHS</u>
Andrew B. MILLER, b.10 Mar 1799
Catherine MILLER, b.30 Oct 1797
Peter SHEADS, Sr, b.13 Jan 1781
Salome TROXCE b.13 Apr 1784
Peter SHEADS, Jr, b.4 Nov 1819
Mary Jane MILLER, b.3 Nov 1826
[-------] SHEADS, b.23 Sep 1848
Alice Jane SHEADS, b.11 Apr 1851
Sarah Salome SHEADS, b.4 Sep 1853
Peter Andrew SHEADS, b.27 Feb 1856
Mary Catherine SHEADS, b.2 Oct 1858
Mary Miller SHEADS, b. 8 Jul 1862
Rufus C. SHEADS, b.6 Mar 1867

John L. SHEADS, b.27 Jun 1869
DEATHS
Andrew B. MILLER, d.14 Oct 1846; aged 47yrs 8mos 4dys
Catherine MILLER, d.1 Aug 1842, aged 44 yrs 8mos 2dys
Peter SHEADS, Sr, d.11 Jun 1848; aged 67yrs 4mos 11dys
Salome SHEADS, d.3 Apr 1860
Peter SHEADS, d.10 Jul 1903; aged 83yrs
Mary J. SHEADS, d.24 Jun [---]; aged 63yrs
William H. SHEADS, d.1 Sep 1903; aged 54yrs 11mos 9dys
Peter A. SHEADS, d.10 May 1899; aged 43yrs 2mos 13dys
Rufus C. SHEADS, d.8 Dec 1914; aged 47yrs 4mos 2dys
DEATHS
Sarah Salom AUGHMBAUGH; d.16 Apr 1925, aged 71yrs 7mos 12dys
Mary Catherine SPANGLER, d.12 Dec 1926; aged 68yrs 2mos 10dys
Alice Jane SHEADS, d.25 Aug 1929, aged 78yrs 4mos 14dys
Alice Meade SHEADS, d.2 Oct 1941; aged 77yrs 9mos 22dys
John L. SHEADS, d.21 Nov 1941; aged 72yrs
Murray M. SHEADS, d.23 Jul 1948; aged 86yrs 15dys
(Misc Bilble Records)

POTTER BIBLE

Transcript of a HOLY BIBLE Published by M. Carey, Philadelphia, 1815. The original was in the possession of William Sherwood Potter, Westfield, NJ

MARRIAGES
William B. POTTER to Catherine Magie WERE, 13 May 1802
David M. POTTER to Elizabeth SHERWOOD, 11 Mar 1840
William Sherwood POTTER to Anna Olivia CARPENTER, 25 Nov 1869
Edgar Culver ADRIANCE to Sarah Catherine POTTER, 19

Oct 1870
Charles Henry POTTER, MD to Eva Adella VOUNT, 22 Jul 1873
Samuel Clard LUM to Anna Elizabeth POTTER, 27 Oct 1875
MARRIAGES sons of William and Catherine POTTER
Joseph POTTER to Susan POTTER, 3 Jan 1829
Samuel S. POTTER to Eleanor W. JOHNSTON, 20 Dec 1825
William DARBY to Jane Magie POTTER, 2 Dec 1832
Stephen S. POTTER to Olivia Sutton HOFFMAN, 22 Nov 1882
David Magie POTTER to Rowena Johnson TEAS, 14 Nov 1894
BIRTHS
William Broadwell POTTER, b.11 Apr 1781
Catherine, his wife, b.5 Jan 1781
Joseph POTTER, b.22 Mar 1803
Samuel Smith POTTER, b.26 Jan 1806
Jane Megie POTTER, b.24 Apr 1810
Catherine Haines POTTER, b.5 Oct 1812
David Magie POTTER, b.13 Sep 1815
Matthias Day POTTER, b.26 Sep 1818
Elizabeth SHERWOOD, wife of David Magie POTTER, b.11 Jan 1818

Children of William and Jane DARBY

Catherine DARBY, b.10 Dec 1834

Children of David and Elizabeth POTTER

William Sherwood POTTER, b.10 Dec 1840
Charles Henry POTTER, b.12 Aug 1842
Hannah Ann POTTER, b.27 Apr 1844
Sarah Catherine POTTER, b.27 Jul 1846
Anna Elizabeth POTTER, b.16 May 1849
David Magie POTTER, b.29 Mar 1851
Stephen Sherwood POTTER, b.25 Nov 1858

Edward Payton POTTER, b.24 Oct 1861; d.12 Mar 1862

Children of Samuel and Eleanor POTTER and Grandchildren of William and Catherine POTTER

Margaret Johnston POTTER, b.28 Aug 1829

William B. POTTER, b.1 Jan 1831

James Josnston POTTER, b.19 Aug 1834

DEATHS

Catherine POTTER, d.12 Apr 1843

Hannah Ann POTTER, d.11 Jun 1844

Jane DARBY, d.16 Mar 1856

Wm DARBY, d. Oct 1856

William B. POTTER, d.19 Apr 1856

David Magie POTTER, d.3 Feb 1879; aged 63yrs 4mos 18dys

Charles Henry POTTER, MD, his son d.6 Aug 1881; aged 38yrs 11mos 25dys

William POTTER, son of David M. & Elizabeth POTTER, d.22 Apr 1901, aged 60yrs

Anna Olivia POTTER, wide of Wm S. Potter, d.20 Apr 1901, aged 60yrs

Edgar C. ADRIANCE, husband of Kate S. POTTER, d.30 Mar 1901

Elizabeth Sherwood POTTER, wife of David Megie POTTER, d.7 Jan 1902, aged 84yrs

Olivia S.H. POTTER, wife of Stephen Sherwood POTTER, d.12 Aug 1922

Sarah Katherine Potter ARDIANCE, wife of Edgar C. ADRIANCE, d. 1924

Anna Elizabeth Potter LUM, wife of Samuel Clark LUM, d.9 May 1924

(Misc Bible Records)

TEAS BIBLE

Transcript of a HOLY BIBLE published by Butler and Williams, 1845. Then in possession of Mrs Fred Alleman, Washington, NJ

MARRIAGES

John TEAS to Rowena JOHNSON, 23 Nov 1837
John TEAS to Ellen H. TICHENOR, 28 Jan 1846
John TEAS to Susan WHALLEY, 18 Jun 1872
Stephen J. TEAS to Catharine KIRKPATRICK, 24 May 1866
William BUCHANAN to Mary Noble TEAS, 23 Oct 1872
Samuel Clark TEAS to Adeline DAY, 19 Feb 1879
David Magie POTTER to Rowena J. TEAS, 14 Nov 1894
Helen Rowena POTTER, dau of David M. POTTER to Frederick Raymond ALLEMAN, 19 Apr 1920
Russell Sherwood POTTER, son of David M. POTTER to Louise BURDORF,31 Dec 1923
Kathryn Teas POTTER, dau of David M. POTTER to Stephen M. WOLLMAN, 29 May 1929
David M. POTTER, Jr, son of David M. POTTER to Erna ADLER, 18 Sep 1929

BIRTHS

Stephen JOHNSON, b.2 Nov 1781
Mary JOHNSON, b.31 Oct 1766
Jesse JOHNSON, b.18 Dec 1810
Rowena JOHNSON, b.1 Mar 1813
Samuel [S or L] JOHNSON, b.24 May 1817
Julia JOHNSON, b.23 Dec 1819
Phoebe JOHNSON, b.24 Mar 1823
John TEAS, b.1 May 1812; Rowena JOHNSON his first wife)
Ellen TICHENOR, his second wife, b.16 Jun 1810
Mary Noble TEAS, b.23 Apr 1839
Stephen Johnson TEAS, b.25 Oct 1840
Mary Noble TEAS, b.7 Dec 1842
Elizabeth Meeker TEAS, b.17 May 1847

Cassie TEAS, wife of S.J. TEAS, b.1 May 1838
Rowena J. TEAS, b.28 Jan 1867
Letitia TEAS, b.10 Feb 1872
Emma TEAS, dau of S.C.T., b.29 Apr 1880
Samuel Clard TEAS, b.6 Feb 1884
Wm BUCHANAN,b.17 May 1842
Laura Mary BUCHANAN, b.22 May 1874
John Russell BUCHANAN, b.8 Oct 1875
Jane Isabella BUCHANAN, b.20 May 1877
Samuel Clark TEAS, Sr, b.16 Aug 1852
David Magie POTTER, b.29 Mar 1851
Helen Rowena POTTER, b.5 Dec 1895
Russell Sherwood POTTER, b.20 Aug 1897
Kathryn Teas POTTER, b.17 Jul 1900
David Magie POTTER, Jr,b.10 Apr 1905
Stephen Johnson POTTER, b.6 Aug 1906
Wm B. POTTER. b.13 Sep 1910
Louise Burdorf, wife of Russell S. POTTER, b.27 Feb 1904
Ann Sherwood POTTER, dau of Russell S. POTTER, b.26 Sep 1914
Stephen M. WOLLMAN, b.22 Oct 1902
Helen Patricia ALLEMAN, b.20 Feb 1921
Frances Winifred ALLEMAN, b.22 May 1922
Virginia Potter ALLEMAN, b.8 Apr 1924
Constance Dunkle ALLEMAN, b.15 Jun 1928

DEATHS

Rowena, wife of John TEAS, d.14 Apr 1845
Mary NOBLE, d.30 Dec 1843
Ellen H. TEAS, d.21 Sep 1863
Letitia, dau of S.J. TEAS, d.24 Aug 1872
Laura Mary BUCHANAN, d.27 Aug 1874
Jane Isabella BUCHANAN, d.27 Jan 1881
Wm BUCHANAN, d. Good Friday 1885

John TEAS, d.5 Oct 1885
Adeline TEAS, d.3 Feb 1887
Samuel Clard TEAS, d.18 Sep 1891
Mary Nobles Teas BUCHANAN, d.25 Dec 1904
Elizabeth M. TEAS, d.12 Sep 1912
Catherine Kirkpatrick TEAS, d.23 May 1917
Stephen Johnson TEAS, d.27 Sep 1925
David KIRKPATRICK, d.8 Dec 1904; aged 73yrs
Mary KIRKPATRICK, d.8 Feb 1910
John KIRKPATRICK, d.24 Dec 1913
David H. KIRKPATRICK, d.21 May 1917
(Misc Bible Files)

ALLEMAN BIBLE

Transcript of a HOLY BIBLE, published by Bible Publishing House, Syracuse, NY, 1882. Then in the possession of Frederick R. Alleman, Washington, NJ

Frederick Henry ALLEMAN married to Elizabeth Anna DUNKLE, 4 Aug 1887, St John's Lutheran Church, Steelton, PA
<u>BIRTHS</u>
Margaret Edith ALLEMAN, 24 Jun 1889
Mary Dunkle ALLEMAN, b.15 Dec 1890
Frederick Raymond ALLEMAN, b.18 Feb 1893
Ruth Elizabeth ALLEMAN, b.29 Jan --
George Mervin ALLEMAN, b.4 May 1901 (the above all born in Steelton, PA)
Elizabeth Viola ALLEMAN, b.30 Jun 1904, Summit, NJ
<u>BIRTHS and DEATHS</u>
Michael Rudy ALLEMAN, b.25 June 1825; d.13 Aug 18760
Leah ROYER, b.16 Apr 1824

Michael Rudy ALLEMAN married to Leah ROYER, 26 Aug 1852
Josiah Andrew DUNKLE, b.11 Sep 1834
Mary BISHOP, b.19 Aug 1838
Josiah A. DUNKLE married to Mary BISHOP
Frederick H. ALLENTON, b.29 Sep 1860, near Middleton
Elizabeth A. DUNKLE, b.3 Feb 1866, Churchville, PA
(Misc Bible Records File)

REYMOLD BIBLE

No Title Page or dates. From Clayton Jefferson Co, NY
FAMILY RECORD
<u>BIRTHS</u>
John M. REYNOLDS, b.12 Mar 1872
Catherine TOBIAS, b.13 Apr 1810
Sarah BENEDICT, b.6 Apr 1822
George W. REYNOLDS, b.17 Jul 1832
Jesse T. REYNOLDS, b.30 Jan 1834
Amos REYNOLDS, b.1 Jun 1836
Laura Anna REYNOLDS, b.19 Sep 1840
John M. REYNOLDS, b.21 Dec 1842
Mary Statira REYNOLDS, b.7 Jul 1845
Philorie S. REYNOLDS, b.22 Feb 1852
Horace G. REYNOLDS, b.18 May 1854
George W. REYNOLDS, b.6 May 1856
<u>MARRIAGES</u>
John M. REYNOLDS to Catherine TOBIAS, 8 Jun 1831
John M. REYNOLDS to Sarah BENEDICT, 4 May 1851
J.S. COLLINS to Leuree R. REYNOLDS, 19 Apr 1860
J.T. REYNOLDS to Mattie C. HUNT, Mar 1862
Amos REYNOLDS to Linda STEVA, Aug 1860

J.M. REYNOLDS to Cora SPENCER, 1880
Philo G. REYNOLDS to Estella M. FOX, 3 Nov 1873
Horace G. REYNOLDS to Cetitia J. LYON of New York City, 23 Jan 1884
George W. REYNOLDS to Mary Z. La VOCK of [---NY], 1 Mar 1888
J.M. REYNOLDS to Mrs Alice M. GOULD, 20 May 1888
A[---] E. COLLINS to May E. THORMAN, 17 May 1888
DEATHS
Mary Stutira REYNOLDS, d.9 Aug 1846, bur Methodist Burial Ground on westside of George Barnett child in St Catherine C.W.
Catherine [--] REYNOLDS, d.12 Dec 1847
George W. REYNOLDS, d.18 Jul 1856, Canada West
George W. REYNOLDS d. 24 Oct 1865
Sarah Catherine REYNOLDS, d. [-] Nov 1865
Philo S[--] REYNOLDS, d.5 Apr 1881
John M. REYNOLDS d.7 Aug [---]
Cora REYNOLDS, d.10 Jun 1886, Washington, KS
John M. COLLINS, d.[-] Jul 1873, Bernett, NE
(Misc Bible Records File)

MANY BIBLE

No Title Page or date;Transcript of a Bible, original copy in posession of Mrs Florence T. Robertson.

BIRTHS
James Harvey MANY, b.10 Jul 1813
Elizabeth CLARK (wife), b.29 Jan 1812
Their Children
Frederick Van Liew MANY, b.4 Aug 1837
James B. MANY, b.16 Nov 1838
Margaretta MANY, b.23 Nov 1840

William H. MANY, b.23 Nov 1842
Eliza Ann MANY, b.9 May 1844
Charles Webb MANY, b.7 Jun 1846
Josephine Augusta MANY, b.19 Apr 1848
Charles Webb MANY, b.17 Nov 1849
Samuel A. MANY, b.23 May 1851
Nathaniel MANY, b.21 Oct 1855

Family of
Isaac Tobias TOWNSEND, b.13 Oct 1839
and
Eliza Ann MANY (wife), b.9 May 1844
Their Children
Charlott Elizabeth TOWNSEND, b.24 Jul 1867
Elihu Hedges TOWNSEND, b.7 Sep 1869
Roma TOWNSEND, b.2 Feb 1872
John Webster TOWNSEND, b.22 May 1875
Aymar TOWNSEND, b.21 Oct 1877
Florence Iola TOWNSEND, b.21 Dec 1881
Avis TOWNSEND, d.6 Sep 1884
Nelson Sawyer TOWNSEND, b.15 Jul 1886

Family of
Florence TOWNSEND and Harvey ROBERTSON
I. Townsend ROBERTSON, b.3 May 1909
Phyllis Charlotte ROBERTSON, b.12 Apr 1915
Revere Harvey ROBERTSON, b.5 Nov 1919

MARRIAGES

James Harvey Many, son of Daniel & Susan Birdsall MANY; married at Cornwell, NY to
Elizabeth CLARK, dau of Cornelius & Elizabeth Wooley CLARK, 23 Nov 1835
Eliza Ann MANY to Isaac Tobias TOWNSEND, 29 Nov 1865

William Henry MANY to Jane E. YOUNG, 24 Apr 1872
Charles Webb MANY to Agnes BENNETT, 6 Jun 1881
Eliha Hedges TOWNSEND to Florence BERGEN, 18 Dec 1892
Charlott Elizabeth TOWNSEND to William David MELCHER, 29 Apr 1893
Aymar TOWNSEND to Amelia WRAITH, 6 Jun 1900
Florence Iola TOWNSEND to Harvey ROBERTSON, 29 May 1906
John Webster TOWNSEND to Edna WILCOX, 17 Mar 1916

DEATHS

Margaretta MANY, d.6 Feb 1843
Charles MANY, d.27 Aug 1847
Samuel MANY, d.29 May 1855
Nathaniel MANY, d.10 May 1856
James Harvey MANY, d.18 Oct 1872
William H. MANY, d.29 Mar 1882
James B. MANY, d. Jun 1884
Frederick Van Liew MANY, d.2 Dec 1885
Elizabeth MANY, d.6 May 1890
Avis TOWNSEND, d.9 Jul 1885
Roma TOWNSEND, d.11 Apr 1891
Isaac T. TOWNSEND, d.10 Oct 1904
Phyllis Charlotte ROBERTSON, d.27 Feb 1917
Eliza Ann Many TOWNSEND, d.5 Sep 1928
William Davis MELCHER, husband of Charlitte TOWNSEND, d.28 Sep 1938
Charlott Townsend MELCHER, dau of Isaac & Eliz; d.21 Oct 1943
Harvey ROBERTSON, husband of Florence TOWNSEND, d.13 Aug 1945

(Misc Bible Records File; 4-106)

SEAY BIBLE

No Title Page or Date. Published by Silas Andrus & Son, Hartford, Transcript; original in possession of Judge Burwell W. Seay, Palmyra, VA

Burwell Warren SEAY, son of B.W. SEAY, b.7 Oct 1856, Fluvanna Co, [VA]
Louisa PORTER, b.4 Nov 1833
Burwell Washington SEAY, b.23 Oct 1792, Fluvanna Co.
Catharine Pumphrey POLLARD, his wife, b.6 Jan 1794, Amelia Co.
Burwell Warren SEAY, b.5 Mar 1832, Powhatan Co
Burwell W. SEAY married to Catherine P. POLLARD, 21 Dec 1820
Burwell W. SEAY married to Louisa A. PORTER, 20 Dec 1854
Burwell W. SEAY, d.8 Sep 1857
Burwell Washington SEAY, d.5 Apr 1868
Catharine P. SEAY, wife of B.W. SEAY, d.17 Jun 1874, aged 80yrs, 5mos
Burwell Warren SEAY, d.14 Jun 1921, aged 64yrs, 8mos
(Misc Bible Records File; 4-222)

DRAKE BIBLE

No Title Page or date; A Transcript of the original in 1922 in the possession of Mary Augusta Cooper Maxon, Marietta, OH

David Grassett DRAKE, b.22 Dec 1759, Orange Co, NY
his wife
Mary Smith DRAKE, b.15 Apr 1768
Their Children

Fanny DRAKE, b.29 May 1788
Sally DRAKE, b.3 Dec 1789
Susan DRAKE, b.22 Dec 1791
Clarissa DRAKE, b.5 Aug 1793
Phebe DRAKE, b.14 Jul 1795
Hannah DRAKE, b.12 Apr 1798
Marie DRAKE, b.23 Jan 1799
Abigail DRAKE, b.15 Apr 1801
Joseph DRAKE, b.5 Aug 1803
Archibald DRAKE, b.29 Mar 1805
Emily DRAKE, b.7 Feb 1807
D. Haynes DRAKE, b.11 Sep 1810
George Washington DRAKE, b.28 Jul 1827
(Misc Bible Records File; 4-325)

ENGLE BIBLE

NEW TESTAMENT, published by D. Hitt & T. Ware, 1815. Original in posession of Miss Virginia Engle, Borsa, KY

MARRIAGES

Peter ENGLE to Margaret, his wife, 22 Aug 1799
Peter ENGLE to Mildred, his wife, 22 JUn 1823
James ENGLE to Elizabeth, his wife, 28 Oct 1824
Thomas J. ENGLE to Eliza, his wife, 23 Feb 1847
James J. STEWART to Alice, his wife, 23 Dec 1847
B.F. ENGLE to Elizabeth, his wife, 19 Sep 1854

BIRTHS

Peter ENGLE, b.20 Nov 1774
Margaret ENGLE, b.15 Mar 1783, wife of Peter
Mildred ENGLE, 2nd wife of Peter, b.29 Jan 1794
Elizabeth ENGLE, wife of B.F. ENGLE, b.3 Apr 1831

Children of Peter & Mildred ENGLE

James ENGLE, b.31 May 1824

Thomas Jefferson ENGLE, b.19 Feb 1826
Benjamin Franklin ENGLE, b.4 Feb 1828
Alice ENGLE, b.18 Feb 1830
Elizabeth ENGLE, b.25 Oct 1832
Fenny Chick ENGLE, b.15 Sep 1836
James J. STEWART, b.22 [---] 1826
Children of Thomas & Eliza ENGLES
James Franklin ENGLE, b.2 Feb 1848
Robert George ENGLE, b.11 Feb 1850
Mildred ENGLE, b.27 Jan 1852
Sarah C. RAMSEY, b.24 Jun 1872
DEATHS
Margaret ENGLE, wife of Peter ENGLE, d.18 Oct 182[-]
George ENGLE, SR, d.31 May 1826; aged 76yrs
Elizabeth ENGLE, wife of George ENGLE, d.2 July 1835; aged 77yrs 11mos
Peter ENGLE, d. 1 Mar 1840, aged 65yrs 9mos
Mildred ENGLE, d.7 Oct 1860, aged 65yrs 9mos 22dys
BIRTHS
Children of F.B. & Elizabeth ENGLE
Nancy Eliza ENGLE, b.18 Sep 1855
Children of George W. & Elizabeth HALE
Sarah Mildred HALE, b.22 Apr 1852
Tabitha Alice HALE, b.19 Aug 1854
Margaret Frances HALE, b.3 Mar 1857
Martha An Elizabeth HALE, b.31 Oct 1859
James Jefferson HALE, b.16 Jul 1862
DEATHS
Nancy Eliza ENGLE, d.22 Sep 1856; aged 1yr 4dys
BIRTHS
Children of Job & Fanny RAMSEY
Mary Elizabeth RAMSEY, b.14 Apr 1861; d.14 Feb 1863
Margaret Alice RAMSEY, b.1 Oct 1862

James Washington RAMSEY, b.30 Dec 1864
(Misc Bible Records File; 4-326)

JORDAN BIBLE

HOLY BIBLE, printed by William W. Harding, Philadelphia, PA 1869

BIRTHS

A.S. JORDAN, 27 Jan 1838
Gertrude WEIGHTMAN, 19 Jul 1848
Julia May JORDAN, 10 May 1868
Georgeanna JORDAN, 15 Jun 1870
Edith May WILLIS, 22 Jan 1896
J.S. WILLIS, Jr, 3 Aug 1861
Mary Helen WILLIS, 18 Aug 1899
Gertrude Irene WILLIS, 8 Mar 1901
Audrey Helen COLLINS, 3 Mar 1928
Joyce May McGEHEE, 14 Aug 1932
Harriett Lynn GABRIEL, 21 Mar 1951
John Wesley GABRIEL, 16 Apr 1953
Kenneth Forrest BOCKEMUEHL, 3 Sep 1954
Robert Henry GABRIEL, 3 Nov 1955

BIRTHS

Harry James GABRIEL, 9 Jan 1959
[Daughters of Harriett GABRIEL]
Jodie Lynn KNIGHT, 6 Jul 1973
Stacy Lane KNIGHT, 27 Nov 1974
[Children of Kenneth Forrest BOCHEMUEHL and Pamela Ann CRAWFORD]
[Grand Children of Joyce May McGEHEE and Robert Russell BOCKEMUEHL]
Brooke Nicole BROCKEMUEHL, 15 Aug 1978
Russell Forrest BOCKEMUEHL, 28 Dec 1979

MARRIAGES
A.S. JORDAN to Gertrude WEIGHTMAN, 3 Jul 1867
B.J. WADSWORTH to George Anna JORDAN, 12 Nov 1887
J.S. WILLIS to Jullia May JORDAN, 23 Sep 1894
Gertrude WADSWORTH to Dan GANDOLFI, 21 Dec 1909
Ida WADSWORTH to Carl HYDE, 30 May 1914
B.J. WADSWORTH to Louise THOMPSON, 19 Mar 1920
Edith May WILLIS to Herbert Hillery McGEHEE, 14 Jun 1922
George W. COLLINS to Irene Willis, 30 Aug 1922
Audrey Helen COLLINS to Harry Joseph GABRIEL, Jr, 5 Jun 1948
Joyce May McGEHEE to Robert Russell BOCKEMUEHL, 13 Jun 1952
Pamela Ann CRAWFORD to Kenneth Forrest BOCKEMUEHL, 9 Oct 1976
DEATHS
Wm B. JORDAN, 15 Sep 1847
Julia A. JORDAN, 14 Dec 1852
Joanna WEIGHTMAN, 19 Dec 1869, New Orleans, LA; age 46yrs
Henry C. JORDAN, 14 Sep 1874
George WEIGHTMAN, 14 Feb 1892
B.J.WADSWORTH, Sr, 22 Jun 1899
Algernon Sidney JORDAN, 15 Mar 1901
Gertrude Weightman JORDAN, 27 Dec 1911
Gertrude Weightman GANDOLFI, 18 Sep 1914
James Samuel WILLIS, Sr, 11 Mar 1912
Mary Elizabeth Wells WILLIS, 7 Mar 1913
George WILLIS, 2 Apr 1915
J.S. WILLIS, Jr, 8 Jul 1922
B.J. WADSWORTH, Jr, 1 Sep 1934
DEATHS

Julia May Jordan WILLIS, 26 Apr 1936; wife of James Samuel WILLIS, Jr
George Wesley COLLINS, 25 Aug, 1936; husband of Gertrude Irene Willis COLLINS
George Anna Jordan WADSWORTH KERN, wife of Benjamin James Wadsworth, Sr & Alonzo D. KERN
Herbert Hillery McGEHEE, 16 Aug 1947; husband of Edith May Willis McGEHEE
Mary Helen WILLIS, b.18 Aug 1899; d.22 May 1957
Edith May Willis McGEHEE, b.22 Jan 1896, Hammond, LA; d.16 Sep 1986, Pontiac, MI
(John Bertrand File)

WILLIS AND HARBOUR BIBLE

HOLY BIBLE, Published by B.Waugh and T. Mason, for the Methodist Episcopal Church, New York, 1833. Original in 1989 in possession of Mrs Irene Collins of Hammond, LA.

FAMILY RECORD

W.R. WILLIS, b.25 Jun 1771, New Jersey; d.13 Jan 1835
Catherine SMITH WILLIS, wife of W.R. WILLIS; b.14 Sep 1772; m. 27 Mar 1792 at Rockaway, NJ; d.19 Aug 1826, Baton Rouge. LA; aged 53yrs 11mos 15dys
William R. WILLIS, Jr b.29 Dec 1792, Morris Co, NJ
Maria Susan WILLIS, b.21 Aug 1794; d.19 Aug 1812
Hannah Eliza WILLIS, b.14 Oct 1796; d.9 Oct 1825, New Orleans
George Washington WILLIS, b.3 Sep 1798; d.7 Oct 1833
James Smith WILLIS, b.16 Jul 1800
Bernard Smith WILLIS, b.11 Oct 1803; d.16 Apr 1834
Alexander Hamilton WILLIS, b.12 May 1808
Frederick Augustus WILLIS, b.28 Feb 1811; d. Feb 1840, in

Texas
Elenora Kean HART m.25 Jan 1824; d. 29 Oct 1825 in St Helena, [LA]
Elenora Louisa WILLIS, dau of Samuel S. & Elenora K. WILLIS, b.17 Oct 1825; d.9 Jan 1826
Charlotte Jane HARBOUR, b.11 Aug 1811; m.1 Dec 1828 to James Smith WILLIS
Ellnora Kenner WILLIS, b.16 Nov 1829; d.5 Jul 1835; dau of J.S. & C.J. WILLIS
Ann Eliza WILLIS, b.6 Sep 1832; d.13 Jan 1833; dau of J.S. & C.J. WILLIS
James Samuel WILLIS, b.17 Nov 1833, son of J.S. & C.J. WILLIS
Pleasant Charles WILLIS, b.28 Dec 1835; d.12 Sep 188[?] 9; son of J.S. & C.J. WILLIS
George Washington WILLIS, b.22 Sep 1837; d.27 Sep 1837; son of J.S. & C.J. WILLIS
Lavinia Louisa WILLIS, b.4 Mar 1839; dau of J.S. & C.J. WILLIS
Augustus Bargess WILLIS, b.18 Sep 1841; d.4 Oct 1878; son of J.S. & C.J. WILLIS
Susan Cornelia WILLIS, b.8 Jan 1844; d.23 Sep 1844; dau of J.S. & C.J. WILLIS
Egenia Lovina WILLIS, b.18 Aug 1845; dau of J.S. & C.J. WILLIS
Charlotte Jane WILLIS, d.8 Aug 1849; aged 37yrs 11mos 29dys
Charles Arnold WILLIS, d.5 Dec 1849; aged 41yrs 6mos 24dys
James SMITH, d.6 Dec 11849; aged 72yrs
James Smith WILLIS, b.16 Jul 1800; d.6 Jul 1852; aged 51yrs 11mos 20dys
Mary E. WELLS, b.5 Aug 1839; m.8 Jul 1858 to James S.

Willis
Lavinia L. WILLIS m.9 Dec 1858 to J.M. TRACY
John P. WILLIS, b.13 May 1859; d.19 Oct 1863; son of J.S. & M.E. WILLIS
James Samuel WILLIS, b.3 Aug 1861; son of J.S. & M.E. WILLIS
Effie Lorena WILLIS, b.11 Jan 1865; d.19 Aug 1869; dau of J.S. & M.E. WILLIS
George Augustus WILLIS, b.19 Aug 1867; son of J.S. & M.E. WILLIS
Minnie Clara WILLIS, b.27 Mar 1870, dau of J.S. & M.E. WILLIS
Walter Sidney WILLIS, b.6 Aug 1872; son ,of J.S. & M.E. WILLIS
Lulu May WILLIS, b.19 Nov 1875; dau of J.S. & M.E. WILLIS
Clellie Maud WILLIS, b.19 Dec 1879
J.S. WILLIS, Sr; d.11 Mar 1912; [b.1836]
Mary E. WILLIS, d.7 Mar 1913; [b.1839]
George A. WILLIS, d.2 Apr 1915
Veva WILLIS, b.17 Dec 1895; d.1 Jan 1922
LuLu WILLIS, b.12 Jan 1898
Lydia WILLIS, b.22 Aug 1900
Samuel HARBOUR, d.25 Dec 1821
Mourning Kenner Dalton HEADON, b.13 Feb 1791
Charlotte Jane HARBOUR, b.11 Aug 1811; dau of Samuel & Mourning HARBOUR
Ann Eliza HARBOUR, b.2 Apr 1813
Pleasant H. HARBOUR, b.30 Apr 1815
Ewell D. HARBOUR; b.13 Mar 1817; d.5 Nov 1819
Samuel D. HARBOUR, b.9 Nov 1819; d.30 Dec 1822
William G. HEADEN, b.18 Oct 1823
George W. HEADEN, b.11 Jul 1825

Emily J. HEADEN, b.7 Feb 1831
Mary T. HEADEN, b.8 Oct 1833
Mary K. HEADEN, b.5 Jul 1821; d.23 Oct 1829
(John Bertrand File)

McGEHEE BIBLE

Original BIBLE burned in a house fire in Mississippi in the early 1900's. The Family records pages had been removed prior to the fire. possibly dated 1861.

BIRTHS
Robert Lea McGEHEE, 9 Dec 1883
two Infants sons b. 28 Mar 1886
Phillip Eugene McGEHEE, 24 Apr 1887
Lillian May McGEHEE, 21 Jul 1889
Infant son 2 Apr 1892
Hillery Herbert McGEHEE, 27 Aug 1893
children of Eugene & Verna
Verna Geraldine McGEHEE, 24 Oct 1920
Phillip Eugene McGEHEE, JR, 2 Sep 1924

J.M. McGEHEE, 5 Feb 1862
Joyce May McGEHEE, b.14 Aug 1932, Memphis, TN
Kenneth Forrest BOCKEMUEHL, b.3 Sep 1954, Detroit, MI
MARRIAGES
Phillip Eugene McGEHEE to Verna Mary LOTTERHOS; 25 Dec 1918
Hillery Herbert McGEHEE to Edith May WILLIS; 14 Jun 1922
Joyce May McGEHEE to Robert Russell BOCKEMUEHL; 13 Jun 1952
Edith May Willia McGEHEE, b.22 Jan 1896
DEATHS

Infant son, 28 Mar 1886
Infant Son, b.& d. 2 Apr 1892
Robert Lea McGEHEE, d.3 Feb 1894
Lillian May McGEHEE, dau; d.13 Mar 1919
Verna Mary McGEHEE, d.3 Sep 1924
Mrs Amanda McGEHEE; d.21 Oct 1926
Philip Eugene McGEHEE, Jr; d.5 May 1927
James Madison McGEHEE [Jr] d.2 Jun 1930
Herbert Hillery McGEHEE, d.16 Aug 1947, Detroit, MI
MEMORANDA
J.M. McGEHEE, Jr; b.5 Feb 1862
Amanda McGEHEE, b.18 Jul 1862
(DeJarnette File)

CANFIELD BIBLE

Bible presented to James R. Canfield by S.S. & M.J. CANFIELD 24 Dec 1895 on his 11th Birthday

MARRIAGE of S.S. CANFIELD of Staton County [Nebraska] to
Mary MATHERS of Harrison Co, IA; 12 Mar 1876 at Stanton, NE
MARRIAGES
Samuel S. CANFIELD to Eliza RANDOLPH, 16 Dec 1869, Cumings Co, NE
Amy R. CANFIELD, dau of Samuel S. & Eliza M. CANFIELD to Curtis E. BEEBE, sep 1888
BIRTHS
Samuel S. CANFIELD, b.10 Dec 1839, Wayne Co, PA
Mary Jane CANFIELD, b.13 Mar 1859, Harrison, IA
Eliza M. Randolph CANFIELD, b.
Amy R. CANFIELD, b.22 Apr 1871

Winona May CANFIELD, b.4 Dec 1878
Louis R. CANFIELD, b.24 Dec 1885
Nellie E. CANFIELD, b.8 Aug 1892
DEATHS
Eliza M. CANFIELD, first wife of Samuel S. CANFIELD, d. Aug 1873
Louis L. CANFIELD, son of S.S. & Mary Jane CANFIELD, d.11 Feb 1882
FAMILY RECORD
Samuel CANFIELD, b.7 Feb 1799; d.12 Mar 1880; m.2 Dec 1821
Sarah Ann SMITH; b.16 Jul 1806; d.4 May 1886
Elizabeth CANFIELD; b.8 Aug 1822; m.12 Jul 1840
David B. CANFIELD; b.21 May 1826; m.5 Jul 1847
John W. CANFIELD; b.19 Feb 1828
Chas W. CANFIELD; b.17 Apr 1830; d.29 Dec 1946
Henry CANFIELD; b.18 May 1833; d.1 Apr 1878
Mary Ann CANFIELD; b.29 Jun 1835; d.24 Jul 1873; m. --57
Geo W. CANFIELD; b.21 Aug 1837; m.26 Apr 1864
Samuel S. CANFIELD; b.10 Dec 1839; d.7 Apr 1925; m. to Eliza 16 Dec 1869; m to Mary Jane 12 Mar 1876
Edward R. CANFIELD; b.30 Dec 1841; m.15 Apr 1866
Louis J. CANFIELD; b.22 Sep 1844; m.6 Nov 1863
Lura [?] CANFIELD; b.28 Sep 1846; d.15 Mar 1852
James C. CANFIELD; b.7 Jul 1848; d.12 Apr 1877
(Alice Gaylord File)

WHITLOCK BIBLE

No Title page or date. The Whitlock Family of Dymond Hollow, PA. The original at one time in the possession of Mr Ernest Dunning, Fort Myers, FL.

BIRTHS
Enoch WHITLOCK, b.4 Oct 1803
Mary WHITLOCK, b.15 Feb 1806
Polly Jane WHITLOCK, b.29 Jul 1826
Martha WHITLOCK, b.10 Aug 1828
Infant b. dead 11 Feb 1831
Washington J. Lyle E. WHITLOCK, b.28 Jun 1832
Christopher C. WHITLOCK, b.5 Feb 1835
Rhoda WHITLOCK, b.31 Dec 1836
Gould WHITLOCK, b.27 Mar 1839
Caroline WHITLOCK, b.[--] Aug 1841
Gertrude WHITLOCK, b. 25 Apr -----
DEATHS
Candace WHITLOCK, d.16 May 1846
Mary WHITLOCK, d.5 Nov 1867
Friend A. WHITLOCK, d.24 Nov 1880
Rhoda WHITLOCK, d.1 Jan 1891
Mary Jane WHITLOCK, d.10 Dec 1900
(Misc Bible File)

DYMOND BIBLE

NEW TESTAMENT, published by Edward W. Miller, Philadelphia, 1866. Original in 1978 in possession of Robert H. Dymond, Sr of Clarks Summit, PA

BIRTHS
John B. DYMOND, b.30 Mar 1820
Mary J. DYMOND, b.29 Jul 1826
Sarah C. DYMOND, b.22 Jan 1846
Martin L. DYMOND, b.22 Sep 1847
Martha DYMOND, b.22 Feb 1849
Frances DYMOND, b.2 Mar 1851
BIRTHS

Abel T. DYMOND, b.8 Oct 1852
Samuel DYMOND, b.17 May 1857
John DYMOND, b.24 Nov 1858
Carrie DYMOND, b.13 Feb 1864
Wayman DYMOND, b.1 Jul 1865
Berton DYMOND, b.5 Mar 1867
DEATHS
Samuel DYMOND
Berton DYMOND, d.17 Aug 1864
John B. DYMOND, Sr; b.17 Apr 1899
(Misc Bible File)

WAYMAN FERRE DYMOND BIBLE

HOLY BIBLE, Published by Bible Publishing House, Syracuse, NY, 1882 . Original in 1978 in possession of Robert H. Dymond of Clarks Summit, PA

MARRIAGE
Wayman F. DYMOND to Mary L. EGGLESTON, 28 Sep 1887
BIRTHS
Wayman F. DYMOND, b.1 Jul 1865, Locksville, PA
Mary L. EGGLESTON, b.[-] Jun 1860, Vernon, PA
CHILDREN
Lee E. DYMOND, b.22 Sep 1888
Howard W. DYMOND, b.20 Oct 1890
Ernest DYMOND, b.9 Apr 1892
Russell S. DYMOND, b.19 Mar 1894
Harold DYMOND, b.21 May 1896
Glenn Austin DYMOND, b.2 Jul 1901
MARRIAGES
Earl DYMOND to Mary Edna WILLIAMS, 11 Nov 1914, Wilkes Barre, PA

Russell S. DYMOND to Grace MITCHELL, 17 Dec 1923, Jacksonville, FL
Glen Austin DYMOND to Marjorie SCHULER, Nov 1923
Glen Austin DYMOND to Effie Orean TRUESDALE
<u>DEATHS</u>
Howard W. DYMOND, d.3 Aug 1893
Ernest DYMOND, d.23 Feb 1895
Harold DYMOND, d.27 Feb 1897
Mary Louise EGGLESTON, d.13 Feb 1952
Russell S. DYMOND, d.28 Feb 1972
Marjorie SCHULER, d.11 Jun 1929
(Misc Bible Records Files)

LUCE / WEED BIBLE
No Title page or date.
<u>BIRTHS</u>
Wm F. LUCE, b.9 Feb 1796
Ann M. LUCE, b.29 Jul 1797
C.F. LUCE, b.30 Oct 1821
N.A. LUCE, b.17 May 1824
William P. LUCE, b.27 Mar 1829
E.S. LUCE, b.4 May 1832
A.E. GOFF, b.26 Dec 1837
Foster W. LUCE, b.20 Mar 1853
Emma E. A. LUCE, b.24 May 1856
Ella M. LUCE
Abbigal E. LUCE
Warren J.E. THURSTIN, b.27 Jul 1860
Ann M.E.THURSTIN, b.17 Nov 1862
Floy E. GOFF, b.9 Jul 1862
Frederick WEED, b.1 Apr 1765
Nancy H. WEED, b.15 Dec 1767

Abigah B. WEED, b.14 Jan 1791
Nancy H. WEED, b.9 Apr 1792
Ann M. WEED, b.29 Jul 1797
Mary E. WEED, b.5 Dec 1799
MARRIAGES
Wm F. LUCE to Ann M. WEED, 7 May 1820
Potter GOFF to Ann M. LUCE, 14 Aug 1836
C.F. LUCE to Miss Menbah LEGGETTE, 15 Jun 1852
George L. THURSTIN to Elizabeth L.O. LUCE, 26 Aug 1855
Algenon E. GOFF to Miss Caroline E. RUSSELL, [date cut off]
DEATHS
Wm F. LUCE,d.25 Aug 1834
Potter GOFF, d.12 Nov 1846
Warren J.E. THURSTIN, d.28 Sep 1863
Ella M. LUCE, d.1 Apr 1861
Frederick WEED, d.17 Sep 1845
Nancy WEED, d.17 Jan 1856
Abjah B. WEED, d.28 Jan 1866
Barnabas A. WEED, d.20 Nov 1871
Manly WEED, d.18 May 1845
Charlotte A. WEED, d.21 Jul 1859
Ann M. GOFF, d.6 Oct 1875
C.F. LUCE, d.26 Mar 1896
N.A.E. LUCE, d.13 Oct 1899
W.P. LUCE, d.26 Jan 1900
E.S. LUCE THURSTON, d.20 Jul 1913
Geo L. THURSTON, d.23 Jan 1926
DEATHS
Fred A. TOZIER, d.6 Feb 1924
(Misc Bible Records File)

ENGLISH BIBLE

No Title Page, certified as from a Hardings Medium Edition Old & New Testament, Published in Philadelphia, 1860. Original about 1955 in possession of George Day

BIRTHS

Wm ENGLISH, b.20 Sep 1793
Margaret MORRISON ENGLISH, b.10 Aug 1799
Children of the Same
Jeremiah ENGLISH, b.26 Sep 1814
Fanny ENGLISH, b.10 May 1816
Elizabeth ENGLISH, b.10 Apr 1817
Margaret ENGLISH, b.10 Nov 1819
John W. ENGLISH, b.6 Mar 1823
William ENGLISH, b.6 Aug 1825
George W. ENGLISH,b.4 Jul 1826
Rachel ENGLISH, b.10 May 1829
Sarah ENGLISH, b.10 May 1830
James ENGLISH, b.10 Mar 1831
Claudius ENGLISH, b.1 Apr 1832
Eli ENGLISH, b.9 Apr 1833
Ann ENGLISH, b.6 Aug 1836
Samuel ENGLISH, b.6 Mar 1839
Caroline ENGLISH, b.20 Feb 1841
(Misc Bible Records file)

TOZIER BIBLE

NEW TESTAMENT Published by Samuel Bagster & Sons, London,n.d.

BIRTHS

F.A. Frederic Ancel TOZIER, b.5 Jan 1851
Mary Abigail THURSTON, b.23 May 1873
Their Children
Gladys Alma TOZIER, b.18 Nov 1894

Frederic Alden TOZIER, b.30 Oct 1896
DEATHS
Fred Ancel TOZIER, d.6 Feb 1924
(Misc Bible Records File)

BOVARD BIBLE I

HOLY BIBLE, published by C. Ewer & T. BEDLINGTON, 1825

Charles BOVARD and Mary CRAWFORD, m. 10 Sep 1805
Charles BOVARD, d.21 Aug 1852
M. BOVARD, d.2 Nov 1856
John L. BOVARD, b.26 Jun 1806
George C. BOVARD, b.16 Oct 1807; d.20 Jan 1852
Fany BOVARD, b.29 Oct 1809; d.7 Apr 1857
Charles BOVARD, b.11 Dec 1811; d.1 Jun 1895
William C. BOVARD, b.17 Mar 1814; d.13 Jun 1904
Jane C. BOVARD, b.25 Sep 1816; d.12 Nov 1893
Mary BOVARD, b.6 Nov 1826; d.13 Dec 1899
Charles BOVARD and Melissa COCHRAN, m.8 Apr 1856
(Misc Bible Records File)

BOVARD BIBLE II

No Title Page , statement made that records are from a Holy Bible Published by Jasper Harding, Philadelphia, 1853
BIRTHS
W.C. BOVARD, b.17 Mar 1814
Jane FITZGERALD, b.7 Aug 1826
Alice Maria BOVARD, b.23 Mar 1854
James Fitzgerald BOVARD, b.29 Nov 1855
Lizzie Jane BOVARD, b.31 May 1857

Paul Bovard McLANE, b.15 Nov 1876
John Fisher McLANE, b.14 Nov 1878
Mary Margaretta McCARTNEY, b.8 Nov 1888
Alice Bovard McCARTNEY, b.26 Apr 1891
James Shearer McCARTNEY, b.21 Jul 1893
Jane Elizabeth McCARTNEY, b.30 Mar 1896
Ada St Clair McCARTNEY, b.11 Nov 1898
MARRIAGES
W.C. BOVARD to Jane FITZGERALD, 20 Jan 1853
Alice Maria BOVARD to Rev Wm W. McLANE, Sep 1875
Lizzie Jane BOVARD to Dr James Shearer McCARTNEY, 21 Jul 1887
DEATHS
James Fitzgerald BOVARD, d.12 Feb 1836
Alice Bovard McLANE, d.8 Nov 1878
Wm. C. BOVARD, d.13 Jun 1904

Mary Margaritta McCARTNEY, b.8 Nov 1888
Alice Bovard McCARTNEY, b.26 Apr 1891
James Shearer McCARTNEY, b.21 Jul 1893
Jane Elizabeth McCARTNEY, b.30 Mar 1896

Jan 5 1898 J.S. McCARTNEY moved with his Family to Washington, PA
Ada St Clair McCARTNEY, b.11 Nov 1989
(Misc Bible Records File)

PERRY BIBLE

No Title Page or Date.

FAMILY RECORD
BIRTHS
James PERRY, b.18 Dec 1791

Marry PERRY, b.20 Sep 1800
Elizabeth PERRY, b.25 Oct 1817
Elloner PERRY, b.25 Jun 1819
John Law PERRY, b.23 Nov 1820
William Scott PERRY, b.12 Jan 1824
Robert Thomas PERRY, b.19 Mar 1826
James Finney PERRY, b.23 Oct 1831
Sophiah PERRY, b.17 Feb 1834
Maryann PERRY, b.8 May 1837
Nancy Jane PERRY, b.22 Apr 184[-]
William Walace PERRY, b.1 Jul 18[--]
Wilson Sutter PERRY, b.11 Apr 1851
<u>MARRIAGES</u>
James PERRY to Mary LAW, 5 Feb 1817
Daniel [B]urket to Elizabeth PERRY, 26 Mar 1830
William WALLACE to Ellen PERRY, 2 Jun 1842
John S. PERRY to Caroline E. HUTCHINSON, Feb ----
William S. PERRY to Ruth KUNCEMAN, 30 Dec 1832
Robert F. PERRY to Harriet HASKARGER, Sep ______
James F. PERRY to Mary E. HUNTER, 2 Sep 1856
John WARTON to Sophia PERRY, 20 Sep 185[-]
Charles PERRY to Mary H. PERRY, 28 Oct 1858
<u>DEATHS</u>
Elizabeth BURKET, d.5 Aug 1853
Sarah E. BURKET, d.11 Apr 185[-]
James Finney PERRY, d.9 Jan 1906
Laura M. PERRY, d.18 Feb 1906
Mary Elizabeth PERRY, d.6 Apr 1918
Lyle F. PERRY, d.30 Nov 1927
David Elimer Simpson PERRY, d.24 Oct 1929, bur. Condersport, PA; aged 68yrs; b.12 Jul 1861
Maud Townley PERRY, d.17 Apr 1945
James PERRY, d.25 Jun 1862

Mary PERRY, d.28 Feb 1879

Simpson D. PERRY married to Maud A. TOWNLEY, 28 Jul 1882, Meadville,PA
DEATHS
Mary Adelaide PERRY, dau of S. & Maud A. PERRY; d.23 Sep 1885, bur on farm in Purdes, NE
Lyle Flower PERRY, son of D.S.D. & Maud A. PERRY; d.30 Nov 1927
Daniel E.D. PERRY, d.24 Oct 1929, Flint, MI
(Misc Bible Records Files)

FARRAR BIBLE

No Title Page. In about 1954 the Bible was in the possession of Bernice Farrar McLaury (Mrs Herbert F.) of Silver Springs, MD.
FAMILY RECORDS BIRTHS
Luther T. FARRAR b.9 Nov 1807
Evehine STANLEY b.15 May 1812
Judson W. FARRAR b.14 Jun 1833
Eugene W. FARRAR b.27 Jul 1835
Julia Adelaide STANDISH b.6 Dec 1835
Emma Caroline STANDISH b.20 Feb 1843
Adelia Evelina STANDISH b.13 Jul 1845
Edward Hiram STANDISH b.3 Jan 1847
Address 23 Apr 1886
E S Eiloer _____
Judson Floyd FARRAR b.4 Sep 1905
Hiram STANDISH b.25 Mar 1809
Walter Gordon, son of Walter E. FARRAR b.12 Dec 1893
Harold Cha MCKEE b.17 Dec 1899
Grace Farrar MCKEE b.25 Jan 1904
Gloria Yale FARRAR b.18 Dec 1897

Jane White FARRAR b.2 Jun 1904

BIRTHS

Eugene H. FARRAR b.22 Jul 1835
Martha Jane CARPENTER b.15 Sep 1845
Garth Elmore FARRAR, son of Luther Carpenter FARRAR b.9 Jun 1890
Julie FARRAR, Dau of L.C.FARRAR b.26 Sep 1891
Martha A. FARRAR, dau of L.C.FARRAR b.4 May 1894
Bernice FARRAR, dau of W.E. FARRAR b.4 Sep 1895
Addie M. FARRAR b.13 Apr 1866
Luther A. FARRAR b.20 Dec 1867
Walter Ernest FARRAR b.27 May 1870
Archie Clifton FARRAR b.9 Dec 1873
Edith Evelyn FARRAR b.14 Mar 1875
Judson Floyd FARRAR b.25 May 1878
Henry Lynn FARRAR b.17 Mar 1881
Dorothy Jane MCKEE b.21 Apr 1893

MARRIAGES

Luther T. FARRAR to Eveline STANLEY 21 Sep 1831
Hiram STANDISH to Eveline FARRAR 11 Jan 1838
Edith E. FARRAR to Joseph E. ALLEN 29 Nov 1894
Edith E. FARRAR to August SCHABEL 17 Jul 1900
Archie Clifton FARRAR to Buelah J. WHITE 29 Jul 1903
Eugene W. FARRAR to Martha Jane CARPENTER 10 Dec 1864
Martha Adalaide FARRAR to David Elnore MCKEE 17 Oct 1879
Luther Carpenter FARRAR to Jenevieve R. RIDDLER 12 Dec 1889
Walter EVERET to Bertha BAILY 1 Mar 1893
Jewell FARRAR to Geo Wm GOAL 5 OIct 1926

DEATHS

Luther T. FARRAR d.18 Jun 1836

Eveline F. STANDISH d.30 May 1847
Judson Floyd FARRAR d.11 May 1905
Garth Elmor FARRAR d.17 Jul 1909
Edith Evelyn FARRAR
Judson W. FARRAR d.18 Jun 1863, Alexandria, DC
Eugene W. FARRAR d.25 Jul 1931
Martha J. FARRAR d.2 Feb 1923
Bertha L. FARRAR d.19 May 1937
Henry Lynn FARRAR
Gordon Walter FARRAR
Walter Everett FARRAR d.9 Jan 1950
(Mics File, 17-313)

BARR BIBLE

HOLY BIBLE, Published by Kimber & Shapples, Philadelphia, n.d. The Bible in 1995 is in the possession of Howard Wheaton Barr, Crown Point, IN

Daza L. BARR Crown Point, IND This was Grandpa Barr's Family Bible
over 100 years old
(at end of The Old Testament)
Ray HEDMAN & Mildred BARR m.3 Aug 1935
Howard BARR & Ethel WASHBURN m.6 Dec 1927 at Gary, IN
Hubert BARR, Jr & Irene BRODIE m. __ Nov 1932
Ronald Washburn BARR, son of Ethel & Howard BARR, b. Gary, IN 28 Jul 1931 (First grandchild in the Samuel Barr, Jr Family
Dixon A. BARR, son of Harold & Matilda BARR b.14 Jan 1932
(on "title" page of New Testament)

Emma Standish BARR d.9 Apr 1937; bur Maplewood, age 94yrs one month 20 days
Harold Standish BARR d.30 Oct 1937, Gary ; bur. Calumet Cemetery; son of Herbert & Jessie BARR
Herbert Stanley BARR, son of Samuel & Emma BARR d.16 Jul 1942, Crown Point, bur. Maplewood, age 73yrs 4m 12ds
FAMILY RECORDS BIRTHS
Samuel BARR b.17 Feb 1809
Sarah DUNLAP b.10 Jul 1813
Mildred BARR, dau of Herbert & Jessie BARR b.16 Jul 1905, Crown Point
Baby BARR, dau of Herbert & Jessie BARR b.1 Nov 1906; d.10 Feb 1907
Howard BARR, son of Harry & Frankie BARR b.14 Nov 1907, Crown Point
Harriet BARR b.5 Sep 1831
Lavina BARR b.17 Jun 1834
Sarah BARR b.4 Mar 1836
Mary Ann BARR b.15 Apr 1837
Samuel A. BARR, Jr b.5 May 1842
MARRIAGES
Samuel BARR & Sarah DUNLAP m.30 Nov 1830 by Rev Shafner, Maryatta
John HOFF & Lavina BARR m.3 Nov 1853 by Rev E. Koke
David Brindle & Sarah BARR m. 13 Dec 1867

Martin BROWN & Maryann BARR m.13 Sep 1872
Clarence W. BARR & Lura STRONG m.14 Jun 1888, Chicago, IL_
Herbert S. BARR & Jessie M. HILL m.4 Mar 1899, Chicago, IL
Fred A. BARR & Edith W. HALL m.18 Dec 1901, Chicago, IL

Harry J. BARR & Frankie A. WHEATON m.11 Jul 1902, Chicago, IL
Harold Standish BARR to Matilda HENNING m.6 Aug 1927, Crown Point
DEATHS
Lovina HOFF d. 3[?] Sep 1854, age 20yrs 2m 2wks 2dys_
Albert HOFF d.14 Jun 1857, age 2yrs 9m 14dys
Harriet BARR d.25 Jan 1864, age 32yrs 4mos 22dys
Samuel BARR d.21 Jun 1887, age 78yrs 4mos 3dys
Sarah BARR d.12 Apr 1891, age 77yrs 9mos 2dys
Samuel A. BARR d.24 Jan 1898, bur Crown Point, age 55yrs 9mos 19dys
Mary Ann BROWN, wife of Martin BROWN d. Naperville, 27 Apr 1900
Martin BROWN d.Naperville 25 Feb 1907, age 75yrs
(blank page "flyleaf")
Lura Strong BARR, wife of Clarence BARR, d.9 Jan 1905 bur Oakwood Cemetery, Chicago
Robert Samuel BARR, son of Fred & Edith BARR d.8 Jun 1909, Chicago, bur.Oak Ridge Cemetery, age 10mos
Martha Ann BARR d.Carlisle Spring 17 Nov 1912 bur Naperville Cemetery, age 16yrs 10mos 20dys
Clarence W. BARR d. Crown Point, IN 30 Sep 1923 bur. Maywood, Crown Point Oldest son of Samuel & Emma BARR
(on New Testament title page)
Leland BARR, son of Herbert Hill & Irene Brody BARR b.3 Aug 1945, Hammond, IN
(on a seperate page)
Joan Ardelle BARR dau of Herbert & Irene BARR b.23 Sep 1937, Gary, IN d. Jun 1941
Robert Christopher BARR son of Ray & Mildred BARR b.16 May 1945

Standish Wheaton BARR son of Howeard & Ethel BARR b.26 Mar 1933 Gary IN
Jon Ray son of Ray & Mildred BARR b.12 Dec 1940
Gene Richard BARR son of Herbert & Irene BARR b.13 Feb 1941 Gary IN
(Misc File, 17-313)

DUNLAP FAMILY BIBLE

THE HOLY BIBLE New York, American Bible Society, 1857 In 1995 the Bible in the possession of Mrs Jean Humphreys Herschburger of Sykesville, MD

BIRTHS
Robert DUNLAP b.23 Jul 1817
Rebeca DUNLAP b.8 Sep 1821
James A. DUNLAP b.18 Jun 1841
John H. DUNLAP b.23 Mar 1844
Samuel B. DUNLAP b.16 Oct 1846
Maryann DUNLAP b.13 Jan 1849
Henry DUNLAP b.29 May 1851
George W. DUNLAP b.8 Dec 1853
Rebecca DUNLAP b.10 Feb 1856
Robert DUNLAP b.3 Jun 1858
DEATHS
Mary Ann DUNLAP d.26 Aug 1850, age 1yr 7mos 19dys
Henry DUNLAP d.14 Jan 1857, age 5yrs 7mos 16dys
Robert DUNLAP, Jr d.2 Jul 1858, age 29dys
Robert DUNLAP Sr d.19 Mar 1889, age 71yrs 7mos 26dys
(extra sheet of records)
BIRTHS
Nancyann DUNLAP b.24 Apr 1802
Susanna DUNLAP b.9 Oct 1803
Mary DUNLAP 20 Jan 1806

John DUNLAP 22 Nov 1807
James DUNLAP b.24 Nov 1809
Sarah DUNLAP b.10 Jul 1813
Elizabeth DUNLAP b.23 Sep 1815
Robert DUNLAP b.23 Jul 1817
DEATHS
Susana HAVNER d.26 Jun 1838, age 34yrs 8mos 17dys
John DUNLAP, Sr d.24 May 1848 age 73yrs 3mos 11dys
Mary Ann DUNLAP d.17 May 1851, age 70yrs 5mos 24dys
Nancy Ann WILLSON d.23 Mar 1861, age 58yrs 10mos 27dys
Mary KOHR d.18 Apr 1874, age 68yrs 2mos 29dys
MARRIAGES
John DUNLAP to Mary Ann ANDERSON 10 Feb 1801 by Rev Ebenezer DICKY, East Nottingham
Fredric HEFFNER to Susan DUNLAP 30 Oct 1824 by Rev Gysquite, Helm TWP
Joseph WILLSON to Nancy Ann DUNLAP 6 Apr 1830 by Rev Sheffner Columbia
James DUNLAP to Sarah FERLL 22 Jul 1830 by Rev Schumacherd York
Samuel BARR to Sarah DUNLAP 30 Nov 1830 by Rev Sheffner Marryatta
David CORE to Mary DUNLAP 24 Oct 1822 by Rev Schmuckerd York
John NEWCOMMER to Elizabeth DUNLAP 14 Feb 1839 by Rev Sencal Manschester TWP
Robert DUNLAP to Rebecch HOFF 11 Aug 1839 by Rev A.H. Lochman York
(Misc File, 17-313)

THE McCULLOUGH FAMILY BIBLE

THE HOLY BIBLE 1817 Brattleborough, Printed for John Holbrook

The copy was from Mrs C. Edward Sparrow, Jr of Baltimore, MD

(on the front Flyleaf)

The Property of James McCullough born 29 Aug 1779 in South Carolina

price $12.00 in 1817

FAMILY RECORDS MARRIAGES

James McCULLOUGH to Catherine LOUW 29 May 1808

James McCULLOUGH to Maria HASBROUCK 27 Jun 1816

Maria HASBROUCK b. 9 Dec 1777

Lucinda ANN (widow of the late ____ McCULLOUGH m. William FICK 13 Mar 1867

MARRIAGES

Jane McCULLOUGH to James HARRIS of Caroline Co, MD 22 Dec 1832

William McCULLOUGH to Ann Jane CHAPMAN 18 Nov 1838

Levi McCULLOUGH to Lucinda A CROSS 7 Oct 1844

William McCULLOUGH to Jennette MILLER 8 Oct 1844

James McCULLOUGH to Elizabeth ELA 23 Feb 1847

David McCULLOUGH, son of Levi to Malinda KENT 29 Mar 1871

Catherine Marah, Dau of late Levi McCULLOUGH to George FREE 26 Sep 1872

William Gardner, son of Levi McCULLOUGH to Harriet Adelia LATHAM 17 Oct 1883

Wm McCULLOUGH to Janet MILLER 8 Oct 1844

BIRTHS

Elizabeth Jane b.10 Nov 1845
Maria b.11 Dec 1847
Ada b.26 Dec 1849
Louisa Mead b.31 Oct 1851
David Dankerby b.13 Dec 1853
James b.15 Apr 1856
Jessie Ann b.25 Dec 1858
William Robert b.30 Jan 1861
Agnes Maud b.2 Mar 1864
William Hasbrouck McCULLOUGH b.30 Apr 1819, New Paltz, Ulster Co, NY
Janet MILLER b.4 Aug 1820 Quebec
(on Flyleaf)
David b.8 Aug 1810
Jane b.3 Nov 1812 by first wife
William b.30 Apr 1819
James b.12 Sep 1820
Levi b.24 Nov 1824 by second wife
<u>BIRTHS</u>
David McCULLOUGH b.8 Aug 1810 my first son
Jane McCLLOUGH b.3 Nov 1812, My dau
Mary Ann McCULLOUGH b.20 Sep 1817, my dau
William McCULLOUGH b.30 Apr 1819, my son
James McCULLOUGH b.12 Sep 1820, my son
Levi McCULLOUGH b.25 Nov 1824, my son
<u>DEATHS</u>
Catherine, my wife d.17 Jun 1815
Mary Ann, my dau by second wife d.30 Apr 1818
My sons William's wife d. 3 Aug 1842
William H. McCULLOUGH d.4 Mar 1892
Janet Miller McCULLOUGH d.25 May 1989, age 77yrs
David Dumkoly McCULLOUGH d.1 May 1901, age 47yrs
<u>BIRTHS</u>

David, son of Levi McCULLOUGH b.25 Aug 1846
James, son of Levi McCULLOUGH b.13 Sep 1847
William G. McCULLOUGH b.13 Jan 1853
Catherine McCULLOUGH b.10 Oct 1854
Ida Jane McCULLOUGH b.18 Oct 1857
Rachel McCULLOUGH b.27 Jun 1862
Edgar Levi McCULLOUGH b.11 Aug 1864
DEATHS
James McCULLOUGH, Sr d.27 Apr 1851, age 72yrs
David McCULLOUGH d.16 Sep 1854, age 43yrs
James McCULLOUGH, Jr d.18 Apr 1855, age 35yrs
James, son of L. McCULLOUGH d.14 Dec 1855, age 8yrs
Mariah, wife of James McCULLOUGH d.14 Jul 1858, age 81
Rachel Louisa , dau of Levi McCULLOUGH d.18 Aug 1864, age 29yrs
Levi McCULLOUGH d.2 Mar 1866, age 41yrs
Edgar Levi, son of Levi McCULLOUGH d.15 May 1867, age 2yrs
Catherine M McCULLOUGH, wife of George FREE d.7 Sep 1881, aged 26yrs 10mos 21dys
BIRTHS
John Edgar, son of George TOLL b.12 Aug 1875
Charles Henry, son of George TOLL b.4 Aug 1878; d.26 Aug 1881, age 3yrs 22dys
James Latham, son of William G. McCULLOUGH b.11 Dec 1884
Frederick William, son of William G. McCULLOUGH b.30 Apr 1886; d.4 Dec 1886, age 7mos
DEATHS
Ida Jane, dau of Levi McCULLOUGH d.5 Mar 1887, age 29yrs 4mos
(Mics File 36-79)

NICHOLS BIBLE

No Title Page

FAMILY RECORDS BIRTHS

G. NICHOLS, son of F & E NICHOLS b.21 Aug 1774
Rebecca NICHOLS, his wife, dau of John & Polly DAVIS b.17 Mar 1776

Their Children

Elizabeth, b.16 Oct 1794
James, b.10 Sep 1796
William, b.23 Aug 1798
George, b.4 May 1801
Garret, b.19 Apr 1803
Felix, b.10 May 1805
Polly Ann, b.18 Jun 1807
Eveline, b.15 Sep 1809
Frederich, b.20 Aug 1811
Nancy, b.21 Jun 1814
Sarah, b.12 Apr 1818

BIRTHS

Frederick NICHOLS, son of G. & Rebecca NICHOLS, b.8 Aug 1811
Angelina, his wife, dau of Jas & Betsy Ann CRUMP,b.13 Sep 1833

Children

Nancy, b.4 Jan 1833
Betsy Ann, b.24 Apr 1835
Robinette, b.19 Mar 1837
Owen S. NICHOLS, b.7 Jun 1839
Henry M. NICHOLS, b.2 Nov 1841
Samuel C. NICHOLS, b.31 Dec 1843
Garret N. NICHOLS, b.20 Sep 1845

DEATHS

B. W. W. RICHARDSON m. to Nancy Y. NICHOLS 19 Jun

1850
Nancy Y. RICHARDSON, wife of B W W RICHARDSON, d.26 Nov 1855, aged 22yrs 10mos 22 dys
Betsy Ann NICHOLS, wife of [_______] d.12 Sep 1853, aged 23yrs 6mos 5 dys
Henry M. NICHOLS, d.2 Apr 1861, aged 19yrs 5mos
Samuel C. NICHOLS, d.11 Jul 1862 [got killed in battle against the Rebels]
MARRIAGES
Frederick NICHOLS, son of G & Rebecca NICHOLS m.19 Jun 1832 to Angelina, dau of Jas & Betsy CRUMP
Frederick B. NICHOLS d.26 Mar 1869; aged 58yrs 7mos 6dys

Attached are two photos of tombstones in the Cane Springs Cemetery, Jasper Co, Missouri
Frederick B, NICHOLS/ Born/ 20 Aug 1811/ Died / 26 Mar 1869
Angeline /Wife of /F.B. NICHOLS/ Born/ 13 Sep 1811/ Died/ 30 Jan 1880
(Ballanger File)

RICHARDSON BIBLE

No Title Page. The pages were removed from to Bible and in 1979 were in the posession of Mrs Lydia Nichols Fullerton of Carthage, MO.
MARRIAGES
Bushrod W. M. RICHARDSON m. 19 Jun 1850 to Nancy Y. NICHOLS
Bushrod W. M. RICHARDSON m.2 Jul 1856 to Robinette M. NICHOLS
BIRTHS
Bushrod W. M. RICHARDSON b.11 May 1823

Nancy Y. RICHARDSON b.4 Jan 1833
Volney F. RICHARDSON b.22 Apr 1851
Orrich RICHARDSON b.19 Mar 1853
Nancy Y. RICHARDSON b.6 Nov 1855
Mary RICHARDSON b.3 May 1866
Ella RICHARDSON b.10 Nov 1869
Bushrod W. M. RICHARDSON, Jr & Sister b.19 Aug 1874
Robinette May RICHARDSON b.19 Mar 1837
<u>DEATHS</u>
Nancy Y. RICHARDSON, wife of B.W.M. RICHARDSON, d.26 Nov 1855; age 22yrs 10mos 22days
Mary RICHARDSON, Dau of Robinette RICHARDSON d.8 Aug 1870, age 4yrs 2n 28dys
Infant dau of BWM & R M RICHARDSON d.2 Oct 1864
B W M RICHARDSON d.17 Mar 1897
B W M RICHARDSON, Jr d,2 Mar 1908
Mrs R, M, RICHARDSON d.18 Apr 1920
(Ballenger file)

CYRUS P. HORTON BIBLE

HOLY BIBLE, Published by American Bible Society, New York 1870
<u>FAMILY RECORDS BIRTHS</u>
Cyrus HORTON b.12 Sep 1812
Harriet N. HORTON b.7 Aug 1818
Cornelia HORTON b.4 Jun 1835
Theon[?] W. HORTON b.22 Jan 1837
Leland HORTON b.23 Dec 1839
Polly HORTON b.14 Sep 1841
Selina HORTON b.17 Nov 1843
Joshua L. HORTON B.31 Jan 1846
William F. HORTON b.2 Jul 1848

Sarah Jane HORTON b.5 Apr 1850
Rose [__] HORTON b.27 Dec 1851
Charles Henry HORTON b.12 May 1853
Ellen HORTON b.15 Mar 1856
J--- Infant b. Apr 1857
(Ballanger File)

O. S. NICHOLS BIBLE

HOLY BIBLE, Published by A. J. Holman & Co, Philadelphia, 1892

MARRIAGES

O. [Owen] S. [Smith] NICHOLS of Jasper Co, MO to G. E. COATS of Lawrence Co, on 30 Nov 1865

BIRTHS

O. S. NICHOLS, b.7 Jun 1837
G.E. NICHOLIS b.6 Feb 1846
Laura M. NICHOLS b.3 Dec 1866
Clement NICHOLS b.25 Jan 1867
William NICHOLS b.23 Nov 1872
Frederick NICHOLS b.25 Apr 1876
Cora NICHOLS b.6 Feb 1879
Burt L. NICHOLS b.23 Oct 1881
Pearl NICHOLS b.29 Sep 1884
Emma May NICHOLS b.29 Dec 1855
Lydia NICHOLS b.3 Jun 1896
[C. E. FULLERTON & FAMILY]
Claud E. FULLERTON b.28 Sep 1888
Lydia FULLERTON b.3 Jan 1890
Claude FULLERTON, Jr b.24 Aug 1918, La Russell, MO
Eugene FULLERTON b.26 Sep 1920, Carthage Mo
Jack Daniel FULLERTON b.14 Aug 1920

MARRIAGES

O. S. NICHOLS to G. S. COATS, 30 Nov 1865
Clements NICHOLS to Mattie RIDDLE, 24 Dec 1890
William NICHOLS to Tillie ROUX, 18 Jan 1899
Cora NICHOLS to L. E. WILLIAMS, 30 Mar 1904
Frederick NICHOLS to Ruby CORNOR, 31 May 1916
Lydia NICHOLS to Claud E. FULLERTON, 20 Nov 1916
DEATHS
Laura H. NICHOLS d.7 Oct 1884
Pearl NICHOLS d.29 Sep 1884
G.E. NICHOLS d.11 Mar 1927
Bart NICHOLS d.31 Jan 1951
Cora WILLIAMS d.31 Mar 1952
Wm NICHOLS d.27 Aug 1957
Frederick NICHOLS d.28 Aug 1958
(Ballenger File)

HUSSEY BIBLE

Copied in 1938 by Mary Symons from the Bible in the possession of Milton Hussey, Zionsville, IN. IN 1961 Bible in possession of Alvin Hussey of Alhambra, CA

FAMILY RECORD BIRTHS
Joseph HUSSEY, son of John & Mary HUSSEY, b.1st dy 10th mo 1815
Sarah HUSSEY, dau of John & Rachel FRAIZER, b.10dy 9th Mo 1820
John HUSSEY, son of Joseph & Sarah, b.15dy 2mo 1840
William HUSSEY, son of Joseph & Sarah, b.30dy 4mo 1842
Martha Jane HUSSEY, dau pof Joseph & Sarah, b.28dy 7mo 1844
Mary HUSSEY, dau of above Parents, b.30dy 6mo 1846
Elizabeth HUSSEY, dau of above parents b.15dy 1mo 1849
Harriet HUSSEY, dau of above parents, b.5dy 11mo 1850

Thomas HUSSEY, son of above parents, b.13dy 1mo 1853
Rachel HUSSEY, dau of above parents, b.1dy 4mo 1855
Franklin HUSSEY, son of above parents, b.18dy 6mo 1858
MILTON HUSSEY, son of above parents, b. 14dy 4mo 1862
MARRIAGES
Joseph HUSSEY to Sarah FRAIZER 8 Feb 1838
William HUSSEY to Hannie JESSUP, 24 Nov 1864
Martha J. HUSSEY to Oliver C. ELLIOTT, 3 Dec 1865
Mary HUSSEY to Martin T. CAREY, 3 Dec 1865
Elizabeth HUSSEY to William CLARK, 21 Apr 1872
Harriet HUSSEY to L. SABIN, 16 Aug 1874
Rachel HUSSEY to John W. JESSUP, 30 Nov 1876
Thomas HUSSEY to Sarepta DAUBENSPECK, 8 Dec 1878
Milton HUSSEY to A. Ella HOFFMAN, 25 Nov 1885
DEATHS
Franklin, son of Joseoh & Sarah HUSSEY, d.17 Mar 1860, aged 1yr 8mo 29dys
John, son of Joseph & Sarah HUSSEY; killed at battle of Chicamauga 19 Sep 1863 Member of 10th Reg Co F. Indiana Vol
Mary H. CAREY, dau of Joseph & Sarah HUSSEY, d.15 May 1877; age 30yrs 10mo 15dys
Joseph HUSSEY d.13 Jul 1896, age 80yrs 9mos 12dys
Sarah HUSSEY, d.6 Dec 1899; aged 79yrs 2mos 26dys
(Ballenger File)

ELLIOTT BIBLE

Records copied in 1938 from a Bible in the possession of Mrs Louis J. Symons of Carmel, IN. In 1961 the Bible in the possession of Robert S. Elliott of Mill Valley, CA
FAMILY RECORDS MARRIAGES
Oliver C. ELLIOTT to Martha Jane HUSSEY 3dy 12mo 1865

Louis J. SYMONS to Sarah MEALISS 4dy 4mo 1894
Frederick H. ELLIOTT to Cora DIXON 16dy 10mo 1901
Thomas M. ELLIOTT to Henrietta Rose SPITZER 5dy 8mo 1903
Alvin S. POWER to Harriet ELLIOTT 11dy 11mo 1908
BIRTHS
Oliver C. ELLIOTT, son of Absalom & Polly M. ELLIOTT, b.12dy 9mo 1844
Martha Jane ELLIOTT, dau of Joseph & Sarah HUSSEY, b.28dy 7mo 1844
Sarah Melissa ELLIOTT, dau of Oliver C. & Martha Jane, b.7dy 6mo 1867
Infant Son of Oliver C. & Martha Jane, b.6dy 10mo 1869
Frederick ELLIOTT, son of Oliver C. & Martha Jane, b.5dy 12mo 1872
Thomas ELLIOTT, son of Oliver C. & Martha J, b.16dy 3mo 1876
Harriett ELLIOTT, dau of Oliver C. & Martha J, b.18dy 10mo 1880
DEATHS
Martha J. ELLIOTT, d.15dy 4mo 1914, aged 69yrs 8mos 17dys
Oliver Cromwell ELLIOTT, d.24dy 2mo 1917
Harriet ELLIOTT POWER, d.9dy 12mo 1918
(Ballenger File)

SYMONS BIBLE

The records in 1938 were copied by Mary Symons from a Bible in the possession of Mrs Louis J. Symons of Carmel IN. IN 1961 the Bible in the possession of late home of Mrs L.J. Symons.

MARRIAGES
Louis J. SYMONS to Sara M. ELLIOTT 4 Apr 1894
J. Malcolm SYMONS to Sara FUNK 17 Oct 1931
Norman G. CRAWFORD to Helen SYMONS 20 May 1933
BIRTHS
Mary SYMONS, dau of Louis J. & Sara E.; b.25 Apr 1898
Infant girl, dau of Louis J. & Sara E., b.19 Mar 1901, d. same day
J. Malcolm SYMON, son of Louis J. & Sara E., b.28 Jan 1904
Helen SYMON, dau of Louis J. & Sara E., b.23 May 1906
DEATHS
Morris SYMONS, d.1 Aug 1913
Martha J. ELLIOTT, d.15 Apr 1914
Oliver C. ELLIOTT, d.23 Feb 1917
Harriet E. POWER, d.9 Dec 1918
Elizabeth C. SYMONS d.5 Mar 1922
Elizabeth H. CLARK, d.23 Mar 1921
Fred ELLIOTT, d.9 Nov 1933 Brother
Louis J. SYMONS, d.4 Oct 1937, age 74yrs
MARRIAGES
Nathan M. SYMONS to Elizabeth C. WILSON 12 Apr 1855
Louis J. SYMONS to Sarah M. ELLIOTT, 4 Apr 1894
Mary SYMONS, dau of Louis & Sarah E. b.25 Apr 1898
Malcolm SYMONS, b.28 Jan 1904
Harry M. SYMONS m. 25 Dec 1895 to Florence DAY
Paul M. SYMONS, son of Harry & Florence
Joseph D. SYMONS, son of Harry & Florence, b.28 Feb 1899; d.13 Jan 1901
Hershel SYMONS, b.31 Jul 1901
Kenneth SYMONS, b.
Nathan M. SYMONS, son of Thomas & Abigail SYMONS, b.4dy 12mo 1829

Elizabeth C. SYMONS, dau of Jonathan & Drusilla WILSON, b.1dy 8mo 1837
Alice D. SYMONS, dau of Nathan M. & Elizabeth C., b.6dy 2mo 1857
Louis J. SYMONS, son of N. M. & E.C. SYMONS, b.21dy 8mo 1863
Henry M. SYMONS, son of N.M. & E.C., b.7dy 4mo 1871
(Ballenger File)

JOHN BROWN BIBLE

No Title Page or Date. Copied from the Monmouth County Historical Society, handed in by Josephine Brown, Keyport, NJ, 22 Mar 1903. Records in possession of Monmouth County Historical Society, NJ and Josephine Brown, Keyport, NJ.

Peter REZEAU
Father, Renee REZEAU
Mother, Anne COURSIER

Susannah REZEAU
Father. Peter REZEAU
Mother, Dorcas GUILBERT

John BROWN m. to Susannah REZEAU
Children of John & Susannah BROWN
Peter, b.24 Jan1737
Mary, b.1 Mar 1739
William, b.30 Sep 1742
James, b.27 Nov 1744
Jacob and John, b.1 Feb 1747

Abraham, b.11 Mar 1749
Benjamin, b.31 Aug 1751
Mary, b.3 Oct 1754
Joshua, b.19 May 1757
Daniel, b.9 Nov 1759
Susannah, b.12 Nov 1762

BROWN FAMILY RECORDS

On a seperate sheet of paper the following records
Jacob O. BROWN, b.23 Sep 1810
Mary Ann CONKLIN, b.28 Nov 1822
Albert BROWN, b.21 Jul 1842
Isabelle BROWN, b.21 Jun 1844
Josiah C. BROWN, b.27 Jan 1847
Lewis BROWN, b.1 Apr 1849
Sophie BROWN, b.27 Oct 1852
Theodore BROWN, b.24 Feb 1855
William C. BROWN, b.6 Mar 1857
Ira BROWN, b.7 Aug 1859
Elmer A. BROWN, b.24 Aug 1864
Mary Louise BROWN, b.24 Sep 1866

Mary Ann BROWN, wife of Jacob O. BROWN, d.6 Nov 1876; aged 52yrs 11mos 1week
Jacob O. BROWN and Mary Ann CONKLIN m. 23 Jun 1841
Jacob O. BROWN, d.11 Aug 1892

ELMER R. BROWN BIBLE

No Title Page or Dates. Copies furnished by Mrs Jacqueline Gerth of Glenview, IL in Sept 1995.

BIRTHS

Jacob O BROWN, b.23 Sep 1810
Mary A. CONKLIN, b.28 Nov 1822
Albert BROWN, b.21 Jul 842
Isabelle C. BROWN, b.21 Jun 1844
Joshiah C. BROWN, b.27 Jan 1847
Lewis BROWN, b.1 Apr 1849
Sophia C. BROWN, b.27 Oct 1852
Theodore C. BROWN, b.24 Feb 1855
William C. BROWN, b.6 Mar 1857
Ira BROWN, b.7 Aug 1859
Elmer R. BROWN, b.24 Aug 1864
Mary L. BROWN, b.24 Sep 1866
Annie M. DUNHAM, b.28 Feb 1866
Chester R. BROWN, b.5 Nov 1893
Jacqueline P. BROWN, b. 4 Oct 1921
Floyd GERTH, b.17 Oct 1920
Persis Hope AGNEW, b.30 Nov 1900, Stilman Valley
Stephen Brown GERTH, b.9 Dec 1946, Evenston, IL

DEATHS

Mary A. BROWN, d.6 Nov 1876
Jacob O. BROWN, d.11 Aug 1892
Mary L. BROWN, d.22 Aug 1900
Albert BROWN, d.19 Jan 1909
Elmer R. BROWN, d.4 Mar 1937
Annie M. DUMBAR, d.21 Nov 1941
(Rene Rezeau file)

Albert de la MONTAGINE BIBLE

HOLY BIBLE Published by American Bible Society, New York, 1851. Copy sent by John Merrill de la Montagne of Bozeman, MT in July 1995.

FAMILY RECORDS - BIRTHS

FAMILY RECORDS

William de la MONTAGINE, b.11 Nov 1788

Jane GRAHAM, b.29 Apr 1795

William de la MONTAGINE and Jane GRAHAME m. 5 Nov 1817

Jane GRAHAME, wife of Wm de la MONTAGINE d.9 Mar 1863, bur in Green[wood]; aged 67yrs 11mos 21dys

Henry MEYER, Father of Ellen A. de la MONTAGINE, b. in Hanover, Gremany 9 Feb 1800; d.28 Dec 1880, Brooklyn

Sarah Gertrude MEYER, dau of Henry MEYER and sister of Ellen dela MONTAGINE, d.9 Feb 1881, age 40yrs at Brooklyn

Albert de la MONTAGINE, b. 5 Dec 1826, City of New York

Ellen Anne MEYER, wife of Albert de la MONTAGINE, b. 18 Feb 1832, in New York City

Albert de la MONTAGINE m. to Ellen Anne MEYER by Rev Isaac Ferris, 11 Dec 1851, New York City

Henry de la MONTAGINE, b.19 Dec 1852; d.6 Jul 1936

Albert de la MONTAGINE, Jr b. 7 Sep 1857

William de la MONTAGINE, b.19 Jul 1861; d. c.1930

Sarah Mollen de la MONTAGINE, b.18 Aug 1868/69, Norwalk, CT

Anne Gertrude de la MONTAGINE

William de la MONTAGINE, Jr, son of Wm & Jane de la MONTAGINE, b.9 Aug 1818; d.5 Sep 1853, aged 35yrs 27dys, bur in Greenwood

Margaret Jan dela MONTAGINE, dua of Wm & Jane

(Grahame) dela MONTAGINE b.30 Dec 1829, d.28 Dec 1859 after a residence of six weeks in the Island of St Thomas West Indies, bur in Greenwood. Wife of William P. WHITMAN
Henry Albert, William, Sarah Moller, Anne Gertrude children of Albert & Ellen Anne de la MONTAGINE Bapt by Dr Howard Crosby, 3 Apr 1873
Anne Gertrude, dau of Albert & Ellen Anne de la MONTAGINE,aged 2yrs 5mos, d at Norwalk, CT 30 Jul 1874 Bur 31 Jul 1874 at Greenwood
Joseph Edward dela MONTAGNE m. Amelia LITTLETON 21 Aug 1876 by Rev A.W. Loomis, DD
Joseph Edward dela MONTAGNE d.1 Sep 1876, San Francisco, CA
(de la Montagine file)

BRETT BIBLE

HOLY BIBLE Self-Pronouncing Edition, no publisher or date.

BIRTHS
John Franklin BRETT 24 Aug 1859
Jessie Cummings BRETT 28 Jul 1872
John Frederick BRETT 27 Jan 1897
William Glade BRETT 27 Dec 1899
Martha Elizabeth BRETT 25 Dec 1901
Charlotte Mae BRETT 30 Nov 1904
George Wendall BRETT 30 May 1912
DEATHS
John Franklin BRETT 30 [26] Nov 1930
Jessie Cummings BRETT 15 Nov 1956
John Frederick BRETT 17 Sep 1899
(Peter Lang File)

GEORGE SNYDER BIBLE

No Title Page or date.

FAMILY RECORDS BIRTHS
George SNYDER 27 Jun 1804
Rhoda LOMEREAUX 23 Jun 1811
Elizabeth SNYDER 3 Jun 1802
Thomas B. SNYDER 3 Jan 1807
Curtis SNYDER 4 Apr 1810
Jacob SNYDER 21 Feb 1813
Phillip SNYDER 25 Apr 1815
La[-]y SNYDER [____] 0, 1817
DEATHS
John H. SNYDER 28 Oct 1819
Fanny SNYDER 15 Mar 1821
Martin B. SNYDER 24 Aug 1824
Phebe SNYDER 20 Jul 1827
Polly R. LOMERAUX 30 Jun 1808
Jemima LOMEREAUX 3 Nov 1809
Joel R. LOMEREAUX 30 Mar 1813
Henry LOMEREAUX 27 Jun 1818
Boy with out name 7 Jul 1817
Temperence LAMEREAUX 19 Dec 1821
BIRTHS
Chester SNYDER 2 Dec 1830
Joel L. SNYDER 4 Nov 1831
Jacob H. SNYDER 5 Nov 1833
Jemima SNYDER 3 Freb 1835
Harriett A. SNYDER 24 Feb 1840
Mary SNYDER 9 Dec 1896
DEATHS
Martha LOMEREAUX 14 Jul 1817
Daniel LOMEREAUX 29 Apr 1830
Henry LOMEREAUX Dec 1818

Jemima LOMEREAUX 1812
Margaret, wife of Peter SNYDER 25 Aug 1848; aged 65yrs 10mos 8dys
Peter SNYDER 1 Feb 1850; aged 70yrs 10mos 29dys
MARRIAGES
George SNYDER to Rhoda LOMEREAUX 20 Apr 1818
BIRTHS
Daniel LOMEREAUX 4 Mar 1785
Martha LINN 18 Mar 1783
Peter SNYDER 2 Mar 1779
Margaret NAEL [?] 17 Oct 1782
DEATHS
Jacob H. SNYDER 3 Oct 183[-]
Joel L SNYDER 25 Jan 1881, aged 29yrs 2mos 21 dys
Chester SNYDER 22 Jul 1882, aged 52yrs 7mos 20dys
Rhoda SNYDER 6 Sep 1891, aged 80yrs 2mos 13 dys
George SNYDER 23 Nov 1892, aged 88yrs 5 mos 26days
(L'AMOUREUX FILE)

SAMUEL DIEHL BIBLE

No Title Page or publication date.

FAMILY RECORDS BIRTHS
Thomas DIEHL, son of Samuel Erwin & Getrude Virginia DIEHL 27 Dec 1889
Ethel DIEHL, dau of Samuel Erwin & Gertrude DIEHL 26 Sep 1891
Earle DIEHL, son of Samuel Erwin & Gertrude DIEHL 17 Jan 1893
Myrtle V. DIEHL, dau of Samuel Erwin and Gertrude Virginia DIEHL 16 Apr 1895
Flora May DIEHL, dau of Samuel Erwin & Gerturde DIEHL 12 May 1896

Samuel Erwin DIEHL JR, som of Samuel Erin and Gertrude Virgina DIEHL 20 Jul 1904
Gertrude Virginia DIEHL, dau of Samuel Erwin & Gertrude Virginia DIEHL 29 Jun 1908
(Jean La Montaigne File)

GEORGE DIEHL BIBLE

No Title page or publication date

BIRTHS

George DIEHL, son of Geo & Catherine DIEHL, 15 Aug 1821, Rockhill TWP
Lydia MOFFLY, dau of Samuel & Charlotte MOFFLY, 13 Sep 1830, Richland TWP
Wilbor Fisk, son of George & Lydia DIEHL, 30 Aug 1851, Montgomery Square, PA
Catherine Elizabeth, dau of George & Lydia DIEHL, 25 Oct 1852 Montgomery Square, PA
Samuel Erwin, son of George & Lydia DIEHL 12 Jul 1855 Norristown, Mont. Co, PA
(Jean La Montaigne File)

DAVIS BIBLE

No Title Page and no publication date.

BIRTHS

Charles Lively DAVIS, 13 Mar 1859, Philada
Rebie DAVIS, dau of Chas L. & Josephine W. C. DAVIS, 6 Jul 1884
Josephine W.C. DAVIS, 7 Nov 1863, Philada
Rebie DAVIS, 6 Jul 1884, Philada
Beatrice DAVIS, 30 May 1886. Philada
Mabel Hirst DAVIS, 15 Jqn 1888, Philada

Euegenia [______], 18 Dec 1890
Charles Lively DAVIS, JR, 1 Dec 1892
Dorothy Anderson DAVIS, 23 Nov 1894, Philada
Joseph De Binder Davis, 18 Oct 1896 East Oqontz, PA
Dabette De Binder DAVIS, 7 Feb 1903
(Jean LaMontaigne File)

PETER W. GRUBBS BIBLE

HOLY BIBLE, published by Thomas Cowperthwait & Co, Philadelphia, 1839

FAMILY RECORDS MARRIAGES

Peter W. GRUBBS & Rebecca A. LEPSCOMBE[?], 10 Apr 1834 by Rev Jas B. Taylor, Hanover Co
John L. GRUBBS & Mary E. WINGFIELD, 14 Apr 1858 by Rev J.B. Jeter, Hanover Co.
Wm Y. LEPSCOMBE & Virginia C. GRUBBS, 23 Dec 1857 by Rev J. Lansing Burrows in Richmond
Abbott E. LLOYD & Virginia Lee LEPSCOMBE, 9 Feb 1886 by Rev George Cooper in City of Richmond
Cary Doran WINGFIELD & Georgia Beauregard GRUBBS, 19 Dec 1889 by RevGeorge Cooper in Richmond
George Barrett SNYDER, Jr & Nannie Winston GRUBBS, 27 Oct 1892 by Rev Geo Cooper, Richmond, VA
Robert Daniel TUCKER, MD & Mary Lewis GRUBBS, (b.11 Feb 1896 by Rev George Cooper, Richmond, VA
James H. BRICE & Ida Dean LIPSCOMBE, ___ 1896 by Rev George Cooper, Richmond
Benjamin Wingfield GRUBBS & Goldie May HARVEY, 7 Feb 1900 by Rev George Cooper, Richmond, VA

BIRTHS

Peter W. GRUBBS, son of Anderson & Susan GRUBBS, 25 Aug 1809, Hanover Co

Rebecca A. LIPSCOMBE, dau of Nathaniel C. & Mary B. Sutton LIPSCOMBE, 22 Feb 1817, Hanover Co

John Lewis GRUBBS , son of Peter W. & Rebecca A. GRUBS, 29 Mar 1835, Hanover Co.

William Washington GRUBBS, son of Peter W. & Rebecca A. GRUBBS, 22 Feb 1837, Hanover Co

DEATHS

Peter Winston GRUBBS, 26 Mar 1885, near city of Richmond, Aged 75yrs 7mos 1dy

Rebecca A. GRUBBS, 31 Jan 1890,aged 72yrs 11mos 9dys, Richmond

John Lewis GRUBBS, 13 Jun 1926, aged 91yrs 2mos 15dys, Richmond

William Washington, son of Peter W. & Rebecca A. GRUBBS 18 Oct 1839, aged 1yr 7mos 29dys, Hanover Co

BIRTHS

Virginia Claisome, dau of Peter W. & Rebecca A. GRUBBS, 29 Nov 1839, Hanover Co

Ida Dean, dau of William Y & Virginia C. LIPSCOMBE, 13 Sep 1858, Richmond

Nannie Winston, dau of John L. & Mary E. GRUBBS, 23 Jan 1859, Richmond

Virginia Lee, dau of Wm Y & Virginia C. LIPSCOMBE, 14 Jul 1860, Isle of Wight Co

Georgia Beauregard, dau of John L & Mary E. GRUBBS, 25 Oct 1860,Prospect Hill Hanover Co

DEATHS

Wm Y. LIPSCOMBE 29 Sep 1863, age 29yrs 10mos of Typhoid Fever, Isle of Wight Co

Infant Child of Wm Y & Virginia C. LIPSCOMBE, 28 Aug 1862, aged 2mos 18dys

Willie Y, dau of late Wm Y & Virginia C. LIPSCOMBE, 16 Jun 1864, aged 9mos 23dys

John Winston, son of Lieut Jno L & Mary E. GRUBBS, 21 Jun 1864, aged 23mos 6dys
Ida Diane LIPSCOMBE, wife of James H. BRICE, 5 Jul 1899, Richmond
BIRTHS
______, dau of Wm Y. & Virginia C. LIPSCOMBE,10 Jun 1862, Isle of Wight Co
John Winston, son of Lieut John L. & Mary E. GRUBBS, 27 May 1862, Richmond
Willie Young, dau of late Wm Y & Virginia C. LIPSCOMBE, 24 Aug 1863, Isle of Wight Co
Mary Lewis, dau of John L. & Mary E. GRUBBS, 10 Dec 1866, Hanover Co
Peter Winston, son of John L. & Mary E. GRUBBS, 18 Dec 1867, Richmond
Benjamin Wingfield, son of John L & Mary E. GRUBBS 4 Oct 1870, Oaklawn, Henrico Co
DEATHS
Mary Eleanor WINGFIELD, wife of John Lewis GRUBBS, 10 Oct 1901, Powhatan Co
Peter Winston GRUBBS, 8 Nov 1889, aged 21yrs 10mos 21dys
Benjamin Wingfield GRUBBS, 31 Jul 1925, Richmond; aged 54yrs 2mos 5dys
(Nicholas La Fontaine File)

EDWARD J. BALLARD BIBLE

No Title Page or publication date.

FAMILY RECORDS MARRIAGES
Edward J. BALLARD of Somerset Co, MD to Eliza Ann SMITH of Alexandria, D.C. 12 Jul 1832
Benjamin B. SNYDER, JR to Mary A. BALLARD, both of

Baltimore City, MD, 15 Nov 1866
Jas H. HOPKINS to Eliza J. BALLARD, both of Baltimore City, MD, 12 Jan 1871
J. Edw BALLARD to S. Louise DORMAN, both of Baltimore, MD, 19 Dec 1879
Wm T. ADREAN to Laura V. BALLARD, 22 Nov 1884, Baltimore, MD
L. McCauley HOPKINS to Mary C. BURTON, 1 May 1904 [entry can't be read clearly]
Edward B. HOPKINS to Olive WILCOX of Texas, 14 Jun 1907
Herbert L. OGIER to Elizabeth Raymond BALLARD, 3 Apr 1907
Nellie Louise BALLARD to George A. BAKER of New York, 19 Jun 1907
<u>BIRTHS</u>
Edward James BALLARD, 29 Apr 1811
Eliza Ann BALLARD, 8 Feb 1813
Mary Eliza, first dau of Edward & Eliza Ann BALLARD, 4 Apr 1833, Alexandria, DC
Arnold Henry Martin, first son of Edward J. & Eliza Ann BALLARD, 13 Apr 1835, Baltimore
Amelia Maria, dau of Edward J.& Eliza Ann BALLARD, 11 Jul 1837, Baltimore
Mary Amelia, thrid dau of Edward J.& Eliza Ann BALLARD, 30 Oct 1839, Baltimore
Eliza Jane, dau of Edward J.& Eliza Ann BALLARD, 4 Nov 1841 , Baltimore
Edward Merriken, second son of Edward J.& Eliza A. BALLARD, 19 Feb 1844, Baltimore
Laura Virginia,fifth dau of Edward J.& Eliza BALLARD, 22 May [____], Baltimore
Sarah Louisa Noble, sixth dau of Edward J & Eliza A.

BALLARD, 25 Sep 1848
Joseph Edward, third son of Edward J. & Eliza A. BALLARD, 17 Mar 1851, Baltimore
William A., fourth son of Edward J. & Eliza A. BALLARD, 19 May 1853
Eloise Baker, second dau of Geo & [__], 7 Feb 1913
Emma Maria, seventh dau of Edward J. & Eliza A. BALLARD, 22 Feb 1855, Baltimore
Mary BALLARD, first dau of B.B. & Mary A., 8 Mar 1867, Baltimore
Emma Amelia, second dau of B. B. & M.A. SNYDER, 14 Mar 1870, Bltimore
Benjamin Berry SNYDER, son of B.B. & M.A. SNYDER, 8 Sep 1872, Baltimore
Jas Edward, first son of Jas L. & Eliza J. HOPKINS, 22 Dec 1872, Baltimore
Louise Ballard OGIER, 7 Feb 1912, dau of Herbert & Bessie O.
DEATHS
Amelia Maria, second dau of Edward J. & Eliza Ann BALLARD, 5 Oct 1838, aged 1yr 2mos 25dys
Mary Eliza, first dau of Edward J. & Eliza Ann BALLARD, 25 Apr 1839, aged 6yrs 21dys
Edward MERRIKEN, second son of Edward J. & Eliza Ann BALLARD, 11 Jan 1848, aged 4yrs
Arnold H., son of Edward J. & Eliza A. BALLARD, 16 Jun 1849, aged 14yrs [-]mos
William A., fourth son of Edward J. & Eliza Ann BALLARD, 18 Aug 1855, age 3mos
Emma Maria, seventh dau of Edward J. & Eliza Ann BALLARD, 19 Jun 1864, aged 9yrs
Edward James, husband of Eliza Ann BALLARD, 13 Apr 1867, aged 56yrs

James Edward, son of Eliza & Jas H. HOPKINS, 20 Jul 1893
Willie SNYDER, son of B.B. & M.A. SNYDER, 10 Feb 1883, aged 1yr 10mos
Wm T. ADREAN,husband of Laura V. ADREAN, 6 Dec 1885
Phillipa SMITH, 13 Oct 1876, Baltimore aged 89yrs 10mos
Jane BREAD,Aug 1864, aged yrs
Eliza A. BALLARD, 17 Jul 1890, aged 77yrs
Eliza Jane Smith, fourth dau of Eliza A. & Edward J. BALLARD, b.4 Nov 1841, d.6 May 1895
James Ballard HOPKINS, youngest son of Harry M. & Mary B. HOPKINS 12 Jul 1906; aged 15mos
William H. SMITH, 20 Aug 1901
Sydney Virginia Douglas, youngest dau of Samuel & Phillipa SMITH, 7 Apr 1909, Washington
Laura Virginia ADREAN, Apr 1939

on a loose page

Taken from a Bible of Edward Ballard now in the possession of Joseph Edward Ballard, Jr. No Title page or date of publication. only a transcript.
Children of Edward & Jane MARTIN born in County Cornwell,England
Edward b. 7 Apr 1770,; d.7 Jun 1829
James b.16 Apr 1772; d.Aug 1836
William b.17 Aug 1774
Jane b.20 Jan 1776; d.11 Aug 1864
Bathani dau b.Jan 1780; d.17 May 1785
Philippi b.Jun 1780; d.11 Jan 1783
Thomas and John (twins) b. Jun 21 1782
Bathani b. Nov 1784; d. Nov 1785
Philippi b.11 Dec 1786; d.13 Oct 1876
Harry b.27 Apr 1789

Richard b.14 May 1791
Children of Philippi MARTIN m. to Samuel SMITH of Berkely Co VA 9 Jun 1808
Mary Jane b.17 Apr 1811
Eliza Ann b.8 Feb 1813
Joseph Fry b. 1 Dec 1814
Henreitta Maria b.28 Nov 1816
William Henry b.3 Oct 1821
Wm Henry b.38 Oct 1823
Sidney Virginia b.29 Oct 1825
Q---M--- ,dau b.20 Oct 1827
(Nicholas LaFontaine File)

THOMAS B. FONTAINE BIBLE

HOLY BIBLE Published by A. Chandler, New York for the American Bible Society, 1830. Transcript of the original in the possession (1979) of Mrs Richard Moses Felts of Springfield, TN.

Thomas B. FONATINE b.12 Mar 1777
Moses A. FONTAINE b.2 Aug 1816
Elizabeth FONTAINE b.3 Apr 1756
Thomas B. FONTAINE b.12 Mar 1777, m. 28 Dec 1809 to Mary WILLIAMS
Their CHILDREN:
Sarah W. FONTAINE b.26 Nov 1810
Elizabeth B. FONTAINE b.15 Sep 1812
Mary Ann W. FONTAINE b.15 May 1815
Moses A. FONTAINE b.2 Aug 1816
Charles FONTAINE b.28 May 1818; d. Jul 1818
Nancy D. FONTAINE b.24 Jun 1819; d.17 Feb 1895
Nancy FONTAINE wife of Thomas B. FONTAINE departed

this life
Thomas B. FONTAINE & Ann WATKINS m. 1825 [second wife]
Their CHILDREN:
Martha E. W. FONTAINE b.20 Dec 1826
Lucy I. FONTAINE b.20 Jun 1829

Thomas B. FONTAINE d. 8 Apr 1850
Henry S. FREY d.30 [24] Dec 1852 [51]
(Jean de La Fontaine File)

ALEXANDER F. ROSE BIBLE

HOLY BIBLE, published by M. Carey, Philadelphia 1813

<u>FAMILY RECORDS MARRIAGES</u>

Alexander Fontaine ROSE & Mildred WASHINGTON, 22 Feb 1810by Rev W. Elliotte of Washington Parish at Montrose, Westmoreland Co, VA
Alexander F. ROSE & Sarah R. FONTAINE (who b.21 Sep 1796) m.16 May 1816 by Rev M. Ford at Beaverdam, Hanover Co
Louisa E. ROSE to John POTTS of Washington City 4 May 1841 by Rev Edward C. McGuire at Hampstead
Edmund F. ROSE to Bittn MURRAY 12 Feb 1845 by Rev John Atkins at Clover Hill, Fauquier Co
Alexander F. ROSE to Lucy Steptoe BLACKWELL 16 Jul 1879 at the Meadows Fauquier Co, VA
James Fontaine ROSE to Constance HAGUE 27 Dec 1915 at Aurora, Ontario, Canada
John Boursiqnot ROSE to Mary Lafsley KEITH 21 Jul 1917 at Dumottar, Fauquier Co., VA

BIRTHS

Alexander Fontaine ROSE, fourth child of Sarah FONTAINE & Charles ROSE, Beltiville, Amhurst Co, VA b.1 Apr 1780

Mildred Washington ROSE, first child of Margaret WILLIAMSON & John ROSE of Westmoreland Co, b.10 Oct 1784

Margaret Maria, first child of Mildred W. & Alexander F. ROSE, b.6 Apr 1811

Jane Lawson, b.18 Dec 1812

Edmund Fontaine, first child of A.F. & Sarah F. ROSE, b.25 Feb 1817

Louisa ROSE b. 12 Mar 1819

Lawrence Berry ROSE, b.27 Mar 1821

Charles ROSE, b.2 May 1823

[Alexander was adopted by me as a middle name after my Fathers death C.A.R.]

BIRTHS

Sarah Rose POTTS, first child of J & L.E. POTTS b.22 Jan 1843

Mary Rose second child of J & L.E. POTTS b.16 Nov 1844

John POTTS, third child of J. & L.E.POTTS, b.27 Mar 1846

Alx F. ROSE, first child of E.F. & Bettie ROSE, b.27 May 1846, Hampstead

Annie Brown, second child of E.F. & Bettie ROSE, b.21 Aug 1848, Hampstead

Louisa ROSE, third child of E.F. & Bettie ROSE, b.28 Mar 1851, Hempstead

John B. ROSE, fourth child of E.F. & Bettie ROSE, b. 22 Feb 1853, Hampstead

DEATHS

Mildred Washington ROSE, wife of Alex F. ROSE, d.20 Feb 1815

Jane Lawson ROSE, d.20 Nov 1817, bur Masons burying

Ground, Fredericksburg (no. 4)
Margaret Maria ROSE, d.3 Oct 1825, Westmoreland Co, bur Family buring ground at Troy on the Rappahannock River
DEATHS
Louisa ROSE, d.25 Feb 1852, bur garden at Hampstead
Bettie ROSE, wife of E.F. ROSE, d. 15 Oct 1862, aged 38yrs
Mary E. ROSE, seventh child of E.F. & Bettie ROSE, b.9 May 1860; d.12 Oct 1865 at Hampstead, bur in Garden next to Mother
John B. ROSE, fourth son of E. Fontaine & Bettie ROSE drowned in the Missouri River at St Louis, MO 11 Jul 1884, bur in lot of Maj W.C. Butler, Bellefountaine Cemetery
Alexander Fontaine ROSE,d. 12 Feb 1831 at Geneva, NY
Sarah Fonatine ROSE, wife of Alexander F. ROSE d. 3 Apr 1865, bur Garden Cemetery at Hampstead
Louisa E. POTTS, d.22 Mar 1891, Alexandria, VA, bur Oak Hill, Georgetown, DC
Edmund Fontaine ROSE, d. Jan 1893 at Hampstead, bur at Hempstead
Annie Brown ROSE, wife of Julian [SKINKER] d. 1900
Thomas S. BRIGGS, d.2 Jun 1910
Sarah Fontaine ROSE, wife of Thomas BRIGGS, d.15 May 1910
Alexander Fontaine ROSE, d.29 Apr 1935, Bealton, VA, bur Warrenton, VA
Lucy Steptoe ROSE, wife of A.F. ROSE, d.22 Mar 1924, bur Warrenton
(Jean dela Fontaine File)

FROST FAMILY BIBLE

No Title Page or publication date.

FAMILY RECORDS MARRIAGES

Elijah M. FROST to Kate C.A. STREET, 17 Oct 1878
Anna Beatrice FROST to Richard HUTCHINSON, 21 Oct 1900
Nellie Street FROST to Isaac SPARKS, 21 Oct 1906
Bailey Stirman FROST to Eunice GRAHAM, 8 May 1910
Mark FROST to Amelia STEP[__], 16 Jun 1925
Sadie SPARKS to Sid CUNNINGHAM, 2 Sep 1931
Paul SPARKS to Jewell Jane SHAW, 29 Jun 1938
<u>DEATHS</u>
Kate C.A. FROST, d.22 Jan 1917, Udmore, OK
E.M. FROST, d.29 Sep 1931 at Belleville, AR
Isaac SPARKS, d.28 Nov 1941, Mill Creek, OK
<u>BIRTHS</u>
Elijah M. FROST, b.16 May 1849
Kate C.A. FROST STREET, b.23 Oct 1852
Nellie Street FROST, b.25 Jul 1879
Anna Beatrice FROST b.14 Mar 1881
Bailey Stirman FROST, b.5 Dec 1882
Rose Maria FROST, b. [__] Sep 1884
Elijah Mark FROST, b.13 Jan 1813
June Frost HUTCHINSON, b.27 Jun 1901
Marion Lee HUTCHINSON, b. 24 Mar 1903
Pauline HUTCHINSON, b.13 Oct 1905
Sanford Elijah HUTCHINSON, b. 3 Nov 1907
Sadie Marion SPARKS, b.11 Aug 1907
Isaac Paul SPARKS, b.27 Jul 1911
Nellie Elmyra SPARKE, b.15 Apr 1916
Frank SPARKS, b.3 Nov 1918
Vesta Vern HUTCHISON, b.19 Oct 1914
Maxine FROST, b.27 May 1916
(Jean dela Fontaine file)

STEPHEN R.FRAIZER BIBLE

NO Title page or date of publication

FAMILY RECORDS BIRTHS

Stephen R. FRAZIER,4 Mar 1821
Sarah A. FRAIZER, 25 Jul 1825
Franklin B. FRAIZER, 11 Jun 1844
R. Russell FRAIZER, 18 May 1846
Stephen R. FRAIZER, Jr, 20 Jul 1848
Ann R. FRAIZER, 6 Dec 1850
Sarah A. FRAIZER, 5 Mar 1852

DEATHS

Stephen R. FRAIZER, 30 Nov 1890, age 69
Sarah A. FRAIZER, 9 Jun 1860, age 34
Franklin B. FRAIZER,d. from wounds rec'd at Vicksburg 19 Jun 1863, aged 19yrs 8dys
R. Russell FRAIZER, 5 May 1905
Sarah A. FRAIZER, 5 Aug 1852

MARRIAGES

Stephen R. FRAIZER to Sarah A. BECKLEY, 28 Sep 1843, by Rev Jeo M. Vincent
Stephen R. FRAIZER to Sarah W. [_____], 14 Nov 1860
(Jean dela Fontaine File)

CAMPBELL G. COWAN FAMILY BIBLE

No Title page or date of publication

FAMILY RECORDS MARRIAGES

Campbell G. COWEN to Elisabeth TANKERSLEY, 15 Feb 1828
John A. COWAN to R. J. BRITE, 30 Sep 1852
Richard T. COWAN to M.C. EIDSON, 16 Feb 1858
Martha A. COWAN to Elz SUTTLE, 18 May 186[-]

Mary E. COWAN to A.B. CHARLES, 11 Oct 186[-]
Rosmrah J. COWAN to J.W. ST[--]K, 16 Feb 18[--]
Maldianette Y. COWAN to S W[______]
Elizabeth J COWAN to J. W. STARK
James G. COWAN to M.F. Bernard[?], 22 Mar 1868

BIRTHS

Mary E. COWAN, 5 Jun 1837
James G. COWAN, 20 Aug 1839
William COWAN, 20 Apr 1841
Martha A. COWAN, 17 May 1843
Maldianette Y. COWAN, 20 Sep 1844
Bertha E. COWAN, 2 Jul 1809
William A. COWAN, 4 Jan 1871
Teulah L. COWAN, 21 Dec 1876

BIRTHS

Campbell G. COWAN, 1 Jan 1807
Elizabeth COWAN, 27 May 1811
John A. COWAN, 21 Dec 1828
Charlotte C. COWAN, 27 Aug 1830
Rasanna J. COWAN, 9 Apr 1832
Richard T. COWAN, 15 Jan 1834
Elisabeth J. COWAN, 5 Oct 1835

DEATHS

Campbell G. COWAN, 8 Mar 1846
Elizabeth COWAN, 28 Jan 1871
William COWAN, 27 Apr 1841
Rosanna J. STARK, 28 Nov 1861
John A. COWAN, [__] May 1863
Charlotte C. BARKER, 16 Feb 1868
Martha A. SUTTLE, 19 Jan 1868
Mary E. CHARLES, 4 Sep 1899
Richard T. COWAN, 27 Jul 1898
James Y COWAN, 22 Jul 1910

Bertha E COWAN, 1 Mar 1871
William A. COWAN, 23 Oct 1940
Luluh Lee COWAN, 25 Jan 1848
(Jean dela Fontaine File)

HENRY S. FREY BIBLE

Transcript from HOLY BIBLE, printed 1844 in New York. At one time in possession of Mrs Houston Dorris of Springfield, TN in about Jan 1979

Henry S. FREY, b.29 Mar 1812
Nancy D. FREY, wife of Henry, b.24 Jun 1819
Henry S. Frey and Nancy D. ------ m.22 Dec 1837
Suzan Catherine FREY, dau of Henry & Nancy D. FREY, b.14 Mar 1840
Martha Ellen FREY, dau of Henry S. & Nancy D. FREY, b.19 May 1842
Mary Elizabeth FREY, dau of Henry S. & Nancy D. FREY, b.19 May 1842
Thomas Ballard FREY, son of Henry S. & Nancy D. FREY, b.25 May 1844
Henry Clay FREY, son of Henry S. & Nancy D. FREY, b.3 Oct 1846
John M. FREY, son of Henry S. & Nancy D. FREY, b.23 Dec 1848
Sarah L. FREY, dau of Henry S and Nancy D. FREY, b.11 Mar 1852
<u>DEATHS</u>
Henry S. FREY, d.30 Dec 1852
Martha E. FREY, d.21 Jun 1861
John M. FREY, d.22 Jan 1891
Nancy D. FREY, d.17 Feb 1895

Sallie L. HYDE, d.9 Apr 1896
Mary E. FARMER, d.3 Feb 1909
Thomas Ballard FREY, d.12 Feb 1926
Susan Catherine FREY, d.30 Jan 1931
Henry Clay FREY, d.13 Dec 1922
BIRTHS
Nancy FREY, 21 Sep 1803
Sally FREY, 25 Jul 1805
Martin FREY, 15 Sep 1807
Martha M. FREY, 22 Sep 1809
Henry S. FREY, 20 Mar 1812
Polly D. FREY, 15 Mar 1816
George W. FREY, 17 Sep 1820
Susan FREY, 5 Oct 1818
John W. FREY, 25 Oct 1822
Willie F. FREY, 9 Nov 1824
Catherine Ann FREY, 6 Jan 1827
(Jean dela Fontaine File; 21-235)

HILL FAMILY BIBLE

HOLY BIBLE, published by Charles H. Yost, Philadelphia, no date
Fly Leaf: Presented by John C.C. HILL to Mrs Jane H. HILL and later presented by her to her daughter Lucy Spring Hill 25 Mar 1881
Marriage Certificate: James Monroe HILL, son of Asa & Elizabeth HILL and Jame Hallowell KERR, dau of Hugh & Lucy KERR at Hermitage, Washington Co, TN the 14 Sep 1843
signed Orseneth Fisher
BIRTHS
James Monroe HILL, son of Asa & Elizabeth HILL, 13 Mar

1818
Jane Hallowell HILL, dau of Hugh and Lucy KERR, 28 Oct 1824
James Leonidas HILL, son of the above, 21 Dec 1844
John William HILL, son of James M. & Jane HILL, 31 Mar 1847
Homer Barkasdale HILL, son of James M. & Jane HILL, 3 Jan 1851
George Augustus Alfred, son of James M, & Jane H. HILL, 23 Mar 1853
Lucy Amanda, dau of James M. & Jane H. HILL
Mary Elizabeth, dau of James M. & Jane H. HILL, 27 Aug 1858
Iola Jane, Dau of James M. & Jane H. HILL, 7 Oct 1858
Frank Webb HILL, son of J.M. & Jane H. HIll, 16 Oct 1862
Nola HILL, dau of James M. & Jane H. HILL, 22 Nov 1867

MARRIAGES

James Monroe HILL to Jane HALLOWELL, 13 Mar 1818
John W. HILL, son of James & Jane HILL to Grace PEARSALL, dau of John Edward and Elizabeth PERSALL,b.18 Sep 1852; m. 6 Apr 1871, by Rev A.B.F. Kerr
James Leonidas HILL to Mary Annie FORDTRAN, dau of Charles & Almeida FORDTRAN; b.25 Oct 1850; m. 6 Sep 1871, by Rev A.B.F. Kerr
Mary Elizabeth HILL to Dr Wilbur Fisk FLEWELLEN, son of Thomas and Frances Maria FLEWELLEN, b.1 Feb 1843 in Georgia; m.11 Apr 1875 by Rev A.B.F. KERR at Spring Hill
George A. Alfred HILL to Mary Annie HILL, m.6 Oct 1875 by Rev R.T. Nabors at Galveston

DEATHS

John C.C. HILL, d.16 Feb 1904, aged 76yrs
Iola Jane , dau of James M. & Jane H. HILL, 14 Dec 1861,

aged 1yr 2mos 1 wk
James Leonidas, eldest son of J.M. & Jane H. HILL, 23 May 1873, Fayette Co, TX; aged 28yrs 5mo,2dys
James Monroe HILL, 14 Feb 1904, Austin, TX; aged 85yrs 11mos 1 day
Jane Hallowell HILL;18 Mar 1905, Austian, TX; aged 80yrs,4 mos 20 dys
(John de La Fontaine File; 24-64)

HILL FAMILY BIBLE II

HOLY BIBLE, Published by G. Lane & P.P. Sandford, New York, 1842

FAMILY RECORDS BIRTHS
James Monroe HILL, son of Asa & Elizabeth HILL, 13 Mar 1818
Jane Hallowell HILL, dau of Hugh & Lucy KERR, 28 Oct 1824
James Leonidas HILL, b.21 Dec 1844
John William Alexander HILL, 21 Mar 1847
Homer Barkesdale HILL, 3 Jan 1851
George Augustus Alfred HILL, 23 Mar 1853
Lucy Amanda HILL, 25 Mar 1855
Mary Elizabeth HILL, 27 Aug 1858
Iola Jane HILL, 7 Oct 1860
Frank HILL, 16 Oct 1862
Nola HILL, 22 Nov 1867
DEATHS
Augustus Thomson , son of Hugh & Lucy KERR, 8 Feb 1880; aged 67yrs 7mos 22dys
Alfred Benjamin Fontaine, youngest son of Lucy & Hugh

KERR, 22 Nov 1881 in San Marcos, Hayes Co, TX; aged 58yrs 10mos 21dys
Amanda Julia THRALL, dau of Hugh & Lucy KERR, 11 Jul 1851, aged 24yrs 8mos 25dys
NOTE: The duplicate entries in these two Bibles were not repeated.
(John de La Fontaine File; 24-64)

ARTHUR FAMILY BIBLE

Notarized copy of a old Bible printed in New York, 1825. Last owned by Ambrose Arthur, Whitley Co, KY.
BIRTHS
Ambrose ARTHUR, b.5 Jun 1776 married to
Jane Gilbert FLETCHER, b.5 Oct 1787
CHILDREN:
Polly F. ARTHUR, b.4 Nov 1812
Thomas ARTHUR, b.25 Jul 1814
Sara Ann ARTHUR, b.4 May 1816
Eby Porter ARTHUR, b.14 May 1819
John Fletcher ARTHUR b.27 Jun 1821
Elizabeth ARTHUR, b.14 May 1823
Belinda Fletcher ARTHUR, b.27 Mar 1825
Edward Fletcher ARTHUR, b.12 Jun 1830

Edward Fletcher ARTHUR, b.12 Jun 1830, Knox Co, KY, m. 1 May 1866 to Susan Emma ROUTT, b.7 Dec 1846, Anderson Co, KY
CHILDREN :
Belinda Jane ARTHUR, b.27 Feb 1867
Arabella Dunlap ARTHUR, b.17 Jun 1868
Ambrose ARTHUR, b.17 Jan 1870
Elizabeth Frances ARTHUR, b.27 Feb 1872

Thomas Shanks ARTHUR, b.23 Dec 1873
William Richard ARTHUR, b.23 Feb 1876
John Morgan ARTHUR, b.27 Apr 1878
Edward ARTHUR and his twin sister,
Emma Susan ARTHUR, b.1 Feb 1881
Rebecca Jessie ARTHUR, b.16 Jun 1883
Claiborne ARTHUR, b.30 Mar 1885
MARRIAGES:
Susannah ARTHUR to Charles STEWART, 25 Sep 1801
Salley ARTHUR to John GOODWIN, 9 Nov 1801
Mary ARTHUR to Brice BAKER, 6 Jan 1804
Ambrose ARTHUR to Jane Gilbert FLETCHER, 22 Jan 1811
Milly ARTHUR to Robert GREGORY, 2 Jun 1814
DEATHS
Sarah ARTHUR, mother of Ambrose ARTHUR, d.3 May 1828, aged 81yrs
Eby FLETCHER (Isabella PORTER), b. Abbeville Dist, SC, the mother of Jane ARTHUR, d.12 Jan 1822
Thomas ARTHUR, b.Caroline Co, VA, father of Ambrose ARTHUR, d.8 Sep 1833, aged 84yrs
John FLETCHER, brother of Jane ARTHUR, d.12 Oct 1834
Belinda MAYS, sister of Jane ARTHUR, d.4 Oct 1841
John FLETCHER, father of Jane ARTHUR, d.16 Mar 1845, aged 85yrs
Edward FLETCHER, brother of Jane ARTHUR, d.5 Apr 1859
Ambrose ARTHUR, d.20 Jul 1859, aged 83yrs 1mo 15dys
Elizabeth LEATH, sister of Ambrsoe ARTHUR, d.12 Oct 1858
Milly GREGORY, sisiter of Ambrsoe ARTHUR, d.10 Sep 1868
Granville ST JOHN, b.1812; d.1893; aged 81yrs
Sarah Ann ST. JOHN, d.1897, aged 81yrs
Jane RODGERS, dau of Granville & Sara Ann ST JOHN, d.26

May 1871
Asa G. RUNYON, husband of Polly ARTHUR RUNYON; d.19 Oct 1857
Elizabeth BAUGHMAN, sister of Ambrose ARTHUR, d.12 Aug 1857
Jane Gilbert FLETCHER ARTHUR, d.4 Dec 1880
(Jean de La Chaumette FIle)

ROUTT FAMILY BIBLE

No title page and no publisher or date

MEMORANDA
Claiborn S. ROUTT, b.29 Feb 1859
Martha Bell ROUTT, b.8 Nov 1855
Marian B. ROUTT, b.23 Mar 1849
Mary F. ROUTT, b.25 Nov 1854
Peter ROUTT, b.28 Jun 1813
Rebekah ROUTT, b.12 Jul 1820
William P. ROUTT, b.9 Mar 1840
Richard G. ROUTT, b.16 Dec 1842
Susan C.ROUTT, b. 7 Dec 1846
Senica M. ROUTT, b.8 Nov 1844

DEATHS
Willis H. MORGAN, d.2 Mar 1878
Martha A. MORGAN, d.4 Sep 1884
Belinda Jane ROUTT, d.18 Jun 1889
Rebecca ROUTT, d.18 Feb 1892
Olliver B[____] N[____], d.8 July 1897
Peter POUTT, d.15 Aug 1904
Martha Belle ROUTT, d.2 Oct 1907
(Jean de La Chaumette File)

WILLIAM PACKER BIBLE

Typescript of a HOLY BIBLE, published by Jasper Harding, Philadelphia, 1845

FAMILY RECORDS MARRIAGES

William and Mary PACKER, m.25 Dec 1828
William and Mary PACKER, m.4 Dec 1847
William and Phoeba Ann PACKER, m. 2 Jun 1853
Mary WOLVERTON, 1st con
Mary McCAN, 2nd con
Phoeba Ann SEBRING, 3rd con
John M. & M. E. PACKER, m.28 Nov 1866

BIRTHS

William PACKER, b.25 Nov 1805
Mary PACKER, consort, b.24 Feb 1809
Elmore PACKER, b.15 Mar 1830
Martin PACKER, b.17 Dec 1832
Urian PACKER, b.11 Nov 1833
Mary Jane PACKER, b.17 Sep 1835
Sarah PACKER, b.23 Oct 1837
Emily PACKER, b.8 Jan 1840

BIRTHS

Alvin PACKER, b.4 Dec 1841
John M. PACKER, b.18 Jun 1843, d.4 Feb 1929, aged 85yrs 7mos
Mary, second Consort of William PACKER, b.1 Aug 1813
Infant Dau of John M. & M. E. PACKER, b.7 Sep 1867
John Wm PACKER, b.28 Oct 1868
Lulu Montez PACKER, b.9 Oct 1870
Ethel PACKER, b.9 Jun 1872
Charity Innez PACKER, b.2 Sep 1974
Herbert S. PACKER, b.5 Apr 1877
Elmore E. PACKER, b.3 Feb 1881
Anna L. PACKER, b. ____ 1882

DEATHS
Sarah PACKER, d.23 Sep 1839
Alvin PACKER, d.8 Jun 1842
Mary, consort of Wm PACKER, d.31 Mar 1846
Mary, second consort of Wm PACKER, d.21 Dec 1852
Martin PACKER, d.2 Jan 1855
William PACKER, d.25 Nov 1864
Infant dau of J M & M E PACKER, d.7 Sep 1867
Ethel PACKER, d.12 May 1876
Charity Innez PACKER, d.30 Apr 1876
Lulu Montez PACKER, d.6 Aug 1876
Anna L. PACKER, d.20 Nov 1882
(Gabriel La Boyteaux File)

ELLIOTT FAMILY BIBLE

HOLY BIBLE, published by H & E Pinney, Cooperstown, 18[-]7

FAMILY RECORDS BIRTHS
Bailey F. ELIOTT, b.1 Jul 1805
Susan ELLIOTT, wife of Bailey T. ELLIOTT, b.19 Dec 1811
George W. ELLIOTT, b.28 Feb 1820
Elizabeth T. ELLIOTT, dau of Bailey & Susan ELLIOTT, b.15 Jul 1828
William H. ELLIOTT, b.3 Jan 1832
George B. ELLIOTT, b.18 Feb 1835
Virginia B. ELLIOTT, b.12 Sep 1836
Isabel H. ELLIOTT, b.24 Feb 1839

DEATHS
Elizabeth F. ELLIOTT, d.10 Sep 1830
George B. ELLIOTT, d.17 Aug 1835
Virginia B. ELLIOTT, d.26 Aug 1837
William H. ELLIOTT, d.10 Sep 1837

Bailey T. ELLIOTT, d.31 [___] 1844, age 40yrs
John H. ELLIOTT, d.11 Oct 1864
Isabela ELLIOTT HOWELL, d.13 Apr 1868
Mrs Susan ELLIOTT, wife of Bailey F ELLIOTT, d.27 Sep 1873
George Bailey ELLIOTT, d.1 Apr 1890
<u>BIRTHS</u>
George B., ELLIOTT, b.28 Aug 1841
John H. ELLIOTT, b.28 Dec 1843
<u>MARRIAGES</u>
Bailey T. ELLIOTT to Susan TABB, 30 Jul 1827
Isabella H. ELLIOTT to Morton B. HOWELL of Nashville, TN, 18 Nov 1858
Susan HOWELL, dau of M B & Isabella H HOWELL, b. 28 Sep 1859
(Gabriel La Boyteaux File)

LABERTEAUX BIBLE

A Notarized transcript of HOLY BIBLE, printed in New York, 1828. In 1968 the present owner was Mrs Laura Peterson of Niles, MI.

<u>DEATHS</u>
Jane LABERTEAUX, d.4 Apr 1822, aged 4yrs 5mos
David LABERTEAUX, d.16 Apr 1826, aged 4mos, 4 dys
Anna VAN BUREN, d.7 May 1853
July 4th Mary Jane d., age 28yrs
Theodore d. 7 Apr 1865
Peter LABERTEAUX, d.7 Oct 1876, aged 80yrs
(Gabriel La Boyteaux File)

ZIMMER BIBLE

A notarized transcript of HOLY BIBLE, published in London, MDCCXLIV. In 968 the current owned was Mrs Laura Peterson, Niles MI.
Sarah POTS, b.22 Nov 1731
Jonathan _____, b.16 __ 1756
Dorithy, dau of Elizabeth Para (or Pary), b.29 Nov 1757
On a seperate sheet of paper in the Bible:
Jermena, b.12 May 1763
Elizabeth, 9 Apr 1765
William, b.23 May 1767
Jacob, b.20 May 1769
Angenitye, b.9 Sep 1771
Geabere, b.7 Jan 1773
On the back cover is written:
Jacob ZIMMER m. 11 Dec to Gemina LABERTEAUX
[Joel] ZIMMER, b.17 Apr 1782
(Gabriel La Boyteaux File)

JOHN CALVIN HAYES FAMILY BIBLE

HOLY BIBLE, published by C. Alexander & Co, Philadelphia, 183[-]
FAMILY RECORD MARRIAGES
John Calvin HAYES to Martha GUILLEBEAU, 1 Dec 1824
Elija B. LEROY to Susan L. HAYES, 30 Mar 1852
BIRTHS
John Calvin HAYES, b.13 Sep 1802
Martha HAYES, b.20 May 1803
Harriett Elizabeth HAYES, b.26 Sep 1825
Joseph Elijah HAYES, b.28 Feb 1827
Mary Jane HAYES, b.16 Dec 1829
Susan Langel HAYES, b.22 Oct 1831

Martha Ann HAYES, b.9 May 1834

DEATHS

Josephus HAYES, d.2 Sep 1829, age 23yrs lacking 19dys
Elizabeth HAYES, d.28 Dec 1831, aged 65yrs 3mos
Joseph Elijah HAYES, d.24 Jun 1835
Mary Jane HAYES, d. --- Mar 1839
John Champion HAYES, d.7 Jun 1847, aged 64yrs lacking 14dys

BIRTHS

Petter James HAYES, b.4 Jan 1837
Sarah Magdalen HAYES, b.11 Nov 1838
Deadborn, 1 Jul 1844
Deadborn, 22 Oct 1845

Age of the young Negros

Kiley, b.-- Dec 1842
Jincy, b.15 Jan 1845
Polly, b.25 Jan 1847
Nathan, b.11 Feb 1849
Jery, b.14 Apr 1852
Tom, b.25 Sep 1854
Esther, b.27 Nov 1857
Susy, b.17 Jun 1859
(Jacques L'Angel File)

THE DELANO FAMILY BIBLE

HOLY BIBLE, published by Henry F. Giere of New York, 1910

FAMILY RECORDS GRANDPARENTS

Joseph Patterson DELANO, b.3 Apr 1824, Westmoreland Co, VA; d.9 Jan 1911, Warsaw, VA
Lucinda Lyell SELF, b.21 Jan 1827, Oldhams, VA; d.17 Jan 1878, Warsaw, VA

Eli Peterson PACKETT, b.20 Dec 1841, Warsaw, VA; d. Nov 1876, Warsaw, VA
Ella Susan SISSON, b.1 Dec 1840; d.10 Sep 1911, both Warsaw, VA
PARENTS
William Joseph DELANO, b.10 Dec 1855, Warsaw, VA; d.10 Jan 1926, Wellfords, VA
Virginia Elizabeth PACKETT, b.4 Jun 1860, Warsaw, VA; d.2 Sep 1932, Wellsfords , VA
married 28 Aug 1878 at Warsaw, VA
CHILDREN
Eli Peterson DELANO, b.29 Apr 1879, d.23 Mar 1956; m. 5 Jun 1901 to Minnie Evelyn KENNEDY
Ella Susan DELANO, b.9 Jul 1882; d.21 Aug 1951; m. 2 Mar 1904 to Emory Eli PACKETT
Cleveland Otis DELANO, b.28 Jul 1884; d.3 Jan 1965; d.16 Apr 1914 to Annie Elizabeth MEESE
Austine DELANO, b.19 Aug 1887; d.12 Jul 1888
George Milton DELANO, b.10 Aug 1889; d.13 May 1970; m. 4 Dec 1912 to Maude Virginia DOUGLAS
Arthur William DELANO, b.18 Dec 1891; m. 4 Sep 1918 to Sadie Virginia DAVIS
Laura Virginia DELANO, b.8 Sep 1893; d.3 Sep 1939; m. 17 Nov 1914 to Edward Carroll GARLAND
Lillie May DELANO, b.25 Aug 1895; m.15 Aug 1917 to Walter Vernon SANDERS
Randolph Ottes DELANO, b.10 Apr 1897; m. 20 Sep 1920 to Bernice Virginia BARNES, (she d.2 Feb 1961
Herbert Packett DELANO, b.7 Sep 1899; m. 1 Apr 1922 to Julia Ann LEWIS
Claud Lyell DELANO, b.25 Aug 1902; m. 30 Jun 1928 to Charlotte B. DAWSON
Minnie Ruth DELANO, b.26 Aug 1904, m. 3 Feb 1927 to

George Milton SNYDER (he d. 29 May 1958)
(Jean de La Noy File)

SARAH DARTT'S BIBLE

A transcript of a bible record, no title page, publisher or date. Other names of interest "George H. DARTT & J.H. DARTT, Kingston, Green Lake, WI, 23 Mar 1872"

FAMILY RECORD

Josiah H. DARTT m 9 Sep 1828 to Mary AYER
Sally P. DARTT m. 13 Sep 1828 to Augustus DOW
Betsey E. DARTT m. 17 Jun 1832 to N. KRAFT
Edward A. DARTT, d.Kingston, WI, bur at Joy, NE, 14 Jul 1910
Franklin E. DARTT, d.Sherwood, Clark Co, WI, bur 16 May 1918 at Montello, WI
Erastus J. DARTT, b.3 Jun 1833; d.22 May 1918, Packwaukee, WI
Royal H. DARTT, b.28 Aug 1834; d.11 Nov 1921, Montello, WI

Josiah H. DART, b.7 Jul 1806; aged 82yrs 7mos 5dys
Sally P. DART, b.1 Jun 1809
Justus N. DART, b.22 Aug 1811, aged 68yrs 11mos 9dys
Betsy E. DART, b.22 May 1816
George H. DART, b.__ Oct 1818
Sharlot C. E. DART, b.3 Sep 1820
Mary J.Dart, b.18 Jul 1822
Schuyler H.E. DARTT, b.24 Nov 1824
Mary A. DARRT, b.16 Mar 1815
Mary AYER, b.8 Jun 1808, age 82yrs 29dys
Josiah DARTT, b.15 Aug 1784, Weatherfield, VT; d.18 Mar 1871, Kingston, Green Lake Co, WI

Sally DARTT, d.27 Dec 1856, Kingston, WI; aged 73yrs,4mos
Sharlot C.E. DART, d.12 Oct 1820
Mary J. DART, d.24 Dec 1824
J. N. DARTT, d. 31 Jul 1880, Germantown, Seward Co, NE; aged 68yrs 11mo 9dys
J. H. DARTT, d.12 Feb 1888, Kingston, Green Lake Co, WI; aged 82yrs 7mos 5dys
E.H.S. DARTT, d.31 Jan 1903, Owatona, MN
Mary DARTT, d.7 Jul 1900, Kingston, Green Lake Co, WI; age 92yrs 29dys
Mary A. DARTT, d.9 Jan 1908,Monteloo, WI; age 92yrs 9mos 24dys
Franklin E. DARTT, d.16 May 1918
Erastus J. DARTT, d.22 May 1918
Edward A. DARTT, d.14 Jul 1910
Royal H. DART, d.11 Nov 1921
(Jean de La Noy File)

THE CARTER FAMILY BIBLE

The Illuminated BIBLE, published by Harper & Brothers, New York, 1846
Abot CARTER m. 8 Apr 1837 to Elizabeth P. JOHNSON
Albert F CARTER m. 30 Apr 1883 to Isabella ELLIS by Rev R.C. Price
George Friend CARTER, b.11 May 1839
Gardiner Fieoths CARTER, b.6 Dec 1840
Elmer Albot CARTER, b.10 Jun 1843
Pauline Augusta CARTER, b.5 Sep 1846
Alice Loring CARTER, b.8 Jun 1849
Albert CARTER, b.13 Jun 1814
Elizabeth P. CARTER, b.24 Dec 1819

Albert Freeman CARTER, b.15 Jan 1855
William D. CARTER, b.14 Jun 1857
(Jean de La Noy File)

JOHN FORDHAM BIBLE

No title page, publisher or date

FAMILY RECORDS BIRTHS
Ezehiel, son of John & Katherine FORDHAM, b.21 Jan 1794
Mary, b.18 Nov 1795
Leah, b.3 Oct 1797
Daren, b.18 Feb 1800
Edwin, b.4 Feb 1802
[_____], b.2 Feb 1804 (page torn)
Elrad, b.16 Feb 1806
John, b.25 Apr 1805
Susanah, b.28 Oct 1809
Alscy, b.21 Aug 1811
Katharine, b.21 Dec 1814
Eleanoa, dau of John & Nancy FORDHAM, b.15 Nov 1821
William G., b.20 Apr 1823
Christopher C., b.12 Aug 1824
Ivey, b.11 Dec 18[__]
Jrey, b.[__] Aug [___]
Jesoy H. FORDHAM, b.10 Jul [____]
Atha LEAK, b.9 Oct 1830
Andrew Jackson FORDHAM, son of Jno & Nancy FORDHAM, b.27 Jan 1832
Nancy FORDHAM, b.20 Dec 1833
Calvin FORDHAM, b.13 Oct 1835
Lewis P. FORDHAM, b.17 Feb 1837
David FORDHAM, b.10 Jun 1839

MARRIAGES

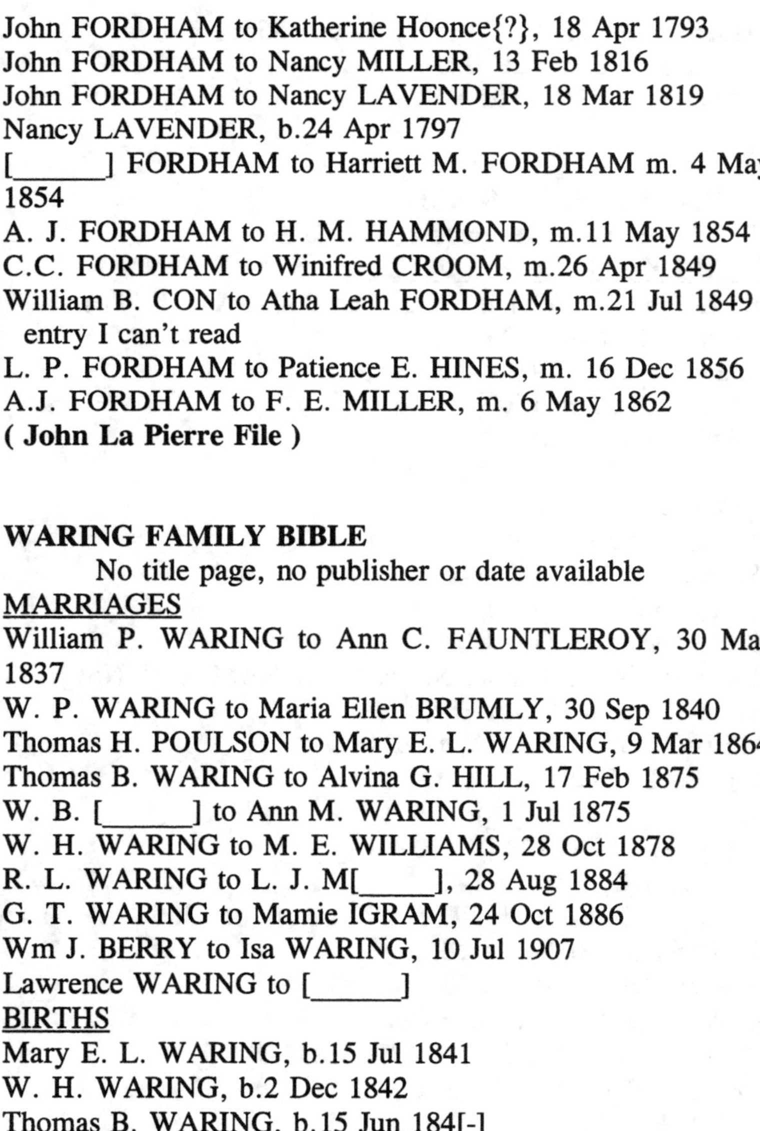

John FORDHAM to Katherine Hoonce{?}, 18 Apr 1793
John FORDHAM to Nancy MILLER, 13 Feb 1816
John FORDHAM to Nancy LAVENDER, 18 Mar 1819
Nancy LAVENDER, b.24 Apr 1797
[______] FORDHAM to Harriett M. FORDHAM m. 4 May 1854
A. J. FORDHAM to H. M. HAMMOND, m.11 May 1854
C.C. FORDHAM to Winifred CROOM, m.26 Apr 1849
William B. CON to Atha Leah FORDHAM, m.21 Jul 1849
entry I can't read
L. P. FORDHAM to Patience E. HINES, m. 16 Dec 1856
A.J. FORDHAM to F. E. MILLER, m. 6 May 1862
(John La Pierre File)

WARING FAMILY BIBLE

No title page, no publisher or date available

MARRIAGES

William P. WARING to Ann C. FAUNTLEROY, 30 Mar 1837
W. P. WARING to Maria Ellen BRUMLY, 30 Sep 1840
Thomas H. POULSON to Mary E. L. WARING, 9 Mar 1864
Thomas B. WARING to Alvina G. HILL, 17 Feb 1875
W. B. [______] to Ann M. WARING, 1 Jul 1875
W. H. WARING to M. E. WILLIAMS, 28 Oct 1878
R. L. WARING to L. J. M[_____], 28 Aug 1884
G. T. WARING to Mamie IGRAM, 24 Oct 1886
Wm J. BERRY to Isa WARING, 10 Jul 1907
Lawrence WARING to [______]

BIRTHS

Mary E. L. WARING, b.15 Jul 1841
W. H. WARING, b.2 Dec 1842
Thomas B. WARING, b.15 Jun 184[-]

Payne WARING, b.17 Mar 1846
J. W. WARING, b.14 Feb 1848
Ann M. WARING, b.19 Feb 1852
L [___] WARING, b.12 Jun 1850
Lucy R. WARING, b.20 Dec 1853
Virginia G. WARING, b.13 Apr 1855
George WARING, b.11 Dec 1857
Robert WARING, b.1 Jan 1860
Frances Ida WARING, b.6 Apr 1862
Lawrence WARING, b.14 Dec 1863
<u>DEATHS</u>
Elizabeth WARING, my Mother, d.7 Feb 1827
John WARING, Sr, d.10 Sep 1857, aged 70yrs
Ann C. WARING, wife of W.P. W., d.23 May 1838, at her Fathers M.G. FAUNTLEROYS; aged 18yrs 2mos
Maria E. WARING, d.19 Apr 1869, Sunny Side; aged 45yrs
Mary E. L. POULSON, dau of W.P. & M.E. WARING, d.5 Feb 1866, on the Eastren Shore; Aged 25yrs
Virginia G. WARING, d.16 Sep 1855; aged 6mos 4dys
Lucy R. WARING, d.31 May 1856; aged 3yrs 11dys
Lowery WARING, d.12 Jun 1856; aged 6yrs 5dys
Payne WARING, d.5 Jul 1856; aged 10yrs 3mos
William Payne WARING, d.19 Dec 1880, aged 69yrs
Wm H. WARING, d.20 Aug 1893
G. T. WARING, d. 9 Jul 1877, Louisville, KY
(Peter Latane File 36-4)

THE GRIGG FAMILY BIBLE

No title page, publisher or date of publication available

<u>FAMILY RECORDS BIRTHS</u>
Isaac GRIGG, b.31 Mar 1821
Mary Adele GRIGG, b.26 Mar 1835

Joseph Franklin GRIGG, b.[--] Oct 1856
James Elliott GRIGG, b.12 Mar 1858
William Montague GRIGG (b.4 Jul 1863
Alfred Stansbury GRIGG (b.24 Mar 1869
Mary Ellen GRIGG, dau of William Montague & Willie HARDIN GRIGG, b.23 Aug 1897
Sallie Maude GRIGG, dau of William Montague & Willis HARDIN GRIGG, b.19 NOv 1899
Myrtle Elliott GRIGG, dau of William Montague & Sallie HARDIN GRIGG, b.16 Feb 1901
Willima Grigg ALLEN, b.7 Sep 1920
James Montague ALLEN, b.26 Oct 1921, Kingston, KY
Mary Elliott ALLEN, b.24 Jan 1926, Kingston, KY
Peggy CASEY, b.3 Jun 1930, Temple, TX
MARRIAGES
Isaac GRIGG to Emeline MONTAGUE, 13 Nov 1851
Isaac GRIGG to Mary A. MONTAGUE, 21 Nov 1855
William M. GRIGG to Willie A. HARDIN, 13 Sep 1896
Alfred S. GREGG to Annie WALKER, 16 Dec 1896
Mary Ellen GRIGG to Rees Roberts ALLEN, 24 Sep 1919
Elliott GRIGG to S. B. CASEY, 1 Jan 1927
DEATHS
Joseph Franklin GRIGG, d.14 [___ ____]
Annie Walker GRIGG, wife of A.S. GRIGG, d.24 Sep 1899, aged 25yrs 3mos 2dys
J.E. GRIGG, d.24 Mar 1904
William Montague GRIGG, d.27 Jul 1941, Waynesboro
Willie Hardin GRIGG, d.4 Aug 1945, Nashville
Emeline GRIGG, the first wife of Isaac GRIGG, d.4 Mar 1852
Isaac GRIGG, d.20 Mar 1901
Mary A. GRIGG, d.26 Oct 1907 {second wife of Isaac}
(Peter Latane File)

HAINES BIBLE

No Title page, publisher or date of publication.

FAMILY RECORD BIRTHS

Susannah HANES, fourth dau of Daniel & Tamer HANES, b. 5 March 1808

Jessee Brion HANES, third son of Daniel & Tamer HANES, b.23 Aug 1810

Rebecca Hill HANES, fifth dau of Daniel & Tamer HANES, b.15 Aug 1814

John Brian HANES, fourth son of Daniel & Tamer HANES, b.12 Feb 1816

James Mann HANES, fifth son of Daniel & Tamer HANES, b.17 Aug 1822

DEATHS

Esther A.P.[-] Le Compte HAINES, concort of Rev James J. HAINES, d.3 Mar 1851, aged 23yrs

Hilda Bryant Haines HESS, wife of Joseph Hoffman HESS, d.9 Nov 1921

Rebecca Hill HAINES, d. 23 May 1891

Sarah HAINES, d.22 Dec 1878

James M. HAINES, d.12 Nov 1874, Port Republic, VA

John Bois LeCompte HAINES, d.28 Dec 1911, Laurel, MD

Adam Averell ROSS, b.14 Nov 1869, [___], Ireland; d.15 Jun 1929

Lucian Boneparte CARPENTER, d.24 Jan 1946

BIRTHS

Daniel HANES, son of Joseph & Abigail HANES, b. 9 Nov 1765 {this Daniel married Tamer Bryant}

William HANES, son of Joseph & Abigail HANES, b.5 Mar 1768

Mary HANES, dau of Joseph & Abigail HANES, b.3 Mar 1770

Joseph HANES, son of Joseph & Abigail HANES, b.27 Sep

1774
Hilda B. HAINES, dau of J.A. & E.A. HAINES, b.25 Aug 1840
Bvis LeCompte HAINES, son of [-] M. HEINES & [----], b.[-] Sep 1848
<u>DEATHS</u>
Nathaniel COVINGTON, 7 Dec 1852
Maria H., wife of Nathaniel COVINGTON, dau of Daniel & Tamer HAINES, d.20 Nov 1841
John B., son of Daniel & Tamer HAINES, d. Tamer HAINES, concort of Daniel HAINES, d.21 Dec 1847, aged 72yrs, {born 1775}
Daniel HAINES Sr, d.26 Sep 1852, aged 76yrs {born 1765}
<u>MARRIAGES</u>
George W. COVINGTON, son of Nathaniel & Maria COVINGTON, b.6 Jan 1834
James H. COVINGTON, son of Nathaniel & Maria COVINGTON, b.20 Aug 1836
Charles A. COVINGTON, son of Nathaniel & Maria COVINGTON, b.25 Oct 1839
Mary Rebecca HAINES, dau of Jos H. & Hulda Bryan HAINES, b.12 May 1876, Wheeler, VA
Adelaide LeCompte, Dau of Jos H. & Hilda Bryant HAINES, b. 22 Feb 1878
Lucian Bonaparte LeCOMPTE, son of L.B. & Adeliade Le C[---], b.30 Jun 1901
two entries are unreadable
<u>MARRIASGES</u>
Willis A. HAINES to Esther L LeCOMPTE, 12 Nov 1845
Joseph Hoffman HESS to Hilda Bryan HAINES, 21 Jun 1875, Baltimore
Adam Averell ROSS, Jr to Mary Rebecca Haines HESS, 24 Oct 1900, Baltimore

Lucian Bonaparte CARPENTER to Adelaide LeCompte HESS, 2 Jun 1900
Thomas Edward ROSS to Adelaide LeCompte Hess CARPENTER, 18 Apr 1906
John Bremer BROWN to Mary Leonora ROSS, 22 May 1926
Lucian B. CARPENTER to Adelaide A. SOUDER, 23 Oct 1926
Edmond du PONT to Averell Adelaide ROSS, 26 Feb 1932
(Michel Le Comte File)

JOSEPH HESS BIBLE

No Title age, publisher or date of publication

FAMILY RECORDS MARRIAGES
Joseph HESS to Ann ROUDABUSH, 17 Sep 1829, by Rev Wm Hank
Elizabeth Margaret HESS to Elijash MATH[---]
Evaline J. HESS to Wm SCOTT, 12 Jan ____
Sarah Adelaide HESS to Lorenzo S. CONRAD, 5 Aug 1857, at Penleton Co, VA, by Rev Robt Smith
Wiliam C. HESS to Bonnie _____
Eliza Ann HESS to Erasume C. KEYS, 1865 by Rev Jos Temple
Jacob H. HESS to
James R. HESS m. in IL
Joseph HESS to Hilda B. HANES, 21 Jun 1875, in Baltimore, by Rev L.T. Haslgh

BIRTHS
Joseph HESS, b.3 Jun 1810
Ann HESS, b.1811
Elizabeth Margaret HESS, b.10 Jan 1831
Evaline Jane HESS, b.17 Nov 1833
Sarah A. HESS, b.22 Aug 1835
William Crawford HESS, b.23 Sep 1837

Jacob Harvey HESS, b.15 Mar 1839
Amanda C. HESS, b.8 Feb 1841
John Albert HESS, b.1843
James Knox Polk HESS, b. Oct 1844
Eliza Ann HESS, b.11 Feb 1847
Mary Ellen HESS, b.10 Oct 1849
Charles Levi HESS, b.5 Sep 185[-]
Joseph [---], b.3 Apr 1854
Mary Rebecca Lewis, dau of Joseph & Hilda H. HESS, b.12 May 1876
(Michel Le Comte File)

JOHN LEFEVER BIBLE

HOLY BIBLE, published by Jesper Harding & Son, Philadelphia, 1858
John LEFEVER, son of Margeret & Jonas LEFEVER, b.12 Nov 1806
Nancy HANSOM, b.2 May 1809
Margaret E. LEFEVER, b.6 Jan 1834
Jonas LEFEVER, b.20 Mar 1836
John Adam LEFEVER, b.15 Aug 1838
Nancy Elizabeth LEFEVER, b.15 Jun 1843
Lizzie, dau of Margaret E. & Nathaniel B. WESTBROOK, b.10 Feb 1855
Nancy Elizabeth, dau of Jonas & Mary T. LEFEVER, b.3 Aug 1862
Elizabeth DUNBAR, b.10 Apr 1897
Mary DUNBAR, b.6 Jan 1899
Thelma DUNBAR, b.27 Apr 1901
Willard [---] DUNBAR, b.17 Oct 1903
Margaret E . LEFEVER m. 1 Oct 1851 to Nathaniel B. WESTBROOK

Jonas LEFEVER m. 19 Oct 1866 to Mary T. WOOLSEY
Shirley, b.31Jan 1842
Maud Elizabeth ALVERSON m,. 29 Apr 1896 to James Watson DUNLAP
John LEFEVER, d.19 Jul 1843, aged 38yrs 3mos
Jacob, infant son of John & Nancy LEFEVER, d. 7 Sep 1840, aged 2dys
Margaret E. WESTBROOK, d.9 Jun 1858
John Adam LEFEVER, d. 24 Jul [___]
Nancy E LEFEVER, d. 27 Apr 1854; aged 1yr 8mos 21dys
Nancy LEFEVER, d.18 Sep 1865; aged 58yrs, 4mos 16dys
(Jacques Leger File)

DOUGLAS HANCOCK MARSHALL FAMILY BIBLE I

Hitchcock's HOLY BIBLE, published by J.A. Wilmore & Co, New York, dated MDCCCLXXXV

FAMILY RECORDS MISCELLANEOUS
D. H. MARSHALL, Sr b.29 Nov 1815
Mary E. MARSHALL, b.15 Jun 1819
Wm G. COLEMAN, b.15 Sep 1830
Mary D. W. COLEMAN, b.15 Jul 1834

BIRTHS
D. C. MARSHALL, b.10 Jul 1859
M. W. MARSHALL, b.25 Mar 18[--]
Mary Elizabeth MARSHALL, b.19 Feb 1890
Wm Douglas MARSHALL, b.7 Jan 1892
Abbott Hancock MARSHALL, b.[-] Nov 1893
Schuyler Benjamin , b.25 Aug 1895
Byron Walker MARSHALL, b. 2 Feb 1898
Baby Isabell MARSHALL, b.23 [_____]

BIRTHS
David Glover MARSHALL, b.22 Mar 1900

Susie Bettie MARSHALL, b.29 Sep 1902
Sarah Gracie MARSHALL, b.21 Feb 1905
Douglas Peruza MARSHALL, b.19 May 1907
Ruby Isabelle MARSHALL, b.25 Jan 1911
<u>MARRIAGES</u>
Douglas Hancock MARSHALL, Jr to Mary WALKER
D. W. MARSHALL m. 19 Dec 1888 to M. W. COLEMAN
Sarah Grace MARSHALL m. 25 Oct 1930 to Willie Cadman RUDD
Susie Betty MARSHALL m. 16 Dec 1939 to Walker JENKINS
Abbitt Hancock MARSAHALL m. 11 Feb 1942 to Virginia SEAL
Ruby Isabella MARSHALL m. 19 Jul 1946 to Joseph Franklin SCOTT
<u>MARRIAGES</u>
Schuyler Benjamin MARSHALL m. 30 Apr 1924 to Virginia CALDWELL
Abbitt Hancock MARSHALL m. 30 Aug 1924 to Margaret Virginia CARTER
David Glover MARSHALL m. 18 Jul 1925 to Irene MARTIN
Byron Walker MARSHALL m. 3 Oct 1925 to Janie Drucilla NICHOLS
William Houghes MARSHALL m. 3 Apr 1926 to Ruth Taylor CALDWELL
<u>DEATHS</u>
Susie E. MARSHALL, d.19 Mar 1898
Wellie COLMAN, d.24 Mar 1900
Mary E. MARSHALL
O. H. MARSHALL, St, d.
Wm C. COLEMAN, d. 16 [--] 1909
Mary [----] COLEMAN, Sr, d.[-] Jul 1910
Margaret MARSHALL, d.29 Jul 19[--]; age 32
<u>DEATHS</u>

D. H. MARSHALL, Jr, d.11 Sep 1914
Mary Elizabeth MARSHALL, d.6 JUn 1951
(Peter LeGrand File; 1-2962)

WILLIAM GLOVER COLEMAN BIBLE

No Title page, publisher or date of publication

FAMILY RECORDS MARRIAGES

Wm G. COLEMAN m. 26 Jun 1850 to Mary ABBITT
T.S. MOSLEY m. 7 Jun 1871 to A. E. JONES
F. W. HUNTER m. [--] Dec 1880 to J. D. COLEMAN
J.B. HUNTER m. 8 Dec 1880 to S. F. COLEMAN
Wm B. MARSHALL m. 5 Apr 1881 to S.E. COLEMAN
S.P. COLEMAN m. 27 Apr 1881 to N. E. MARSHALL
George A. COLEMAN m. 24 Sep 1884 to J.E. ABBITT
D. H. MARSHALL m. 19 Dec 1888 to M. WALKER
[---] BROOKS m. 8 Aug 1892 to Alice [_____]
W.G. COLEMAN 5 Apr 1893

BIRTHS

S.A.E. COLEMAN, b.22 Aug 1852
G. Abbitt COLEMAN, b.29 May 1854
S.P. COLEMAN, b.6 May 1856
Isabella & Fanny, b.10 Jun 1858
Susan E. COLEMAN, b.29 Sep 1862
Wm G. COLEMAN, Jr, b. 6 Jul 1866
Mary J.W. COLEMAN, b.25 Mar 1870
Lucy A. COLEMAN, b.9 Aug 187[--]
Mary Olive JONES, b.16 Jun 1872
Wm Douglas MARSHALL, b.20 May 1885
(Peter LeGrand File; 1-2962)

VAN NESS FAMILY BIBLE

No Title page, publisher or date of publication.

FAMILY RECORDS DEATHS

Samuel VAN NESS, d. 1849
Charles H. VAN NESS, d.6 May 1856
Caroline VAN NESS, d.17 Nov 1869
Jane VAN NESS, d.29 Oct 1871
John R. VAN NESS, d.2 Apr 1872
Isaac J. VAN NESS d. 27 Jan 1886
Mrs Mary P. SUMNER, d.6 May 1878, aged 67yrs 6mos 6dys
Mrs Jane PEER, d.8 Jan 1879, aged 56yrs

BIRTHS

Mary R. VAN NESS, b.30 Mar 1838
John R. VAN NESS, b.13 Apr 1839
Caroline VAN NESS, b.5 Nov 1840
Jane VAN NESS, b.13 Jan 1843
Samuel VAN NESS, b.7 Feb 1847
Charles H. VAN NESS, b.13 Aug 1854
Isaac J. VAN NESS, b.4 Aug 1813
Ann ROOME, b.20 Dec 1812

Mr Isaac J. VANNESS m. 14 May 1836 to Miss Ann ROOME

on a seperate sheet of paper the following:
Peter VAN NESS, b.13 Sep 1730
Hester VAN NESS, b.8 Feb 1732; d.13 Oct 1820
Peter VAN NESS, d.4 Aug 1820
Harriet VAN NESS, wife of Peter VAN NESS, d.12 Mar 1797; aged 64yrs
(Claude Le Maistre File; 4-455)

DRAPER FAMILY BIBLE

Transcript of HOLY BIBLE, published by A.J. HOLMAN & Co.; 1878

BIRTHS

Allen DRAPER, b.24 Jul 1851, St Albans, VT
Carline M. DRAPER, b.25 Nov 1851, Franklin, VT
Harry I. DRAPER, b.30 Dec 1880, Charlestown, MA

MARRIAGES

Harry I. DRAPER m. 13 Jan 1910 to Anna L. STOWE

DEATHS

Carline M. TOWLE DRAPER, d.22 Mar 1932, aged 81yrs
Allen DRAPER, d.25 Jan 1940, aged 89yrs

Allen DRAPER of Berkshire m.26 Oct 1879 to Carlie M. TOWLE of Franklin, VT by Rev S. Donaldson
(Johan LeMercier File)

BOWMAN FAMILY BIBLE

No Title page or publisher, no date of publication

FAMILY RECORD BIRTHS

Hannah M. BOWMAN, 7 Apr 1825, Westford; d.5 Aug 1826
Sophia H. BOWMAN, b.20 May 1830, Franklin VT; d. 29 Aug 1884; aged 54yrs, 3mos
Clara BOWMAN, b.7 Mar 1834
Lucia BOWMAN, b.8 Oct 1840
Martha E. HAYWOOD, b. [---------]

MARRIAGES

Henry BOMAN m. 28 Aug 1817 to Sophia HASELTON at Westford, VT, by Rev Lemeon Permele
Electa BROWN m. 1818 to Samuel HAYWOOD, who died
Electa HAYWOOD m. 31 Dec 1818 to Henry BOWMAN
Esther BARNET m. [---] 1831 to Henry BOWMAN
Narcissus TOWLE m. 3 Jul 1859 to Henry BOWMAN at East

Franklin, VT by J.S. Mott
BIRTHS
Electra BROWN, b.24 Dec 1798, Jerico, VT; d.30 Apr 1836, Franklin, VT; aged 38yrs
Esther BARNET, b.5 Mar 1802, Woodstock; d.27 Feb 1850, Franklin; aged 78yrs
Henry BOWMAN, b.28 Oct 1791; d. 19 Apr 1871, Franklin, VT
Sophia HASELTON, b. Jan 1795; d.23 Apr 1827, Westford, VT; aged 33yrs
Henry H. BOWMAN, b.2 Oct 1818, Westford, VT; d.13 Jul 1882, St Albans
David H. BOWMAN, 30 Jun 1820; d.25 Nov 1843; aged 24yrs
(Johan LeMercier File)

CANNEY FAMILY BIBLE

Transcript of Holy Bible, no title page, publisher or date of publication
In 1960 the Bible in the possession of Mr John Canney of Seattle, WA

James CANEY, b.10 Feb 1794; d.5 Aug 1865
Bleinda COPP, b.12 Oct 1796; d.4 Oct 1854
Havilah D. CANNEY, b.20 Mar 1821; d.12 Dec 1904
Isaac N. CANNEY, b.26 Nov 1822; d.3 Oct 1845
Elizabeth C. CANNEY, b.25 Jun 1829; d.20 Jan 1885
Thomas J. CANNEY, b.27 Oct 1831; d.24 Feb 1913
Ivory B. CANNEY, b.3 Jul 1836; d.6 May 1839
Ida H. CANNEY, b.2 Oct 1858
MARRIAGES
James CANNEY m. 3 Jun 1819 to Belinda COPP

James CANNEY m. 31 Dec 1854 to Mary BRIARD
Thomas J. CANNEY m. 15 Mar 1856 to Julia A. SMITH

Thomas J. CANNEY, b.27 Oct 1831; d.24 Feb 1913
Julia A. SMITH, b.7 Oct 1835; d.31 May 1905
Fred CANNEY, b.15 May 1857; d.1 May 1915
Frank S. CANNEY, b.17 Oct 1858; d.21 Mar 1898
John Beebe CANNEY, b.15 Sep 1860; d.26 Apr 1914
Flora H. CANNEY, b.23 Apr 1862
George H. CANNEY, b.12 Oct 1863; d.22 Mar 1876
Bessie L. CANNEY, b.11 Jun 1867
(Johan Le Mercier File; 5-127)

STEVENS FAMILY BIBLE

HOLY BIBLE, published by American Bible Society, New York; 1857

FAMILY RECORDS BIRTHS
Nelson S. STEVENS, b.28 May 1837
Mary A. HUMPHREY, b.1 Dec 1845
Cora Etta STEVENS, b.7 Jan 1864
Henry Dwight STEVENS, b.31 Jul 1865
Mary Edith STEVENS, b.27 Dec 1866
Charles Boyd STEVENS, b.30 Dec 1869
Clarence Stillman HATT, b.11 Jul 1887
Rafe Nelson HATT, b.11 Nov 1889
Mary Frances STEVENS, b.8 Apr 1897
Helen Marian STEVENS, b.30 Apr 1898
Chas Nelson STEVENS, b.24 Oct 1898
Edith Mary STEVENS, b.17 May [---]
Earle Maynard STEVENS, b.9 Oct 1908
DEATHS

Nelson S. STEVENS, d.10 Oct 1906
Henry Dwight STEVENS, d.14 Aug 1919
Shirley Marie WASS, d.13 Jan 1928
MARRIAGES
Nelson S. STEVENS m. 10 Mar 1863 to Mary A. HUMPHREY
William W. HATT m. 6 Oct 1886 to Cora E. STEVENS
Dwight H. STEVENS m. 18 Apr 1892 to Abbie E. YOUNG
Eldron H. STEVENS m.14 Jan 1896 to Cora E. HATT
Chas B. STEVENS m. 8 Sep 1897 to Grace M. WASHBURN
Frank R. ANDREWS m. 28 May 1918 to Cora E STEVENS
Clarence P. HATT m. 25 Jan 1874 to Ida M. NORTON FISCHER
Rafe Nelson HATT m. 9 Mar 1908 to [______]
Ralph C. WASS m. 13 Sep 1919 to Helen M. STEVENS
Robert E. CLEAVES, Jr m. 30 Jun 1920 to Mary F STEVENS
Chas Nelson STEVENS m. 6 Sep 1920 to Mary Diana PECKHAM
Norton Anson WOODSUM m. 27 Aug 1922 to Edith Mary STEVENS
Earle Maynard STEVENS m. 31 Oct 1935 to Florence Leola SMALLIDGE
(Johan LeMercier File)

W. B. W. HOWE BIBLE

HOLY BIBLE, published by E. H. HUNTER & Co; 1850

FAMILY RECORDS MARRIAGES

Rev W.B.W. HOWE m. 12 Dec 1850 to Catherine G. EDWARDS at St Philips Church by Rt Rev C.E. Gadsden,

Charleston, SC
William Bell White HOWE, b. 31 Mar 1823, Ceceruncut, NH
Catherine Gadsden EDWARDS, b.9 Nov 1827, Charleston, SC
W.B.W. HOWE, Jr m. 4 May 1880 to Louisa P. KING in St Philips Church
Jas Blake HOWE m. 25 Feb 1886 to Rose Butler FORD, Summersmith, SC, by Rt Rev W.B.W. HOWE
Christopher G. HOWE m. 23 Dec 1908 to Martha FASTER, Summersmith, SC
BIRTHS
Wm Bell White HOWE, b.2 Nov 1851, Charleston, SC
Gadsden Edwards HOWE, b.5 Nov 1854, Charleston, SC
Harriet Edwards HOWE, b.22 Feb 1857, St Johns Berkley, SC
James Blake HOWE, b.7 Jul 1860, Charleston, SC
Catherine Gadsden HOWE, b.23 Sep 1862, Darlington Dist, SC
Christopher Gadsden HOWE, b.16 Feb ____
John Badlan HOWE, b.9 Sep 1866, Charleston, SC
W.B.W. HOWE, b.27 Jul 1881, Charleston, SC
(Anthonie Le Roux File)

RAYMOND - GROGAN BIBLE

New Testament, published by C.P. Barnes & C. Cropper, Cincinnati; 1837
Charlotte A, GROGAN, b.23 Sep 1851
Mary L. GROGAN, b.20 Mar 1853; d.19 Apr 1853
George L. GROGAN, d.30 Dec 1853
Lily May KEENAN, b.21 May 1861; 27 May 1880
Lotta A. GROGAN m. 4 Jul 1876 to Thos W. RAYMOND
'young' RAYMOND, b.17 May 1878
Blake RAYMOND, b.7 Apr 1880
Mary V. CARPENTER m.30 Dec 1850 to George L.

GROGEN
M. V. GROGAN m. 2 Jul 1859 to N. E. KEENAN
(Jean Le Roux File)

DANIEL RAYMOND BIBLE

HOLY BIBLE, published by American Bible Society, New York, 1845

FAMILY RECORDS BIRTHS
Daniel RAYMOND, B.25 Jan 1807
Jane Maria BONTE, b.25 Jun 1812
Eliza Maria RAYMOND, b.25 Aug 1834
Christean Bonte RAYMOND, b.9 Apr 1836
Peter RAYMOND, b.10 Nov 1837
Mary Elizabeth RAYMOND, b.23 Oct 1839
Samuel RAYMOND, b.23 Jun 1842

BIRTHS
Sarah Jane RAYMOND, b.2 Mar 1845
Cornelia Maria RAYMOND, b.17 May 1849
Lydia E. VANHOUTEN, b.22 Nov 1823
Thomas Walter, son of D & Lydia E. RAYMONDS, b.30 May 1852
Ella, adopted dau of Daniel & Lydia E. RAYMOND, b.16 Nov 1862, near Bridgeport, AL

MARRIAGE
Daniel RAYMOND m. 30 Oct 1833 to Jane Maria BONTE, by Rev J. M. Trimble
Daniel RAYMOND m. 3 Jun 1850 to Lydia E. VANHOUTEN, by Rev R.O. Spencer

DEATHS
Eliza Maria RAYMOND, d.21 Apr 1835 (poisend (sic) by mistake)
Christean Bonte RAYMOND, d.9 Jan 1839

Mary Elizabeth RAYMOND, d.16 Nov 1840
Cornelia Maria RAYMOND, d.17 May 1850, Dayton, OH
Jane M., concort of D. RAYMOND, d.27 Jul 1849
Ella, adopted dau of Daniel & Lydia E. RAYMONDS, d.5 Aug 1882
Daniel RAYMOND, d.28Aug 1886
Thomas Walter RAYMOND, d.14 May 1923
(Jean Le Roux File)

ALCEUS DAY BIBLE

No Title Page, no publisher or date of publication

BIRTHS

Alceus Ballon DAY, b.25 Nov 1830, Woonsocket, RI
Ellen M. CLOWARD, b.15 Jul 1842, Wilmington, DL
Ellis Cloward DAY, b.15 Aug 1863, Wilmington, DE
Anna Driggs DAY, b.5 Jul 1867, Wilmington, DE
Ruthellen Moore DAY, b.2 Apr 1872, Mount Carmel, PA
Alceus Ballon DAY, Jr, b.26 Dec 1871, Mount Carmel, PA
Nelly Cloward DAY, b.2 Feb 1874, Mount Carmel, PA

MARRIAGES

Alceus B. DAY m. 7 Nov 1864 to Ella M. CLOWARD, by Rev Geo H. Condron, Wilmington, DE
John Neely RHOADS, MD m.10 Oct 1888 to Anna Driggs DAY, by Rev Philip L. Jones, Philadelphia, PA
Oren Edwin KENDALL m.7 Jun 1900 to Ruthella Moore DAY by Rev Dr Philip L. Jones, Philadelphia, PA
Margaret Cloward DAY, b. 12 Mar 1877, Mount Carmel, PA
Jesse Mason DAY, b.4 Jul 1880, Mount Carmel, PA
(Jean Le Roux File; 1-2268)

THOMAS CLOWARD FAMILY

No Title Page, Publisher or date of Publication

FAMILY RECORD BIRTHS

Children of Thomas & Eliza Jane CLOWARD
William Henry CLOWARD, b.26 Oct 1839
Ella Mary CLOWARD, b.15 Jul 1842
Anna Dushane CLOWARD, b.28 Oct 1847
Emilie Banning CLOWARD, b.7 Jun 1856
Thomas CLOWARD, b.29 Apr 1812
Eliza Jane DUSHANE, b.28 May 1818

BIRTHS

Children of Thomas & Margaret CLOWARD
James CLOWARD, b.24 Jul 1796
John CLOWARD, b.24 Dec 1797
Margaret CLOWARD, b.1 Apr 1800
William W. CLOWARD, b.10 Aug 1804
Thomas P. CLOWARD, b.10 May 1806
Elizabeth CLOWARD, b.11 Jun 1807
Justice CLOWARD, b.4 Jul 1809
Thomas CLOWARD, b.29 Apr 1812
Anna CLOWARD, b.10 Mar 1815
Susanna CLOWARD, b.13 Aug 1817
Mary Ann CLOWARD, b.11 Oct 1802
Amelia Ann CLOWARD, b.18 Oct 1823
(Jean Le Roux File; 1-2268)

WILLIAM L. ROBERTS BIBLE

No Title Page, no publisher or date of publication.

BIRTHS

William L. ROBERTS, b.7 Aug 1816
Susan E. ROBERTS, b.18 Dec 1826
Eleanor F. ROBERTS, b.7 Apr 1843
John M. ROBERTS, b.25 Dec 1844

Jane M. ROBERTS, b.2 Apr 1847
William L. ROBERTS, b.25 Oct 1848
Susan F. ROBERTS, 31 Dec 1850
Leonard D. ROBERTS, b.16 Feb 1854
Ophelia ROBERTS, b.22 Apr 1860
MARRIAGES
William L. ROBERTS m. 15 May 1842 to Susan E. DEXTER
entry can not read
Frances G. ROBERTS m. [--] Oct 1919 to Hazel BOWER
(Jean L'Escayer File)

CHARLES WEST FAMILY BIBLE

New Testament, published by A. Chandler for the American Bible Society, New York, 1834

FAMILY RECORDS BIRTHS
Charles WEST, b.19 Nov 1790, Myrtlegrove, Liberty Co, GA
Sarah Evelyn NEPHEW, b. 10 Jun 1796, Julianton, McIntoch Co, GA
Charles William WEST, first child of Charles & Sarah E. WEST, b.19 Jan 1815, Savannah, GA
Hannah Eliza , second child, b.7 Jun 1817, Savannah, Liberty Co, GA
Susan Caroline; third child, b.11 Jan 1819. Lunbury, Liberty Co, GA
Mary Catherine, fourth child, b.14 Apr 1821, Ceylon, McIntosh Co, GA
James Nephew, fifth child, b.5 Apr 1823, Ceylon, GA
Elizabeth Monroe, sixth child, b.9 Jul 1824, Baisden Bluff, McIntosh Co, GA
Clifford Amanda Stiles, seventh child, b.26 Oct 1827, Sunbury, Liberty Co.GA
MARRIAGE

Charles WEST m.27 Jan 1814 to Sarah E. NEPHEW, by Rev Wm M. West, Manchester, McIntosh Co, GA
Hannah E. WEST m. Oct 1836 to David ANDERSON
Charles W. WEST m. 23 Oct 1840 to Eliza A. WHITEHEAD
Mary C. WEST m. 4 Jun 1845 to Henry Holcombe TUCKER
James N. WEST m. 16 Sep 1846 to Isabella D. ATCHISON
Clifford G. WEST m. 5 Feb 1848 to John H.POWERS
Maria L. WEST, m.8 Dec 1858
Joseph J. WEST m. 16 Jul 1807 to Annie M. ROGERS

<u>BIRTHS</u>

Sarah Evelyn Snow, eighth child; 5 Jan 1830, Lunburg
Joseph Jones, ninth child, b.17 Mar 1832, Walthourille, Liberty Co
Maria Louise, ten child ;19 Jan 1835, Walthourville, Liberty Co,

<u>DEATHS</u>

Susan Caroline WEST, d.24 Aug 1829, Sunburg
Hannah E. ANDERSON, d.8 Jun 1837, Walthourville
Elizabeth Monroe WEST, d.29 Nov 1844, Westmoreland, Houston Co, GA
Mary Catherine TUCKER, d.9 May 1847, Monroe Co, GA
Sarah Evelyn L. WEST, d.3 Sep 1847, Hayesville, GA
Sarah Evelyn WEST, d.19 Aug 1857, aged 59yrs
Charles WEST, d.9 Sep 1855, Saratoga Springs, NY, aged 64yrs
Clifford S. WEST, d.2 Dec 1890
(Jacques LeSerrurier File)

WEST FAMILY BIBLE

NEW TESTAMENT, published by Daniel D. Smith, New York, 1829

<u>FAMILY RECORDS MARRIAGES</u>

James Kevin WEST m. 16 Sep 1846 to Isabella D. ATCHISON
Charles Alexander LUCAS m. 3 Feb 1870 to Mary Evelyn WEST
Charles Stewart WEST m. 2 Mar 1876 to Julia G. HEADLER
Hamilton A. WEST m. 15 May 1878 to Sallie Mead DAVEN, Galveston, TX
Alfred W. MARSHALL m. 29 Jun 1880 to Sarah Rosseter WEST
Barrington R. WEST m. 11 Dec 1888 to Lucie C. SCOTT, Lexington, KY

BIRTHS

Isabella Denison ATCHISON, b.27 Oct 1828
May Evelyn WEST, b.19 Sep 1847
Hamilton Atchison WEST, b.30 Mar 1849
Charles Stewart WEST, b.9 Jan 1852
Barrington King WEST, b.17 Nov 1856
Sarah Rossetter WEST, b.7 Dec 1859
Georgia Bartow WEST, 26 Jun 1862
James Kevin WEST, Jr, b.15 Feb 1866
Henry Granville OSBORN, b.15 Jul 1833 [Entry crossed out]
James Nephew WEST, b.5 Apr 1823
Belle Atchison WEST, b.26 Dec 1869
Joseph Gignilliatt WEST, b.5 Jul 1872
Clifford Louise WEST, b.30 Mar 1874

BIRTHS

Hamilton ATCHISON, Jr, b.11 Jun 1799
Sarah ROSSETTER, b.16 Jan 1811
Sarah Rossetter, wife of Hamilton ATCHISON, d.9 Mar 1870, Louisville, KY
James Nephew WEST, husband of I.D. ATCHISON, d.12 Apr 1875
Isabella ATCHISON, wife of James N. WEST, d. 25 Oct

1888, Bellevue, Lexington, KY
DEATHS
Hamilton ATCHISON, d.8 May 1842
Hamilton ATCHISON, Sr, d.15 May 1844
Mrs Susannah CLAYTON, d.10 Sep 1829
Mrs Elizabeth GOIFFIN, d.3 Nov 1840
Appleton ROSSETTER, d.2 Nov 1840
(Jacques LeSerrurier File)

TARNEAURE BIBLE

No Title page, publisher or date of publication.

FAMILY RECORDS BIRTHS
John TURNEAURE, b.26 Dec 1804
Marie MABIE, b.10 Jan 1806
Mary Maria TURNEAURE, b.11 May 1827
Giles TURNEAURE, b.18 Jun 1829
Amanda TURNEAURE, b.9 Feb 1831
Jacob Mabie TURNEAURE, b.16 Jul 1833
Pernillia Mabie TURNEAURE, b.11 Jan 1835
Albert Kuiller TURNEAURE, b.9 Jan 1838
MARRIAGES
John TURNEAURE m. 12 Jan 1826 to Maria MABIE
Mary M. TURNEAURE, m. 14 Nov 1841 to James M. GOODHUE
Giles TURNEAURE m. to Sopleronia MAY
Amanda TURNEAURE, m. 18 Jan 1851 to Charles HOME
Jacob M. TURNEAURE, m.[---] 1876 to Sarah RICE[?]
Perimilla TURNEAURE, m. to Halememann MAY
Albert K. TURNEAURE, m. 10 Oct 1860 to Emily BYINGTON
(Pierre de Neir Mabille File)

MAYBEE FAMILY BIBLE

No Title Page, no publisher or date of publication.

FAMILY REGISTER

Jesse D. MAYBEE, m. 17 Feb 1853 to Martha Ann BEARDSLEY
Jesse D. MAYBEE, b.24 Oct 1829
Martha Ann BEARDSLEY, b.27 Aug 1830
Sarah Allena MAYBEE, b.20 Feb 1854
Milindia MAYBEE, b.1 Oct 1856
John MAYBEE, b.25 Feb 1859
Alice Isabella MAYBEE, b.23 Sep 1861
Melinda J. MAYBEE, d. 16 Dec 1864
Mary McGeyor MAYBEE, b.18 Dec 1865
Sarah Ellen MAYBEE, m. 20 Dec 1876 to Elmer ROBBINS
John MAYBEE, m. 5 Dec 1883 to Elizabeth CRAMER
Alice Isabelle MAYBEE, m.18 Jan 1883 to James JONE
Mary M. MAYBEE, m.29 May 1884 to C.U. BIGELOW
Mary M. BIGELOW, d.22 Jul 1899
Melinda MAYBEE, d.11 Apr 1870
John MAYBEE, d.10 Aug 1898
Jesse D. MAYBEE, d.17 Nov 1898
Martha A. MAYBEE, d.12 Sep 1904
William C[ramer] MAYBEE, b.1 May 1886
F[lora] Fay MAYBEE, b.27 Apr 1889
James R[ussell] MAYBEE, b.15 Jun 1896
Elmer G[eorge] ROBBINS, b.7 Feb 1849; d.8 Feb 1901
Homer E[lmer] ROBBINS, b.5 Jun 1881
Mabelle L. ROBBINS, b.21 Dec 1883
Frederick Nolton BIGELOW, b.22 Oct 1885
Jesse Maybee BIGELOW, b.10 Aug 1888
Dr Nolton BIGELOW, d.13 Feb 1924
Alice Isabel JONES, d.23 Oct 1924

John MAYBEE, d.5 Nov 1927
Elizabeth MAYBEE, d.22 Jan 1939
Mabelle L. ROBBINS, m.21 Jun 1905 to Charles A. SINK
Isabelle MAYBEE, b.17 Dec __
Marion HODGES, b.17 Sep
James E. HODGES, b.9 Nov
Robert Cramer HODGES, b. 1 Dec
Charlotte Ann MAYBEE, b.22 Feb 1927
John MAYBEE, b.26 Jan 1806
Milindia BEARDSLEY, b. 29 Nov 1802
John MAYBEE, m. 2 Jan 1829 to Milindia BEARDSLEY
Jesse D. MAYBEE, b.21 Oct 1829
John Morison MAYBEE, b.1 Nov 1839
John Morison MAYBEE, d.3 Nov 1839
(Pierre de Neir Mabille File ; 6-262)

COVEY FAMILY BIBLE

A transcript of HOLY BIBLE, Published by the American Bible Society, New York, 1859. In Nov 1979 belonged to Ruth Hartson of White Plaines, NY.

"this book was given to Sarah S. COVEY by her Mother, Margaret ABRAM 1862; June
1960"

DEATHS

Caroline Almira COVEY, d.27 Dec 1845
Celestia Belinda COVEY, d.13 Sep 1860
Sarah S. COVEY, d.12 May 1864 [9]
Lyman L. COVEY, d.12 Feb 1872
Lorinda A. COVEY, d.1 Apr 1879
William W. THOMPSON, d.26 Sep 1899
William A. THOMPSON, d.3 Jun 1902
Phoenix Newton DEUEL, d.21 Apr 1904

Abram L. COVEY, d.17 Jul 1917
William H. COVEY, d.25 Aug 1918
Daniel L. JOHNSON, d.4 Feb 1923
Ella B. VEEDER, d.18 Jul 1928
Lyman L. COVEY, d.15 Apr 1929
Philip Noble JOHNSTON, d.28 Jun 1948
Caroline Cornelia Covey JOHNSTON, d.13 Aug 1852
MARRIAGES
Lyman S. COVEY m.18 Dec 1842 to Sarah S. ABRAM
Amelia M. COVEY m. 15 Feb 1870 to Phoenix N. DEUEL
Miranda M. COVEY m.3 Dec 1873 to William W. THOMPSON
Eunice B. COVER m.4 Oct 1878 to Irving W. ROWE
Ella E. COVEY m.2 Sep 1884 to Aaron B. VEEDER
Eugenia C. COVEY m. 2 Jun 1886 to William BOSTWICK
Carrie C. COVEY m.24 Apr 1889 to Daniel L. JOHNSON
Abram L. COVEY m.2 Jun 1885 to Lina H. GRENAER
Lyman L. COVEY m.10 Jun 1903 to Agnes Bell BRUCE
Paul Covey JOHNSTON m.1 Aug 1916 to Ethel Clare HUBERLE
BIRTHS
Lyman Lewis COVEY, b.19 Nov 1816
Sarah Sophia ABRAM, b.25 Oct 1823
Caroline Almira COVEY, b.27 Sep 1843
Celestia Belinda COVEY, b.27 Dec 1844
Margaret Amelia COVEY, b.21 May 1846
Mary Miranda COVEY, b.18 Jan 1848
Ella Elizabeth COVEY, b.23 Dec 1849
Abram Levi COVEY, b.24 Nov 1851
Lorine Almira COVEY, b.26 Aug 1853
Caloline Cornelia COVEY, b.24 Nov 1855
William Haslem COVEY, b.26 Jul 1854
Eugene Celestia COVEY, b.7 May 1859

(Pierre de Neir Mabille file)

HINES FAMILY BIBLE

HOLY BIBLE, published by J. Towar & D.M. Hogan; Hogan & Co, Pittsburgh / Philadelphia, 1830

FAMILY RECORDS MARRIAGES

Peter R. HINES, m.18 Feb 1834 to Sarah MACKIN
Peter R. HINES, m.22 Mar 1842 to Emma J. SNOW
Peter R. HINES, Jr, m.30 Apr 1966 to Ellen FAULCON, dau of Dr R.T. FAULCON

MARRIAGES

R.L. HESTON, m. 30 Dec 1888 to Lolu Ellen HINES
W.T. MORCOCK m. 12 Dec 1909 to Annie Ellen FLSTON

BIRTHS

Harvey HINES, son of Sarah & Peter R. HINES, b.15 Jul 1835
Peter [---] HINES, son of Emma & Peter [--] HINES, b.7 Jan 1843
Harvey HINES, son of Ellen & Peter R. HINES,Jr b.25 Jul 1867
Lula Ellen HINES, dau of Ellen & Peter R. HINES, Jr, b.26 Jan 1870
Rosa Falconer HINES, dau of Ellen & Peter R. HINES, Jr, b.11 Dec 1872
Annie Ellen ALSTON, dau of Lula & R.L. ALSTON, b.7 Apr 1890
Robert Lea ALSTON, Jr, b.14 Aug 1891
Crowelf Hines ALSTON, b.7 May 1894
Harvey Claud ALSTON, b.15 Nov 1896
Lula Mariam ALSTON, b.20 Jun 1899

DEATHS

Sarah HINES, wife of Peter R. HINES, d.25 Oct 1837

Harvey HINES, son of Sarah & Peter R. HINES, d.17 Sep 1864
Peter R. HINES,Sr, d.19 Jul 1880
Emma J. HINES, wife of P.R. HINES, Jr d. [----] 1886
Rosa Falconer HINES, d.2 Mar 1880
Lula E. ALSTON, d.18 Mar 1901
Harvey L. HINES, d.27 Jun 1901
P. R. HINES, son of Emma & P.R. HINES, Jr, d.19 Jan 1908
Mary Ellen HINES, wife of Peter R. HINES, Jr, d.21 Mar 1924
(Gideon Macon File)

EDWIN HUNT MASON BIBLE

HOLY BIBLE, published by Jesper Harding, Philadelphia, 1851

BIRTHS

Edwin Hunt MACON, b.28 Feb 1803
Harriett Marshall MACON, b.22 Jan 1805
L[-----] Amansa GRINER, b.6 May 1809
Robert Adams JONES, 31 Jan 1801
Thomas Grimes MACON, b.16 Nov 1824
Alethea Jane JONES, b.6 Feb 1929
Lillias Iwanona MACON, b.31 May 1851
Robert Edwin MACON, b.16 Dec 1853
Hattie MACON and Mattie MACON (Twines), b.1 Apr 1856
Mary Willihmina MACON, b.10 Jan 1859
Emily Caroline CULBERTSON, wife of Thomas G. MACON, b.8 Sep 1848
Arthur MACON, b.4 Dec 1867
Thomas David MACON, b.20 Jul 1870
Eva Glover MACON, b.10 Jan 1873
Katie Valeria MACON, b.17 Jul 1875

J[_____] Oslin MACON, b.[---] 1878 in Harris Co , GA
Karl MACON, b.25 Mar 1882
Emegine MACON, b.10 Feb 1885
Lora MACON, 10 Nov 1889
MARRIAGES
EDWIN Hunt MACON m.1 Nov 1821 to Letia Amanda GRIMES
Robert Adams JONES m.6 Oct 1825 to Harriet Cardwell MACON
Thomas Grimes MACON m. 4 Jan 1848 to Alerthes Jane JONES
Thomas Grimes MACON m.27 Sep 1866 to Emily Caroine CULBERTSON
William R TUCK m. 19 Jan 1875 to Martha MACON
Arthur MACON, m.22 Apr 1891 to Lillian N. GAREY
DEATHS
Edwin Hunt MACON, d.5 Feb 1841
Robert Adams JONES, d.20 Mar 1843
Lillian Iwonona MACON, d.14 Jun 1854; aged 3yrs, 15dys
Harriett H. M. JONES, d.10 Apr 1855
Mary W. MACON, d.3 Feb 1860
Lillias Amanda MACON, d.2 Aug 1861
Alethea Jane MACON, d.5 Jun 1865
Thomas Grimes MACON, d.27 Dec 1893
Robert Edwin MACON, d.24 Jan 1896
Robert George [Steoberg ?_]; d.29 Sep 1902
Emegene MACON, d.18 Jan 1909
three entries very blurred, unreadable.
(Gideon Macon File)

SIMON TAFT BIBLE

HOLY BIBLE, published by J.L. READ & Son,

Pittsburgh, n.d. The originals in 1991 were in the possession of Georgia A. Johnson Snider of Tomah, WI.

FAMILY RECORDS BIRTHS

Simon B. TAFT, b.18 July 1802
Eliza BEDFORD, b.10 Jul 1805
Catherine DYE, b.19 Mar 1805
Albert B. TAFT, b.18 Oct 1823
Lucy E. TAFT, b.18 Aug 1825
Eliza Ann TAFT, b.29 Jun 1827
Maryett TAFT, b.22 Sep 1829
Furaney L. TAFT, b.22 Mar 1832
Priscilla F. TAFT, b.17 Nov 1834
Delia L. TAFT, b.26 Sep 1837
Simon D. TAFT, b.26 Aug 1842
George W. WHITNEY, b.6 May 1845
Wilson WOODWARD, b.31 Dec 1831
Delia L. TAFT, b.26 Sep 1826
married 25 Feb 1855
Anna Eliza, b.27 Aug 1856
Deistaing Taft WOODWARD, b.13 Sept 1858
Priscilla Flavilla WOORDARD, b.23 Aug 1862
Annie Violletta WOODARD, 19 Oct 1864
Delia Lovina WOODWARD, b.15 Jun 1867
Kitty Lennive WOODARD, b.20 Apr 1871
Wilson D. WOODARD, b.1 Nov 1876

MARRIAGES

Simon B. TAFT m.13 Feb 1811 to Eliza BEDFORD
Simon B. TAFT m. 20 Mar 1831 to Catherine DYE, his second wife
Wilson WOODARD m. 25 Feb 1855 to Delia L. TAFT
Byran JOHNSON, m.6 Nov ---- to Anna Eliza WOODARD
Distaing Taft WOODARD to Mati JOHNSON
Frank L. JOHNSON, m.9 May ---- to Priscilla F. WOODARD

Frank WANDERVEST, m.25 Dec ___ to Annis Violette WOODWARD
Wm Henry MOSSE to Delia Lavina WOODARD
Estes N. PURDY, m.20 Oct 1898 to Kettie J. WOODARD
Wilson D. WOODARD, m. Mar 1899 to Maud JUDD
Gilbert WOODARD, m.17 Oct [---] to Lurany L. TAFT
DEATHS
Eliza TAFT, d.17 Nov 1830
Mary TAFT, d.25 Mar 1837
Elizabeth Ann WHITNEY, d.20 Dec 1846
Simon A. TAFT, d.11 May 1847
Priscilla F. HALL, d.3 Nov 1857
S. B. TAFT, d.11 Jun 1877
Lucy E. WHITNEY, d.17 Sep 1884
Lurancy Taft WOODARD, d.9 Jun 1906
Delia Taft WOODARD, d.7 Dec 1905
Wilson WOODARD, d.5 Feb 1933
George W. WHITNEY, d.6 May 1851
Charles HALL
Gilbert WOODARD, d.6 Jun 1885
Charles H. WHITNEY, d.4 Feb 1881
George D. WHITNEY, d.20 Mar 188[6]
Catherine Dye TAFT, d.20 Feb 1888
Priscilla Woodard JOHNSON, 15 Oct 1900
Distaing Tafy WOODARD
(Hester Mahieu File)

RAGAN - SHEPARD BIBLE

Hitchcock's HOLY BIBLE, published by A.J. Joshnson, New York, MDCCCLXXII
FAMILY RECORD BIRTHS
James RAGAN, b.13 Nov 1793

Sally WICKHAM, b.16 Apr 1803
Ransom RAGAN, b.19 Jul 1823
John T. RAGAN, b.19 Jul 1826
Cynthia RAGAN, b.20 Aug 1829
Roxy Ann RAGAN, b.22 Jun 1831
Children of Ransom and Sophia RAGAN
George James RAGAN, b.12 Apr 1849
Arthur Josiah RAGAN, b.22 Mar 1858
Dora May RAGAN, b.27 Aug 1860
Mary D. SMITH, b.22 Dec 1829
Marselles SEARLS, b.12 Jun 1828
Hellen D. SEARLE, b.20 Sep 1858
Cora Elva SEARLE, b.22 Jun 1863
<u>BIRTHS</u>
George SHEPARD, b.17 Oct 1798
Mary A. STAPLIN, b.2 Jan 1804
Mary O. SHEPARD, b.13 Jul 1823
Theadora E. SHEPARD, b.8 Mar 1825
Esther S. SHEPARD, b.21 Jan 1827
Sophia A. SHEPARD, b.25 Apr 1828
Theressa E. SHEPARD, b.8 Mar 1831
Achsah S. SHEPARD, b.8 Jan 1834
George W. SHEPARD, b.26 Jan 1836
Otis A. SHEPARD, b.13 Jul 1837
Eunice A. SHEPARD, b.16 Nov 1836
Emma V. SHEPARD, b.20 Jun 1844
Charles J. SHEPARD, b.29 Mar 1848
<u>DEATHS</u>
George James RAGAN, d.15 Nov 1875
Arthur Josiah RAGAN, d.17 Apr 1899
Dora May Ragan MARTIN, d.29 Dec 1810; aged 50yrs, 4mos 2sry
Ransom RAGAN, d.10 Sep 1888

Cynthia SEARLS, d.7 Dec 1886
Sally RAGAN, d.14 Feb 1846
Roxy Ann RAGAN, d.12 Feb 1851
Janes RAGAN, d.14 Dec 1865
Abraham WICKHAM, d.13 Jan 1863, aged 86yrs
(Hester Mahieu File)

JACOB WICKER BIBLE

HOLY BIBLE, published by Mark & Charles KERR, Edinburgh, MDCCXCV

MARRIAGES

Jacob WICKER m. 15 Nov 1790 to Asenath KINGSLEY at Northhampton by Rev Solemon Williams
George F. WICKER m. [_] March 1821 to Jerusha SMITH at Burlington by Rev Nathaniel Gague
William Frederick WICKER m. 5 Jul 1821 to Cmlla BRYINGTON at Carlotte by Rev Mr Yorke
Maria WICKER m. 29 Apr 1827 to John D. PERRIGO
Lawrence S. WICKER m. 28 Sep 1828 to Eliza M. THOMPSON in Cincinnati, OH
Asenath WICKER m. 15 Jun 1829 to Isaac H. PERRIGO at Middlebury Vt.

BIRTHS

William F. WICKER, b.2 Jan 1798 at Northampton, MA
Geo Franklin WICKER, b.1 Feb 1800
Lucy WICKER, b.28 Feb 1802
Maria W., b.12 May 1804
Lawrence [_] W., b.6 Jan 1806
Asenath W. b. 23 Nov 1808
(Hester Mahieu File)

ISAAC H. PERRIGO BIBLE

HOLY BIBLE, published by Jesper Harding & Sons, Philadelphis, 1857

BIRTHS

Isaac H. PERRIGO, b.10 Sep 1807, Ticonderoga, NY
Asenath WICKER, b.23 Nov 1808, Northampton, MA
Julia M. PERRIGO, b.8 Mar 1830, Berlington, VT
John D. PERRIGO, b.21 Sep 1832, Burligton, VT
John F. PERRIGO, b.25 Jan 1835, Gomermean, NY
Emily A. PERRIGO, b.15 Jan 1838, Governean, NY
Charles H. PERRIGO, b.1 Oct 1842, Governean, NY
George W. PERRIGO, b.18 Sep 1843 Lockport, NY
written by J. H. PERRIGO
Mary Asenath Van DUZEE, b.3 Dec 1860, Debugue, IA
Emily Bigelow LOFFRING, b.2 Aug 1915
adopted Emily Bigelow DICKS,

MARRIAGES

Isaac H. PERRIGO m. 15 Jun 1829 to Asenath WICKER, Middleburg, VT, by Rev J.V. Nichols
A.H. SOUTHWORTH m. 31 Jan 1849 to Julia M. PERRIGO, Lockport, NY
Alanzo I. VANDUGEE m. 1 Jun 1809 to Emily PERRIGO
Chas H. PERRIGO m. [?] May 1864 to Mary CAMPTON, Lockport, NY
Alenzo PERRIGO m. 27 Nov 1866 to [___]minia BIRDSOE, Lockport, NY
written by J. H. PERRIGO
Mary Asenaih VAN DUGEE m. 29 Sep 1887 to Isaac Stanffes BIGELOW, MD
Emily BIGELOW m.1 Oct 1914 to Glenn Harrison TOPPING
Emily Bigelow TOFFING m. 27 Sep 1919 to James Laurence DICKS, St Louis, MO
Emily DICK m. 5 Jun 1936 to W. H. GOLGER

DEATHS
John Dean PERRIGO, d.22 Mar 1834, aged 1yr 6mos
John Franklin PERRIGO, d.8 Apr 1842, aged 7yrs, Governour, NY
Emily A. VAN DUGEE, d.7 Apr 1865, Debuque, IA
Asenath PERRIGO, d.1 Sep 1872, aged 63yrs 8mos 7dys, Hudson, IL
Isaac H. PERRIGO, d.25 [___] 1875, Lockport, NY; aged 67yrs 1mo 15dys
George H. PERRIGO, d.4 Feb 1892
Julia M. SOUTHWORTH, d.20 Aug 1888
Charles H. PERRIGO, d.31 Jan 1907
Alanzo John VAN DUZEE, d.15 Nov 1912, aged 78yrs 10mos

Mary Crumpton PERRIGO, d.26 Nov 1927
(Hester Mahieu File)

WILLARD PURDY GRAVES BIBLE

No title page, no publisher or date of publication

BIRTHS
Willard Purdy GRAVES, b.31 Jul 1838 [______]
Lucy Melvina LIBBY, b.20 Nov 1838, Jay, Maine
Willard GRAVES, Jr, b.26 Sep 1865, Alexandria, VA
Myrtilla Melvina GRAVES, b.4 Mar 1868
Herbert Cornelius GRAVES, b.17 Aug 1869
Lucy Mariah GRAVES, b.3 Aug 1871
Mary Ellen GRAVES, b.14 Aug 1873
Asenath Moon GRAVES, b.10 Sep 1875
Willard Purdy GRAVES, Jr, b.3 Feb 1878
MARRIAGES
Willard Purdy GRAVES m. 19 Dec 1864 to Lucy Melvina

LIBBY, by Rev Wallace, Manchester, NH
Herbert C. GRAVES, m.4 Sep 1894 to Edith WALTER, by Dr Alexander Gibson, Washington DC
Mary Ellen GRAVES, m. 25 Jun 1902 to Fred M. McGROW, by Dr Frank Brook, Alexandria, VA
Asenath Moore GRAVES m. 29 May 1905 to George Albert CHADWICK, by Rev Dr F.J. Brooke, Alexandria, VA
DEATHS
Willard GRAVES, Jr, d.14 Feb 1866
Lucy Melvina GRAVES, d.26 Feb 1912
Willard P. GRAVES, Jr, d.20 Jun 1913
Herbert C. GRAVES, d.26 Jul 1919, England
Willard Purdy GRAVES, Jr, d.12 Jan 1922
Myrtilla Melvina GRAVES, d.7 Dec 1839
Lucy Mariah GRAVES, d.27 Jun 1946
Mary Ellen GRAVES, d.24 Jul 1946
(Hester Mahieu Files)

WILLIAM PRICE FAMILY BIBLE

HOLY BIBLE, published by Jesper Harding Philadelphia, 1851
FAMILY RECORD MARRIAGES
William PRICE m.1 Jan 1847 to Mary STARKEY
William PRICE, m.8 Mar 1851 to Lovina BADGER
BIRTHS
Eliza Jane PRICE, b.27 Aug 1851
Erastus McClure PRICE, b.28 Jan 1853
David Elry PRICE, b.6 Jun 1854
Oliver Carey PRICE, b.15 Jan 1856
Uretta Gurnsey PRICE, b.22 Apr 1858
Mary Jane PRICE, b.19 Sep 1849
William PRICE, b. 22 Mar 1821

Lovina PRICE, b.19 Apr 1823
James Lacey PRICE, b.11 Dec 1860
Lucy Maria PRICE, b.30 Aug 1864
George Washington PRICE, b.19 Nov 1866
Melton L. PRICE, 21 Dec 1869
DEATHS
Mary PRICE, d. Sep 1849
Eliza Jane PRICE, d.29 Aug 1851
Lucy Marrah PRICE, d.4 Apr 1866
Mary Jane PRICE, d.3 Oct 1866
George W. PRICE, d.30 Jul 1867
Erasrus McClure PRICE, d.29 Aug 1868
entry can not be read
William E. PRICE, d.8 Aug 1892
entry not readable
Oliver Carey PRICE, d. May 1929
(Theodores Malott File)

SENTENCY FAMILY BIBLE

Transcript of a OLD TESTAMENT, published by Mathew Carey, Philadelphia, 27 Oct 1802. At one time the Bible was in the possession of Miss Anna Frank, of Maysville, KY

Copied 6 Jan 1983 by Lula Jane Crain Feller from the "Family File" at the Kentucky State Historical Society Library, Frankfort, KY

BIRTHS
John SENTENCY, b.20 Dec 1766
Elizabeth SENTENCY, b.17 Sep 1772
Have Issue
Thomas SENTENCY, b.11 Mar 1793

Joab SENTENCY, b.6 Dec 1794
Nancy SENTENCY, b.5 Apr 1797
Jacob SENTENCY, b.8 Jun 1799
Catherine SENTENCY, b.3 Apr 1802
Charity SENTENCY, b.30 Aug 1804
Mary SENTENCY, b.7 Jul 1807
Clara SENTENCY, b.13 Dec 1812

Mary HOUGHTON, b.5 Feb 1757
William HOUGHTON, b.25 Sep 1757
Aaron HOUGHTON, b.19 Apr 1761
Sarah HOUGHTON, b.19 Nov 1767
Belchell [?] HOUGHTON, b.17 Feb 1771
Joab HOUGHTON, b.24 Feb 1773
John SENTENCY, son of Jacob & Elizabeth, b.10 Oct 1817
Thomas SENTENCY, son of Joab & Elizabeth, b.16 May 1819
Emily SENTENCY, dau of Thomas & Nancy SENTENCY, b.19 Mar 1813
Elissaan SENTENCY, dau of Thomas and Nancy SENTENCY, b.8 Jan 1815
Martha Cone CURBY, b.25 Feb 1831
Elizabeth CASE, b.5 Apr 1818
Walter CASE, b.17 Jul 1820
Spencer CLARK, b.8 Sep 1817
Elizabeth SENTENCY, dau of Joab & Elizabeth, b.10 Dec 1820
Nancy SENTENCY, dau of Thomas & Nancy, b.16 Sep 1817
James SENTENCY, son of Thomas & [______], b.16 Mar 1821
Nancy SENTENCY, dau of Joab SENTENCY. b.6 Mar 1823
Martha Ann THOMAS, b.3 Feb 1842
John William CASE, son of Walter S. & Maria L. CASE,

d.16 Apr 1854
Jos. Frank CASE, son of Walter S. & Maris L. CASE. b.7 Jun 1858
A son of Walter S. & Maria L. CASE, still born 2 Nov 1855
<u>MARRIAGES</u>
John SENTENCY m. 4 Apr 1792 to Elizabeth HOUGHTON
Thomas SENTENCY m.16 May 1812 to Nancy CURBY
Joab SENTENCY m.4 Aug 1816 to Elizabeth GOINGS
Walter CASE m. 25 Mar 1816 to Nancy SENTENCY
James CURBY m.30 Jan 1823 to Catherine SENTENCEY
Lewis SENTENCY m.7 May 1829 to Mary B. SENTENEY
Walter S. CASE m.24 Feb 1850 to Maria L. THROCKMORTON
<u>DEATHS</u>
Jacob SENTENCY, son of John & Elizabeth, d.23 Aug 1800; aged 1yr 2mo 15dys
Walter CASE, d.21 Jan 1820
Nancy SENTENCY, concort of Thomas SENTENCY, d.22 Mar 1821
James SENTENCY, son of Thomas & Nancy, d.25 Mar 1821
Catherine CURBY, d.28 Feb 1831,; aged 28yrs 11mos 4dys
Joseph JACOBS, d.20 Mar 1830; aged 8dys
John SENTENCY, Sr, d.25 May 1836; aged 70yrs 4mos 25dys
Nancy CASE, d.27 Oct 1849; aged 52yrs 6mos 22dys
Jos Frank CASE, son of Walter & Maria L. CASE; d.18 Aug 1860; aged 3yrs
(Henri Marchand)

GOODALL - WILLIAMS BIBLE

HOLY BIBLE, published by A. J. HOLMAN & Co, Philadelphia, 1879

Marriage Certificate page:
Frank M. GOODALL of Nashville, TN m. 9 Aug 1870 at Bay St Louis, MS to Anna J. WILLIAMS of Bay St Louis, MS; by Rev Alexander Marks

BIRTHS

Frank Montgomery GOODALL, b.2 Sep 1843, Sparta, TN
Anna Jerellien WILLIAMS, b.1 Oct 1849, Bay St Louis
Blanche Mitchele GOODALL, b.23 May 1872, Nashville, TN
Frank Louis GOODALL, b.6 Nov 1874, Nashville, TN
Anna J[_____] GOODELL, b.21 Apr 1877, Nashville, TN
Jessie Williams GOODALL, b.19 Feb 1879
Robert Montgomery GOODALL, b.10 Jun 1881
Cornelia D[___] GOODALL, b.28 Feb 1885
Richard Gott WILLIAMS, b.1786; d.1878 m. 12 Dec 1812 to Catherine HOLDER, b.1797; d.1884
Cornelia A. MARTIN, b.13 Jun 1827
Dr John Holder WILLIAMS, b.27 Nov 1813; d.27 Aug 1850
John Lewis GOODALL, b.15 Jun 1815; d.2 Aug 1858; m.11 May 1842 to Jane Montgomery SIMPSON, b.7 Mar 1826; d.Sep 1906

DEATHS

John Holder WILLIAMS, d.27 Sep 1853, Bay St Louis, MS
John Lewis GOODALL, d.21 Aug 1858, Smithville, TN
John MARTIN, d.29 Sep 1876, Bay St Louis, MS
Cornelia A. MARTIN, d.22 Mar 1885, Nashville, TN
Frank Montgomery GOODALL, d.1 Apr 1888, San Antonio, TX
Frank Lewis GOODALL, d.30 May 1890, Nashville, TN
Alfred Blackman BATTLE, Jr; d.17 Jan 1910. Nashville, TN
James Ethelbert HOUK, d. May 1929, Nashville, TN
Anna J. Williams GOODALL, d.13 Apr 1930, Nashville, TN
Alfred Blackman BATTLE, d.8 Dec 1943, Nashville
Robert Montgomery GOODALL, d.21 Jan 1949, Nashville

Blance Goodall BATTLE, wife of Albert B. BATTLE, d.4 Sep 1951, Nashville
Horace J. BARNES, husband of Anna G. BARNES, d.26 Jan 1952; Pulaski, TN

Jessie Goodall HOUK, wife of Joa E. HOUT, d. Sept __________, Nashville
(Nicholas Martin file, 21-222)

JOHN FEILD BIBLE

transcript of Bible Records, No title page, no publisher or date of publication, in Nov 1964 original in possession of Meade Feild Cox

BIRTHS

John FEILDS, b.10 Jul 1791
Mary Harriett BOLING, b.21 Nov 1810
Hume FEILD, b.10 Nov 1829
Ellen Meade FEILD, b.16 May 1831
Harriet Bolling FEILD, b.19 Jul 1833
John Alexander FEILD, b.22 Feb 1835
William Meade FEILD, b.15 May 1837
Richard Channing FEILD, b.7 Jul 1839
Susan Ann FEILD, b.31 Mar 1841
Mildred Bolling FEILD, b.25 Mar 1843
Sarah Jones FEILD, b.8 Jul 1845
Emily Mather FEILD, b.10 Apr 1847

FAMILY RECORDS BIRTHS

George S. FEILD, b.7 Apr 1836
Susan Ann FEILD, b.31 Mar 1841
George FEILD, Jr, b.16 Mar 1859
Harriet Bolling FEILD, b.17 Dec 1860
Lucy Meade FEILD, b.29 Mar 1862

Spotswood Bolling FEILD, b.17 Dec 1863
Susie Pryor FEILD, b.13 Feb 1867
Minna Jones FEILD, b.1 Sep 1868
David Meade FEILD, b.31 May 1872
Bessie Louise FEILD, b.27 Dec 1877
MARRIAGES
John FEILD m.23 Oct 1828 to Mary Harriett BOLLING
Hume FEILD m.28 Oct 1851 to Lucy Osborne JONES
Andrew Meade FEILD m.3 Oct 1852 to Ellen Meade FEILD
George S. FEILD m.16 Dec 1857 to Susan A. FEILD
DEATHS
Harriet Bolling FEILD, dau of John & Mary H. FEILD, d.5 Aug 1834
Sarah Jones FEILD, d.16 Jul 1846
John FEILD, d.26 Sep 1851
Richard Channing FEILD, d.29 Jul 1853
Harriet Bolling, dau of G.S. & S.A. FEILD, d.4 Feb 1863; aged 3yrs
Lucy Meade FEILD, d.30 Jun 1865
(Nicholas Martin File)

GEORGE FEILD BIBLE

Transcript from a Old Bible, no title page, note it was published in Edinburgh, Scotland,1795. Copied by Meade Feild Cox in November 1961 at Laurel Brook, Virginia.

George FEILD m. 5 Nov 1818 to Lucy A. G. DUNN
George FEILD, b.20 Jan 1796
Lucy A.G. FEILD, b.1 Dec 1801
George Spotswood FEILD, b.7 Apr 1836
Dr George Spotswood FEILD, d.24 Dec 1891
Dr George FEILD, d.7 Jun 1861, aged 65yrs

Lucy A.G. FEILD, d.10 Apr 1863, aged 61yrs 4mos 20dys
(Nicholas Martian File)

RUSSELL FAMILY BIBLE

From the flyleaf of a old Bible, No Title page, no publisher or date of publication.

James RUSSELL, Jr, b.30 Nov 1771
Ann THROCKMORTON, b.17 Dec 1772
James RUSSELL m. 15 Oct 1795 to Ann THROCKMORTON
Thomas RUSSELL, b.7 Sep 1796
James Blackburn RUSSELL, b.7 Sep 1798
Mary Ann RUSSELL, b.6 Nov 1800; d.24 Sep 1804
Hannah Throckmorton RUSSELL, b.6 Feb 1803; d.13 Oct 1804
Ann RUSSELL, wife, d.26 Mar 1807, aged 34yrs 3mos 9dys
James RUSSELL, d.29 Aug 1808, aged 36yrs 10mos 29dys
(Nicholas Martin File)

WILEY FAMILY BIBLE

Holy Bible, no title page, no publiher or date of publication

<u>BIRTHS</u>

Brothers of W.C. WILEY
Ishem G. WILEY, b. 14 Oct 1837
F.B. WILEY, b.23 Dec 1839
George H. WILEY, b.27 May 1842
William WILEY, Father of C.C. WILEY, b.2 Oct 1802
Joseph Jack RUTHERFORD, halfbrother of W.C. WILEY, b.24 Mar 1858
G.H. WILEY, d.29 Oct 1904

Father Wm MARSHALL, d.23 Mar 1881, aged 73yrs
Wm C. WILEY,b.19 Nov 1835
Mary MARSHALL WILEY, b.5 Oct 1831
Wm A. WILEY, b.3 Oct 1860
Lucinda WILEY, b.3 Aug 1862
Celeste Leonie WILEY, b.29 Apr 1865
Charles WILEY, b.25 Jun 1867
Lucinda WILEY, Mother of W.C. WILEY, b.15 Feb 1810
Sons of W. and M. WILEY
Francis M. WILEY, b.23 Jul 1871
Lewis Henry WILEY, b.4 Sep 1873
grandchildren
Mildred WILEY, b.3 Jun 1894
Chester WILEY, b.10 Sep 1891
Viola WILEY, b.18 Aug 1903
<u>DEATHS</u>
Wm WILEY, father of W.C. WILEY, d.17 May 1843
Joseph G. RUTHERFORD, killed 26 Mar 1861
Joseph RUTHERFORD the father of J.G. RUTHERFORD, d.20 Dec 1851
Lucinda WILEY, d.10 Jan 1899; aged 88yrs 10mos 26dys
Isham [____] WILEY, d.12 Jan 1909, aged 71yrs 30s 1dys
Bertha WILEY, d.
Lucinda WILEY, dau of W.C. & Mary WILEY, d.3 Nov 1893, aged 31yrs 3mos
Charles WILEY, d.15 Mar 1895, aged 24yrs 2mos 10dys
Leona WILEY, d.15 Apr 1903
Mary Moorhead WILEY, d.19 May 1906; aged 74yrs 7mos 14dys Mother
William Charles WILEY, d.19 Jan 1925; aged 89yrs 2mos Father
William M. WILEY, son of Wm & Mary, b.1860; d. Mar 1927

MARRIAGES
Wm C. WILEY m. 25 Dec 1859 to Mary MARSHALL
Charles WILEY m. 2 Nov 1890 to Mary E. WHITMEN
Lewis H. WILEY m.30 Sep 1902 to Stella PAYNE
Francis Maynard WILEY m.15 Jun 1905 to Bertha HAM
Wm WILEY 1827 to Lucinda LEWIS at Cincinnati
Lucinda LEWIS, Father killed at battle of New Orleans 1815
(Nicholas Martian File)

GRAY FAMILY BIBLE

HOLY BIBLE, published by American Bible Society, New York, 1850. The original was in the possession of Mrs Parker P. Gray or Ramer, AL

FAMILY RECORDS BIRTHS
Parker GRAY, b.23 May 1830
N.U. GRAY, b.18 Jan 1826
May H. GRAY, b.2 Jul 1843
Annie GRAY, b.2 Nov 1843
MARRIAGES
Parker GRAY m. 20 Nov 1849 to N. U. TOWNSEND
Parker GRAY m.6 Nov 1860 to Mary HOUGH
Parker GRAY m. 23 Jun 1880 to Jessie GRIER
DEATHS
Nellie M. GRAY, d.[--] Oct 1884
[entry can't read] d.18 Jun 1877; aged 33yrs 11mos 26dys
Minnie Gray EDEN, d.18 Oct 1898; aged 27yrs 9mo 27dys
Parker GRAY, d.9 Feb 1901; aged 70yrs 8mos 16dys
BIRTHS
Eli B. GRAY, b.14 Feb 1851
John GRAY, Jr, b.12 May 1853
Martha Oliver GRAY, b.28 Sep 1861
John Thomas GRAY, b.3 Aug 1863

Saly Urettn Josephine GRAY, b.26 Mar 1865
Lewis Chapel GRAY, b.25 Mar 1867
entry cant't read
Parker Pertillon GRAY, b.19 Jan 1869
Minnie Joe GRAY, b.21 Dec 1870
Maggie Lillian GRAY, b.15 Feb 1873
Mollie Jeanette GRAY, b.1 Jan 187[-]
(Nicholas Martian File)

HINES FAMILY BIBLE

HOLY BIBLE, published by American Bible Society, New York, 1869

FAMILY RECORD BIRTHS

I.A. HINES, b.10 Jun 1839, Macon, GA
Roas Alfriend HINES, b.4 May 1851, Sparta, GA
Mary Emily HINES, b.24 Nov 1870, Wooten Station
Roas Mary HINES, b.7 Sep 1872, Sparta, GA; d.26 Nov 1947, West Palm Beach, FL
Bessie HINES, b.20 Jan 1876, Albany, GA
Julia HINES, b.14 Jun 1878, Albany, GA; d.3 Feb 1960, West Palm Beach, FL
Augustus H. HINES, b.27 Sep 1880, Albany, GA; d.1881

MARRIAGES

Iverson A. HINES m. 18 Jan 1870 to Roas A. ALFRIEND, at Wooten's Station, Lee Co, GA
Algemon James LITTLE m.18 Aug 1896 to Bessie HINES, Albany, GA
Walter B. WHITAKER m. 14 Jun 1897 to Julia Alfriend HINES, Elberton, GA
(Nicholas Martian File)

LITTLE FAMILY BIBLE

NEW TESTAMENT, published by John E. Potter & Co, Philadelphia, n.d.

FAMILY RECORD MARRIAGES

Sidney D. LITTLE m. 22 Oct 1850 to Elizabeth TATUM, LaGrange, GA by Rev Oatis Smith

Kate Elizabeth LITTLE m. 4 Oct 1888 to Francis Marion GAINES, Elberton, GA

Algemon James LITTLE m. Aug 1896 to Bessie HAINES

Sidney Dekalb LITTLE m. to Bobbie HOWELL at Atlanta, GA

BIRTHS

Sidney D. LITTLE, fourth child, third son of Kinchen & Christeen LITTLE, b.29 Jan 1825, Putnam Co, GA

Elizabeth TATUN, fourth dau of Peter & Nancy E. TATUM, b.11 May 1828, Putnan Co, GA

Emma Chappell LITTLE, child of Sidney D. & Elizabeth LITTLE, b.16 Jun 1852, Long Cane, GA

Walter Clarence LITTLE, b.5 Oct 1854, Near LaGrange, GA

Ida Christeen, b.17 Oct 1856, LaGrange

Fourth heir a dau (called Lump) b.14 Jun 1859, LaGrange

Kate Elizabeth, b.13 Jan 1862, LaGrange

Algenon James, b.4 Jul 1864, LaGrange

Sidney DeKalb, b.22 Mar 1871, LaGrange

Anna Dickison LITTLE, dau of S.D. & Bobbie LITTLE, b. at Atlanta, GA

(Nicholas Martian File)

POSEY - THORNTON PRAYER BOOK

BOOK OF COMMON PRAYER for the Church of

England , published by Joseph Bentham, Cambridge, 1764
On the Fly Leaf
Mary A POSEY
Mary P. HALL's Book presented her by her beloved Mother, 26 Jun 1824
This book was brought from England by Maj George THORNTON, grandfather to Mrs HALL

John POSEY m. 25 Jan 1792 to Lucy Frances THORNTON, Spotsylvania, by Rev Wm Stephenson
Mary RAMISON, their First Dau, b.22 Jan 1797
Thomas Lloyd POSEY. their first son, b.16 Feb 1801
George Anna Thornton POSEY, dau b.5 Sep 1803
John Francis POSEY, second son, b.26 Oct 1805
George Anna T. POSEY, second Dau d.21 Nov 180[-]
William Thornton POSEY, third son of Lucy & John, b.1 Feb 1808
Ruebon Mountfort POSEY, fourth son, b.17 Feb 1810
Martha Ann Thompson POSEY,b.13 Feb 1815
Alexander Hamilton POSEY, fifth son, b.14 Jun 1817
Addison Thornton, sixth son, b.17 Oct 1819
Lloyd POSEY, b.23 Nov 1822; d.12 Dec 1822
(Nicholas Martian File)

TALLEY FAMILY BIBLE

HOLY BIBLE, no title page, no publisher or date of publication

BIRTHS

William TALLEY, b.3 May 1853
Jane TALLEY, b.3 Nov 1854
Mary TALLEY, b.10 Jul 1856

James TALLEY, b.9 Jan 1859
Wilino TALLEY, b.20 Nov 1862
Vernecia TALLEY, b.25 Jul 1829
Susan RAY, b.9 Oct 1845
Andrew TALLEY, b.1 Mar 1869
Levi RAY, b.22 Mar 1869
Martha TALLEY, b.22 Dec 1877
G.W. TALLEY, b.10 Mar 1879
John TALLEY, b.9 Aug 1880
Charlie, b.19 Dec 1881
Sarah TALLEY, b.28 Jan 1883
Warren TALLEY, b.10 Sep 1884
Jesse TALLEY, 19 Jul 1886

MARRIAGES

William TALLEY m.11 Mar 1877 to Susan RAY
Sarah F. TALLEY m. 30 Apr 1899 to Fred WILCOX
George W. TALLEY m.28 Nov 1900 to Leala TILLEY
Warren TALLEY m.19 Jul 1905 to Riby ALTON

DEATHS

Pernecia TALLEY, d.4 Jun 1875
William TALLEY, d.14 Oct 1865
Benjaman TALLEY, d.6 Mar 1865
Maria TALLEY, d.9 Feb 1864
Charley TALLEY, b.12 Mar 1882
Jessie TALLEY, d.20 Jul 1886
William TALLEY, d.29 Jan 1919
Jane Talley CLARK, d.14 Mar 1938
William CLARK, d.14 Jan 1936
John TALLEY, d.1932
Warren TALLEY, d.1934
(Gabriel Maupin File)

ASA W. MAUPIN BIBLE

HOLY BIBLE, no title page, no publisher or date of publication

MARRIAGES

Asa W. MAUPIN m. May 1894 to Pearl May WARD
Claude Victor MAUPIN m. 10 Jun 1903 to Lita May CARTER
N. Clouen MAUPIN m.3 Aug 1904 to Lottie P. YOUNG
Bayard S. MAUPIN m.3 Jun 1908 to Ethel May MANSFIELD
Alonzo R. MAUPIN m. Dec 1908 to Mary Elise JOHN
Nora Beulah MAUPIN m. 28 Mar 1917 to Ralph BATCHELDER

BIRTHS

Napoleon Crawford MAUPIN, b.29 Jul 1837
Mildred Ellen MAUPIN, b.20 Aug 1844
Asa William MAUPIN, b.10 Dec 1873
Bayard Shannon MAUPIN, b.22 Jun 1875
Claude Victor MAUPIN, b.29 Oct 1877
Napoleon Cloren MAUPIN, b.5 Oct 1879
Nora Beulah MAUPIN, b.11 May 1883
Alanzo Roscoe MAUPIN, b.18 May 1884

Marriage Certificate

Napoleon Crawford MAUPIN m. 2 Jan 1873 to Mildred Ellen MAUPIN, by Oliver Brown

DEATHS

Asa William MAUPIN, d.22 Sep 1896
Napoleon Crawford MAUPIN, d.9 Feb 1906
Venable MAUPIN, d.8 Jul 1906, infant dau of Napoleon Cloren & Lottie Young MAUPIN
Mildred Ellen MAUPIN, d.20 Feb 1912

(Gabriel Maupin File)

EDNAH DONNELL BIBLE

NEW TESTAMENT. published by American Bible Society, New York, 1846

<u>FAMILY RECORD MARRIAGES</u>

Ednah DONELL m. 27 Oct 1814 to Polly ANDRES
Jane L. DONNELL m. 18 Oct 1842 to Isac SPARKS
Beggy L. DONNELL m. 25 Jan 1848 to John W. WYNNE
Betsy Ann DONNELL m. 10 Mar 1848 to John H. NEUS

<u>BIRTHS</u>

Ednah DONNELL, b.20 Jan 1789
Polley DONNELL, b.20 Dec 1794
James A. DONNELL, b.4 Oct 1815
Jane L. DONNELL, b.25 Aug 1817
Peggy L. DONNELL, 21 Dec 1819
William M. DONNELL, b.30 Dec 1822
Betsy Ann DONNELL, b.16 Jun 1825
John Hall DONNELL, b.16 Sep 1827
John H. NEW, b.21 Oct 1821
Elizabeth Ann NEW, b.16 Jun 1825
J.W.A. NEW, b.9 Apr 1849
N.L. NEW, b.15 Dec 1850
Sarh Loutica NEW, b.8 Sep 1853
Lauiza Jane NEW, b.10 Aug 1855
Pleaent LeRoy NEW, b.13 May 1858

<u>BIRTHS</u>

[____] DONNELL, b.[--] Sep 1851
William M. [____________]
Madison M. NEW, b.11 Jan 1861
Horace Lee NEW, b.13 Aug 1863

<u>DEATHS</u>

Ednah DONNELL, d.18 Sep 1831
William M. DONNELL, d.12 Feb 1834
Margaret L. WYNNE, d.16 Apr 1850

James A. DONNELL, d.21 Jun 1850
Mary DONNELL, d.1 Aug 1853
Sarah L NEW, d.21 Mar 1854
L.H. DONNELL, d.31 Oct 1861
(Gabriel Maupin File)

JOHN MILLER REID FAMILY BIBLE

HOLY BILE, published by M'Carty & Davis, Philadelphia,1834. The Bble at one time in the possession of Mrs Thomas Billingsley, of Henry, TN

FAMILY RECORD MARRIAGES
J. M. REID m. 9 Sep 1825 to E. M. DINWIDDIE
Ann Eliza REID m. 14 Jan 1847 to Daniel M. LANKFORD
Garland J. REID m. 11 Mar 1851 to Mary HANNA
W.A. THOMAS m.1 Mar 1880 to Ethel REID

BIRTHS
John M. REID, b.27 Oct 1801
Elizabeth M. REID, b.16 Nov 1802
Sidney C. REID, b.27 Sep 1824
Ann Eliza REID, b.24 Nov 1829
Elizabeth Ann LANKFORD, b.11 Nov 1847
John Henry [_____] b. 8 Mar 1849

DEATHS
John M. REID, d.12 Sep 1842
Sidney C. REID, d.3 Sep 1844
James H. REID, d.19 Oct 1862
Gartand J. REID, d.24 Sep 1864, in battle
Elizabeth M. CARSON, d.7 Oct 1864

BIRTHS
John William REID, b.3 Jan 1855
Cynthia Jane REID, b.20 Feb 1857
Sarah Ethel REID, b.8 Mar 1859

James Henry REID, b.14 Jul 1861
Sidney Lee JOHNSON, b.9 Aug 1868
Annie, little dau of W.A. & Ethel THOMAS, b.17 Jul 1891
Virgia Lee THOMAS, b.19 Mar 1895
DEATHS
Mrs Ethel Reid THOMAS, d.9 Oct 1936
BIRTHS of Negroes
Mary Jane , b.21 Jan 1836
Henry, b.23 Nov 1837
Albert & Jane b. 20 Aug 1840
Martha Ann, b.1 Feb 1843
Daniel b.7 Aug 1846
Thomas, b.5 Jul 1848
Taby, b.27 Dec 1855
Willis, b.4 Mar 1862
Thomas Jefferson, b.27 Dec 1843
DEATHS
Henry, a negro d.19 Aug 1835
Jane , a negro, d.18 [__] 1840
(Gabriel Maupin File)

FOLEY FAMILY BIBLE

COMPREHENSIVE BIBLE, published by Robinson & Franklin, New York, 1839

FAMILY REGISTER BIRTHS
Wm D. FOLEY, b.1 May 1823
Jas S. FOLEY, Jr, b.5 Jun 1824
Anna FOLEY b,4 Nov 1825
Henry Geo FOLEY, b.27 Jul 1829
Henry Geo FOLEY, twin brother of [___] Rebecca FOLEY, b.10 Dec 1830
Matilda FOLEY, b.2 Jun 1835

Thos Robinson FOLEY, b.22 Aug 1835
Samuel Dawson FOLEY, b.11 Feb 1838
Andrew FOLEY, b.12 Mar 1839
Eleanor Laurette FOLEY, b.12 Aug 1841
<u>BIRTHS</u>
Anna Maria MAUPIN, b.15 Nov 1845
William MAUPIN, b.18 May 1847
[____] Foley MAUPIN, b.13 Mar 1849
Edward Griffith MAUPIN, b.18 Dec 1850
Matilda D. MAUPIN, b. 21 Dec 1852
Samuel Dawson MAUPIN, b.11 Mar 1855
Mary [__] MAUPIN, b.19 Nov 1856
[_____] MAUPIN, b.21 Oct 1858
Ruth MAUPIN, b.15 Feb 1860
Geo W. MAUPIN, b.26 Nov 1861
<u>MARRIAGES</u>
Jas.S. FOLEY m. 23 Apr 1821 to Anna DAWSON
Anna FOLEY, dau of the above, b.1 Mar 1825, m. 10 Dec 1844 to Wm G. MAUPIN
[___] Foley, dau of James S. & Anna DAWSON FOLEY, b.2 Jun 1834, m. 8 Apr 1868 to Capt [___] W. BAILEY, USA; d.17 Oct 1870
Ellen F. FOLEY, dau of James S. & Anna Dawson FOLEY, b.12 Aug 1841, m. 13 Nov 1868 to I. J. HOWARD; d. Oct 1883
(Gabriel Maupin File)

CROSBY FAMILY BIBLE

NEW TESTAMENT, published by Mark & Charles KERR, Edinburgh, MDCCXCIII
Uriel CROSBY, son of George CROSBY & Sary, his wife, b. 19 Aug 1738, Stafford Co, VA; d.8 Feb 1799

Susannah CROSBY, dau of Thos CONWAY & Elizabeth, his wife, b.15 Mar 17[_]5; d.19 Aug 1806
Uriel & Susannah CROSBY, m. 11 Jan 1764
Anne CROSBY, dau of Uriel & Susannah CROSBY, b.16 Oct 1764
Frances CROSBY, dau of Uriel & Susannah CROSBY, b.19 Jan 1766
George CROSBY, son of Uriel & Susannah CROSBY, b.4 Sep 1767
Sally CROSBY, dau of Uriel & Susannah CROSBY, b.11 Jan 1769
Elizabeth CROSBY, dau of Uriel & Susannah CROSBY, b.1 Dec 1770
Susannah CROSBY, dau of Uriel & Susannah CROSBY, b.22 Aug 1772
Mary CROSBY, dau of Uriel & Susannah CROSBY, b.14 Sep 1774
Thomas CROSBY, son of Uriel & Susannah CROSBY, b.5 Apr 1776
Lydda CROSBY, dau of Uriel & Susannah CROSBY, b.28 Nov 1777
Peggy CROSBY, dau of Uriel & Susannah CROSBY, b.12 Nov 1779
Nancy CROSBY, dau of Uriel & Susannah CROSBY, b.7 Feb 1784 (entry crossed out)
Rebekah and William CROSBY, dau and son of Uriel & Susannah CROSBY, b.7 Dec 1781
Nancy CROSBY, dau of Uriel & Susannah CROSBY, b.7 Feb 1781
Jinney CROSBY, dau of Uriel & Susannah CROSBY, b.21 Mar 1787

Uriel CROSBY, d.8 Feb 1799

Susannah CROSBY, d.19 Aug 1806
Peggy CROSBY, dau d.24 Mar 1808
Lydda DAVIS, dau of Uriel & Susannah CROSBY, d.12 Apr 1814
Mary BRYAN, dau of Uriel & Susannah CROSBY, d.18 Mar 1816
William CROSBY, son of Urile & Susannah CROSBY, d.9 Sep 1817
Elizabeth COFMAN, dau of Uriel & Susannah CROSBY, d.20 Jan 1819
FRancis FRISTOE, dau of Uriel & Susannah CROSBY, d.12 Nov 1820
Jinney HORNER, dau of Uriel & Susannah CROSBY, d.20 Mar 1827
Nancy SMITH, dau of Uriel & Susannah CROSBY, d.13 Sep 1838
two entries very faded and can't be read
George CROSBY, son of Uriel & Susannah CROSBY, d.7 Sep 1851
(Michael Mauzy File)

GRANT FAMILY BIBLE

NEW TESTAMENT, published by Alden, Beardsley & Co, Auburn, 1851

FAMILY RECORD MARRIAGES
R.J. GRANT m. 17 Nov 1852 to Evaline COZBY
Richard J. GRANT m. 4 Nov 1855 to Elizabeth FOSTER
C. K. MAUZY m. 14 Aug 1860 to Elizabeth GRANT
W. E. HOGE m. 30 Nov 1887 to Rhoda MAUZY
BIRTHS
R.J. GRANT, b.10 Dec 1826
Evaline GRANT, b.12 May 1833

Elizabeth FOSTER, b.17 Jan 1831
William Foster GRANT, son of R.J. & Elizabeth GRANT, b.19 Aug 18[__]
DEATHS
Evaline GRANT, d.7 Oct 1853
William F. GRANT, d.19 Feb 1857, aged 6mos
R.J. GRANT, d.16 Jan 1858
C.K. MAUZY, d.13 Aug 1896
Mrs Elizabeth MAUZY, d.28 Dec 19078
W.E. HOGE, d.14 Jan 1928
BIRTHS
Rhoda MAUZY, b.12 Oct 1861
Charles MAUZY, b.15 Oct 1863
Robert MAUZY, b.17 Jan 1866
William MAUZY, b. Jul 1868
(Michael Mauzy File)

ADAM MEHN GERMAN BIBLE

BIBLIA a old German Language Bible no publication date noted
Translation of the records as follows.
In the year 1770 I, Adam MEHN, was married to Abelohen (Apollonia) WEIL
In 1772 our Daughter Elizabeth was born on the 27th of March
IN 1774 our son John Frederick was born on [_page torn__] April
In the year 1785 our daughter Maria Magdalena was born on 22 [_page torn_]
In the year 1792 our son John George was born on the 29th of July
Mary Elizabeth MAIN was born 4 Apr 1845
John George, son of George A. MAIN, b.29 Jul 1792; d.30

Aug 1878; aged 86yrs, 1mo 1dy
(Francis Louis Michel File)

SCOTT FAMILY BIBLE
NEW TESTAMENT, published by William Jackson & William Dawson, Oxford, 1795. Original owned at one time by Mrs John M. Southhall, Richmond, VA,

Charles A, SCOTT, b.17 Jan 1777
Elizabeth L. HUDSON, b.2 Aug 1778
the above married 25 May 1800
Ann Eliza SCOTT, b.17 Mar 1802
William Alexander SCOTT, b.25 Jun 1803
Frances SCOTT, b.16 Feb 1805
Samuel SCOTT, b.4 Jan 1808
Charles SCOTT, b.21 Feb 1810
Daniel SCOTT, b.6 Feb 1812
Martha SCOTT, b. Apr 1814
Mary SCOTT, b.7 Feb 1816
John Lewis SCOTT, b.8 Nov 1817
Edward SCOTT, b.7 Apr 1820

Elizabeth L. SCOTT, d.29 Sep 1830
Charles A. SCOTT m. 3 Jul 1832 to Anne H. GAY
Powhatan Gay SCOTT, son of Charles A. & Anne H. SCOTT,b.27 Jan 1836
Charles A. SCOTT, d.5 Mar 1843
(Paul Micou File)

GEORGE NEALE, SR BIBLE
Transcript of Bible Records, no Title Page, no publisher

or date of publication.

MARRIAGES

George NEALE m.13 Dec 1792 to Sarah ____
Elizabeth CREEL, dau of the above, m.8 May 1814
Lewis NEALE, son of above, m.20 Apr 1815
Lucy CREEL, dau of the above , m. 4 Oct 1818
William NEALE, son of the above, m. 15 Apr 1821
George NEALE, Jr m. 4 Mar 1824 to Elizabeth LEWIS
Sarah E. CREEL, dau of Dr D. CREEL, m.25 Dec 1839
Sarah E. CREEL, dau of Alexander H. CREEL, m.19 Dec 1849

BIRTHS

George NEALE, b.10 Jan 1772
Sarah NEALE, wife of George, b.29 Apr 1776
Lucy NEALE, dau of above, b.14 Dec 1795
Lewis NEALE, son of above, b.17 Oct 1793
Betsy NEALE, dau of above, b.4 Jan 1798
William NEALE, son of above, b.14 Feb 1800
George NEALE, son of above, b.11 Jun 1802
George L. NEALE, son of George NEALE, Jr & Elizabeth L. NEALE, b.3 Dec 1824
Elizabeth L. NEALE, dau of George NEALE, Jr & Elizabeth LEWIS NEALE, b.5 Oct 1826
Edwin H. CREEL, b.9 May 1817
Alexander M. CREEL, b.20 Jun 1819
Sarah CREEL, b.26 Aug 1823
(Paul Micou File)

GOOD BIBLE

HOLY BIBLE, no title page, no publisher or pulication date

FAMILY RECORD BIRTHS

D.M. GOOD, b.12 Dec 1812
Leah R. GOOD, b.29 May 1814
Wm Carroll GOOD, b.13 Sep 1834
Wm Carroll GOOD, b.24 Aug 1837
Mary Augusta GOOD, b.9 May 1841
Willson Kramer GOOD, b.12 Mar 1844
Solon Lyeurgus GOOD, b.19 Jul 1847
James Lucius McNabb GOOD, b.8 Jan 1850
Margaret Emma GOOD, b.17 Dec 1853
Charles Clinton GOOD, b.8 Jul 1856
U.S. Grant GOOD, b.16 Aug 1865
Orrell Jesse GOOD, b.12 Apr 1867
Clemanthe Cadiz GOOD, b.10 Mar 1868
Elizabeth A. SHUNK, b.13 May 1834
Dennis Slayton GOOD, b.21 Aug 1874
David M. GOOD, b.27 Jul 1871
(Michael Musser File)

FRENCH BIBLE

HOLY BIBLE, no Title Page, no publisher or date of publication.

FAMILY RECORD   BIRTHS

Samuel W. FRENCH, son of Eveline & Amos B. FRENCH, b.14 Jan 1820
Leah G. FRENCH, dau of Rachel & John FRANKS, b.25 Sep 1824
Albert FRENCH, son of Leah & Samule W. FRENCH, b. 20 Jun 1842
Eveline FRENCH, dau of Leah & Samuel W. FRENCH, b.18 Sep 1844
John FRANKS, b.17 Jun 1787
Rachel OSTRANDER, b.3 Apr 1788

Stephen FRANKS, d.15 Dec 1806
Jonathan FRANKS, b.31 May 1817
Eliza Margaret FRANKS, b.28 Jun 1820
Leah Jemima FRANKS, b.25 Sep 1823
Catherine Jane FRANKS, b.19 Nov 1829
MARRIAGES
Greenbush March 18th John FRANKS to Rachel OSTRANDER
(Peter Ostrander File)

GARDNER BIBLE
Transcript HOLY BIBLE, Published by Harper & Brothers, New York, 1846
In 1971 the original in possession of Wells D. Gardner of Queens, NY
MARRIAGES
William GARDNER m. 3 Jul 1839 to Eliza M. FRANK
Thomas H. GARDNER m. 29 Feb 1868 to Sarah NEALS
Caleb W. GARDNER m. 12 Aug 1871 to Emily M. MARROW
Peter GARDNER m. 4 Oct 1871 to Rachel E. GARDNER
BIRTHS
William, b.22 Oct 1818
Eliza M. FRANK, b.25 Jun 1820
Thomas Henry GARDNER, b.4 Aug 1840
John Stephen GARDNER, b.8 Feb 1843
Caleb GARDNER, b.27 Sep 1845
Rachel E. GARDNER, b.22 Apr 1848
Edgar Wells GARDNER, b.5 Jan 1851
GRANDCHILDREN
Julia GARDNER, b.25 Nov 1868
William GARDNER, b.12 Jan 1870

Grace GARDNER, b.6 Dec 1871
Annie GARDNER, b.28 Feb 1873
Homer GARDNER, b.11 Oct 1874
Edna GARDNER, b.18 Dec 1877
Ella GARDNER, b.12 May q882
Vesta GARDNER, b.13 Sep 1885
William E. GARDNER, b.6 Jun 1872
Emily M GARDNER, b.12 Aug 1876
Burett C. GARDNER, b.27 Jun 1889
Frederick M. GARDNER, b.5 Nov 1894
Wells F. GARDNER, 26 Oct 1872
DEATHS
Edgar Wells GARDNER, d.15 Mar 1851
William GARDNER, d.5 May 1896

BIRTHS
Children of Thomas C & Willompee Bogert GARDNER
Dow [Douw] B. GARDNER, b.19 Aug 1799
Thomas GARDNER, b.28 Jul 1801
Maria GARDNER, b.16 Mar 1803
Bornt GARDNER, b.18 Jun 1806
Cornelia GARDNER, b.25 Jun 1808
Caleb GARDNER, b.26 Aug 1810
Alida GARDNER, 5 Sep 1812
Garit [Garret V.S.] GARDNER, b.22 Apr 1816
William GARDNER, 21 Oct 1818'
Agnes GARDNER, b.10 Jan 1820
(Peter Ostrander File)

PERRINE BIBLE

HOLY BIBLE, No Title Page, no publisher or date of publication
BIRTHS

Charles H. PERRINE, b.30 Dec 1845
Sarah E. PERRINE, b.23 Oct 1855
Mary F. PERRINE, b.3 Mar 1870
John E. PERRINE, b.[-] Oct 1874
Rosalee PERRINE, b. May [_____]
Jessie May PERRINE, b.2 Mar 1884
Wayne Crawford, b.25 Sep 1904
Carl Edward PERRINE, b.14 Jan 1910
Howard PERRINE, b.[--] Apr 1908
Alta PERRINE, b.9 Jul [----]
remainder of page can't be read poor xerox copy
(Pierre Perrine File)

NEGLEY FAMILY BIBLE

HOLY BIBLE, published by American Bible Society, New York, 1864. Original was in the possession (1960) of Lulu Negley Painter, Monmouth, IL

FAMILY RECORD BIRTHS
Jacob S. NEGLEY, b.4 Dec 1830
Mary A. NEGLEY, b.3 Sep 1834
William P. NEGLEY, b.3 Oct 1855
John F. NEGLEY, b.13 Apr 1857
Elden C. NEGLEY, b.2 Mar 1859
Mary Ida NEGLEY, b.2 Apr 1861
Daniel P. NEGLEY, b.11 Jul 1865
Albert N. & Almer L. NEGLEY, b.2 May 1869
Joseph NEGLEY, b.2 Jan 1873
Abraham S. Abslem NEGLDEY, b.4 Sep 1875
Henry NEGLEY, b.4 Jun 1879

MARRIAGES
Jacob S. NEGLEY m. 28 Nov 1854 to Mary A. PERRINE
William P. NEGLEY m. 30 Jan 1878 to Anna E. FREEMAN

Mary Idez NEGELY m. 12 Feb 1880 to Charles B. VANDORIN
John G. NEGLEY m. 10 Sep 1890 to Maggie Marys WILLSON
Daniel P. NEGLEY, m.26 Jan 1891 to Sophia KROPFF
Albert N. NEGLEY m. 14 Dec 1893 to Cora May BEEMAN
J.S. NEGLEY came to Illinois in 1852 (May the 15th)
(Pierre Perrine File)

PERRINE FAMILY BIBLE

HOLY BIBLE, no title page, no publisher or date of publication listed.

FAMILY RECORDS MARRIAGES
Daniel PERRINE m. 8 Jan 1823 to Eleanor NEVIUS
William PERRINE m. 4 Jan 1844 to Aletty A. BROKAW
William G. HILL m. 8 Feb 1844 to Elizabeth PERRINE
Jacob A. NEGLEY m.8 Sep 1858 to Sarah PERRINE
Joseph NEVIUS m. 11 Jan 1798 to Elizabeth DRUNUN
John NEGLEY m. 25 Feb 1830 to Catherine SLYDER
Daniel O. NEGLEY m. 12 Jan 1854 to Susan HINKEL
Mary E. NEGLEY m. 9 Feb 1854 to Abraham WILSON
Jacob S. NEGLEY m.28 Nov 1854 to Mary A. PERRINE
Eliab L. NEGLEY m.23 Oct 1860 to Mrs Mary E. CAMPBELL
Eveline C. NEGLEY m.26 Feb 1861 to Abraham HESS
Louisa C. NEGLEY m. 27 Feb 1866 to John HOOKE
John F. NEGLEY, m.15 Sep 1874 to Sarrah V. IDE

BIRTHS
Eleanor NEVIUE, b.10 Jan 1804
Daniel PERRINE, b.21 Feb 1802
William PERRINE, b.28 Dec 1824
Joseph N. PERRINE, b.4 Apr 1829

James PERRINE, b.12 Dec 1831
Absalom PERRINE, b.2 Sep 1837
Sarah PERRINE, b.21 May 1840
Eleanor PERRINE, b.6 Dec 1842
Daniel PERRINE, b.4 Mar 1846
David PERRINE, b.4 May 1849
Elizabeth PERRINE, b.20 Nov 1826
Mary A. PERRINE, b.3 Sep 1834
John C. NEGLEY, b.5 Sep 1801
Catherine SLYDER, b.6 Jun 1811
Jacob S. NEGLEY, b.4 Dec 1830
Daniel O. NEGLEY, b.15 Sep 1832
Marry E. NEGLEY, b.5 Mar 1834
Lydia NEGLEY, b.21 Feb 1836
Eliab L. NEGLEY, b.9 Dec 1837
Rosanah NEGLEY, b.10 Sep 1839
Eviline C. NEGLEY, b.20 Nov 1841
Simon F. NEGLEY, b.9 Oct 1845
John F. NEGLEY, b.10 Oct 1846
Louisa C. NEGLEY, b.6 Apr 1849
DEATHS
Eleanor PERRINE, d.29 Apr 1876
Joseph PERRINE, d.3 Jul 1876
James PERRINE, b.7 May 1879
Daniel PERRINE, d.26 Feb 1884
(Pierre Perrine File, 12-2)

LEE BIBLE

HOLY BIBLE, No publisher, place or date of publication
Joshua LEE, b.14 May 1770
Theodore LEE, b.21 May 1780

Hannah LEE, b.3 Jul 1819
Isabella LEE, b.16 Aug 1825
David Written House LEE, b.8 Feb 1801
Alexander D. LEE, b.7 Apr 1802
Mathew P. LEE, b.4 Sep 1804
Margaretta LEE, b.20 Apr 1807
Jane LEE, d.29 Sep 1809
Mary A, LEE, b.12 Oct 1811
John LEE, b.17 Apr 1814
Sarah E. LEE, b.31 Oct 1816
[____] LEE & Jane S. LEE m. 20 Mar 1834
Hamner LEE, b.3 Jul 1819
Catherine Isabel LEE b.16 Aug 1825
John A. HAVANDER and Rooda A. LEE were married 16 Jun 1854
Rhoda BEAUMONT, d.22 Sep 1846
Edward BEAUMONT, d.25 Jul 1861
Rhoda Ann FREEMAN, d.8 May 1863
John LEE, d.11 Sep 1864
John A. HAVANDER m. 16 Jun 1853 to Roda A. LEE
John James LEE m. 22 Feb 1865 to Varginia G. MORAN
William W. LEE m. 25 Apr 1865 to Nancy C. NELSON
Richard H. GRIMES m. 16 Apr 1867 to Martha A. LEE
Joseph Feer GINES, b.1 Aug 1868
Thomas BEVENS m. 15 [___] 1877 to Seluh A. FREEMAN
John LEE b. [-] April 1814
Vine Tealanh LEE, b.[-] Mar 1819
Rhoda Ann C. LEE, b.27 Nov 1836
William Werth LEE, b.6 Nov 1842
John James LEE, b.[-] Sep 1845
Alberta Malisa LEE, b.15 Jul 1848
Alice Canzady LEE, b.24 May 1851
Edward BEAUMONT, b.11 Sep 1800; m.7 Nov 1815 to

Rhoda BEAUMONT, b.25 Jul 1789
Delah S. FREEMAN, b,.17 Sep 1857
Willa Bell FREEMAN, b. 23 Jul 1858
Samuel MORAN m. 17 Feb 1876 to Willa Bell FREEMAN
George T. LYLES m. 27 Sep 1877 to Alice C. LEE
Martha M. GRIMES d.24 Dec 1884; aged 42yrs,4mo 9dys
Francis L. LYLES, d.10 May 1886
Alice C. LYLES, d.28 Sep 1893; aged 42yrs 4mos 4dys
Jane S. LEE, d.9 Sep 1904; aged 85yrs 9mos 9dys
(Pierre Perrine File, 40-6)

PECK BIBLE

Transcript HOLY BIBLE, published by William W. Harding, Philadelphia, 1868. The original in 1960 in the possession of George H. Bonsall of Quincy, MA

MARRIAGES

Theodore M. PECK m. 29 Dec 1864 to Susan HOWELL
Ellen Douglass PECK m. 23 Dec 1891 to Geo H. BONSALL
Martha Baldwin PECK m. 25 Oct 1894 to E. Fred KNAPP
Frederic Malcolm KNAPP m.8 Oct 1921 to Katherine FARNSWORTH
George Hubert BONSALL m. 3 Jun 1922 to Grace Pratt MILLER

BIRTHS

Theodore M. PECK, b.25 Apr 1837
Susan HOWELL, b.24 Dec 1841
Mary Louisa PECK, b.30 Sep 1865
Martha Baldwin PECK, b.9 Jan 1867
Ellen DOUGLASS PECK, b.28 Sep 1868
Anna Howell PECK, b.5 Jan 1872
Margaret Frances PECK, 18 Jul 1876
Geo H. BONSALL, b.20 Aug 1861

Ellen Douglas PECK, b.28 Sep 1868
Geo Herbert BONSALL, b.26 Aug 1894
Helen Peck BONSALL, b.6 Jun 1896
E. Fred KNAPP, b.21 May 1868
Martha Baldwin PECK, b.9 Jan 1867
Frederic Malcolm KNAPP, b.5 Jul 1897
DEATHS
Anna Howell PECK, d.26 Nov 1873
Theodore M. PECK, d.15 Dec 1897, Mentone, CA
Margaret Frances PECK, d.13 Mar 1903
(Pierre Perrine File, 23-24)

BEENE BIBLE

HOLY BIBLE, published by James A. BILL, Philadelphis, n.d.

FAMILY RECORDS MARRIAGES
Obadiah BEENE, son of Robert BEENE, b.15 Dec 1785
Barbara BEENE, wife of Obiadiah, b.22 Mar 1771
Nancy BEENE, dau of Obidiah BEENE, b.14 Feb 1809
Martha BEENE, 31 Jan 1811
Samuel BEENE, b.4 Jul 1813
Elizabeth BEENE, b.28 Dec 1814
O. R. BEENE, b.10 Dec 1816
Milly BEENE, b.14 Nov 1818
Rhoda BEENE, b.10 Apr 1820
Sarah BEENE, b.15 Sep 182[-]
Polly BEENE, b.1 Nor 1824
Barbara BEENE, b.28 Mar 1825
Anna W. BEENE, b. 9 Dec _____
(Robert Pickens File)

HOSMER FAMILY BIBLE

HOLY BIBLE, published by Jesper Harding, Philadelphia, 1853

BIRTHS

Gustavus Pomeroy HOSMER, b.2 Aug 1819, Avon, NY
Mary Elizabeth JOHNSON, b.23 Oct 1818, Onandaga, NY
Henry Cuyler HOSMER, b.24 Apr 1843, Albany, NY
Arthur Livingston HOSMER, b.13 May 1846, Albany, NY
Jeannie Martin HOSMER, b.19 Oct 1850, Albany, NY
Robert Townsend HOSMER, b.31 May 1855, Buffalo, NY
Gustavus P. HOSMER, Jr, b.28 Sep 1856, Buffalo, NY

MARRIAGES

Gustavus Pomeroy HOSMER m. 18 Nov 1841 to Mary Elizabeth JOHNSON, by Rev W.J. Kip (Episcopal)
Gustavus Pomeroy HOSMER m. 2 Oct 1861 to Mary Elizabeth BOILEAU, Meadville, PA by Rev Wm Look (Baptist)

DEATHS

Mary Elizabeth HOSMER, d.23 Aug 1858, Buffalo, NY, aged 39yrs 10mos (remains removed to Lockport Nov 1881)
Henry Cuyler HOSMER, d.24 Feb 1883; aged 39yrs 10mos, buried Loskport, NY
Robert Townsend HOSMER, d.21 Jul 1889, Lockport, NY; age 34yrs 1mo 21dys
Gustavus Pomeroy HOSMER, d.11 Nov 1891, Lockport, NY; aged 72yrs 3mos 21dys
Jeannie Hosmer EMERSON, d.22 Mar 1896, Providence, RI; aged 45yrs 5mos 3dys
(Henri Quesnil File)

LAWRENCE BIBLE

HOLY BIBLE, published by Moore, Wilstach, Keys & Co, Cincinnati, 1857

BIRTHS

[Children of Jadah M. LAWRENCE & Alice Jennett THOMPSON]

Eliza Ann LAWRENCE, b.8 Dec 1830, Toronto, C.W.

Caroline Matilda LAWRENCE, b.17 Mar 1833, Toronto, C.W.

Paul Henry LAWRENCE, b.8 Feb 1836, [_____] C.W.

Orilia Jane LAWRENCE, b.9 Jan 1838, Orilia, C.W.

Frank Pacificus LAWRENCE, b.2 Jul 1840, Su St Marie, MI

Charles James Lieter LAWRENCE, b.18 Sep 1842, Racine, WI

Edward Otho [_____] LAWRENCE, b.10 Aug 1844, Racine, WI

Walter Licingus LAWRENCE, b.17 Feb 1847, Racine, WI

Hester Ann [___] LAWRENCE, b.14 Apr 1849, Racine, WI

Delia Maria LAWRENCE, b.18 Nov 1851, Racine, WI

George Ralph LAWRENCE, b.1 Dec 1858, Racine, WI

Mary Morris Francis LAWRENCE, b.29 Nov 1859, Racine, WI

Mary Emily MILLER, b.5 Aug 1848, Waukesha, WI

Laura Eunice MILLER, b.28 Nov 1851, Wyocena, WI

Wesson Gage MILLER, b.26 Feb 1858, Janesville, WI

[Children of Frank P. LAWRENCE and Mary Emily MILLER]

Maude Valeria LAWRENCE, b.31 Aug 1866, Fond du Lac, WI

Cushman K. LAWRENCE, b.9 Jun 1871, Racine, WI

Burtie LAWRENCE, b.14 Jun 1872, Racine, WI

Clarence Gage LAWRENCE, b.14 Jun 1876, Union Grove, WI

Frankie L. LAWRENCE, b.1 Jan 1881, Utica, NE

[Children of Frank P. LAWRENCE and Lora A. SMITH]

Lora Jeannette LAWRENCE, b.17 Jun 1889, Lincoln, NE

Helen Irene LAWRENCE, b.9 Aug 1890, Lincoln, NE
(Henri Quesnil File)

VAN HARLINGEN BIBLE

Transcripts from two HOLY BIBLES. First Published by William Elliott, New York, 1809. Second published by the American Bible Society, New York, 1857.

MARRIAGES

John VAN HARLINGEN, Jr m. 15 Sep 1774 to Eleanor SCHUREMAN
Mary VAN HARLINGEN m. to Abraham F. DITMARS
Elizabeth VAN HARLINGEN m. to Uriah LOTT
Rensye VAN HARLINGEN m. to Jacques CARTELYOU
Margaret VAN HARLINGEN m.31 Jan 1815 to Staats VAN SANTVOORD
John VAN HARLINGEN m.18 Feb 1813 to Catherine LAWSON
John VAN HARLINGEN, m secondly 15 Oct 1831 to Mrs Mary CUMMINS, dau of Peter & Rachel PERLEE
George VAN HARLINGEN, son of Jno & Mary VAN HARLINGEN, m. 16 Dec 1858 to Sallie E. CLARK
John VAN HARLINGEN m. third 3 Feb 1870 to Lydia Ann KOOGLE
Lydia A. KOOGLE, third wife of John VAN HARLINGEN, b.17 Dec 1823, Lebanon

BIRTHS

Ferdinand Schureman VAN HARLINGEN, b.18 Oct 1821
William Lawson VAN HARLINGEN, b.29 Feb 1824
John VAN HARLINGEN, fifth son, b.21 May 1826
Edward VAN HARLINGEN, 6th son, b.8 Jan 1828
Augustus Taylor VAN HARLINGEN, 7th son, b.5 Dec 1829

George Hardy VAN HARLINGEN, 1st son of John and Mary VAN HARLINGEN, b.24 Aug 1832

DEATHS

Elizabeth VAN HARLINGEN, d.16 Feb 1782, age 10mos 11dys

Anna VAN HARLINGEN, d.19 Oct 1801, aged 11yrs 1mo 7dys

Abraham DITMARS, d.

Uriah LOTT, d.5 Nov 1817

John VAN HARLINGEN, Sr, d.25 Apr 1825, New Brunswick, NJ; aged 69yrs 4mos 7dys [b.18 Dec 1755]

DEATHS

Uriah Lott VAN HARLINGEN, d.7 Oct 1825, Belleville, NJ; aged 7yrs 11mos 24dys

Augustus Taylor VAN HARLINGEN, d.13 Mar 1830, Lebenon, OH; aged 3mos 8dys

Catherine VAN HARLINGEN, d.14 Mar 1831, Lebenon, Warren Co, OH; aged 35yrs 6mos 1dy

Eleanor VAN HARLINGEN, d.6 May 1833, Lebenon, Warren Co, OH; aged 17yrs 9mos 12dys

Mary VAN HARLINGEN, second wife of John VAN HARLINGEN, d.6 Mar ----, Lebenon, OH; aged 67yrs

John VAN HARLINGEN, MD, d.30 Sep 1886, Lebenon, OH; aged 94yrs 7mos 11dys

Mrs Ann LAWSON, d.18 Dec 1858, Cambridge City, IN

Ferdinand S. VAN HARLINGEN, d.8 Feb 1883, Sharonville

John Van HARLINGEN's wife d. 6 Mar 1883, San Francisco

Dr Lewis DRAKE, d.30 Jul 1851

Rev J.J. HILL, d.11 Nov 1885

BIRTHS

Jno VAN HARLINGEN, b.19 Feb 1792, New Brunswick, NJ

Catherine LAWSON, b.____, New Brunswick

James MITCHELL, b. ______, PA

Jane WILSON, b.___, PA
Edward M. VAN HARLINGEN, b.8 Jan 1828, Lebenon, Warren Co, OH
Sarah Jane MITCHELL, b.12 Jul 1836, London, Madison Co, OH
James Mitchell VAN HARLINGEN, son of E.M. & Sarah J. VAN HARLINGEN, b.9 Nov 1858, London, Madison Co, OH
Edward McClimans VAN HARLINGEN, son of E.M. & Sarah J. VAN HARLINGEN, b.2 Dec 1860, London, Madison Co, OH
Kitty VAN HARLINGEN, first dau/3rd child; of E.M. & Sarah J. VAN HARLINGEN, b.8 Feb 1864, London, Madison Co, OH
John Russell VAN HARLINGEN, 4th child, third son of E.M. & Sarah J. VAN HARLINGEN, b.15 Jul 1866, London, Madison Co, OH
MARRIAGES
E. M. VAN HARLINGEN m. 9 Feb 1858 to Sarah Jane MITCHELL, London, OH, by Rev J.J. Hill
James Mitchell VAN HARLINGEN m. 4 Oct 1883 to Alice DUNMORE, Greensburg, IN, by Rev Robert Sloss
Kitty VAN HARLINGEN m. to Dr George FEE
John R. VAN HARLINGEN m. 17 Dec 1890 to Margaret KING, Columbus, IN
Louise VAN HARLINGEN m.29 Jun 1910 to Royal Eason INGERSOLL, Atlanta, GA, by Rev Richard Orme Flinn
DEATHS
Catherine VAN HARLINGEN, d.14 Mar 1831, Lebenon, Warren Co, OH
Mary VAN HARLINGEN, second wife of Jno VAN HARLINGEN, d.6 Mar 1865, Lenanon, Warren Co, OH
Sarah Jane VAN HARLINGEN, d.29 Apr 1883, Richmond, IN

Edward M. VAN HARLINGEN, d.29 Dec 1914, Indianapolis; bur. London, OH; aged 86yrs 11mos 21dys
Edward McClimand VAN HARLINGEN; d.Roosevelt Hospital, New York City
James MITCHELL, d.2 Sep 1856
Jane Wilson MITCHELL, d. 1831, London, Madison Co, OH
Alice Dunsmore VAN HARLINGEN, d.12 Sep 1935, Atlanta, GA
James Mitchell VAN HARLINGEN, d.23 Mar 1941, Washington DC
(Joris Rapalje File)

OGDEN BIBLE

NEW TESTAMENT, published by W. & H. Merriam, Troy, NY, 1846

FAMIY RECORD MARRIAGES
John OGDEN m. 22 Aug 1839 to Rachel HOAGLAND, Canadice, Ontario Co, NY
Henry OGDEN m. 8 Apr 1869
Robert J. OGDEN m. 7 Nov 1924 to Lucy STARLING

BIRTHS
John OGDEN, b.23 Jun 1817, Kent Litchfield Co, CT
Rachel OGDEN, b.24 Mar 1820

Children
Henry OGDEN, b.1 Aug 1841
[__]aine OGDEN, b.4 Oct 1842
[__]obert R. OGDEN, b.7 Sep 1844
Eleanor P. OGDEN, b.30 Sep 1846
Hoppy A. OGDEN, b.1 Aug 1849 (attached a photo of tombstone: "wife of P.B. WAGONER, d.9 Mar 1901)
Frank OGDEN, b.30 Nov 1851
Willie A. OGDEN, b.23 Jun 1853

John OGDEN, b.25 Feb 1855
Rachel A. OGDEN, b.4 Oct 1859
(Joris Rpalje File)

PENNINGTON BIBLE

HOLY BIBLE, no title page, no publisher or date of publication.

FAMILY RECORDS BIRTHS

The Children of James H. PENNINGTON & Martha Jane PENNINGTON, his wife
John J. PENNINGTON, b.10 Dec 1842
James Lawrence PENNINGTON, b.30 May 1845
Frances Marion PENNINGTON, b.6 May 1847
Henry Ludlow PENNINGTON, b.23 Nov 1849
Mary Hollen PENNINGTON, b.12 May 1852
Samuel Claland PENNINGTON, b.10 Oct 1854
Sarah Catherine PENNINGTON, b.14 Feb 1854
Liston PENNINGTON, b.23 Apr 1859
Emily Adella PENNINGTON, b.26 Jul 1861
Lee Roberta PENNINGTON, b.13 Jul 1864

BIRTHS

Catherine PENNINGTON, dau of John L. PENNINGTON and Sarah his wife, b.13 May 1810
Louisa Ann PENNINGTON, dau of John J. PENNINGTON & Sarah, his wife, b.11 Aug 1812
Elizabeth PENNINGTON, dau of John J. PENNINGTON & Sarah, his wife, b.1 May 1815
James H. PENNINGTON, son of John J. PENNINGTON & Sarah, his wife, b.18 Feb 1817
Sarah A. PENNINGTON, dau of John J. PENNINGTON & Sarah, his wife, b.15 Oct 1818

MARRIAGES

John J. PENNINGTON m. 2 Mar 1809 to Sarah HOLDING
Henry MILLER m.3 Jan 1828 to Catherine PENNINGTON
Andrew LYSINGER m. 30 May 1830 to Louisa A. PENNINGTON
Nicholas L.B. PRYOR m. 20 Nov 1836 to Elizabeth PENNINGTON
James H. PENNINGTON m. 17 Jan 1842 to Martha Jane PRYOR
Horace T. ROBERTS m. 9 Jan 1843 to Sarah Ann PENNINGTON
Marion F. PENNINGTON
Lee Roberts PENNINGTON m. 4 Oct 1893 to Mary Larine HULETT
Lee Roberts PENNINGTON, Jr m. 17 Jan 1920 to Catherine CARTER
Walter Carlton PENNINGTON m. 14 Dec 1921 to Dorothy M REED
Samuel Hulbert PENNINGTON, m.31 Dec 1923 to Margaret KRIEL

<u>DEATHS</u>

Elizabeth PRYOR, d.22 Nov 1838
John J. PENNINGTON, d.28 Feb 1845
Sarah PENNINGTON, d.
Martha Jane PENNINGTON, d.3 Oct 187[2]
James H. PENNINGTON, d.29 Sep 1887
James H. PENNINGTON, d.28 Sep [----]
John J. PENNINGTON, 24 Jul 1924 (son of Jas H.)
John J. PENNINGTON, d.5 Oct 1918

<u>DEATHS</u>

Rebecca E. STEPHENS, wife of James B. STEPHENS, d.2 Feb 1862
James Thomas STEPHENS, son of James B. & Rebecca E. STEPHENS, his wife, d.19 Aug 1864

James B. STEPHENS, d. Aug 1916, aged 84yrs 5mos
Liston PENNINGTON, d.12 Oct 1933;aged 74yrs 6mos
Ann S. PENNINGTON, d.23 Jul 1951
BIRTHS
Martha Rebecca , dau of Linton & Annie PENNINGTON, b.15 Jul 1889
James Stevens, son of Liston & Anie PENNINGTON, b.14 Jan 1892
Victor Power, son of Liston & Annie PENNINGTON, b.19 Dec 1892
MARRIAGES
James B. STEVENS m. 15 Mar 1859 to Rebecca E. THOMAS
James B. STEVENS m. 9 Feb 1869 to Juliet M. HURN
Liston PENNINGTON m. 10 Feb 1886 to Annie STEVENS
(Joris Rapalje file)

MOORE BIBLE

HOLY BIBLE, no title page, no publisher or date of publication
BIRTHS
Thomas M. MOORE, b.5 Nov 1830, Brown Co, OH
Catherine MOORE, b.10 Sep 1833, Baltimore, MD
Mary E. MOORE, b.23 Dec 1852, Georgetown, Brown Co, OH
Philip M. MOORE, b.14 Dec 1854, Georgetown, Brown Co, OH
Emma J. MOORE, b.4 Feb 1857, Georgetown, Brown Co, OH
Charles E. MOORE, b.16 Jun 1859, Georgetown, Brown Co, OH
Mattie B. MOORE, b.14 Sep 1864, Georgetown, Brown Co, OH

William T. MOORE, b.4 Feb 1864, Higginsport, Brown Co, OH
Alfred L. MOORE, b.6 Oct 1867, Higginsport, Brown Co, OH
Harry S MOORE
MARRIAGES
Thomas M. MOORE m. 26 Dec 1850 to Catherine MILLER, Georgetown, Brown Co, OH, by Chas W. Reed
(Joris Rapalje File)

FREELAND BIBLE

HOLY BIBLE, published by Moore, Wilstach & Baldwin, Cincinnati, n.d.

BIRTHS
Richard J. FREELAND, b.25 Jun 1801
Elizabeth FREELAND, b.2 Jan 1813
John R. FREELAND, b.8 Mar 1830
William FREELAND, b.26 Mar 1832
James FREELAND, b.16 Oct 1834
Letty Ann FREELAND, b.9 Apr 1837
Phebe Ellen FREELAND, b.9 Feb 1840
Margaret FREELAND, b.11 May 1842
Charles M. FREELAND, b.21 Aug 1844
Mary A. FREELAND, b.10 Nov 1846
Elizabeth FREELAND, b.6 Aug 1849
Phebe Jane FREELAND, b.23 Jul 1857
William Keifer FREELAND, b.7 May 1870
Edith L. FREELAND b.2 Oct 1872
Elisha P. FREELAND, b.11 Nov 1874
Clarence B. FREELAND, b.12 Nov 1878
John R. FREELAND, b.21 Apr 1881
Amy E. FREELAND, b.11 Sep 1883

DEATHS
Elisha POST, d.24 Mar 1815
Richard FREELAND, d.22 Apr 1878
Mrs Betsey FREELAND, d.17 Oct 1876
Pheby Jane FREELAND, d.20 Mar 1879
William SPEAKER, d.9 Apr 1876
Eletta Post SPEAKER, d.10 Oct 1897
old Grandmother POST (Charity POST), d.3 Jan 1857; aged 74yrs
PARENTS RECORD MOTHER
William SPEAKER, b.27 Jan 1814
Eletta Post SPEAKER, b.3 Oct 1822
Charity E. SPEAKER, b.19 Sep 1845
John SPEAKER, b.19 Jan [____]
Mary A. SPEAKER, b.5 Sep 1849
Abigail A. SPEAKER, b.9 May 1852
Sarah E. SPEAKER, b.3 Jan 1855
Charles C. SPEAKER, b.11 May 1857
Martha SPEAKER, b.11 Dec 1860
Levi W. SPEAKER, b.4 Apr 1863
Emma L. SPEAKER, b.6 Jul 1866
MARRIAGES
Charles M. FREELAND m. 31 Dec 1816 to Charity E. SPEAKER
William K. FREELAND m. 7 May 1892 to Etta J. VANDERHOOF
Samuel T. CLARK m. 5 Aug 1908 to Amy E. FREELAND
(Joris Rapalje File)

JOHN THOMAS JONES BIBLE

HOLY BIBLE, published by Judd, Loomis & Co.,

Hartford, 1836. The originals in 1963 in possession of Wayne Van Leer Jones of Houston, TX.

FAMILY REGISTER BIRTHS

Michael JONES, b.19 May 1781
Mary JONES, b.6 Sep 1788, in Maryland
John Thomas JONES, b.4 Jul 1812, Gallatin Co, IL
Hannah Marie JONES, b.19 Dec 1813, Manchester, England
Martha Hannah JONES, b.19 Dec 1834, Gallatin Co, IL
Mary Sophia JONES, b.13 Sep 1836
William Pinkney JONES, b.23 Jul 1838
[____] Michael JONES, b.[--] Feb 1840
Emma Letichia JONES, b.23 Oct 1842
Basil Henry JONES, b.11 Nov 1844,
John Anthony JONES, b.10 Aug 1846
Harriet Sydney JONES, b.15 Apr 1848
-------still born [--] Jul 1850
Robert [___] JONES 15 Jul 18[__]
Can not read the remainder of this page.

MARRIAGES

Michael and Mary JONES m. 6 Aug 1811
John Thomas JONES m. 1 Mar 1834 to Hannah Marie DOCKER
Martha Hannah JONES m. 4 Jul 1853 to Franklin L. RHOADS
Mary Sophia JONES m. 6 Mar 1855 to William L. CALDWELL

DEATHS

Mary JONES, d.10 Feb 1839, aged 50yrs 5mos 4dys, member of Presbyterian Church, Shawneetown, IL
William Pinkney JONES, d.[_____] 1840, aged 2yrs 24dys
[___] Michael JONES, son of F.W. & M.H. JONES, d.6 Jul 1844
still born baby, son of J.T. & M.H. JONES, d.7 Jul 1850

John Thomas JONES, d.5 Apr 1863, Shawneetown, IL; aged 50yrs 9mos 1dy
Hannah Maria JONES, widow of John T.;, d.3 Sep 1863, Shawneetown, IL; aged 49yrs 8mos 15dys
Susannah JONES, dau of Michael & [___] JONES, d. ______ [--]
Michael JONES, d.5 Jan 1845; aged 63yrs 7mos 17dys
Caroline JONES, d. _________
Sabina JONES, d.15 Oct 1855, St Vinvcent School, [___] Co, KY; aged 15yrs 6mos 24dys
Michael JONES, d.26 Mar 1856, Shaweneetown, IL
(Joris Rapalje File)

COSBEY BIBLE

HOLY BIBLE, published by Ziegler & McCurdy, 1872

MARRIAGE CONTRACT

David L. COSBEY of East Sycamore m.16 Mar 1854 to Barbara A. HETZLER, of Indian Hill, by Rev Mr Elliot

MARRIAGES

David L. COSBEY m. 1 Feb 1849 to Hannah J. LYON
David L. COSBEY m. 16 Mar 1854 to Barbara A. HETZLER
Alvia T. DENMAN m. 24 Dec 1874 to Catherine B. COSBEY
Wm R. GOULD m. 30 Dec 1886 to Laura A. COSBEY
John F. HEITMEYER m. 13 Jan 1881 to Elizabeth E. COSBEY
Eugene M. PIERSON m. 15 Feb 1883 to Lena A. COSBEY

BIRTHS

Children of David L. and Barbara A. COSBEY
Alice Jane COSBEY, b.3 Nov 1849
Catherine B. COSBEY, b.7 Jan 1855
Laura Ann COSBEY, b.28 May 1857
Elizabeth Ellen COSBEY, b.4 May 1859

Clara Elvira COSBEY, b.26 Apr 1861
Lena A. COSBEY, b.14 Dec 1863
Jesse Edward COSBEY, b.9 Mar 1871
DEATHS
Hannah J. CROSBEY, wife of David L. COSBEY, d.20 Nov 1849, aged 24yrs
Jesse Edward COSBEY, d.15 Dec 1871, son of David L & Barabra A. COSBEY
Catherine B. DENMAN, d.23 Apr 1879
Clara E. COSBEY, d.7 Jun 1879
Elizabeth Ellen HEITMEYER, d.31 Jul 1901
John HEITMEYER, d.27 Feb 1936
David L. COSBEY, d.7 May 1903
Mrs Barbara COSBEY, d.1 Dec 1930, wife of David COSBEY
Laura A. GOULD, d.26 Aug 1937, wife of W.R. GOULD
MEMORANDA
David L. COSBEY, b.26 Dec 1825; son of Samuel & Eleanor COSBEY
Barbara A.HETZLER, b.31 Dec 1830, dau of Jseph & Elizabeth HETZLER
(Joris Rapalje File)

WILLIAM WOODRUFF BIBLE

transcript copied by Mrs Edmund Labbe of Portland OR. No title page , no publisher or date of publication.
Elizabeth HARVEYE, dau of Thomas & J. HARVEYE, b. 14 Aug 1730, Wakefield, Bucks Co,PA
John CORYEL, son of Emanuel CORYELL, and Sarah, his wife, b.12 Jun 1730; d.13 Dec 1799
Emanuel CORYELL, first son of John & Elizabeth CORYELL, b,24 Oct 1753, Amwell, NJ
Sarah CORYELL, second child of John & Elizabeth

CORYELL, b.5 Feb 1756, wife of Robert LANNING

ROBERT LANNING BIBLE

Transcript copied by Mrs Edmund LABBE. No Title Page, No publisher or date of publication.

Robert LANNING, b.24 Feb 1747; d.4 Oct 1828; aged 81yrs 8mos 4dys

Sarah CORYELL, wife of Robert LANNING, b.5 Feb 1756; d.15 Sep 1839

Sarah LANNING, dau of Robert & Sarah LANNING, b.10 Mar 1788; d.11 Nov 1864; wife of William READING

Rebecca READING, dau of William & Sarah READING, b.4 Mar 1813; d.26 Nov 1883; m. 10 Apr 1831 to Samuel WOODRUFF; m/2 10 Dec 1840 to John DERRY

Sarah Maria WOODRUFF, dau of Samuel & Rebecca WOODRUFF, b.3 Apr 1833, Flanders, NJ; d.24 Jan 1878; m 9 Dec 1857 to Augustus Delaniere TAPPEN

TAPPEN BIBLE

Transcript, copied by Mrs Edmund Labbe of Portland, OR from originals in her possession. No Title Page, no publisher or date of publication.

<u>BIRTHS</u>

ALbert A. TAPPEN, b.24 Jul 1807

Jane B. BUTLER, b.27 Jul 1809

Samuel D. WOODRUFF

Rebecca READING, b.4 Mar 1813

Augustus Dalamere TAPPEN, b.3 Apr 1832

Sarah Maria WOODRUFF, b.3 Apr 1833

George Horace TAPPEN, b.10 Nov 1858

Fanny Elizabeth TAPPEN, b.24 Nov 1860

Mary Rebecca TAPPEN, b.6 Feb 1863

Reading Woodruff TAPPEN, b.1 Apr 1865

Eugene Woodruff TAPPEN, b.9 Dec 1866
Helen Augusta TAPPEN, b.11 Aug 1869
Olive Lake TAPPEN, b.19 Feb 1872
Albert Erdman TAPPEN, b.6 Apr 1874
Jane Broadwell TAPPEN, b.9 Aug 1876 (adopted by Dr & Mrs Frederick W. OWEN; m. Fred'k P. MUDGE
(Joris Rapalje File, 2-439)

HADDOCK BIBLE

HOLY BIBLE, no title page, no publisher or date of publication.

FAMILY RECORD
William F. HADDOCK, b.10 Dec 1861
Henry B. HADDOCK, b.17 Dec 1865
John J. HADDOCK, b.22 Jul 1867
Josephine A. HADDOCK, b.21 Dec 1871
Betty P. HADDOCK, b.27 Sep 1874
[_______] HADDOCK, b.24 Jan 1879
Ora S. HADDOCK, b.12 Apr 1881
(Abram Ramy File)

JAMES E. RAMEY FAMILY RECORD

Family records xeroxed form a small booklet
James E & Austialie RAMEY's Family Record
James Edwin RAMEY, b.2 Jul 1839, Lyon Co, KY; d.3 Mar 1901, Carroll Co, IA
Australia DUVALL, b.18 Jul 1838, Williamson Co, TN
James Edwin RAMEY m. 18 Oct 1860 to Australia DUVALL, Trigg Co,
KY
Phillander RAMEY, b.28 Sep 1861, Trigg Co, KY

Lucian RAMEY, b.6 Aug 1863, Trigg Co, KY; d.20 Sep 1864
Frederick RAMEY, b.20 Jun 1865; d.13 Oct 1866, Trigg Co, KY
Irene E. RAMEY, b.8 Sep 1867, Lyon Co, KY
Elbert W. RAMEY, b.20 Mar 1870, Trigg Co, KY
Sidney RAMEY, b.4 Feb 1873, Bates Co, MO
Edwin RAMEY, b.30 Mar 1875, Benton Co, IA
Alice M. RAMEY, b.27 Aug 1876, Benton Co, IA; d,25 Jan 1904, Green Co, IA, aged 27yrs 4mos 29dys

Elbert W. RAMEY m. 25 Jul 1894 to Julia E. PHIPPS, Guthrie Co, IA
Julia E. PHIPPS, b.9 Sep 187[-], Benton Co, IA; d.24 Oct 1901, Glidden, IA; aged 31yrs 15dys
Melbourn C. RAMEY, b.31 May 1896, Glidden, IA
Flossie Myrtle RAMEY, b.10 Mar 1898, Glidden, IA
Lillian Bernice RAMEY, b.19 Oct 1900, Glidden, IA

Sidney RAMEY m. 17 Aug 1898 to Bertha L. DAY, Glidden, Carroll Co, IA
Bertha L. DAY, b. 28 Jul 1879, Bureau Co, IL
Merle Alice RAMEY, b.5 Aug 1899, Glidden, IA
J. Roland RAMEY, b.8 Mar 1903, Glidden, IA
Zelma Benetta RAMEY, b.4 Jun 1907, Glidden, IA
Irma Leah RAMEY, b.5 Sep 1909, Glidden, IA
(Abram Ramy File; 15-56)

THOMAS RUNYAN FAMILY BIBLE

HOLY BIBLE No Title Page, no publisher or date of publication.

FAMILY RECORD MARRIAGES

Thomas RUNYAN m. 28 Nov 1824 to Ruth PALMAR

BIRTHS
Thomas RUNYAN, the son of Elder Thomas RUNYAN, b.17 Aug 1800
Ruth PALMAR, b.9 Apr 1802
The children of Thomas & Ruth RUNYAN
Rachel, b.11 May 1826
Ahimaaz, b.1 Apr 1829
William, 24 Jun 1831
Elizabeth Jane, b.22 Feb 1833
Joseph, b.1 Oct 1836
Phinehas, b.29 Jul 1839
Charlotte, b.8 Jul 1842
Ann, b.11 Jun 1845

Mary Martha, dau of Thomas & Lydia RUNYAN, b.5 Sep 1848
appearing to be from a different Bible:
FAMILY RECORD BIRTHS
Bessie Belle RUNYAN, b.23 Oct 1870
Lilie Blanch RUNYAN, b.21 Dec 1873
Judson RUNYAN, b.10 Jun 1875
DEATHS
Bessie B. RUNYAN, d.22 Apr 1912
Earl Landon DICKEN, d.22 May 1912
Elmer A. DICKEN, d.5 Dec 1916
Caroline Amy Mellott RUNYAN, d.15 Dec 1928
(Vincent Runyan File)

BURTIS BARBER FAMILY BIBLE

HOLY BIBLE, no title page, no publisher or date of publication
FAMILY RECORD BIRTHS

Burtis BARBER, son of William & Ann BARBER, b.28d 3mo 1788
Mercy BARBER, dau of Henry & Lydia ALLEN, b.2d 4mo 1794
Edward BARBER, son of Burtis & Mercy BARBER, b.23d 10mo 1813
Samuel E. BARBER, son of Burtis & Mercy BARBER, b.29d 8mo 1815
Lydia Ann BARBER, dau of Burtis & Mercy BARBER, b.18d 11mo 1817
Hannah BARBER, dau of Burtis & Mercy BARBER, b.4d 4mo 1819
Henry BARBER, son of Burtis & Mercy BARBER, b.22d 5mo 1821
William BARBER, son of Burtis & Mercy BARBER, b.22d 8mo 1823
John Wright BARBER, son of Burtis & Mercy BARBER, b.5d 9mo 1825
Charles C. BARBER, son of Burtis & Mercy BARBER, b.15d 6mo 1828
Burtis BARBER, son of Burtis & Mercy BARBER, b.12d 11mo 1831
DEATHS
Lydia Ann BARBER, dau of Burtis & Mercy BARBER, d.9d 1mo 1838; aged nearly 21yrs
Hannah BARBER, dau of Burtis & Mercy BARBER, d.8d 10m 1819
Burtis BARBER, son of Burtis & Mercy Barber, d. ___
MARRIAGES
Burtis BARBER m. 10d 10mo 1811 to Mercy ALLEN
Edward BARBER m. 3d 12mo 1835 to Ann T THORN
Samuel BARBER m. 3d 6mo 1841 to Mary OWEN
Henry BARBER m. 20d 7mo 1843 to Ann CHAPMAN

William BARBER m. to Hannah BASSETT
John W. BARBER m. 27d 2mo 1851 to Ann SOMERS
Charles C. BARBER m. 3d 2mo 1853 to Jilielma SOMERS
DEATHS
Mercy BARBER, d.19d 5mo 1854
Burtis BARBER, d.12d 9mo 1857
(Misc Bible Records file)

EDGERTON FAMILY BIBLE

HOLY BIBLE, published by H.& E. Phinney, Cooperstown, NY, 1831. The original in the possession of Rev Travis DuPriest, Racine, WI
inside the front cover:
Roger EDGERTON m.29 Sep 1744 to Betsy COLE
Lucy EDGERTON m. 25 Feb 1811 to Daniel HAGLIS
Calvin EDGERTON m. 25 Nov 1822 to Betsy MANNING
Hiram EDGERTON m. 22 Sep 1827 to Sally PAYNE
Lois EDGERTON m.4 May 1828 to Charles CASEY
Hial EDGERTON m. Jan 1829 to Lydia EDGERTON
Calvin EDGERTON m. 20 Oct 18[__]
Albert EDGERTON m. 19 Sep 1844 to Rebecca CLARK
BIRTHS
Roger EDGERTON, b.12 Dec 1761
Betsy EDGERTON, b.16 Apr 1771
William EDGERTON, b.1 Jan 1790
Lucy EDGERTON, b.7 Apr 1792
William E. EDGERTON, b.25 Sep 1794
Calvin EDGERTON, b.19 Jul 1797
Hiat EDGERTON, b.28 Feb 1799
Hail EDGERTON, b.29 Mar 1801
Lois T. EDGERTON, b.30 Aug 1805
Hiram EDGERTON, b.18 Jul 1809

Erastus EDGERTON, b.23 Jul 1811
Albert EDGERTON, b.20 Apr 1815
DEATHS
William EDGERTON, son of R & BETSY, d.11 Mar 1791
William C. EDGERTON, d.5 Nov 1810
Hial EDGERTON, d. Oct 1799
Erastus EDGERTON, d.Oct 1813
Betsy EDGERTON, wife of Calvin, d.1Nov 1829
Lucy WYLIE, d.10 Jun 1837
Lois CAREY, d.10 Feb 1838
Hail EDGERTON, d.17 Jun 1854
Roger EDGERTON, d.24 May 1844, aged 82yrs 5mos 12dys
Betsy EDGERTON,relict of Roger EDGERTON, d.4 Jun 1854; aged 83yrs 1mo 19dys

From what appears to be a second EDGERTON BIBLE:
FAMILY RECORD, BIRTHS
George W. EDGERTON, b.8 Oct 1825
Julia S. EDGERTON, b.17 Jul 1827
Henry [-] EDGERTON, b.4 Dec 1855
Hial A. EDGERTON, b.8 Feb 1858
Jennie EDGERTON, b.20 Apr 1860
William E, EDGERTON, b.16 May 1861
Carrie EDGERTON, b.23 Jun 1863
Emma J. EDGERTON, b.29 May 1865
Alfred L. EDGERTON, b.1 Mar 1890
Ruth EDGERTON, b.30 Mar 1891
Mildred J. EDGERTON, b.25 Jun 1892
Edna M. EDGERTON, b.24 Aug 1900
MARRIAGES
George W. EDGERTON m. 12 Nov 1851 to Julia S. PORTER
William E. EDGERTON m. 3 Oct 1888 to Mary E. BECKWITH

DEATHS
Henry L. EDGERTON, d.14 Mar 1860
Hial H. EDGERTON, d.25 Feb 1860
Geo W. EDGERTON, d.19 Jun 1891
Julia S. EDGERTON, d.26 Feb 1900
Alfred L. EDGERTON, d.22 Aug 1913
Jennie EDGERTON, d.8 Feb 1919
Mary E.B. EDGERTON, d.22 Sep 1923
Carrie EDGERTON, d.8 Aug 1935
Emma J. EDGERTON, d.27 Sep 1939
(Pierre LeGrande File)

HOUTS BIBLE

HOLY BIBLE, published by Case, Lockwood & Co, Hartford, 1866

BIRTHS
John William HOUTS, b.4 Oct 1860
Charles Clarence HOUTS, b.20 Oct 1862
George Elsworth HOUTS, b.30 Dec 1863
James Sherman HOUTS, b.30 Jul 1866
Mary Ann HOUTS, b.8 Oct 1868
Lemuel HOUTS, b.20 Jan 1871
(Sebastian Royer File)

HOUTS BIBLE II

Holy Bible, No title page, no publisher or date of publication listed

Copied Dec 1971 at home of Ernest T. HOUTZ, Denver, CO

FAMILY RECORD BIRTHS
John HOUTS, b.16 Nov 1830
Jacob HOUTS, b.9 Mar 1833

William HOUTS, b.22 Jan 1835
Nancy HOUTS, b.28 Jan 1837
George HOUTS, b.21 Apr 1839
Maryann HOUTS, b.10 Dec 1840
Ely HOUTS, b.14 Feb 1842
James P. HOUTS, b.23 May 1844
Sarah Elizabeth HOUTS, b.16 Jul 1846
Elan HOUTS, b.9 Jul 1848
(Sebastian Royer File)

SWAIN BIBLE

HOLY BIBLE, no title page, no publisher or date of publication listed.

FAMILY RECORDS BIRTHS

Edward SWAIN, son of Anthony & Abby W. SAWIN, b.4 Jan 1846
Maria Louisa COREY, dau of Horatio N. & Mary G. COREY, b.10 Aug 1846
Mary Wood, dau of Edward & Maria Louisa SWAIN, b.20 Apr 1871
Anna, dau of Edward & Maria Louisa SWAIN, b.26 Sep 1872
Edward, son of Edward & Maria Louisa SWAIN, b.22 Jun 1874
Louisa, dau of Edward & Maria Louisa SWAIN, b.11 Sep 1875
Horace Corey, son of Edward & Maria Louisa SWAIN, b.21 Jun 1877
Joseph Warner, son of Edward & Maria Louisa SWAIN,b.23 May 1882

MARRIAGES

Edward SWAIN m. 11 Jun 1870 to Maria Louisa COREY, Bristol, PA

Anna SWAIN, dau of Edward & Maria Louisa SWAIN, m. 17 Apr 1907 to Symington Phillip LANDRETH
Edward SWAIN, Jr, son of Edward & Maria Louisa SWAIN, m.2 Oct 1911 to Helen L. MERRICK
Joseph Warner SWAIN, Jr, son of Edward & Maria Louisa SWAIN, m. 28 Oct 1916 to Jean McClinton GUITERIR [?]
DEATHS
Edward SWAIN, son of Anthony & Abby SWAIN, d.7 Feb 1905; aged 89yrs 1mo
Horace Corey SWAIN, son of Edward & Maria Louisa SWAIN, d.14 Jun 1913; aged 35yrs 11mos 23dys
(Reuel Pierre Rulon File)

JULIAN FAMILY BIBLE

Holy Bible, no title page, no publisher or date of publication available.
MARRIAGES
Isaac JULIAN, b.2 Apr 1786
Nancy JULIAN, b.22 Sep 1788
Barbara JULIAN, b.2 Nov 1806
Susan JULIAN, b.6 Jun 1808
Polly JULIAN, b.12 Aug 1810
Sarah JULIAN, b.29 Jul 1812
Rene C. JULIAN, b.25 May 1817
Samuel R.W. JULIAN, b.31 Oct 1819
Stephen H. JULIAN, b.4 Apr 1822
Nancy J. JULIAN, b.23 Jul 1824
Keziah E. JULIAN, b.23 Jul 1826
BIRTHS
Isaac P. JULIAN, b.17 Jan 1831
Clementine N. JULIAN, b.15 Feb 1833
Sarah S. JULIAN, b.23 Jan 1850

Nancy J. M. JULIAN, b.13 Dec 1851
Stephen E. JULIAN, b.3 Apr 1854
Susan C. JULIAN, b.9 Jan 1857
William S. JULIAN, b.7 May 1859
Mary M. JULIAN, b.6 Dec 1861
[____] C. JULIAN, b.1 Oct 1864
John E. JULIAN, b.9 Jun 1867
Alta A. JULIAN, b.25 Nov 1869
Isaac T. JULIAN, b.8 Aug 1872
Vesta L JULIAN, b.30 Mar 1876
Isaac Pipton JULIAN, b.8 Jan 1893 (entry crossed out)
(Rene St Julian File, 18-105)

BOHAN JULIAN FAMILY BIBLE

Transcript HOLY BIBLE, no title page, no publisher or date of publication available. Bible owned at one time by Fred W. Julian, Franklinville, NC.

page 1

Isaac JULIAN, b.12 Oct 1804
John JULIAN, b.24 Aug 1806
Martha JULIAN, b.19 Apr 1809
Betsy JULIAN, b.11 Apr 1811
Elinor JULIAN, b.17 Jun 1813
W. Gaston JULIAN, b.18 [13] Jun 1817
Alfred JULIAN, b.18 Feb 1820
Tobias JULIAN, b.26 Aug 1825
Rene White JULIAN, b.4 Jan 1828

Page 2

Bohan JULIAN, d.28 Mar 1861, aged 83yrs 7mos 6dys
T.C. JULIAN, d.25 Feb 1910; aged 84yrs 6mos
Jane JULIAN, d.12 Apr 1864, aged 77yrs, 1mo 26dys
John JULIAN, d.14 Nov 1863, aged 57yrs 2mo 21dys

Wm G. JULIAN, d.13 Apr 1874; aged 56yrs 10mos
Isaac JULIAN, d.25 Oct 1872, aged 68yrs 13dys
Elizabeth DOUGAN, d.6 Oct 1874; aged 63yrs 5mos 25dys
Eleanor ROBINS, d.24 Oct 1865; aged 52yrs 4mos 7dys
Page 3
Alfred JULIAN, d.19 Sep 1876, aged 56yrs 7mos 1dy
Martha HINSHAW, d.11 Jul 1881, aged 72yrs 2mos 22dys
Eleanor ROBBINS, d.24 Oct 1865, aged 52yrs 4mo 7dys
Isaac JULIAN, d.25 Oct 1872, aged 68yrs 13dys
Bohan JULIAN, b.22 Aug 1777
Jane JULIAN, b.17 Feb 1787; m. 14 Nov 1803
Isaac JULIAN, b.12 Oct 1804
John JULIAN, b.24 Aug 1806
Martha JULIAN, b.19 Apr 1809
Betsy JULIAN, b.11 Apr 1811
Eleanor JULIAN, b.17 Jun 1813
Gaston JULIAN, b.19 Jun 1817
Alfred JULIAN, b.18 Feb 1820
Tobias JULIAN, b.26 Aug 1825

From a paper in the Bohan Julian Bible, apparently a record of the family of this brother, Tobias.

Tobias JULIAN, Sr, b.26 May 1779
Esther MORGAN, his wife, b.8 May 1779
Bohan, their son, b.28 Nov 1800
Sally JULIAN, b.27 Apr 1803
Howgil JULIAN, b.8 Jan 1806
Lewis JULIAN, b.27 Jun 1808
Polly JULIAN, b.26 Jan 1812
Esther JULIAN, b.11 Mar 1818
J.P. JULIAN, b.18 Apr 1820

Tobias JULIAN, d.16 Feb 1852
Esther JULIAN, his wife, d.14 Feb 1855

Esther JULIAN, dau, d.6 Sep 1833
J.P JULIAN, son, d.20 Jan 1883
Bohan, son, d.4 Feb 1850
(Rene St Julian File)

JAMES SECORD SMITH FAMILY BIBLE

HOLY BIBLE, published by W.A. Burnham, Syracuse, NY, 1868.

<u>BIRTHS</u>
James Secord SMITH, b.30 Dec 1823, Niagara TWP
Susan Maria HODGKINSON, b.4 Jul 1829, Grantham TWP
John Elias SMITH, b.25 Jan 1850, Grantham TWP
Robert William SMITH, b.20 Nov 1851, Thorold TWP
Wilford Lawrence SMITH, b.29 Apr 1855, Granstham TWP
<u>BIRTHS</u>
Elizabeth Cristania SMITH, b.25 Jun 1858, Grantham TWP
James Maitland SMITH, b.4 Jun 1861, Grinsby TWP
Lieuas Edward SMITH, b.9 Feb 1865, Burford TWP
Susan Margaret SMITH, b.18 Jun 1868, Burford TWP
Charles Henry SMITH, b.13 Oct 1872, Burford TWP
<u>MARRIAGES</u>
Robert Wm SMITH m.27 Sep 1876 to Maggie BROWN, in London
Jno F. DYNES m. 8 Feb 1877 to Elizabeth C. SMITH
James M. SMITH m. 3 Dec 1883 to Selena QUXTON
<u>MARRIAGES</u>
James Secord SMITH m. 12 Dec 1848 to Susan Maria HODGKINSON, St Catherines
John E.S. SMITH m. 19 Aug 1876 to Mary A. [_____]; Beamsville
Wilford H. SMITH m. __ Oct 1875 to Annie BRAGG, Tilsonburg

DEATHS
James Secord SMITH, killed 10 Feb 1895
Elizabeth Cristania DYES, d.9 Jul 1890, St Williams
Susan Marie SMITH, 19 Oct 1896, Knoxville, TN
Robert Wm SMITH, killed 14 Dec 1903 ,Syracuse, NY
Wilfred Lawrence SMITH, killed 28 Feb 1907, Shawnee, OK
DEATHS
James Maitland SMITH, d.8 Jan 1911, St Thomas
(Ambroise Sicord File)

PORTER FAMILY BIBLE

NEW TESTAMENT, Published by American Bible Society, New York, 1854

FAMILY RECORDS DEATHS
Samuel PORTER, d.1 Jul 1833
Robert PORTER, d.28 Feb 1836
Jordan PORTER, d.11 Feb 1860
Burton Sanders PORTER, d.21 Sep 1861, near Manassas
Harrell PORTER, d.1 May 1870
Catherine PORTER, d.8 May 1872
David J. PORTER, b.13 Nov 1880
John PORTER, b.9 Feb 1892
BIRTHS
Gordan PORTER, b.22 Dec 1807
Catherine PORTER, b.24 Dec 1807
Susan PORTER, b.31 Mar 1827
Felix PORTER, b.12 Feb 1829
Samuel PORTER, b.25 Apr 1831
Robert PORTER, b.20 Jul 1833
John A. PORTER, b.17 Sep 1836
Burton S. PORTER, b.17 Dec 1838
Eliza J. PORTER, b.21 Feb 1841

Harrell PORTER, b.20 Jul 1843
Catherine A. PORTER, b.10 Jun 1846
<u>BIRTHS</u>
Harrell PORTER, son of Harrell & Melinda PORTER, b.1 Apr 1864
Nancy Victoria PORTER, b.11 Nov 1866
Mary Jane PORTER, b.7 May 1868
John William PORTER, b.28 Aug 1870
Daniel Jordan PORTER, son of [----] & Susan PORTER, b.23 Sep 1866
<u>MARRIAGES</u>
Jordan PORTER m. 5 Feb 1826 to Catherine FLANAGEN
Robert PORTER m. 27 Feb 1845 to Susan PORTER
Felix PORTER m. 24 Aug 1848 to Matilda Ann HUDDLE
John A. PORTER m. 6 Oct 1855 to Mary E. PEARMEN
Harrell PORTER m. 24 Feb 1861 to Melinda E. DAVIDSON
Catherine A. PORTER m. 29 Sep 1864 to F.M. BARKER
Nathan DYER m. 29 Dec 1872 to Eliza J. PORTER
(Abraham Sublet File)

PITTMAN BIBLE

NEW TESTAMENT, published by the American Bible Society, New York, 1830.

Mary PITTMAN, b. 29 Mar 1830
Micagah PITTMAN, b.16 May 1813
Noami PITTMAN, b.4 Dec 1814
Susan Jane PITTMAN, b.29 Aug 1833
Sally Ann PITTMAN, b.[__] Apr 1835
Nancy PITTMAN, b.22 Jan 1837
William PITTMAN, b.25 Mar 1839
Margaret Jane PITTMAN, b.6 Jul 1841

Jesse PITTMAN, b.6 Oct 1843
M[__]ger PITTMAN, b.22 May 1845
Naomi PITTMAN, b.16 Jan 1852
Naomi PITTMAN, d.29 Jul 1852
William PITTMAN, d. 8 May 1858
Pinsey PITTMAN, b.10 Aug 1857
Gilly Ann PITTMAN, b.6 Oct 1860
George LONGWORTH m. 10 Sep 1874 to Tinsey [Jane] PITTMAN
George LONGWORTH, son of Naomi WELCH, b.1822, VA
Naomi WELCH m. to William LONGWORTH
Naomi WELCH, dau of Samuel WELCH & Vrsula PORTER
(Abraham Sublet File)

WOOLRIDGE BIBLE

HOLY BIBLE, no title page, no publisher or date of publication. Original appears to have been found in National Archives Group15A W22686 (?).

FAMILY RECORDS MARRIAGES

Josiah WOOLRIDGE m. 24 Feb 1784 to Martha WOOLRIDGE
the above couples married Descendants
Major CHEATAM Martha CHEATAM
Joseph WHITE Mary WHITE
Samuel WOOLREIDGE David WOOLRIDGE
Rebecca WOOLRIDGE Lucy WOOLRIDGE
Morgan WOOLRIDGE, b.12 Nov 1830
John Thomas WOOLRIDGE, b.8 Jan 1831
Martha [____] WOOLRIDGE, b. Jun 1832
Josiah WOOLRIDGE, b.15 Nov 1755
Martha WOOLRIDGE, b.5 May 1754
(Abraham Sublet File)

THOMAS BIBLE

HOLY BIBLE, published by H. & E. Phinney, Cooperstown, NY, 1845.

FAMILY RECORDS BIRTHS

John E. THOMAS, son of Samuel THOMAS, b.26 Apr 1805

Halida THOMAS, dau of George JONES, b.19 May 1816

glued in "obituary' for: John E. THOMAS, d,. age 75yrs, b. Mddle Neck, burial in Presbyterian Cemetery

[_______] d. [_____] 1879; bur Dec 11 1879

Anna R. THOMAS, dau of John E. THOMAS & Matilda, his wife, b.3 Feb 1838

Matilda J. THOMAS, dau of John E. THOMAS & Matilda, his wife, b.27 Aug 1839

Hannah E. THOMAS, dau of J.E. THOMAS & Matilda, his wife, b. 30 Aug 1841

Lettia C. THOMAS, dau of J.E. THOMAS & Matilda, his wife, b.18 Feb 1844

DEATHS

Alford Coockman THOMAS, son of John E. THOMAS & Matilda, his wife, d.28 May 1850

Hilum Nap THOMAS, d.7 Jul 1854

John E. THOMAS, d.8 Dec 1879; bur 11 Dec 1879

Mary E. BROWN, dau of George A. BROWN & Elizabeth BROWN, d.3 Aug 1879

Matilda THOMAS, wife of the late John E. THOMAS, d.5 Jan 1900

Lettie, b.18 Feb 1849; d.4 Dec 1917

Hannah E. BROWN, d. 10 Jun 1923

Mary Frances THOMAS, d.17 Nov 1934

(Andris Souplis File)

CORSON BIBLE

HOLY BIBLE, no publisher, no place or date of publication

FAMILY RECORD BIRTHS

A[___] CORSON, b.2[-] Mar 1808
Janet CORSON, b.10 Sep 1868
Alan CORSON, b.13 Jul 1876
Alan CORSON, Jr, b.7 Jul 1904
Burton Francis CORSON, b. [--] Oct ____

DEATHS

Catherine FRANCIS, d.12 Jun 1842
Margaret CORSON, d.13 Dec 1848
Alan CORSON, d.19 Apr 1855
Margaret FRANCIS, d.25 May 1857
Elizabeth CORSON, d.1 Oct 1894
Thomas F. CORSON, d.29 May 1902
Isabella F. CORSON, d.26 Mar 1924

BIRTHS

Thomas SHIELDS, b.19 Oct 1796
Hannah FRANCIS, b.28 Sep 1801
Isabella F. CORSON, b.4,Apr 1847

DEATHS

John CORSON, b.20 Nov 1797
Joseph FRANCIS, b.29 Dec 1799
Isabella FRANCIS, b.5 Feb 1802
Thomas FRANCIS, b.8 Sep 1811
Elizabeth FRANCIS, b.7 Oct 1813

(Poncet Stelle File)

TRABUE BIBLE

HOLY BIBLE, no publisher, no place or date of publication

FAMILY RECORDS DEATHS

N.M.TRABUE, d.3 Dec 1855
Elizabeth TRABUE, d.27 Jan 1834, Schuyler Co.
Mary TRABUE, d.25 Aug 1835, Sangemore Co (?)
Mary SHUTTER, d.15 Apr 1858
W.C. TRABUE, brother, d.27 Apr 1888
Jacob Benjamin TRABUE, d.29 Oct 1855
Malinda TRABUE, d.1 Mar 1864
Hannah Frances TRABUE, d.19 Oct 1864
Pheba Melinda TRABUE, d.31 Mar 1865
E.A. TRABUE, wife of N.A.; d.28 Aug 1868
N.M. TRABUE, d.14 Apr 1865
N.A. LUX, d.16 Nov 1883

MARRIAGES

N.A. TRABUE m. 26 Oct 1848 to Melinda SHUTTER
N.A. TRABUE m. 31 Jan 1866 to Emely Addaline GOSN
N.A. TRABUE m. 15 Aug 1869 to Mary B[____]

BIRTHS

N.M. TRABUE, b.7 Sep 1799
Elizabeth WATSON, wife of N.M. TRABUE, b.26 Jan 1803
N.A. TRABUE, b.12 Dec 1825, Washington Co, IN
Melinda TRABUE, b.11 Oct 1829, Washington Co, IN
John Henry Maxey TRABUE, b.5 Sep 1849, Mou[__] Co, IL
Mary Elizabeth TRABUE, b.4 Oct 1851, Moulton Co, IL
Jacob Benjamin TRABUE, b.23 Mar 1854, Moulton Co, IL
Hannah Francis TRABUE, b.21 Apr 1857, Moulton Co, IL
N.A. LUX, b.2 Nov 1869, Piatt Co (?)
William C. TRABUE, b.3 May 1859, Peatt Co, IL
Susan Almarinda TRABUE, b.19 Jun 1861, Piatt Co, IL
Pheba Melinda TRABUE, b.5 Mar 1864, Moulton, Co, IL
Emily A. TRABUE, b.1 Oct 1843
Cora A. TRABUE, b.20 Jan 1867, Bennent

(Antoine Trabue File)

GILBERT STRANG BIBLE

Transcript, HOLY BIBLE, printed by Thomas Baskett, London, 1756. Original in Jul 1957 in possession of Jasper S. Allard, Jr of East Orange, NJ.

First Page

Gilbert BROWN m. 10 Dec 1799 to Elizabeth STRANG, by Rev Samuel Haskell

Major Gilbert BROWN, d.27 Dec 1820, aged 61yrs

Elizabeth BROWN, widow of Gilbert BROWN, b.27 May 1767

Daniel STRANG, father of Elizabeth BROWN, d.6 Jul 1822, aged 97yrs

Joseph STRANG, son of Daniel STRANG, d.31 May 1819, aged 49yrs

Elizabeth ISENHART, mother of Gilbert BROWN, d.25 Jan 1806

Margaret BROWN, d.7 Jan 1819

Elizabeth BROWN, d.8 Jun 1838

Gilbert B. STRANG m.27 Oct 1845 to Irene DOWNES, Sag Harbor, L.I.

Emma STRANG, b.19 Jan 1847, Sag Harbor, L.I.

Henry STRANG, father of Gilbert STRANG, d.17 [16] Apr 1853

Second Page

G.B. STRANG, b.27 Sep 1817

Gilbert Brown STRANG, b. Town of Rye, Westchester Co.

Irene DOWNES, wife of G.B. STRANG, b. 17 May 18[__], River Head

Emma STRANG, b.19 Jan 1847, Sag Harbor, L.I.

Third Page

Gilbert B. STRANG, b.17 Sep 1817, Rye
Irene STRANG ___
Emma B. STRANG, b.19 Jan 1847, Sag Harbor, L.I.
Ella STRANG,,b.6 Feb 1853, New York City
Lucy Ada STRANG, b.2 Sep 1853, Jersey City
Maria Banks STRANG, 9 May 1864, New York City
Eva STRANG & Alice STRANG, b.10 Jan 1871, New York City
(Daniel Streing File; 2-516)

JOSEPH COMMANDER BIBLE

HOLY BIBLE, published by American Bible Society, New York, 1850.

<u>FAMILY RECORD</u>

Joseph COMMANDER m. 14 Dec 1847 to Emily C.K. RAMSEY, by Rev Wm Reed, Pasquotank Co, NC
Joseph COMMANDER, son of Joseph & Parthenia COMMANDER, b.21 Jul 1823, Perquimans Co, NC
Emily C. K. RAMSEY, dau of Ric'd H. & Jacamine RAMSEY, b.3 Dec 1825, Sussex Co, VA
(James Thelaball File)

COMMANDER BIBLE II

HOLY BIBLE, no publisher, no place or date of publication

<u>FAMILY RECORDS DEATHS</u>

Richard H. RAMSEY, d.9 Aug 1862, aged 72yrs
Jacamine H. RAMSEY, wife of R.H., d.25 Jan 1837, aged 37yrs
Joseph Walter Cary, son of Joseph & Emily COMMANDER, d.18 Aug 1852

Carl Clifton, son of Joseph & Emily COMMANDER, d.4 Jul 1853
Mana Elgin, son of Joseph & Emily COMMANDER, d.19 Feb 1858
Sarah Joseph, dau of Joseph & Emily COMMANDER, d.15 Aug 1862
[_____] H[__], dau of Joseph & Emily COMMANDER, d.4 Oct 1861 (?)
Richard Henry, son of Joseph & Emily COMMANDER, d.29 Apr 1865, aged 16yrs 6mos
Sallie Wheetbee, Infant dau of Joseph & Emily COMMANDER, d.8 Aug 1865, aged 1yr 8mo
Minnie May, infant dau of Joseph & Emily COMMANDER, d.8 Sep 1867, aged 7mos
(James Thelaball File)

HINES BIBLE

HOLY BIBLE, Published by Towar, J.& D.M. HOGAN, Philadelphia, 1830

<u>FAMILY RECORD MARRIAGES</u>

Peter R. HINES m. 18 Feb 1834 to Sarah MACNIN
Peter R, HINES m.12 Mar 1842 to Emma J. SNOW
Peter R. HINES, Jr m. 30 Apr 1866 to Ellen FAULCON, dau of Dr R.T. FAULCON

<u>BIRTHS</u>

Harvey HINES, son of Sarah & Peter R. HINES, b.15 Jan 1835
Peter R. HINES, son of Emma & Peter R. HINES, b.7 Jan 1843
Harvey HINES, son of Ellen & Peter R. HINES, JR, b.25 Jul 1867

<u>MARRIAGES</u>

R.L. ALSTON m. 30 Dec 1888 to Lula Ellen HINES
next entry can't be read
BIRTHS
Robert Lea ALSTON, Jr, b.14 Aug 1891
Crowell Hines ALSTON, b.7 May 1894
Harvey Claude ALSTON, b.15 Nov 1896
Lula Marian ALSTON, b.28 Jun 1899
BIRTHS
Lula Ellen HINES, dau of Ellen & Peter R. HINES, b.26 Jan 1870
Rosa Falconer HINES, dau of Ellen & Peter R. HINES, b.11 Dec 1872
Annie Ellen ALSTON, dau of Lula & R.L. ALSTON, b.7 Apr 1890
DEATHS
Sarah HINES, wife of Peter R. HINES, d.25 Oct 1837
Harvey HINES, son of Sarah & Peter R. HINES, d.17 Sep 1864
Peter R. HINES, Sr, d.19 Jul 1880
Emma J. HINES, relict of P.R. HINES,Sr, d.11 May 1886
DEATHS
P.R. HINES, son of Emma & P.R. HINES, d.19 Jan 1908
Mary Ellen HINES, wife of Peter R. HINES, Jr, d.21 Mar 19024
DEATHS
Rosa Falconer HINES, d.2 Mar 1880
Lula E. ALSTON, d.18 Mar 1901
Harvey L. HINES, d.27 Jun 1901
(James Thelaball File)

TILLOU - FREEMAN BIBLE

transcript, HOLY BIBLE, published by American Bible

Society, New York, 1869. The original at one time in possession of Ralph Peck Tillou of South Orange, NJ.

MARRIAGES

Joseph Brown TILLOU m. 5 Feb 1801 to Mary BROWN (could be FREEMAN)
Abijah Freeman TILLOU m. 4 Nov 1840 to Pamelia BROWN
Rodney Wilber TILLOU m. 22 May 1860 to Eliza KNORR
Daniel W. TILLOU m. 20 Jun 1883 to Lucy Sanger WOOD
Samuel Brown TILLOU m. Feb 1880/81 to Elizabeth JACKSON (widow of Morris BROWN)
Samuel Brown TILLOU m. Feb 1901 to Francis JACKSON
Ralph Peck TILLOU m. 3 Oct 1942 to Grace WILSON

BIRTHS

Amos FREEMAN, Sr, b.31 Oct 1748
Mary Crane FREEMAN, wife of Amos, Sr, b.2 Nov 1747
Achsah FREEMAN, b.18 Nov 1773
Keziah FREEMAN, b.1 Dec 1775
Timothy FREEMAN, b.28 Sep 1778
Samuel FREEMAN, b.28 Aug 1780
Mary FREEMAN, b.2 Apr 1782
Amos FREEMAN, Jr, b.14 Nov 1784
Achsah FREEMAN, b.11 Nov 1786
John E. FREEMAN, b.27 Dec 1809
James Willi.FREEMAN, b.29 Jul 1805
Abijah FREEMAN, b.9 Jan 1789
Lucetta FREEMAN, b.24 Feb 1793
Joseph Brown TILLOU, b.18 Dec 1773
Mary FREEMAN, b.2 Apr 1781, wife of Joseph Brown TILLOU
Joseph Morris TILLOU, b.11 Jun 1806
Mary TILLOU, b.3 Jun 1808
Abijah Freeman TILLOU, b.3 Oct 1810
Charles TILLOU, b.22 Mar 1813

Job Brown TILLOU, b.3 Mar 1815

BIRTHS

Daniel Bosworth TILLOU & Lucetta TILLOU, b.19 Nov 1817
Rodney Wilber TILLOU, b.19 Nov 1821
Pamelia Brown TILLOU, wife of Abijah Freeman TILLOU, b.7 Sep 1810
Mary Ellen TILLOU, b.27 Aug 1841
Samuel Brown TILLOU, b.25 Jul 1846
Daniel Webster TILLOU, b.8 Aug 1850
Abijah Morris TILLOU, b.6 Aug 1854
Elizabeth Knorr TILLOU, wife of Rodney W. TILLOU, b.12 Aug 1836
Hattie Anna TILLOU, b.6 Mar 1861
Amma TILLOU, b.21 Oct 1863
Alice Bassett TILLOU, b.22 May 1865
Ralph Peck TILLOU, b.10 Nov 1889
Daniel Wilson TILLOU, son of Ralph Peck TILLOU, b.7 May 1944

DEATHS

Joseph Brown TILLOU, d.20 Nov 1860
Mary Freeman TILLOU, d.9 Oct 1854
Joseph Morris TILLOU, d.11 Aug 1830
Eliza WININS, d.12 Jan 1850
Charles TILLOU & Dau Lucetta, d.5 Oct 1854
Daniel Bosworth TILLOU, d.23 Sep 1855
Achsah FREEMAN, d. Jan 1861
Lucetta TILLOU, d.26 Dec 1867
Mary TILLOU, d.8 Dec 1871
Eliza TILLOU, d.17 May 1885
Pamelia B. TILLOU, d.9 Sep 1879
Abijah F. TILLOU, d.21 Feb 1904
Lucy Sanger TILLOU, wife of Daniel Webster TILLOU, d.21 Sep 1903

Job B. TILLOU, d.2 Mar 1911
Hetsre Mandeville TILLOU, d.4 May 1909
Charles Wood TILLOU, d.12 Jun 1884
Daniel Bosworth TILLOU, d. Nov 1859
Lucetta TILLOU, d.3 Feb 1885
Mary FREEMAN, d.21 Feb 1830
Amos FREEMAN, d.13 Apr 1833
Samuel FREEMAN, d.31 Dec 1835
Amos FREEMAN, d.23 Nov 1838
James F. Wm FREEMAN, d. 1876
Mary, wife of Joseph TILLOU, d.9 Oct 1854
Joseph B. TILLOU, d.20 Nov 1860
John S. LOBAR, d.28 Apr 1880
Rodney W. TILLOU, d.22 Nov 1901
Samuel Brown TILLOU, d.7 Sep 1941
(Pierre Tilbiou File)

TURNER FAMILY BIBLE

HOLY BIBLE, no title page, no publisher or date of publication

FAMILY RECORD MARRIAGES
JOHN TURNER, m.22 Nov 1813 to Margret SLEE
Births
Eliza W. TURNER, b.14 Dec 1834
Henrietta TURNER, b.15 Dec 1836
Benjamin G. TURNER, b.2 Jun 1839
Thomas M. TURNER, b.30 Nov 1841
William H.TURNER, b.27 Jan 1843
Caroline A. TURNER, b.3 Jun 1847
Sarah TURNER, d.15 Mar 1820
William TURNER, d.11 Mar 1831
Henry TURNER, d.9 Mar 1843

John TURNER, d.17 Oct 1854
Eliza W.A. WILSON, d.16 Nov 1859
Margaret TURNER, d.29 Sep 1864
Ann G. KINKADE, d.6 Jan 1868
George TURNER, d.10 Jun 1870
John TURNER, 26 Sep 1872
Jane WILLISTON, d.6 Jun 1885
Mary A. SHERIDAN, d.13 Jul 1897
Joseph TURNER, d.28 Nov 1899
Benjamin G. TURNER, d.12 Apr 1907
Thomas M. TURNER, d.24 May 1917
Etta MEAD, d.18 Jan 1919
Sarah HAWES, d.Sep 1913
W. Henry TURNER, 23 Feb 1920
Caroline Agusta Turner RICE, d.16 March 1931
(Daniel Tourneur File)

MARSHALL - NEWBERRY BIBLE

HOLY BIBLE, published by Mark & Charles KERR, Glasgow, MDCCXCVII

half page end of Apocrypha

John C. MARSHALL, b._____; d.27 Mar 1800
John, son of John & Elizabeth MARSHALL, d.9 Oct 1805
Elizabeth TURNER, b.12 Oct 1769
Elizabeth NEWBERRY, the same, d.3 Feb 1822
Leweretia TURNER, d. Jun 1776, aged 33yrs
Thomas TURNER, d.24 Feb 181[_]; aged 81yrs
Elizabeth MARSHALL, d.5 Feb 1823
[__________], b.13 Jan 1837
Thomas TURNER, d.24 Feb 1779; aged 87yrs

John MARSHALL, b.19 Nov 1789

Thomas MARSHALL, b.29 Nov 1791
Isaac MARSHALL, b.22 Mar 1794
James MARSHALL, b.22 Jul 1796
Eliza MARSHALL, b.21 May 1799
John MARSHALL m. 20 Nov 1806 to Elizabeth MARSHALL
John B. NEWBERRY, b.3 Nov 1807
Wm H. NEWBERRY, b.20 Feb 1811
John B. NEWBERRYm. 12 Nov 1829 to Elizabeth [____]
John C. NEWBERRY, b.25 Feb 1831; d.19 Mar 1833
Wm Henry NEWBERRY, b.31 Aug 1833; d.31 Jul 1834
Ann Elizabeth NEWBERRY, b.6 Jan 183[_]

BIRTHS

John B. NEWBERRY, b.3 Nov 1807, Newport, DE
Elizabeth CONNER, b.15 Apr 1809, wife of John Bennett NEWBERRY

MARRIAGES

John B. NEWBERRY m. 12 Nov 1829 to Elizabeth CONNOR

BIRTHS

John C. NEWBERRY, b.25 Feb 1831
William H. NEWBERRY, b.31 Aug 1833
Ann Elizabeth NEWBERRY, b.4 Jan 1835
John C. NEWBERRY, Jr, b.13 Dec 1837
Amandar NEWBERRY, b.29 Jun 1840
Virginia NEWBERRY, b.29 Aug 1844
William Henry NEWBERRY, b.29 Aug 1844

DEATHS

John C, NEWBERRY, son of John B. & Elizabeth NEWBERRY; d.19 Mar 1833
William H. NEWBERRY, son of John B. & Elizabeth NEWBERRY, d.31 Jul 1834
William Henry NEWBERRY, son of John B. & Elizabeth NEWBERRY, d.10 May 1856
Amanda Van Pely Newberry HEWES, d.3 Apr 1868

Franklin HEWES, son of Amanda & George Whitfield HEWES, d.7 Feb 1866
George Whitfield HEWES, d.8 Apr 1876
John NEWBERRY, d.7 Apr 1854, aged 74yrs
John B. NEWBERRY, d.15 Dec 1858, aged 52yrs
Catherine CHAMBERS, d.28 Jun 1849, aged 83yrs
Elizabeth NEWBERRY, d.28 May 1885, aged 76yrs
John Chambers NEWBERRY, d.9 Mar 1892
Sarah Olivia NEWBERRY, wife of John Chambers NEWBERRY, d.21 Dec 1896
George Neely RANDALL, husband of Ann Elizabeth NEWBERRY RANDALL, d.7 Mar 1873, aged 21yrs
Bloomfield Moors NEWBERRY, son of John Chambers NEWBERRY and Sarah Olivia, d.16 Jun 1911
Ann Elizabeth RANDALL, wife of George Neely RANDALL, d.[____]
(Daniel TOURNEUR File)

HARBERT RINGO FAMILY BIBLE

NEW TESTAMENT, published by H.E. Phinney, Cooperstown, NY, 1828. THe original in possession of Carl L. Owen of Kennewick, WA

<u>BIRTHS</u>
Cornelious J. RINGO, b.11 Sep 1753
Sarah RINGO, b.14 Jul 1774
Robert Lee RINGO, b.7 Aug 1865
John Gribble RINGO, b.19 Sep 1868
Archibald Walter RINGO, b.4 Oct 1877
Nancy Jane RINGO, b.15 Mar 1860
Andrew Jackson RINGO, b.18 Aug 1871
Martha RINGO, b.25 Oct 1860
George Burtis RINGO, b.26 May 1880

Edward Franklin RINGO, b.5 May 1882
Elmer Lorin RINGO, b.17 Oct 1880
Joseph Luceine RINGO, b.15 Aug 1882
<u>DEATHS</u>
Cornelious RINGO, d.30 Sep 1836
Sarah RINGO, d.18 Aug 1843
Archibald Walter RINGO, d.4 Sep 1878
Elmer Lorin RINGO, d.18 Aug 1881
James RINGO, d.19 Nov 1882
Joseph RINGO, d.3 May 1881
Emma Magary RINGO, d.9 Aug 1863
Milda Jane RINGO, d.20 May 1875
Huldah A. RINGO, d.1 Sep 1878
Harbert C. RINGO, d.15 Mar 1894
<u>MARRIAGES</u>
Joseph RINGO m.21 Aug 1828 to Mrs Mary RANSDALL
Harbert C. RINGO m.15 Aug 1850 to Huldah A. KNIGHT
H.C. RINGO m.2 Feb 1879 to Martha TODD
Franklin W. VAUGHAN m. 28 Oct 1868 to Mary E. RINGO
Jos D. RINGO m. 8 Nov 1876 to Nancy J. NOYER
<u>BIRTHS</u>
Joseph RINGO, b.3 Oct 18[06]
Mary RINGO, b.2 Dec 1798
Harbert Cornelius RINGO, b.4 Aug 1829
Joseph Preston RINGO, b.11 Oct 1834
Archibald Davis RINGO, b.14 Oct 1835
Mary Elen RINGO, b.27 Oct 1851
Joseph Davis RINGO, b.10 Sep 1853
Huldah Ann RINGO, b.31 Jul 1833
Milda Jane RINGO, b.6 Jul 1857
Emma Magary, b.16 Jun 1860
William Harbert RINGO, b.26 Aug 1862
<u>BIRTHS</u>

Cora A. RINGO, b.18 Apr 1884
Hattie E. RINGO, b.20 Apr 1885
Roy Ringo, b.3 Feb 1890
DEATHS
Martha RINGO, d.10 May 1941
Roy RINGO, d.29 Nov 1953
George Burtis RINGO, d.2 May 1959
Hattie Elenor RINGO, d.4 Aug 1961
(Pierre Trego File)

DE TURK BIBLE

HOLY BIBLE, published by Samuel D. Burlock & Co, Philadelphia, n.d.

BIRTHS
Louis Philipp DE TURK, b.13 Nov 1836, Burks Co, PA
Mary Emeline DE TURK, b.12 Nov 1854, Morgan Co, IN
Eugene DE TURK, b.16 Jan 1861, Morgan Co, IN
Lydia DE TURK, b.1 Jul 1877, Morgan Co, IN
Mabel DE TURK, b.3 May 1879, Morgan Co, IN
Harry DE TURK, b.13 May 1883, Morgan Co, IN
MARRIAGES
Louis Philipp DE TURK m. 20 May 1875 to Mary E. CRAMER
Eugene DE TURK m. 27 Oct 1886 to Viola WETHERTY
W.A. RINHER m. 17 Mar 1897 to Lydia DE TURK
Matt Y. MOUIEAL m.2 Mar 1901 to Mabel DE TURK
Harry DE TURK m.15 Nov 1905 to Kathryn SMOCK
Aloheus J. KINNEAR m.20 Nov 1905 to Mary E. DE TURK
Harry A. DE TURK m. 8 Jun 1917 to Anna F. Waynman STALEY
DEATHS
Louis Philipp DE TURK, d.5 Jun 1896, Martinville, IN

Kathryn S. DE TURK, d. Jun 1913, Coffeyville, KS
Lydia D. RINKER, d.1921, Dallas, TX
Mary Emeline KINNEAR, d.24 Jun 1925, Martinville, IN
(Jacob De Turk File)

RICHARD LOESCH BIBLE

HOLY BIBLE, no title page, no publisher or date of publication given. At one time the Bible in the possession of William H. Loesch.

BIRTHS

Richard C. LOESCH, b.13 Mar 1828, Bethabara, NC
Fanny BOWMAN, (now LOESCH) b.26 Dec 1830, Kinnettles, Scotland
Richard C. LOESCH, Jr, b.26 Oct 1851, New York City
Henry Augustus LOESCH, b.8 Sep 1853, Hoboken, NJ
Ella Maria LOESCH, b.25 Apr 1855, Hoboken, NJ
Fannie Gertrude LOESCH, b.23 Sep 1854, South Bergen, [NJ]
Horace Holden LOESCH, b.4 Nov 1859, Bergen, NJ
Jessie Olivia LOESCH, b.9 Jul 1962, Bergen, NJ
Charles Arthur LOESCH, b.12 Jan 1865, Bergen, NJ
Charlotte Ameila LOESCH, b.5 Aug 1867, Bergen, NJ
William Henry LOESCH, b.27 Jan 1872, Jersey City Heights, NJ

MARRIAGES

Richard C. LOESCH, m. 12 Sep 1850 to Fanny BOWMAN, both of New York City. m. at Florida (Scotch Bush, Montgomery Co, NY), by Rev Mr Stevenson.
Richard C. LOESCH, Jr m. 30 Apr 1874 to Bessie (Elizth) GLUECK, dau of the late Jacob GLUECK. m.at St John Free Church, Jersey City Heights, by Rev N.S. Rulison
William HOLME m. 24 May 1882 to Fannie G. LOESCH, Jersey City, NJ

Francis SAUNDERS m. 13 Oct 1888 to Jessie O. LOESCH, Jersey City, NJ
Charles A. LOESCH m. 7 Oct 1890 to Lena M. VREELAND
William H. LOESCH m. 11 Jan 1899 to Lorene J. SHUMWAY
(Abraham Vautrin; 2-233)

ALEXANDER WOTEN BIBLE

NEW TESTAMENT, published by American Bible Society, New York, 1886. In 1971 the Bible in possession of Helen Shaw Foltz of Van Wert, OH.

FAMILY RECORD BIRTHS
Alexander WOTEN, b.23 Jul 1849
Jane WOTEN, b.21 Jan 1849
Eliza WOTEN, b.21 Aug 1868
Hugh WOTEN, b.13 Mar 1870
Rhoda WOTEN, b.13 Jul 1871
Mary WOTEN, b.16 Oct 1872
Emma Jane WOTEN, b.2 May 1874
Tuella WOTEN, b.9 Oct 1875
Alexander Hamelton WOTEN, b.8 Sep 1878
MARRIAGES
Alexander WOTEN m. 15 Dec 1867 to Jane McDANIEL
Eliza WOTEN m. 19 Apr 1885 to Jesse SHAW
Rhoda WOTEN m. 26 Oct 1887 to John CROW
Mary WOTEN m. 7 Oct 1891 to Charley A. RAGER
Emma B. WOTEN m. 3 Mar 1895 to Orson T. SHAW
DEATHS
Tuella RAGERS, d.8 May 1904 ; aged 28yrs 6mos 29dys
Mary RAGERS, d.24 Mar 1908; aged 35yrs 5mos 8dys

Tuella WOTEN m. [-] Nov 1895 to Harry RAGERS

Hugh WOTEM m. 11 Nov 1896 to Olie DECAMP
Alexander H. WOTEN m. 13 Aug 1902 to Edna HARTZOG
Mary RAGER m. 8 Mar 1905 to Harry E. RAGER
(NOTE: In order to understand this Record note that two Rager brothers married two Woten sisters. Both couples had families. One brother died and one sister died then the remaining two married and they had children)
(Abraham Vautrin)

PEARCE FAMILY BIBLE

NEW TESTAMENT, published by the American Bible Society, New York, 1850. The original in the possession of Roy Van Pearce Collins, of Cario, IL, in Jun 1883.

FAMILY RECORDS DEATHS
John Wright PEARCE, d.29 Aug 1845
Martha PEARCE, d.8 Jan 1854
William Milton PEARCE, d.8 Oct 1861
Margaret PEARCE, d.27 Aug 1862
William PEARCE, d.8 Jul 1864
L. J. PEARCE, d.4 Jan 1878
Cynthia FARIS[?],nee PEARCE, d.21 Dec 1892
Mary WATKINS, nee PEARCE, d.21 Jun 1918
Elizabeth HERRIN, nee PEARCE, d.13 May 1920

BIRTHS
Lemuel Jackson PEARCE, b.27 Nov 1828
Elizabeth PEARCE, b.22 Jan 1832
John Wright PEARCE, b.20 May 1834
Mary Jane PEARCE, b.31 Dec 1836
Cynthia PEARCE, b.10 Apr 1839
Sarah PEARCE, b.27 Sep 1842
Bertha PEARCE, [-----] 1845
[______] PEARCE, b.15 Mar 1849

Emily Francis PEARCE, b.15 Feb 1852
William Milton PEARCE, b.30 Apr 1859
Joseph R. PLANT, 27 Jan 1841
Thomas PEARCE, b.4 Dec 1761
William PEARCE, b.13 Feb 1801
Margaret PEARCE, b.26 Dec 1811

MARRIAGES

William PEARCE m. 21 Nov 1827 to Margaret GRAY
George W. HERRIN m.25 Dec 1850 to Elizabeth PEARCE
Lemuel J. PEARCE m. 3 Apr 1851 to Sarah Ann HOBBS
Moses HERRIN m. 30 Dec 1852 to Mary Jane PEARCE
Jame TWIFS m. 2 Feb 1860 to Cynthia C. PEARCE
Joseph R. PLANT m. 4 Jun 1863 to Sarah E. PEARCE
Hannah E. PEARCE m. 25 Aug 1869 to Samuel H. CH [_____]

(Jean Vermeille File)

ABRAHAM SCHUYLER BIBLE

Transcript, HOLY BIBLE, published by M. Carey, Philadelphia, 1815. At one time in the possession of Florence E. Young of Beachwood, NJ.

MARRIAGES

Abraham SCHUYLER m. 23 Apr 1815 to Sally M. SUTHERLAND, Plymouth, Chenango Co, NY

BIRTHS

Abraham SCHUYLER, b.29 Mar 1789, Minden, Montgomery Co, NY
Sally Melinda SUTHERLAND, b.3 Feb 1793, Duanesburg, Albany Co, NY
Nelson Simon SCHUYLER, b.11 May 1816 , Sullivan, Madison Co, NY
Juliana Isabella SCHUYLER, b.13 Jul 1820, Millersburg, Upper Paxton Twp, Dauphin Co, PA

Henrietta, b.12 May 1825, Monroe Co, NY
a son, b.12 May 1825; d.17 Jul 1825
DEATHS
Abraham SCHUYLER, d.20 Oct 1828, Mendon, Monroe Co, NY
Juliana Isabella SCHUYLER, d.8 Feb 1832, Mendon, Monroe Co, NY
(William Vigne File)

WILLIAM H. SOOY BIBLE

HOLY BIBLE, no publisher, no place or publication, or publication
date.
BIRTHS
William H. SOOY, b.27 Jun 1847
Sarah E. SOOY, b.7 Oct 1852
Samuel Horace SOOY, b.27 May 1873
Tetta SOOY, b.26 Mar 1876
William Leander SOOY, b.24 Feb 1878
Amanda Edna SOOY, b.16 Jun 1880
John E. Carey SOOY, b.6 Dec 1882
Anna D. SOOY, b.24 Aug 1877
second wife of S.H. SOOY
Hannah D. SOOY, b.24 Dec 1850; second wife of W.H. SOOY
DEATHS
Sarah E. SOOY, wife of William H. SOOY, d.15 Apr 1883
Amanda E. BROWN (nee SOOY), dau of William H. & Sarah E. SOOY, d.28 Jul 1912, aged 32yrs
Wm H. SOOY, d.10 May 1920; aged 72yrs 10mos 22dys
Hannah D. SOOY, wife of Wm H. SOOY, d.13 Apr 1921; aged 70yrs 3mos 19dys

Emily Amelia Mary SOOY, wife of Samuel Harace SOOY, d.12 Feb 1926; aged 47yrs
Samuel Horace SOOY, d.14 Jul 1961
Anna Dorthy SOOY, 2nd wife of Samuel Horace SOOY, d.11 Mar 1941; aged 64yrs
Benjamin SOOY, d.16 Sep 1872, aged 53yrs
Eunice B. SOOY, wife of Ben SOOY, d.30 Mar 1902, b.6 Jan 1824, bur Green Bank, NJ
(William Vigne File)

GIBBS FAMILY BIBLE

HOLY BIBLE, no publisher, no place of publication or date of publication given.

FAMILY RECORD MISCELLANEOUS
W.C. GIBBS, b.8 Sep 1839
Sallie E. BELL, b.12 Apr 1847
M.S. BELL, b.22 Aug 1848
Craig Hendrix ROSS, b.29 Jul 1878
William Thoroughgood WEST, b.3 Apr 1909
MARRIAGES
W.C. GIBBS m. 3 Oct 1865 to Sallie E. BELL
W.C. GIBBS m. 10 Jan 1876 to Martha S. BELL
Minnie Bell GIBBS m. 30 Dec 1890 to Wm Carrick RUTHERFORD
Roberta Annie GIBBS m. 30 Jun 1892 to Frank L. McCALL
Chas Russell GIBBS m. 28 Nov 1907 to Lula Elizabeth HAYNES
Mary Crawford GIBBS m. 6 Sep 1909 to Craig Hendrix ROSS
Sarah Holbrook GIBBS m. 21 Apr 1915 to Thomas Grayson CAMPBELL
Mossie R. RUTHERFORD m. 20 Oct 1920 to Lofton Lewis BROCK

BIRTHS
Minnie Bell GIBBS, b.3 Oct 1866
Annie Roberts GIBBS, b.27 Mar 1869
Drew Brady GIBBS, b.30 Jun 1871
Sucky Julia GIBBS, b.4 Nov 1876
Myrtle Easton GIBBS, b.27 Mar 1879
J. Mary Crawford GIBBS, b.16 Dec 1882 (Mayme GIBBS)
Charles Russell GIBBS, b.21 Sep 1885
BIRTHS
Sara Irene GIBBS, b.10 Jul 1888
Craig Gibbs ROSS. b. 20 Jun 1910
Martha Cornelia ROSS, b.5 Sep 1918
Mossie R. RUTHERFORD, b.12 Jun 1894
Jessie May RUTHERFORD, 24 Nov 1897
Billie Gibbs RUTHERFORD, b.15 Feb 1901
DEATHS
Sallie E. Bell GIBBS, d.2 Nov 1873
Martha S. BELL, d.4 Feb 1891
Myrtle Easton GIBBS, d.17 Aug 1882
Roberts A. GIBBS, d. Mar 1804
William Carroll GIBBS, d.20 Oct 1917
(William Witt File; 21-297)

SAMUEL H. BELL BIBLE

HOLY BIBLE, no Title Page, no publihser, no place of publication or date of publication

FAMILY RECORD MARRIAGE
Samuel H. BELL, b.8 Jun 1811; m.14 Apr 1835 to Charlotte HAMMER, b.8 Jan 1816
Margery C. LEGG, b.4 Oct 1820 m. 9 Jan 1845 to Samuel N. BELL
BIRTHS

Mary Ann BELL, b.17 Apr 1837
James Washington BELL, b.6 Sep 1839
William Montgomery BELL, b.5 Mar 1841
Charlotte Eleanor Jane BELL, b.8 May 1843
Samuel Alexander Jackson BELL, b.8 May 1843
Sarah Elizabeth BELL, b.12 Apr 1847
Martha Soffonus BELL, b.22 Aug 1848
Nancy Luvenia, b.28 Aug 1851
John W. BELL, 30 Apr 1852
Marjory A. BELL, b.28 Jul 1854
Rufus H. BELL, b.21 Nov 1856
Marriet [___] BELL, b.10 May 1860
DEATHS
Charlotte BELL, d.8 May 1843
Charlotte E. J. BELL, d.21 Sep 1843
Samuel A. J. BELL, d.21 Sep 1843
Nancy Lavenia BELL, d.11 Nov 1850
John W. BELL, d.16 Aug 1854
Harriet M. BELL, d.30 May 1860
Sarah Elizabeth GIBBS, d.2 Nov 1873
(William Witt File)

INDEX

C

D

G

H

I

L

M

N

O

P

Q

R

S

T

www.ingramcontent.com/pod-product-compliance
Lightning Source LLC
Chambersburg PA
CBHW071220290426
44108CB00013B/1240

* 9 7 8 0 8 0 6 3 4 6 3 6 6 *